AFRICANA MODERN LIBRARY

No. 13

General Editor: PROFESSOR E. U. ESSIEN-UDOM
University of Ibadan, Nigeria

HOLY JOHNSON

JAMES JOHNSON AS A YOUNG MAN

HOLY JOHNSON

Pioneer of African Nationalism, 1836 - 1917

BY

E. A. AYANDELE

B.A. Ph.D. (London)

Professor of History, University of Ibadan

FRANK CASS & CO LTD

1970

First published in 1970 by
FRANK CASS & COMPANY LIMITED
67 Great Russell Street, London WC1B 3BT

Copyright © 1970 E. A. Ayandele

ISBN 0 7146 1743 1

Printed in Great Britain by
Clarke, Doble & Brendon, Ltd.,
Plymouth

For

OYEBIMPE

CONTENTS

LIST OF ILLUSTRATIONS

LIST OF MAPS

ACKNOWLEDGEMENTS

WE should like to make acknowledgement to the following for the use of photographs: to the Church Missionary Society for permission to reproduce the photographs of James Johnson, J. A. Payne and Dr. O. Johnson; to the Board of Trustees Glover Memorial Hall, Lagos, for permission to reproduce the portrait of James Johnson; to Allen & Unwin of London for permission to reproduce the photograph of John Pope Hennessy from the book *Verandah*; to Dr. J. O. Lucas of Lagos for permission to reproduce the photograph of Captain J. P. L. Davies; to Oxford University Press for permission to reproduce the photograph of E. W. Blyden from the book *Edward Wilmot Blyden* and to Bishop Samuel Charles Phillips for permission to reproduce the photograph of R. B. Blaize.

ABBREVIATIONS

C.M.S.   Church Missionary Society Archives

M.M.A.   Methodist Missionary Society Archives

B.M.S.S. Brooke's Manuscripts (C.M.S.)

S.M.A.   Society of African Missions' Archives Rome

M.P.   Morel Papers

L.P.   Lugard Papers

A.P.S.   Aborigines Protection Society

P.P.   Parliamentary Papers

C.O.   Colonial Office

F.O.   Foreign Office

S.L.A.   Sierra Leone National Archives

N.A.   National Archives, Nigeria

PREFACE

HARDLY had James Johnson expired in May 1917 than the hope was expressed that a biography of this pioneer of African nationalism would not be delayed. From all account and as the uniquely profuse tributes that accompanied his death clearly testify, he was a rare but popular personality who occupied an olympian height in matters of morality and patriotism. For half a century this idealist of British West Africa commanded undiminished universal respect among Africans and Europeans even when they disapproved of his irrepressible passion, his puritanical outlook, his dogmatism, his sphinx-like resoluteness, his anti-white vituperations and his quixotism. For the Sierra Leonians he was "Wonderful Johnson", for Nigerians "Holy Johnson", for the authorities of the Church Missionary Society the "Pope" of Nigeria, for those who knew him in Britain a "saint".

Though he left behind no evil that might have lived after him his good was interred with his bones. His activities and ideas, which essentially anticipated those of the well-known nationalist leaders of the inter-war years and of post-independence statesmen, were completely forgotten until only very recently. So deep was the vault in which James Johnson was buried that on the eve of political sovereignty by Nigeria and Sierra Leone, when the graves of the nineteenth century dreamers of this crucial event in the evolution of the continent were uncovered, the remains of this early prophet of African independence went unmentioned.

Two factors would seem to account for the total eclipse of James Johnson. First, he left behind no self-advertisement in the form of publications of monumental value such as have perpetuated the names of E. W. Blyden, J. Casely Hayford, J. M. Sarbah and J. B. Horton, whose works are now being reprinted by Frank Cass. Second, naturally, biographies of the nationalist crusaders and independence-winners of present day Africa have absorbed the interest and attention of writers. These writers do not perceive that Abdel Nasser, Habib Bourguiba, Ben Bella, Leopold Senghor, Kwame Nkrumah, Nnamdi Azikiwe, Obafemi Awolowo, Julius Nyerere, Jomo Kenyatta and Kenneth Kaunda—to name a few—

11

are architects rather than fathers of independence, winners rather than beginners or originators. All over Africa, both before and during the colonial occupation of the continent, lettered and unlettered individuals and peoples had prepared the way for the well-advertised patriots of the last half century.

However it is better late than never. Thanks to enormously rich archival materials, it has been possible in this book to partially exhume and resuscitate one of the earliest of the literate prophets and pioneers of African nationalism—James Johnson. It is no more than a pioneer study. Were his personal papers available this unveiling of James Johnson's life would have run into several volumes. Nevertheless the author is persuaded that ample revelations have been made in this book to stimulate and to justify interest in the writing of biographical nineteenth century African personalities. The author is convinced that biographies can enrich and deepen our knowledge of the African past in a way no other kind of historical writing can: it compels authors to generalise less and, in the case of West Africa in the years covered by James Johnson's life, it enables the historian to operate in the wider West African, rather than the narrower provincial, spectrum. For, far more than the post-World War I African educated elite, their predecessors were cosmopolitan and West African, in their outlook; they were veritable West Africans. Unlike the present-day educated elite, narrow ethnic or tribal affinities and loyalty to narrow territorial frontiers were much less weighty than allegiance to Africa in general and West Africa in particular.

This fact can be abundantly illustrated. Dr. J. B. Horton, born of Ibo parentage in Sierra Leone Colony, spent the most eventful years of his 'political' life pleading the cause of the Fanti of the Gold Coast, apart from demanding social and political reforms on the platform of West Africa; scores of *Saro* from Lagos and Sierra Leone sojourned in the Niger Basin, among ethnic groups unrelated to them, as traders and missionary agents. Institutions linked together the four enclaves that were to become British West Africa. Until the founding of the first secondary grammar school on the Gold Coast in 1876 the C.M.S. Grammar School in Freetown was patronised by the Gold Coasters, just as, until the founding of university institutions on the Gold Coast and in Nigeria after the Second World War, Fourah Bay College served all West Africa. In the civil service J. B. Horton served in all the four colonies; Blyden and Dr. Obadiah Johnson in Sierra Leone and Nigeria. The vitality of the prevalent West African-ness of those days may be judged from the desire of leaders of elite opinion to know parts of British West Africa outside their own areas. Mojola Agbebi travelled to Liberia and Sierra Leone, Casely Hayford and Edward

Blyden to all the colonies; Herbert Macaulay of Nigeria corresponded with people in the Gold Coast, Sierra Leone and Liberia.

All this indicates that from about the middle of the nineteenth
century to the early years of British rule in this century West Africa
was in a sense a unit, a unit demanding a history of its own. This
biography belongs to this West African context. James Johnson
was a representative of some of its spirit, values and aspirations.
It is hoped that other characteristics of this West African society,
partially and broadly revealed in Robert W. July, *The Origins of
Modern African Thought*, London, 1968, will be brought to the
knowledge of the academic world by studies of the *dramatis
personae* that embodied them.

From the point of view of sources this work has been denied
the support of its character's personal papers; intensive searches for
them have been futile but not frustrating. The absence of these
documents have in several ways imposed limitations on the details
of this portrait. One would have liked to have included personal
touches such as James Johnson's habits of work and hobbies, his
fun and mannerisms, his standard of living and family budgets, his
family relationships and friendships. Fortunately little is obscure
about his public life and career, thanks to his penchant for calling
a spade by its name. His letters, journals, addresses, memoranda,
newspaper articles and sermons—which taken together are stagger-
ingly enormous—bear the imprint of an extrovert unloading his
mind and of a gifted observer recording much of all that met his
eyes.

This work would not have been ready for the press now or assume
this shape but for the invaluable co-operation of archivists,
librarians and scholars in West Africa and Britain. Among the
archivists, I wish to mention in particular Miss Rosemary Keen of
the Church Missionary Society; the often changing archivists of the
Methodist Missionary Society; the officials of the Public Record
Office, London; the late Mr. L. C. Gwam of the National Archives,
Nigeria, and Mrs. Gladys Sheriff of the Sierra Leone National
Archives. During my field work in Sierra Leone in July and August
1967 various individuals were kind and patiently helpful. The
Registrar of Fourah Bay College, Mr. M. R. O. Garber, and his
wife over-welcomed me with their hospitality; the Right Reverend
N. C. O. Scott, Bishop of Sierra Leone, spared time for interviews
and exerted himself to obtain for me a copy of the rare little
autobiography of James Johnson; the Reverend J. I. Johnson of
Benguema, a Lokoh who became an adopted member of the Johnson household, gave me tips about the genealogy of James Johnson,
confirmed and embroidered by the manuscript of the family left
behind by the late Bishop T. S. Johnson. To the latter's son, the

Reverend Eva Johnson, I here record my appreciation of his kindness in letting me peruse the document. Lastly I should not forget
to thank my colleague, Dr. J. B. Webster, for putting at my disposal
copies of the correspondence between James Johnson and J. K.
Coker, one of the former's admirers who broke away from Breadfruit Church in 1901 in sympathy with its inspirer.

My gratitude to three academic seniors in Ibadan is beyond
words. Professor E. U. Essien-Udom, Editor of the Frank Cass
Africana Modern Library Series, encouraged me with his enthusiasm for the research and impressed me with a desire that has
been consuming him for some time—that the frontier of African
Political Science should be pushed back into the nineteenth century
and beyond. He read through the entire manuscript with admirable
patience and gave me the benefit of informed criticism. Professor
E. B. Idowu, whose unflagging encouragement has all along been
a fillip, read a few chapters with a meticulousness that I found
truly beneficial. Lastly, though not the least, Professor J. F. Ade
Ajayi, in spite of overwhelming commitments, strained himself and
his time to go through a number of chapters and offered extremely
valuable suggestions that resulted in a better focusing on James
Johnson than I had achieved originally.

With benefit to myself I compelled two of my colleagues, Dr.
J. B. Webster and Dr. T. N. Tamuno, to each read a chapter
cognate to their research interests. My appreciation of the help of
my kind friend, Mr. Christopher Fyfe, can be judged from the fact
that I drafted the first two chapters in London in the summer of
1967 purposely to have the benefit of his advice and unrivalled
knowledge of Sierra Leone.

Finally I wish to thank the authorities of the University of
Ibadan for financing my trips to Sierra Leone and London. And
to my brother, Mr. Victor A. Ayandele, who did the final typing
I say thank you.

E. A. Ayandele

History Department,
University of Ibadan,
6 June 1968.

CHAPTER ONE

TWIN CHILD: FORMATIVE YEARS

> I have been asked to tell the story of my life; and I am glad to do so; because whilst there is nothing in it that I should speak of as fascinating or romantic, yet I do think it may serve to show how God often over-rules evil for good, . . . how He works in ways little expected to convert men to Himself and to use them to bring the life-giving knowledge of His son to those who are perishing in ignorance and sin.
>
> James Johnson addressing an
> audience in Ireland in 1908.

THE precise date when James Johnson was brought into this world may never be known. This may seem strange to scholars familiar with the impressive and considerably detailed documentary materials on the Waterloo District of the Sierra Leone Colony, where he was born, among which marriage licences provide some clue to the birthdate of many contemporaries older than he.[1] But there is nothing unusual about the absence from the records of any account concerning his birth. However it has one significance: it indicates the nature of his origins. For had his parents been literate or people of substance, in close contact with the C.M.S. or Wesleyan missionaries, the journal-makers of those days, or had he been born in the coastal area of Freetown which was under the close surveillance of the Colonial Government, his birth might have received attention. But both his father and mother were obscure, unlettered, poor and inconsequential frontier settlers, a class of people incapable of appreciating the necessity for birth-recording.

But it is clear beyond doubt that James Johnson had been living several years before 1840, the date ascribed him by the obituaries of his death, and before 1838, the year perpetuated in the expensive and prominent statue in St. George Cathedral, Freetown, commissioned to his memory by his Benguema countrymen. For the records reveal that not only was he in school in 1843 but also he was by this date a mature boy, intelligent enough to read the Bible, master "very well" the compound rules of Arithmetic, and able to take down dictation.[2] In those days of poor diet, relatively slow rate of maturity and little advantage for young children to enter school, James Johnson could scarcely have been less than seven years in 1843. In all probability, then, he was born about 1835.

The mist about his birth begins to clear away as one probes his origins. He was born in a tiny village, Kakanda Town, mid-way between Benguema and Campbell Town, only a few miles south of Waterloo.[3] Kakanda Town was within the twenty-five mile long and ten-mile wide peninsula which British philanthropists had located in 1787 and which from about 1809 onwards became the dumping ground for the medley of West African slaves originally intended for the New World but eventually rescued on the high seas by the British navy. His parents belonged to the Yoruba nation, the singularly culturally and linguistically homogeneous stock inhabiting the south-western portion of Nigeria. Their antecedents, a knowledge of which considerably influenced the development of their only son, is fascinating. The father was an Ijesha from Akure, the easternmost out-post of the Ijesha branch of the Yoruba nation into which the Edo, makers of Benin Empire, had intruded for centuries; the mother was an Ijebu from Ijebu-Ode, the seat of the paramount ruler of the Ijebu Kingdom. Both parents claimed royal blood, the father remotely with the Ilesha monarchy, the mother closely with the Awujale stool.

They were both victims of the perennial warfare that engulfed most of Southern Nigeria west of the Niger in the first half of the nineteenth century, the father of the inter-tribal conflict between the Yoruba and the Edo, and the mother of the intra-tribal war that marked the last days of the Old Oyo Empire. Both were adult and family people at the time of their enslavement, the father possessing several wives, the mother a husband with several children.[4] Both were fortunate to be liberated by the British and deposited in Freetown, though at different times, the father after some spell of service in Benin City.

It is possible to determine approximately when the father arrived in Sierra Leone Colony: it is said that he derived the name Johnson from the famous German missionary, W. A. B. Johnson of Regent, whose activities spanned the period 1816 to 1823. But James Johnson's father receives no mention in the missionary's memoirs.[5] His illiteracy was undoubtedly a handicap, preventing him from being able to take advantage of the various facilities put at the disposal of liberated Africans by the British Government. Unlike Ajayi Crowther and other relatively younger people, James Johnson's father was too old to begin an education that could lead to a career in the Church or in the administration, an advantage taken by his sister, much his junior, who went to Charlotte school. Nor does his name occur in the long list of liberated Africans who learned a trade, such as carpentry, smithery, masonry, shingle-making or cultivation on farms allotted and supervised by the Colonial Government.[6]

There is evidence that he did not stay permanently in any settlement until he finally decided on Benguema, a further indication that he had neither a good nor a stable career. From Regent he moved from one village to another, including Kakanda Town, until finally he settled down at Benguema, a frontier outpost which liberated Aku (Yoruba) forcibly took from the Mende indigenes in the thirties. The village itself bore the Mende name Jengbeima, derived from the river near the village. The river, which was an emblem of worship, contained in abundance a type of fish known as Jengbe. After dislodging the Mende from the village, and pushing them to present-day Samuel Town, the name was Yorubalised into Gbongboima and ultimately anglicised by the British to Benguema.[7] This settlement, which today is a ghost of its former self, was very suitable and rewarded labour so abundantly that people began to flock there not only from the rank of newly liberated Africans, but also from the older settlements nearer Freetown. Apart from cassada, arrowroot, ginger, potatoes and cereals, Benguema began to specialise in fruit trees. Benguema had another attraction. It was blessed with the best form of grass for house-roofing, a factor which led at least a cousin of James Johnson to leave Regent for the frontier village.

James Johnson's father's instability was not only physical; he changed his denominational allegiance as well. For at the time James Johnson was born he had ceased to be an Anglican; he had become a member of the West African Methodist organisation, the body that had broken away from the Wesleyans in 1821,[8] and which was the first separatist African Church in the history of Christian missions in modern Africa.

It was in such circumstances that James Johnson's parents were married again. James was the first of a pair of twins and the only son of the remarried Johnsons. In later years two other children, both female, were added. The twins—James and Eliza—gave more anxiety than joy to their parents and posed a serious problem. In Akure the practice was to kill twins, in the belief that they belonged to the devil. Had James not been born under the British flag, he would never have been permitted to live. The parents found themselves on the horns of a dilemma, but as they were wondering what to do a fellow Akure recaptive, who had become a constable, warned them that the strong hand of the British Government would never countenance a fulfilment of Akure law in Sierra Leone Colony.[9] The other alternative open to them was to apply another custom prevalent in the rest of the Yoruba country and which was employed in similar circumstances—that of the worship of *ibeji*, the god of twins, in order to ensure the welfare and continued existence of the two children. Therefore an altar was built and sacrifices began to be made to the god of twins by the entire family, the children participating.

The duality of the religious loyalty of the parents of these twins should not surprise us, nor was it peculiar to them. As it is clearly established by documents, the majority of the liberated Africans in the Colony in the early years were external conformists in the Church and the adherents of the traditional beliefs of their race in the inner recesses of their homes. This state of affairs can be easily understood. On the one hand, external conformity to Christian worship was easier among the liberated slaves than among any other group of Africans in the pre-scramble era: missionaries found them the easiest to convert. Uprooted from their ethnic groups and forced to live together in a common territory, the attachment of these liberated Africans to traditional religion was bound to be weakened in the new environment of the colony. Secondly, the rescue of their body by the British Government elicited from the people a spontaneous disposition toward the doctrine so patently encouraged by their liberators. Indeed many of them might have lost faith in the traditional gods that had failed so signally to protect them from the terrific physical sufferings of the Middle Passage.

But on the other hand, as Christian missions were to learn, outward conformity did not mean inward acquiescence. It would have been nothing short of a miracle if the liberated slaves had been completely severed from their roots. Moreover, there needed to be a long period of acclimatisation for these people to understand and appreciate the inner values of Christianity, in the light of their experience. Nor should it be forgotten that a large proportion of these recaptives were, like James Johnson's parents, elderly folk who had been so drilled in traditional religion that it would have been difficult for them to understand a new religion. Above all, the way and manner in which these recaptives were grouped in the Colony along ethnic lines made possible a revivification and revitalisation of some old customs. And, as a study of the Colony in the first half of the nineteenth century has revealed, the togetherness of the Yoruba in the various settlements in the colony made it possible for them to cling to their religion and culture with a tenacity bewildering to contemporary observers.[10] It was a state of affairs that James Johnson was to mourn throughout his life in Sierra Leone.

The Benguema in which James Johnson grew into boyhood was especially suited for the flourishing and persistence of many of the divinities of Yoruba worship. The god of thunder, *Shango*, was well represented, although the weekly Friday worship and parade were grander in neighbouring Waterloo; Benguema also boasted of Ifa diviners. The *Egungun* Cult, physically represented by robed figures who are believed to be ancestral spirits, was not only strong there but its head, until his conversion to Christianity, was a cousin of James Johnson, James Benjamin Johnson, who was an *Oje*, that is a priest. J. B. Johnson used to represent Benguema in the cult's meetings at Hastings, another settlement south of Waterloo.[11] Above all there was the cult of witches and wizards, comprising fourteen members, nine of whom became Christians. The activities of this cult, which involved surreptitious killing of several people in the village, actually became in March 1849 an open scandal—an event which James Johnson should have witnessed.[12]

Moreover Benguema society, like all the villages in the interior of the Colony, was an unstable and lawless society in the forties. Although the majority of its inhabitants were Yoruba, about nine other groups were also represented. Inter-ethnic tension was inevitable and often it developed into open warfare. The Benguema Aku in particular were very aggressive and several times in the forties they joined with their fellow tribesmen in Waterloo in physical engagement against the Ibo and "Calabar", whom they accused of "Chopping" an Aku "almost every year".[13]

Indeed the necessity of maintaining the peace in the Eastern District, that is the Waterloo District, of which Benguema was a part, had been a problem for the Colonial government about the time James Johnson was born. In 1838 a comprehensive administrative and social improvement programme was launched for the area. The number of constables was increased from one to three and the Manager, one G. W. Nicol, was given the following instruction that was eventually to apply to all the District: "to appoint one Headman over every ten families who shall be able to account for their number, *their condition, produce of their labour*, births and deaths and General [*sic*] conduct. Over ten such Headsmen or tithesmen please appoint a hundredth censor or centenary who must be able to read and write, and who will furnish you with the result of their censorship. The object of this division is to obtain (among other things) . . . the arrangement of all petty disputes, punishment of crimes of whatever degree as the minor offences can easily be disposed of in a summary manner and those of a heinous nature sent to the sessions."[14]

By the time this new arrangement was applied to Benguema the social and tribal problems had grown serious, as the police records of the District clearly testify. In fact the instructions quoted above were probably never enforced. The village people had their own self-government, which was inevitably associated with traditional religious practices. Crime became rife, involving a larger number of people as the population grew, mainly through fresh settlers. True, many of these crimes were petty—larceny, pilfering, assaults and burglary—but a few acts of murder were committed as well. A gaoler had been appointed in 1838, and in 1853 alone a total number of fifty-five people had to be sent to prison. Among them was one James Johnson, convicted for stealing on 21 November and sentenced to thirty days' imprisonment. It is extremely doubtful whether this bearer of the name James Johnson was Holy Johnson. For one thing James Johnson was in the Grammar School and this conviction would have disqualified him for admission to Fourah Bay College in June 1854. However this evidence cannot be dismissed entirely, as knowledge of this event might have been unknown to C.M.S. authorities, and as the records indicate clearly that the culprit was from Benguema.

It is against the social background described above that we should understand the growth of James Johnson. In the meantime his social and religious life were being altered by education. He was sent to the school of the West African Methodist organisation in the village of Campbell Town, because this African Church had no school in Benguema, then a monopoly of the C.M.S. It is not known for how long he stayed in the school, but it is recorded that his father was baptised again in the Anglican communion in February 1847,[15] by which time James had transferred to the C.M.S. school in St. Matthews Parish. Campbell Town school was considered an excellent school. It received some attention from the Government which contributed to the salary of the teachers. As elsewhere in the Colony the method of education was the Lancastrian, or Monitorial, system, by which the pupils were divided into small classes. The children's lessons were taught by constant repetition, and they were initiated in writing by practising on slates. From this school James became familiar with the scriptures by the constant repetition of passages from them, as well as by singing psalms, hymns and reciting the catechism. It is worthy of note that among his colleagues in Campbell Town school was Henry Johnson who was to become Archdeacon of the Upper Niger, and G. J. Macaulay, later an Archdeacon in Sierra Leone.

Short though it was, James Johnson's association with the West

African Methodist body left a permanent effect upon his thinking. This organisation became a perennial fountain of inspiration for him. For after its break from the Wesleyan Mission in 1821 the members of this African Church displayed an energy and a liberality that brought success, especially in the villages, surpassing that of the C.M.S. and other alien missions. It was these African Methodists who founded the Samaria Church, Bethesda, Bethel and Tabernacle, and took the gospel to York, Tombo, Kent, Murray Town (where James Johnson's father became a member), Benguema and Banana Islands.

The success of these African Methodists, labelled as "wild Africans" by their Mission disparagers, can be noted from the fact that as early as 1829 the C.M.S. missionaries were so alarmed at the outburst of their activities and its results that a petition was presented to the Colonial Government about them. The villages had been the exclusive monopoly of the C.M.S. "Of late years, however," says the Annual Report for 1829, "the state of things has undergone an alteration. The Liberated African villages have been visited by independence Teachers, and not without success. Such Teachers have administered the ordinances in Liberated African villages. Their men, though without education, and with little sound knowledge of religious truth, possess the gift of an animating address with a large stock of scriptural expressions. They trouble not, we should think, their people with much instruction, but give decided encouragement to the vehement outward manifestations of inward excitement before adverted to, as evidences of the work of grace within. Thus meeting the taste of the people, they will possess an advantage over us on the very outset; and the dependence of such ministers on their congregations will, no doubt, be as recommendatory to the system of independency among the Africans as it has proved among other nations."[16]

Indeed the West African Methodists became popular with the people because their activities showed evidence of African racial consciousness and independence of mind. The congregations, who controlled their ministers, "have valued themselves not a little on their independence in matters of Church government".[17] At a time when the established missions had only thatched churches in the villages the adherents of the African organisation were prepared to volunteer labour and money for "places of worship superior to what the Colonial Government has hitherto afforded them" (C.M.S. churches in the villages).[18]

For Holy Johnson the West African Methodist movement was an indication of the capacity of Africans to understand Christianity, spread the gospel, direct their affairs and bear their burden, without any connection with or any help from any foreign body. Moreover, in his judgment, it had other advantages for Africans. It inculcated in the converts the principles of self-help, self-reliance, dignity and racial pride. By the time he became an ordained priest of the Anglican communion in 1863, James Johnson had become irrevocably convinced that any Christian mission that did not leave Africans to be independent in this way was not only hampering the cause of Christianity in Africa but undermining the natural racial consciousness of Africans as well.

Hardly had he transferred to the C.M.S. primary school in Benguema than he began to manifest the deep spiritual impulses that never abandoned him for the rest of his life. He began to take seriously and literally the stories rammed into his head at school. It was too early for a boy of his age to be able to understand the substance of the tenets of the Christian faith. On being taught one day the First and Second commandments—the ones forbidding idol worship—he began to think that he himself and his parents had been guilty of sin against God and he resolved to stamp idolatry out of the family. Torn between the loyalties demanded from individuals by the two commandments and the other demanded from children to their parents he devised a clever trick that would reconcile the conflict. He unburdened his mind to his teacher and told him of the time when the propitiation of *ibeji* spirit used to take place.[19] The parents were not to know that he was behind the conspiracy. At about seven o'clock on 24 December 1847, the teacher walked in, and met the Johnson family "in the act of worshipping country fashion as they said". This teacher's journals are best allowed to speak: "this country fashion consists of three small pots almost full of water with kolas and some other mixed things put into each of them, and placed in the hollow of a round wall about two feet high, at the south-west corner of the house in the piazza. I also met a large goat tied close by, and ready to be offered up, a bason [*sic*] full of palm oil, besides some other articles, the owner himself with another man who was not a Christian, were just beginning offering these things to this country fashion before I arrived; two yams and about eight ripe bananas were already placed before it. They seemed to be very surprised and alarmed at my coming, they would try to hide the articles from me, but it was too late, because there was a bright light hanging up in the piazza over them, however the owner of the house rose up immediately in anger, and carried the goat back into the house. What are these things for? I asked. I am making country fashion for my two children who are twins (whom he showed to me close by, they are belonging to our school). What good can this do to your children? I asked. This country fashion can do so much good for my children, it keeps them always from sickness and death."[20]

Although the teacher upbraided James Johnson's father for his unblushing hypocrisy and destroyed the altar, the trick had failed. For his father soon rebuilt the altar and restored the gods. The persistence of his parents in idol-worship drove their son into becoming an iconoclast. One day when they were out of the house James cleared away the images and all propitiatory accessories, turning them into ashes. Never again, claimed James Johnson, did idolatry exist in his family.[21]

From childhood James Johnson had indicated a quality that was not to desert him in life—a sense of independent judgment and action. Apart from the step he took in destroying the *ibeji* idols he once refused to obey an instruction of his father. A teacher transferred to Kent had desired to take him along, under the excuse that if the boy lived with him his school-work would progress. The father and teacher had concluded an agreement behind James Johnson's back. When he was told to go he politely refused, observing that his friends who lived with masters rather than with their parents were as a rule late and irregular in attendance. And there the matter ended.[22]

The opportunities for learning, which James Johnson enjoyed through the benevolence of the Church Missionary Society, further strengthened his inclination to religion. First, since he was poor, he could have the luxury of a grammar school education only if he chose the Church for his career. The only Grammar School in the Colony was opened in Regent Square, Freetown, on 25 March 1845. This he entered as a C.M.S. scholar in 1851. It was a matter of luck and because of his character that he was given a place (the only one out of thirteen in his class at St. Matthew School). For he was not the brightest boy in his class. However it is said that from boyhood he had learned to employ his own words rather than quote others, a practice he retained for the rest of his life. At the Grammar School he had the opportunity to widen his horizon by the instructions he received in English Grammar and Composition, Greek, Mathematics, Geography with the use of the Globe and Mapping, Bible History, Astronomy, the Thirty-Nine Articles, English History, Writing, Recitation and Music. He also did a course in industrial education by participating in farming four hours a day and taking his turn in the ginning of cotton produced in a six-acre plantation. Nevertheless he made the best of his years as a student. He was a lover of books and he read extensively outside the classroom. None of his class-mates in this institution was to attain the quality of his mind or reach the height of his fame in Church and State. He was the first product of the Grammar School to achieve the status of Assistant Bishop.

But apart from the fact that he had no alternative to the Christian ministry as a C.M.S. scholar, it seems that the Church was the best place for his temper and outlook. On his confession he had from childhood dedicated himself to the cause of religion, to the extent that he used to practise homiletics by mimicking preachers at the back of his father's house, preaching to imaginary congregations.

On 1 June 1854 he was withdrawn to Fourah Bay Institution, which had been founded in 1827 and later became the clergy-producing machine of the C.M.S. in West Africa until the end of the Second World War. He was the one hundred and twenty-fifth student to enter the Institution. According to the judgment of Edward Jones, the Negro Principal of the Institution from 1841 to 1858, James Johnson and his colleague, T. C. John, who were the only students admitted in 1854, had a more comprehensive and more thorough course than any of their predecessors. They read the Greek Testament twice over, learned considerable Hebrew, studied English History up to the reign of Queen Anne and familiarised themselves with a bit of "Euclid, Geometry and Algebra". Of course, as should be expected, their training was predominantly in the Anglican brand of theology.[23] He graduated from the Institution on 3 December 1858.

He was appointed to a tutorship at the Grammar School and we are fortunate in knowing the impression he made upon some of his students during his short career there. His religious fervour was noted to be very impressive. His mind, we are told, was always occupied by theology and it was his practice to pray on his knees, in a room where he could be spied upon, three times a day. He would stop his students' dinner if they did their homework badly, in the belief that they had done it out of playfulness.[24]

The fanatical piety and narrowmindedness on matters of dogma that he was to exhibit throughout his life were to a certain extent based on some of his experiences out of the classroom. This was particularly the case in respect to slavery, against which he nursed the bitterest aversion. As a child his parents had filled his ears with the horrors of slave raiding in Southern Nigeria and the wickedness of the society which sold them across the Atlantic and how they had eventually arrived in Freetown naked.[25] His mother related to him the bitter experience of the Middle Passage and the suicide committed by many of her companions in the slave ship. Later in the sixties James Johnson used to witness the disembarkation of liberated Africans in Kent, just as he had witnessed their settlement at Benguema. Also in his youth he was so appalled by the revelations contained in T. F. Buxton, *The Slave Trade and Its Remedy* that he swore to devote himself to the regeneration of his Negro brethren.[26]

It should be stressed that James Johnson's spiritual growth was neither sudden nor without flaws until after his Fourah Bay studentship. As pointed out earlier he might have been convicted of an act of stealing towards the end of 1854. Nor did he lack sexual emotions. In March of the same year, that is before he entered Fourah Bay and at the rather tender age of about nineteen, his name was mentioned in respect of one Rachel Garnon, an old student of C.M.S. Female Institution.[27] They were expected to marry, but for reasons which are still to be discovered, the marriage, which had been announced, did not take place. In the first report on him in Fourah Bay Institution, the Principal, the Reverend E. D. Jones, wrote of him as being less impressive in character than his colleague, T. C. John.[28] Even as late as 1868 a C.M.S. agent, Dr. G. T. Manley, who had just been released from an asylum, suspected that James Johnson was *in liaison* with his wife and was getting involved in the semantics of freemasons.[29]

James Johnson is himself the best witness to the fact that his spiritual metamorphosis was by no means complete until after he had left Fourah Bay and was serving as a Catechist in Kent between 1860 and 1863. How this fulfilment to his dedication to the Christian faith occurred is best seen in his own words: "It was in connection with the work in that district [of Kent] that I became a converted man in heart, that I yielded myself to the Lord Jesus Christ as my Master. I was preparing a Bible lesson for my class of school children on a particular occasion. I was reading with them the Book of Zechariah, and while I was preparing my lesson on the 3rd and 4th chapters of that book the Lord spoke to me as my Saviour, and within that week at a Holy Communion service I found salvation. My heart was filled with joy and gladness and thankfulness. That gave a different colour to my teaching and preaching at the time. On that occasion the joy and gladness of personal salvation led me to offer myself to God that He might send me out as a missionary among heathen people. . . . I conceived the idea of working among the people who did not know of the Saviour at all, and telling them of Jesus and the great Salvation He had wrought for mankind."[31]

Such unique spiritual experience vouchsafed to James Johnson, it may be stressed, has been shared by the truly saintly figures of Church History in circumstances not dissimilar. Both Francis of Assisi and Augustine of Hippo, to mention just two, were in their early lives far more profligate than James Johnson.

Though as a teacher he was on a salary of only 30 shillings a month, he refused to be attracted away from the Christian Church in 1862 to a secular situation that would have started him on a scale of nine pounds a month.[32] He was made a Catechist in 1863, the twenty-third African in Sierra Leone since 1830, and was located under a European superintendent at Christ Church, Pademba Road. His appointment marked a definite turning point in his life. Henceforward the holiness that was to be attached to him was increasingly visible. His life became one of incredible austerity. Theology became his main mental pre-occupation; morality was henceforward an absolute reality and came before logic. He became a puritan in the strict sense and a fundamentalist in his theological position—what he described as "pure and simple Christianity". This constituted the Truth, the whole Truth, the revealed Truth, to which he was to direct the inner minds of all people and all races for the rest of his life. For it he endured hardships, he debated, he split hairs, he crusaded.

From 1863 his vision was fixed; he never lost it and he never added to it. He was to describe as "arrogance" the later Victorian school of thought which scientifically questioned the basic tenets of the Christian faith. From now on religion meant for him a complete surrender to the dogmas of the Christian faith, a Christianity so pure that charms and other social habits of Africans not in strict conformity with this new faith could have no right to exist. His standpoint in life henceforward was absolutely scriptural. The Bible, he said, came to men from heaven and its morality was "the purest and finest".[33] This total commitment, it is easy to perceive, places Holy Johnson among the Christian idealists whose thoughts and outlook are often out of touch with the world of mortals.

Indeed so complete was his surrender to Christianity that he began to manifest characteristics that might be described as anti-social. He became incapable of wit or humour, hardly ever to laugh for the rest of his life. Man as an end in himself did not exist, except as an instrument for the furtherance of God's will and the fulfilment of His purpose. Humility was his watchword, emphasising that man *per se* deserved no praise, which was only due to God, "the Maker not the instrument".[34] For him there could be no hero —and he had none, nor any conception of the omnipotent genius in history.

Indeed if ever a thoroughly Christianised man appeared in West Africa in Victorian and Edwardian times, that man was James Johnson. He never acted surreptitiously; he would never backbite or say behind any individual, black or white, what he would not say to his face. Word and action were fused in him. It can hardly be surprising that a man of this kind was rare and that he was to remain from 1863 onwards a lonely voice in the wilderness, perpetually in conflict with society and his age, admonishing always, rarely ever commending.

His journals and letters six years after his appointment as catechist are a great testimony to the transformed nature of his character and relentless crusade he had to fight against the godlessness of his age. In his judgment the times were out of joint and he considered it his duty to put them right. Particularly galling was the sexual immorality in which he saw the womenfolk of Sierra Leone Colony wallowing. Therefore he collected together young women whom he dosed with "moral philosophy", organised a Dorcas Society to whose members he gave "plain lectures in Scripture, Church profane history, Natural and Moral Philosophy", and compelled them to write essays on these.[35] He found odious and incompatible with his own understanding of Christianity the gregariousness of the Sierra Leonians who saw nothing inconsistent with their adopted faith in their convivialities connected with indigenous marriage and burial customs. He condemned, as promoters of immorality, the "companies" into which individuals of both sexes grouped themselves for mutual benefit. He was constantly mourning that hypocrisy, and formal mouth devotion to Christianity should continue to abound in the British Colony. Nor could be understand why there should be "heathens" in the territory. By 1866, when his efforts to change people into genuine Christians had not produced the quick and complete results he had anticipated, he had to lament: "It is no easy work to root out heathenism from the minds of our people: at the sound of every heathen drum they seem to think fondly of olden days."[36] A year later no improvement in the state of religiosity was in sight: "With many of our worshippers religion is only a matter of form and fashion: some of our members I fear are strangers to true piety."[37]

So concerned was he with the tone of behaviour in the Colony that he even paid attention to remarks in conversations in the streets to detect lewd pronouncements. His standard of morality and piety became too severe for several members of his Church, who accused him of inflicting them with long sermons and ceaseless emphasis on immorality and drunkenness.[38]

Sierra Leone men and women of James Johnson's youthful days were not wilfully degenerate. To some extent they were victims of the environment of the Colony. Colony-born citizens neglected agriculture, which was considered to be beneath their dignity. Nor could the soil yield enough to lower food prices. Unemployment began to stare young men in the face in the sixties. The clerical appointments which they wanted being unavailable they became traders and at one stage began to prefer prison, where they were assured of food, to a life of idleness and starvation. This was particularly so between 1865 and 1868 when provision prices rocketed by about 300 per cent and the African members of the C.M.S., including James Johnson, had to plead for increased salaries.[39] Ladies, too, became victims of the situation. Though educated there were not enough positions in the civil service to absorb all of them; in vain did James Johnson apply to the Colonial Government on the behalf of many. They had no alternative to the unprofitable retail trade which, as James Johnson observed, brought them "in a whole month something less than nothing".[40] Since in addition to their needs they also had to take care of their poor parents they had no choice but to "constantly fall into the sin of fornication and adultery".[41]

James Johnson's puritanism was not confined to his fellow countrymen alone. He applied it to himself as well. His first letter to Henry Venn, the Honorary Secretary of the C.M.S., whose pro-African policies had already endeared him to James Johnson, was on a personal matter. He wanted to marry, but his partner must be an ideal woman. A bad marriage "will disgrace my ministry, lessen my influence, weaken my efforts and present no edifying example to the Church".[42] He was having "great difficulty" in getting "a pious and properly educated young woman". Not that there was a shortage of literary ladies, but in his estimation none was suitable for a minister of the Gospel. A careful search eventually revealed "in every way a worthy person"; her parents were in Lagos and he persuaded them to send their daughter to England for training in a Mission School. Friends had undertaken to pay the passage there and back but there was no means of maintaining her in England. A request for help was therefore made to the C.M.S.[43] But since the C.M.S. would not help he literally starved himself to send and maintain this girl at Acocks Green, near Birmingham. But in 1868 she died of a chill.

The dignity, Christian resignation and philosophic calmness with which James Johnson took this terrible blow—which he said nearly sent him insane—is worthy of note: "Whilst I pray for grace to submit to his chastening rod and take with patience that which he has been pleased to lay upon me, I humbly beg him to sanctify it that I may be thereby weaned from the world, kept from the paths of sin and led to be devoted to his service."[44] This tragedy turned him into an ascetic of a rare kind for the age in which he lived. A highly principled man, he refused to marry until (twenty-seven years later) he came across a lady of his spiritual taste and level. This was Sabina, a daughter of J. S. Leigh, an Egba *Saro* and one of the most prosperous businessmen of his day. The death of his fiancée in 1868 may have prejudiced James Johnson against the British climate and culture as detrimental to his race, and in subsequent years he was to reiterate the opinion, time and again, that the best form of education for the people of West Africa could be obtained only in Africa itself.

Until his ordination to priesthood in December 1866, James Johnson's influence was concentrated in the parish rather than in the church. Although he was a probationery, a mere assistant to European missionaries, his work attracted the special attention of the Church Missionary Society to the extent that his entire journals in these years were published. He occupied himself with visiting the sick, converting "heathens" and returning backsliders to the fold. James Johnson's method of evangelisation was to meet individuals at home or accost them on the street, and to remind them of their sinful ways and to warn them of God's impending wrath if they should not amend their character. He was never tired of visiting both his parishioners and those for whom the Church was a remote world. His patience was inexhaustible when listening to the opinions of potential converts, particularly as his superior earning enabled him to rebut these completely. He was incredibly persuasive. His quiet talk had a powerful effect upon the individual man and the individual woman, when acting in his position as their spiritual guide and adviser. He made the men and women feel that each of them was an object of personal interest to him, for to each individual were manifest the tenderness of his heart, his considerate affection, his sweet reasonableness. No man or woman, whatever his errors, was left unattended by him.

His evangelistic ability can be illustrated by his successful conversion of John Macaulay, alias King Macaulay. John Macaulay was a Muslim-born Hausa who by 1863 had resided in the Colony for forty-eight years and who had become the most popular man in Freetown and king of the Aku. Until October 1863, when he was afflicted with a severe sickness, he had led "a very immoral life and followed all heathen practices".[45] This extreme illness was fully exploited by James Johnson who, to everybody's surprise, converted him to Christianity to the extent that he turned away his concubines and became a member of Christ Church.

Hardly had James Johnson taken over the full control of Christ Church than he established an elaborate system of sin-detection. It was a hierarchical system at the top of which he stood as general overseer. At the base the entire church community was divided into twelve classes, under twelve leaders. The community was divided according to spiritual fervour. The fresh convert must pass through a probationary period of at least three years; if his life conformed to Christian tenets he became a full communicant. Communicants who sold liquor were excluded from full membership "till they give up the trade".[46] There were a number of adherents who had to be probationers for upwards of ten years for whom James Johnson mourned "continually that I have not been able to move them".[47] Leaders were people of a patently exemplary life. Their responsibility was enormous. The District of Pademba Road was divided between them and they had to watch the action, the movement, the thoughts and the statements of members both at home and at work. As James Johnson put it, their duty was to seek out "every case of sin".[48] Each week every act of misbehaviour was reviewed and punishment meted out. Later on female overseers were also appointed. The wheat and tares were separated, and the backsliders formed into a separate class at the very bottom of the hierarchy.

It was a spy system reminiscent of sixteenth century Massachusetts and Geneva, and it was the system that James Johnson was to use throughout his long career, in Lagos, in Abeokuta and in Ibadan. It would have been a device too rigorous for many members of any Christian organisation.

It was not only in Freetown in general and in Christ Church in particular that James Johnson sought to promote the growth of a puritanical kind of spirit, but it also prevailed in his family, and in this respect a brief look should be taken at the Johnson home. For it is devotion to the Christian Church that distinguishes James Johnson's family from the innumerable Johnsons in Sierra Leone. The family had two branches, one of which is now extinct. James Johnson's father was not the only victim of the slave trade. A sister of his, said to be related to the royal family of Ilesha, was captured about the same time as James Johnson's father.[49] Trained at the Girls' School at Charlotte she married one Agbogey, a liberated African under the care of the famous W. A. B. Johnson of Regent. He also bore the name of Johnson. One of her children was James Benjamin Johnson and was thus a first cousin of James Johnson. The two branches constituted themselves into one household and the two cousins grew together under the same roof. J. B. Johnson's life was destined to add to the intense Christian atmosphere of the Johnson family.

In his early years J. B. Johnson was a supercargo connected with the fleet of canoes which every week conveyed goods from Waterloo to Freetown. He changed in later years to become a farmer, specialising in fruit trees. His vast land of fifty acres is today in possession of the Reverend James Ingham Johnson, a Lokoh who was offered to J. B. Johnson as a foster child.[50] Less fortunate than James Johnson, in the sense that he had no formal education, J. B. Johnson learned reading and writing and became "a very enthusiastic Lay Reader"[51] in St. Matthew Church, Benguema. The story of his conversion from the *Egungun* cult to Christianity is of interest. One day whilst on his way to a meeting of *Ojes* at Hastings, just before the railway crossing at Waterloo and not far from where the Government hospital stands today,[52] he swooned and heard:

> Hark my soul, it is the Lord;
> 'Tis thy Saviour, hear His word;
> Jesus speaks, and speaks to thee;
> Say, poor sinner, lov'st thou me?

These words are a song by William Cowper (1731-1800) which became his favourite. From this spot members of his cult carried him to their grove, but when he regained consciousness he swore to be a Christian and henceforward became the bitterest enemy of the *Egungun* cult. According to the Reverend J. I. Johnson piousness and prayerfulness prevailed in the home of the Johnsons. One of the children of J. B. Johnson was the late Bishop T. S. Johnson, who took after the pious life of his father and uncle, forcing the C.M.S. to accept him for a Church career, in spite of his small stature and loss of an eye. His son, Evan Johnson, who is maintaining himself out of the instituion he is running, is at this moment of writing saving to train himself for a career in the Church.

It was the sad fortune of James Johnson's branch of the family that very few members remain. He himself died childless even though, having lost a wife in 1900 and being over sixty years of age, he had not lost hope of having a child should he ever marry again. Two of his three sisters, Mrs. Forbes and Mrs. Sali Cole, married and settled down in Freetown but they likewise had no children. The third appears to have had a daughter but in the last months of his life James Johnson began to fear that this daughter, his niece, would be unable to have children.[53]

But to return to James Johnson's early life. One formative and decisive influence on him in the early years is worthy of attention. He became a victim of sentimental loyalty and attachment to the Church Missionary Society and its interests, and this lasted throughout his life and career, excepting the year 1891 when he led a nationalist rebellion against the treatment meted by the Society to Bishop Samuel Ajayi Crowther in that year. He had a lasting deep sense of gratitude to the Society which had given him the opportunity to enjoy a decent living and play his part in the improvement of his people. This is the point that eluded his contemporaries to whom he seemed an enigma, a kind of Jekyll and Hyde character.

True if he were to be tested by his pronouncements alone, particularly in the second half of the nineteenth century, this opinion of him would seem to have some substance. For instance he was the earliest and the most outspoken advocate of an African Church which would be African in personnel, in liturgy, in hymnology, in

rituals, in theology and in forms accommodating to the racial peculiarities and customs of Africans compatible with the verities of the
Christian faith. The logical step for a man who entertained these
ideas, one would expect, was that he would translate them into
action by founding an African Church with himself as the Primate.
In fact he was the inspirer, if not the main cause, of many of the
secessions from the Anglican Church in Nigeria. But James Johnson
never abandoned the Church Missionary Society and even condemned all secessions from the Anglican Communion as unfortunate
events against the interests of the Negro Race. In practical terms his
African Church would be a contradiction in terms, since Anglicanism would form the nucleus. No less noteworthy is the fact that
James Johnson's theology from his formative years was completely
saturated with Anglicanism; consequently his attitude was often
sectarian. Other Christians outside the Anglican communion he dismissed as "Dissenters", and Roman Catholics were not Christians
at all but idolaters. Dissenters, he said, should not have any *locus
standi* in human society. Quoting an Anglican divine in order to
jibe at the Wesleyans in Sierra Leone he declared on one occasion:
"If the vessel of the Church of England goes to the bottom, the
cabin of dissenters will go with it."[54]

But viewed through Johnson's eyes he was not deliberately so
double-faced. In the sixties, and for the rest of his life too, he had
a grandiose and fixed conception of the Church Missionary Society
that may seem to our generation naïve, if not ridiculous. In his
view this missionary organisation epitomised undiluted altruism and
was the providential agency for the achievement of all the aspirations of the African patriots of the nineteenth century. As he saw
it the Society was committed to achieving the following objects—
to educate Africans in all fields of human endeavour to the highest
standard, to convert them to genuine Christianity, to raise Africa
to the material and social standards of contemporary England, to
put the educated elite in the highest positions of trust and responsibility, even over Europeans of less ability than Africans, to fight
for the political emancipation of the continent and to prove to
the disparagers of the Negro Race that, given equal opportunities,
the latter were the "normal equals" of other races of mankind.

Nor was this all. This Society, in partnership with the British,
should suppress slavery, put an end to inter-tribal warfare and
teach Africans to be able to govern themselves. No conditions were
to be attached to the discharge of this commitment. The reason
for this, said James Johnson, was that by participating so zealously
in depopulating and humiliating Africans in the transatlantic
slave trade the British had inflicted on Africa so serious a wound
that no exertions on their part could heal the wound and atone

for the sins committed.[55] Therefore the Society, as well as the British, could not have a purpose and an interest of their own.

It requires no imagination to perceive that this was a one-sided view which, with the possible exception of Henry Venn, could hardly be shared by the most pro-African philanthropists in nineteenth century Britain and how much less by missionaries in Africa. Little wonder then that by 1874 James Johnson had begun to disagree with British leaders in Church and State in Sierra Leone about the reason for the British presence in West Africa.

NOTES

1. S.L.A. *Liberated African Department Letter Book* (in several volumes).
2. *Ibid.*, "Report of School Campbell Town October 1843" in *Manager for 2nd Eastern District/Waterloo* (Record Book 1842 to 1854).
3. Bishop T. S. Johnson, "Biographical Notes" in possession of his son, the Rev. Evan Johnson, Freetown.
4. James Johnson, *A Brief Outline of the Story of my Life*, London, 1908, p. 7.
5. Rev. William Jowett (Ed.), *A Memoir of the Rev. W. A. B. Johnson*, London, Seeley Service, 1852.
6. S.L.A., cf. records of the Liberated African Department.
7. Local history given to the writer on Wednesday, 2 August 1967 at 52 Liverpool Street, Benguema, by the Rev. James Ingham Johnson.
8. For an account of this organisation see Christopher Fyfe, "The West African Methodists in the Nineteenth Century". *The Sierra Leone Bulletin of Religion*, Vol. 3, No. 1, 1961, pp. 22-28.
9. James Johnson, *op. cit.*, p. 10.
10. Christopher Fyfe, *A History of Sierra Leone*, O.U.P., 1962, pp. 186-7, 292-3; J. E. Peterson, *Freetown: A Study of the Dynamics of Liberated African Society, 1807-1870*, Ph.D. Northwestern, July 1963, pp. 293-4.
11. C.M.S. CAI/094, C. T. Frey, *Journals*, Entry 20 January 1850; CAI/0228, J. H. Wilson, *Journals*, Entry 28 February 1848.
12. C.M.S. CAI/094, C. T. Frey, *Journals*, Entry 14 March 1849; CAI/0228, J. H. Wilson, *Journals*, Entries 10 and 20 March 1849.
13. C.M.S. CAI/094, C. T. Frey, *Journals*, Entries 28 December 1843, 2 January 1844.
14. S.L.A., Volume 7, *Liberated African Department Letter Book*, 22 August 1837 to 15 February 1842.
15. C.M.S. CA1/0228, J. H. Wilson, *Journals*, Entry 24 December 1847.
16. C.M.S. CA1/07, *Annual Report*, 1829.
17. *Ibid.*
18. *Ibid.*
19. James Johnson, *op. cit.*, p. 14.
20. C.M.S. CA1/0228, J. H. Wilson, *Journals*, Entry 24 December 1847.

21. James Johnson, *op. cit.*, p. 16.
22. *Sierra Leone Weekly News*, 9/6/1917: T. S. Johnson's evidence.
23. C.M.S. CA1/0129, E. Jones, "Report for the half-year ending 14 April 1858".
24. A.B.C. Sibthorpe, *The History of Sierra Leone*, Third Edition, 1906, pp. 168-169.
25. James Johnson, *op. cit.*, p. 8.
26. *Jubilee Volume of the Sierra Leone Native Church*, London, 1917, pp. 86-7: Reminiscences by James Johnson, February 1913.
27. A.B.C. Sibthorpe, *op. cit.*, p. 204.
28. C.M.S. CA1/0129, Report dated 10/4/1855.
29. C.M.S. CA1/0144, G. T. Manley to Secretary, 14/9/1868.
31. James Johnson, *op. cit.*, p. 17.
32. C.M.S. CA1/03, E. D. Jones to Secretaries, 21/5/1863.
33. C.O.267/317, "The Fifty-fifth Annual Report of the Sierra Leone Auxiliary Bible Society, 1871" by James Johnson.
34. *Lagos Times*, 24/1/1891.
35. C.M.S. CA1/0123, James Johnson to Henry Venn, 15/4/1869.
36. *Ibid.*, James Johnson, *Journals*, March 1866.
37. *Ibid.*, James Johnson, *Journals*, October 1867.
38. C.M.S. CA1/0123, James Johnson, *Journals*, September 1864 and October 1867.
39. C.M.S. CA1/02, James Johnson and others to Finance Committee, 25/7/1869.
40. C.M.S. CA1/0123, James Johnson, *Journals*, October 1868.
41. *Ibid.*
42. *Ibid.*
43. C.M.S. CA1/0123, James Johnson to Henry Venn, 20/12/1867.
44. *Ibid.*, *Journals*, October 1868.
45. *Ibid.*, *Journals*, March 1863.
46. *Ibid.*, James Johnson to Secretary, 15/4/1869.
47. *Ibid.*
48. *Ibid.*
49. Bishop T. S. Johnson, *op. cit.*
50. Pointed out to writer 2 August 1967.
51. Bishop T. S. Johnson, *op. cit.*
52. Visited by writer 2 August 1967.
53. T. J. Thompson, *The Jubilee and Centenary Volume of Fourah Bay College*, Freetown, 1930, pp. 154-155, copy of James Johnson's will.
54. *The Day Spring and Sierra Leone Reporter*, 8 & 15 January 1869, Vol. 1, No. 19.
55. C.M.S. CAI/0123, James Johnson to M. Taylor and others, 19/4/1873; C.O. 269/369, James Johnson to Sir Henry Holland, 26/7/1887.

CHAPTER TWO

STORMY PETREL IN SIERRA LEONE I

> We continually cherish the remembrance of the days of former native independence and glory and are anxious to convince our enemies, open and covert, that we are not destitute of the elements of individual and national greatness. But we see nothing around us which we can call our own in the true sense of the term; nothing that shows an independent native capability excepting that infant Native Pastorate institution. For this reason and the conviction that we have that it is capable of being made a mighty instrument to develop the principles which create and strengthen a nation we cleave to it.
>
> James Johnson to Sir John Pope-Hennessy
> 6/12/1872

WHILST James Johnson was brooding over the low tone of morality and the mere churchianity of the world around him, events, momentous in the experience of its inhabitants, were being enacted in the Colony of Sierra Leone. Three of these events were of crucial significance. In 1861 the Church Missionary Society launched an experiment, the first of its kind in its history, by creating a Native Pastorate from nine of its churches—thereby devolving some measure of self-government on the African clergy and laymen. Two years later the British administration also began an experiment— again the first of its kind in Negro British Africa—by taking Africans into greater partnership in state deliberations, through the appointment of a liberated African, John Ezzidio,[1] to membership of the Legislative Council.

These two experiments owed nothing to the initiative of Africans; they were acts of benevolent paternalism and magnanimity on the part of the British rulers in Church and State. But the third—the Industrial Exhibition of 1865, which advertised the industrial skill and economic potentialities of the Colony to the world in imitation of Britain's Great Exhibition of 1851—was the effort of European and African leaders of the community. James Johnson was not among the originators of this event, nor did he contribute as much as a penny to the total sum of £727 2s. 6d. which was raised to make the occasion a success and to which a large number of Europeans and the educated African elite subscribed generously.[2] Although he participated in the Exhibition, he did so in a queer and ridiculous fashion. Whilst people like Bishop Samuel Ajayi Crowther, R. B. Blaize (a Government printer), J. B. Horton (the distinguished medical surgeon), and even an old pupil, A. B. C. Sibthorpe (the Kukuruku historian), showed their skill and won prizes, all that James Johnson contributed was a gourd presented in its raw natural form.[3]

Indeed James Johnson was a man of no consequence in society and politics in these early years. Leadership was in the hands of liberated Africans, independent and successful businessmen in their own right—people like John Ezzidio, Syble Boyle, Henry Lumpkins (senior) and William Grant. In the Anglican Church he was a mere auxiliary—a Catechist—under European bosses. It was not until December 1866 that he was fully ordained and not until 1870 that he was in full control of Christ Church, Pademba, and District. Of much greater influence was James Quaker, one of his teachers in the Grammar School, who eventually became principal of that institution and Secretary of the Native Pastorate.

But between 1868 and 1874 James Johnson's stature in the community increased enormously. By 1872 he, and he alone, was member of all the four committees of the Anglican Church.[4] Moreover not only did he make an excursion into the limelight but he also assumed the role of spokesman for the entire community in the Colony and began to pose as champion of the true interests of the Negro Race. As observed by his ecclesiastical superior, James Johnson was by 1874 not only "an intelligent labourer in the cause of Christ and his countrymen" but he was the "chosen champion"[5] of the grievances of his countrymen against the policies being pursued by the British rulers in Church and State. In these years his opinion was not only endorsed but also echoed by the African members of the Legislative Council and by Sir John Pope Hennessy, Governor of the West African Settlements from 1872 to 1873; he became leader of a nationalistic movement within and without the Anglican community; he became a subject of editorial attention and had begun to be a columnist, and for some time editor, of a newspaper extremely distasteful to Europeans. For the latter, particularly those in the C.M.S. and Wesleyan missions, he had become a *persona non grata*. His desire, they alleged, was to see the departure from the Colony of European missionaries and administrative officials.[6]

And yet the spirit to champion the cause of his countrymen had been in James Johnson before he became a public figure. In Kent, before he was made a Catechist in 1863, he had overcome the opposition of the European administrator who would not treat him as his equal.[7] He was already indicating in his letters and journals the strength of his character. It would appear that he was aware of the proceedings of the Anthropological Institute of London, at which the Negroes were arrogantly and offhandedly described in derogatory terms as an inferior species of the human race, with biological differences from the supposedly superior Caucasoid species, for he had protested as early as 1864 against this pernicious doctrine.[8] Simultaneously, too, he had begun to notice and to commend the pro-African activities of Henry Venn, the man largely responsible for the training of a number of West African educated elite in commercial, naval, literary, professional, technical and ecclesiastical fields.[9] He had also begun to denounce Roman Catholicism as an enemy of the true interests of the Negro Race.[10] According to him "Romanism" was an emasculator of the reasoning faculty of Man, a breeder of authoritarian ecclesiastics and, through the Index, a killer of Man's freedom of will and choice to read whatever he liked, including the works of people like Martin Luther and Melancthon.

James Johnson's first major public appearance was in connection with the Native Pastorate question. This institution had been established in 1861 by the C.M.S. in accordance with the principles which Henry Venn had enunciated as being in the best interest of missionary expansion in Africa and Asia. The supreme objective of missions, declared the C.M.S. Secretary, was the spread of the gospel and not pastoral ministration. Once converts had been obtained and had gathered in heathen lands and once Churches were formed, native agents should be left with the pastoral work and the churches organised into Native Pastorates. At every stage the natives should be urged to bear their burden and progressively encouraged to administer their affairs, until such a time when subvention from the Parent Society would cease and control by European missionaries would also terminate. The congregations should then be left alone and the missions move to the "regions beyond" to repeat the process all over again. The ultimate aim was the development of Native Episcopate. As the official organ of the Society, the *Church Missionary Intelligencer*, put it at the time of the formation of the Native Pastorate of Sierra Leone, its objective was "to render them (native Christians) self-ministering, self-supporting, and self-propagating churches, with their own native pastorate, and except in colonies where European and native races are associated, their own native Episcopate."[11]

Since Henry Venn's theory of Church government was to be resolved by James Johnson into political and nationalistic factors, it is essential to define clearly the extent of the influence on him of Henry Venn's theory. Although Venn recognised the existence of nationalistic instincts in Africans and the necessity of the Church to come to terms with it, he did not see himself presiding over the liquidation of the C.M.S. missionary empire. Judging from the articles of the constitution designed for the Native Pastorate of Sierra Leone it is clear that, for Venn, an "independent" Native Episcopate would imply neither a complete severance from the parent body, nor ecclesiastical independence from Lambeth Palace, nor a sacrifice of the essential doctrines of the Church of Engand, nor a breakaway from the Anglican Communion. Moreover he emphasised that the process towards the goal was to be evolutionary rather than revolutionary.

It was an evolution that was demanded by the circumstances of Sierra Leone in the sixties. For the Native Pastorate scheme, which at the beginning comprised nine churches (excluding James Johnson's church) was, from the financial viewpoint, a venture based more on fantasy and confidence than on empirical data. Its estimated revenue of £1,600 per annum was never to be half reached in the next decade, in spite of the liberality of many of its supporters. Income stood at first at around £500, rising gradually to just over £700 in 1870, and was only barely sufficient to pay the salaries of its clerical and lay staff.[12] From the start it depended on the C.M.S. for an annual subvention of £300 which, according to Venn's theory, should diminish as the Pastorate learned to bear more and more of its burden. Not only did the hope of this subsidy recede with years but it also became clear that a sum of no less than £500 would be required every year for church and school repairs.

It was in such circumstances that the Church Committee, the Pastorate's executive which comprised Europeans and Africans, decided that they should accept what they were offered annually from the Colony's chest. To the agents both of the C.M.S. and the Native Pastorate this decision was not only natural but also just. State and Church, that is the Colonial Government and the Anglican Church, were only different parts of one Body;[13] they were the Established Church, in a position not dissimilar to that of the Church of England in Britain. Nor were they just being presumptuous. Since the British Government had taken over the Settlement, the Anglican Church had been institutionally linked with the Colonial Government, first through the Colonial Chaplain and since

1852 through the Bishop, both of whom were appointees of the British Government.

It is against this background that the ease with which application for public funds was successful should be understood. Samuel Wensley Blackall, the Governor who approved an annual grant of £500, through the Legislative Council, had no qualms that he was doing anything out of order. Indeed he was enthusiastic towards the Native Pastorate for another reason. He saw in the institution an agency for "the real development of self-reliance among the natives on a subject most important to their interests."[14] He not only contributed liberally to the funds but also accepted the office of President of the Pastorate.[15]

The attention and financial aid being lavished on the Native Pastorate by the Colonial Government were a patent demonstration of partisanship. It was a strengthening of the organic link between Church and State in a way prejudicial to the interests of other Christian communities. It was a blatant misappropriation of the taxes of the community, which included—though in a small number—'pagans' and Muslims. Nor was the existence of the Pastorate an unmixed blessing even for the Anglican community in the Colony. Potentially it was a divisive factor, breaking the Anglican body into two: the Pastorate and the C.M.S. For the clergymen and school teachers of the Pastorate owed their allegiance to the Africans, who paid their salaries, while African agents outside the Pastorate were payees of the C.M.S. with loyalty to the Society, under the jurisdiction of European missionaries.

However the potentially fissiparous element in the Native Pastorate for the Anglican community and the Colony did not begin to appear until 1868. Prior to this date relations with the C.M.S. had been very smooth indeed. There was no question of the Pastorate viewing itself as a separate entity, but as a child with the umbilical cord which connected it with its parent remaining intact. This "umbilical cord" was represented by the Bishop who was Chairman of the Church Committee. In fact the European missionaries were fully integrated into the administration of the Pastorate and co-operated to see that it was a success. Not only were members of the Pastorate determined to remain Anglican but they also were profuse in their gratitude to the Church Missionary Society. As the Pastorate's clergymen memorialised their Parent: "The separation we hope, is merely outward; invariably we shall still be united in the indissoluble bonds of the Gospel—on our part by respect, affection and gratitude; on your part, we trust, by your prayerful sympathy, counsel and guidance."[16]

Two individuals had different conceptions of the Native Pastorate, one within and the other without the Anglican Communion.

Respectively they were James Johnson and Benjamin Tregaskis, Superintendent of the Wesleyan Mission in Sierra Leone from 1864 to 1874. They became the bitterest enemies, the one as arch-defender, the other as the eternal foe of the institution.

James Johnson and Benjamin Tregaskis differed in both personality and ideology. Tregaskis was old enough to be Johnson's father, having been a missionary in the West Indies before James Johnson entered the primary school. The one was, *vis-à-vis* other Christian groups, an Anglican bigot whose "sectarian annoyances" rendered the Wesleyan clergymen very "sore";[17] the other was a Wesleyan of the deepest hue for whom the apostolic doctrine of the Church of England was gall and wormwood.[18] For the one the C.M.S. were the only true friends of Africa, for the other only the Wesleyans.[19] James Johnson believed in the Established Church, that is the Native Pastorate, the Wesleyan leader in the Disestablished Church. Both professed to be working in the true interests of the Negro Race. While James Johnson believed that the African was the best identifier of his true interests and should be the only agent (with European money and training) to achieve these interests, Benjamin Tregaskis held the view that the white man could discern these interests and be part of the agency for their realisation. For the African leader the European was to be a mere tool for Africans; for the Wesleyan Superintendent the races should work together if the Liberian kind of "retrogression" was to be avoided.[20] Lastly James Johnson's conception of the Church for West Africa was very narrow and exclusive; it was to be for Africans only. In contrast that of the Wesleyan leader was more elastic, more catholic in outlook; in Africa the Church should include all races, but control was to emanate from the Wesleyan Conference in England. Although Tregaskis was not opposed to the principle of a Native Pastorate he believed a Native Church would have to wait for a remote future.[21]

There was an irony about the termination of the duel between these contrasting characters. James Johnson defended the Pastorate with a zeal that degenerated to an anti-C.M.S. and anti-European crusade, and he became too extreme for many of his followers who perceived the shaky financial state of the institution and he found himself deserted by most of his African supporters. Benjamin Tregaskis, who started as the bitterest opponent of the Native Pastorate, ended up as the defender of the European race with the tacit approval of the C.M.S. European missionaries.

James Johnson's conception of the Pastorate was different from that of the agents of the institution mentioned earlier. For him there was no question of the institution being just a lackey of the Church Missionary Society, and receiving their orders, "counsel and guidance". Rather, in his conviction, it was a separate organisation with a distinct identity of its own, and should strike along independent lines. The umbilical cord had been severed: it was "quite an independent institution".[22] Evidence of its separate identity was manifest in the fact that it had a constitution different from that of the C.M.S.; that it was a settled Church and not a missionary organisation; that its clerical and lay appointments were made by members of the clergy and laymen of the Pastorate, whilst the actions and decisions of the local committees of the Pastorate were final, beyond the veto of the Church Missionary Society; that the ministry was purely African, responsible only to the Bishop and the Pastorate Church. He looked forward to the day when the Native Pastorate would evolve its own theology, its own hymns and liturgy, for "the Church of England *is not our own*".[23] The prayer book, he was to say in later years, was to be one in which prayer for Queen Victoria would be replaced with prayer for African rulers.[24] "While we value our connection with England and use the services of valuable European Bishops", he informed a Governor of the Colony, "I say that the use of the services of a native prelate and our liturgy and canon is a mere question of time".[25]

Furthermore his conception of the Native Pastorate was not just one of ecclesiastical or religious independence. He saw in Henry Venn's principles of Church government infinite possibilities for the emancipation of Africa from alien rule and the training of Africans in the European art of self-government. From this time onwards James Johnson was confounded by the intrusion of Europeans into Africa and the seizure and annexation of some parts of the continent—including Sierra Leone and Lagos—which "is by divine right the Africans".[26] As years went by James Johnson could not understand by what right, "except that of might",[27] Europeans could begin to lord authority over Africans. Therefore he deplored the British establishment along the West coast of Africa and the supersession of the traditional rulers by the white intruders. All around him in the Colony he saw the white intruders as rulers in Church and State. For him this was a kind of imperialism which even in these early years he had found unpalatable and he continued to romanticise the "days of former native independence and glory",[28] when Africans were the directors of their own affairs.

The Native Pastorate was for James Johnson an institution that would achieve several worthy ends for the glory of Africa and of Africans. Firstly it would become a training ground for Africans in the cultivation of virtues such as self-dignity, self-reliance and desire for self-government. True they would tax themselves to the hilt in order to possess these virtues, and to become absolutely independent of European tutorship and to spread Christianity alone on their continent; their suffering would be overcompensated by the ecstasy and nobleness of independence, self-respect and manliness. From the sixties onwards he became impatient of the continuing foreign control of his people; he hated, as a mark of slavery, every sign of this foreign relationship. Through the committees, school boards and church committees on which they served and to which they elected their representatives, Africans would be able to display their ability to organise, to administer, to order their destiny and thereby convince the disparagers of the Negro Race, "our enemies, open and covert, that we are not destitute of the elements of individual and national greatness".[29]

Secondly, the Native Pastorate was an institution of crucial significance for James Johnson because it was "capable of creating and diffusing the principle that creates and sustains an independent Christian nation".[30] It was an embryo, a nucleus, for a continental African Church, Africanised from top to bottom in its hierarchy, forms and theology. As he declared: "The desire to have an independent church closely follows the knowledge that we are a distinct race, existing under peculiar circumstances and possessing peculiar characteristics, the desire to preserve this distinction uninjured, the conviction that it would materially contribute to give a purely native character and power to our religious profession, and that the arrangements of foreign Churches made to suit their own local circumstances can hardly be expected to suit our own in all their details."[31] Europeans, James Johnson said, were to be completely excluded because they were not only a different race, with interests at variance with those of Africans, but their continued presence in Africa would produce the effect of depriving the Negro Race of their natural endowments such as "the superior physique, the manly independence, the courage and bravery, the daring and self-reliance, and the readiness to face difficulties".[32]

Above all the Native Pastorate was in James Johnson's view the first institutional process in the evolution of Pan-Africanism. It was "the centre of Christian Civilization to all Africa";[32a] it was also "truly the Church of the people, the foundation of an extensive African Church",[33] the instrument "for the development of a future African existence". Eventually the institution would embrace Christians of all persuasions, deal a mortal blow to sectarianism, "a lamentable evil",[33a] a fissiparous factor vitiating the emergence of a monolithic continental African Church and society and the growth of African solidarity.

We should pause a while for a consideration of this kind of exposition of nationalist ideas through the agency of the Church. It is of great significance in the history of African nationalism generally and of West Africa in particular. It indicates that, contrary to the impression of political analysts, African nationalism, particularly in West Africa, had been in existence at least a generation before the era of the Scramble. Nor was it negative. It was purposeful, constructive and remarkably anticipatory of such ideas that statesmen of post-colonial Africa were to express. It shows clearly that even before the European powers began to divide the continent and its peoples among themselves, and in spite of the mental and cultural enslavement in which the first generation of the educated elite were pushed by the formal Western-type education of European imperial presence, yet from the beginning there were not wanting individuals among these educated elite who recognised Africa and her peoples as an entity, and who wished that her sovereignty had never been violated. There were also among them individuals who wished for and envisaged a united Africa and African people and who hoped to see her brought to an age of science and technology.

It was an incipient form of nationalism, but nevertheless of great importance. Like the unlettered rulers and peoples who physically resisted the intrusion of the white man in the nineteenth century, the educated elite of the first generation, of whom James Johnson was one in West Africa, never failed to retain nationalistic instincts. Their nationalism was the beginning of a process that was to become more marked in the colonial era. True there was in the educated elite of this pre-Scramble period a sense of gratitude to their colonial mentors, who had made them what they were, and had given them a new status which put them way above their unlettered countrymen and rulers; yet they had a sense of separateness from the governors. This feeling which was impressively symbolised in James Johnson is now a neglected theme of African nationalism.

The forum chosen, in West Africa earlier than in other parts of the continent, was the Christian Church. This was in the logic of history. In several ways the Church was the incubator of African nationalism. It was in the Christian Church that the talents of the educated elite were first detected and developed; it was in the Church that they first began to imbibe the concept of equality of all men and of all races; it was in the Church that they first began to perceive that the cultural and mental attainment of the white man was not beyond the reach of the African; it was in the Church that responsibility which required initiative, administrative ability and independence from the white man's physical control, could be and was actually enjoyed; it was in the Church that African opinion about the running of the affairs of an institution was first sought by white rulers, or demanded by Africans themselves, and obtained;

it was in the Church that the laity learned the principle of elective representation; it was in the Church that the laity saw the class fees in terms of taxes, and demanded ultimate say in administrative matters on the basis of their financial power, claiming the right to control their finances and the agents whose salaries they paid.

It is against this potentiality in the Church for the rise of African nationalism that the earliest manifestations of nationalist movements in West Africa, indeed in all Africa, should be understood. In this sense James Johnson was no more than a symbol. It should be noted that before his birth the Church had been producing many of the nationalistic concomitants of missionary propaganda mentioned above. The founders of the West African Methodist Church into which, it will be remembered, he was born, had claimed the right to be the final controller of their affairs, had condemned the authoritarianism of the European missionary and had seen themselves as African Methodists, "an independent body of people of all other Methodists in the world".[34]

However, far more than any other individual both before and after him James Johnson was the greatest, the most vocal and the most systematic exponent of an African nationalism with the Christian Church as its base. It was he who built around this institution the most grandiose and the most comprehensive religio-political ideology. The term that best describes his nationalistic thoughts and activities and those of his supporters all over West Africa is Ethiopianism, which derived from the word Ethiopia which they themselves used to symbolise the whole of Africa. For they saw Africa as the Biblical Ethiopia which "shall soon stretch forth her hands unto God", and Africans as Ethiopians. The Negroes in the New World were Ethiopians, Africans in exile, as James Johnson put it, in a land "in which they cannot under any possible circumstances, exist as a distinct nation".[35] But their Ethiopianism is quite different from the popular one associated with Central, Eastern and Southern Africa.[36]

One of the characteristics of West African Ethiopianism, as symbolised by James Johnson, was that it rested on the foundation of Christianity, the verities and moral canons of which would be the touchstone by which the African State and its peoples would be assessed. Unlike Central and Southern Africa there was no question of using the physical, organised Church as an instrument for the propagation of anti-white sentiments or as the safety-valve for a psychological and emotional escape from the world of social grievances against their white masters. West African Ethiopianism was positive, constructive and optimistic. It demanded that Africans must first of all be, in the spiritual sense, genuine Christians.[37] As

James Johnson conceived it, the African glorious past dated only from the time of the earliest Christian Church in North Africa, when bishoprics were filled by Africans and intellectual divines such as Tertullian, Augustine and Cyprian, people in their days greater than contemporary Europeans, were produced and commanded the respect of Christendom.[38] According to James Johnson, Africa lost her great moment in history when the North African Church failed to spread this faith to the rest of the continent and the North African society failed to accept it as the way of life. The consequence of this failure, he said, was that by divine will and punishment, Africa lapsed to the Dark Ages. As he put it: "Africa has been the basest of kingdoms: the judgment of the Lord has rested upon her for her negligence to disseminate Christian truth in the days of her spiritual glory and she had stood long deprived of it".[39]

According to his philosophy of history it was because Europe accepted Christianity, making it the way of life for all members of society, that the Western countries became great. In James Johnson's view Christianity was the key to the storehouse of worldly bliss, technical marvels and eternal salvation. Because of this Africa must disown Islam and traditional religion and return to the worship of Jehovah. Not until Africa did this, he said, would she be able to claim and assert equality with other countries and count for something in the transactions of human affairs; not until then would the millennium arrive "and the greater days of the Negro Race shall exceed the former". As he declared publicly in 1867:

Africa is to rise once more; Ethiopia is to stretch out her hands unto God, her tears are to be wiped off her eyes; her candlestick is to be replaced; her scores of cathedrals and Bishops are to be restored, her Christian colleges are to be re-established, her native literature is to revive, and science again is to dwell in her, the word of the Lord above all is to cover her as the waters do the mighty deep: where this shall be the case then she will take her place with the most Christian, civilized and intelligent nations of the Earth. The Native Church of this Colony is expected to do this work.[40]

Secondly, West African Ethiopianism rested on an expectancy, a sudden arrival of the millennium.[41] In Church and State it was expected that the British would surrender control in a matter of one generation. In the State, according to James Johnson, the recommendation of the Parliamentary Committee of 1865, that the British should withdraw from all their West African settlements, should be implemented at once. For the rest of the century he never ceased to denounce what he considered the slow pace of social and intellectual development of Africans by the British and the latter's failure to evolve a clear-cut comprehensive programme of training Africans to "eventually govern themselves". As to the Church he expected that by 1917, at the latest, there would be flourishing "an extended native Church presided over by a large number of African Bishops, and ministered to by ministers of Ham's race",[42] and Africans would be witnesses of "Mohammedanism and heathenism dethroned and Immanuel's authority universally acknowledged".[43]

In the sixties and early seventies when the British rulers in Church and State were being exceptionally liberal in the training and appointment of tens of the educated elite to positions of trust and responsibility the Ethiopians believed that this policy would last for ever. Consequently every such appointment tended to be magnified out of its real value and significance. For instance, the Niger Mission of Bishop Ajayi Crowther, with all its African staff, was construed by the executive of the Native Pastorate as evidence that Ethiopia had begun to stretch forth her hands unto God and particular emphasis was laid on the limitlessness of the territorial extent of his diocese and his vast power, which, they said, were greater than those of any European Bishop in recorded history.[44]

Thirdly, West African Ethiopianism was based on the assumption and conviction that, as Henry Venn was ready to do, European missionaries would wholeheartedly co-operate in the implementation of this African vision. It was believed by the Ethiopians that the European missionaries would perceive the merits of their vision, that it was in the interest of Christianity itself. As a newspaper editorialised: "The conviction is deepening and extending both among thinking Europeans and intelligent Natives that the great work of opening Africa to civilization and Christianity must devolve, for the most part, upon the African, that the European will have an essential, but by no means the greatest or most honourable part in this work, that the discipline to which the African race has been subjected for centuries was providentially directed to this end".[45] Race, it was being argued, could not be divorced from missionary enterprise. Moreover, the Ethiopians believed that the European missionaries were in Africa to help, and that their purpose or conception of how best to Christianise Africans could not legitimately be different from the Ethiopians' own.

The implication of this belief was that in contrast to the Ethiopianism of other parts of the continent, West African Ethiopianism was not an anti-white manifestation. Rather its success was expected by the Ethiopians to depend on the working together of the two races, the Europeans being mere instruments for the training of the elite and for the granting of financial aid. When in later years this African assumption was belied by events, tension developed between the races and there began a struggle for positions in Church administration. But there was no question of secession with James Johnson. Ever loyal to the British Crown and eternally grateful to the Church Missionary Society he never became anti-white. What he detested was the racial arrogance of many of the missionaries in West Africa, their exclusiveness and patronising attitude, their failure to see themselves as temporary sojourners whose tutorship was required only for a period of time. He also believed that it was these missionaries, rather than the Church Missionary Society, that should be blamed for the disharmony that occurred in the relations of both races from time to time.[46] His main aim was to claim equality of the races, to persuade the European rulers in Church and State to perceive and acknowledge that Africans were the "normal equals" of all other races. He did not hate the mixing of the races as such, at least until Africans should have been sufficiently trained to be absolutely independent, but he wished that both in Church and State Europeans with less ability than Africans should gladly serve under the latter.[47]

Paralleled with the development of the Ethiopian Continental African Church came the evolution of the African State. In James Johnson's view state paternalism was as bad as ecclesiastical paternalism. As he reflected in later years, the British Administrations in Sierra Leone and Lagos were guilty of killing the spirit of manliness and independence in the Africans by superseding the indigenous authorities.[48] Therefore the British should not extend their rule into the interior. In the enclaves in which the British had established themselves Africans should be given training by means of a self-governing municipality in which they would elect their rulers. The elective principle should be introduced into the Legislative Councils in West Africa by the British, whose ordained task there was to train Africans to be "eventually able to govern themselves".[49] The African State was to be manned by thoroughly christianised statesmen who would base promotion in the civil service on a code of Christian ethics.[50] In this State Christianity would be the only religion; polygamy, slavery and slave-raiding would be abolished, inter-tribal warfare would cease to exist and the spirit of militarism would be outlawed.

Between 1868 and 1874 James Johnson's personality became more powerful outside the purely religious and ecclesiastical circles in Sierra Leone. The response to the Native Pastorate scheme had begun to take a political turn. The institution ceased to behave exactly as the European missionaries had expected. Its creation generated a feeling of confidence and self-dignity in the Africans. In spite of the profusion of their gratitude to the C.M.S. Parent

D

Committee the Society and the Native Pastorate were in a sense physically and administratively two separate bodies. The interests and aims of the two bodies did not need to be identical. By 1868 the Africans had begun to act as a group; they had become critical of the European members. The latter remained undisguisedly paternalistic and patronising in their attitude to their African wards. The Scriptural doctrine of brotherhood of all races before God did not create in them the sentiment of equality. The Africans were expected to appreciate the enormous sacrifices they, Europeans, were making at the expense of their health in a treacherous climate to educate, Christianise and "civilise" these beneficiaries of British philanthropy. Indeed some of them were wont to make remarks very irritating to Africans. Such remarks had led James Johnson to the conviction that, as he openly declared in a conference in 1868, "it is a *natural impossibility* for a *white* man to love a *black* man".[51]

To the delight of Benjamin Tregaskis, an arch-enemy of Venn's devolution of power on Africans, there openly occurred what he described as "an outbreak" between the European missionaries and their African wards; the missionaries, the Wesleyan Chairman reported, "are culminating [*sic*]".[52] The Africans accused the Europeans of being highhanded and behaved to their mentors in such a manner that, as the Bishop's Commissary reported it: "Had we been their greatest foes, their sworn and avowed enemies, they could not have behaved with greater violence."[53] So deplorable was their behaviour that the man whose love and principles were the main source of their inspiration, Henry Venn, had to warn them that they were very much in a haste and that he trembled "to think of the confusion and calamities into which the native Church would be plunged by a premature severance from the C.M.S."[54]

Venn's pleas were brushed aside. The Native Pastorate persisted in moving along nationalistic lines, in many cases quoting James Johnson's phrases. In its official report for 1870 the Executive declared that the Pastorate was, according to their conception, "a revivification of the early African Churches so much celebrated in Ecclesiastical History, and would fain hope, that the West African Church will under God, rise to greater grandeur than the Church of the North, and present to the dark and benighted tribes of this vast but as yet unknown continent a better type of Christianity. . . . Ethiopia is beginning to stretch out her hands unto God".[55]

The rift between the Europeans and Africans began to acquire a racial tinge. Indeed the Africans had the temerity to inform Bishop Cheetham, that as far as they were concerned he was racially Bishop for the Europeans alone and only institutionally Bishop of the Native Pastorate.[56] So pervasive was James Johnson's influence that James Quaker, hitherto regarded by the C.M.S. as a moderate and the person on whom Henry Venn had entertained hopes for leadership, became infected with it. "The general feeling here", James Quaker was daring enough to write, "is that all the Europeans *who do not love the Africans* should go away".[57]

The reaction of the European missionaries to the assertiveness of their wards was one of regret and bitter resentment at what appeared to be base ingratitude. They began to regret that the Native Pastorate had ever been created and Henry Venn was blamed for the unpleasant situation in which they found themselves. As Benjamin Tregaskis reported it: "The European men say that old Venn is madly set on this Native affairs [*sic*], and nothing that can be said can make him reflect. They will pay for it."[58] Henceforward the enthusiasm of the missionaries for the institution declined. As far as the European missionaries were concerned their wards were immature and self-conceited, hardly in a position to know what were the best African interests. The Native Church was an infant, needing the fostering care and wise guidance of experienced European missionaries, who were inheritors of a "Christian" tradition of several centuries' standing. As an irate organisation in Britain had to warn these prematurely self-conceited ingrates: "We beseech you to reflect to whom, under God, the *Native Church owes its very existence*, and who they were, who brought to the oppressed African, *liberty*, *light*, *education*, above all the Glorious Gospel?"[59]

Of greater interest for us is the fact that the controversy ceased to be an Anglican affair; it transcended ecclesiastical and religious frontiers. Leading Africans of all denominations, including Wesleyans, began to see the Native Pastorate in predominantly racial and nationalistic terms. When in 1872 opposition to the institution was no longer confined to Benjamin Tregaskis with his powerful press and "parabolic posters"[60] all over the town and was carried to the legislative chambers by an African protégé and Methodist sectarian, Samuel Lewis (later Sir), Acting Attorney General, all the three nominated unofficial African members supported the grant,[61] as they were to do in subsequent years. The arguments of these members of the Legislative Council and the interdenominational body that drew up a memorandum against the enemies of the Native Pastorate are interesting not only because they echo James Johnson's views but because they anticipated the ideas hitherto credited solely to the founders of the United Native African Church in Lagos in 1891. Institutionalised Christianity, they argued, was alien to them and had failed to win the deep and intense religious instincts of Africans.[62] Moreover, by its numerous sects it was abetting the balkanisation of Africa. The Native Pastorate

would wipe out sectarianism and harmonise African culture with
the Christianity of the Bible. They declared: "But we look forward
to the time when a religion of fully developed social power will
spring up among us; when the religious formulae and system
instead of being dull and profitless will be a source of joy and
strength; when mere denominational questions introduced from
abroad will sink into their proper subordination; when the hope
and power that spring from a people's harmony, the reverence for
something higher than man, which comes from a people finding
out and following their own will and instincts, will have their
proper influence. To hasten that time, and aid in bringing about
such results, is the aim and purpose of the Native Pastorate."[63]

The racial tension over the Pastorate developed into a kind of
press war. Both sides launched news media to capture the reading
public. The Europeans were anxious to forestall any African
initiative. Bishop Cheetham founded *Home and Mission*, published
in England but printed by the Grammar School.[64] The Africans for
their part launched the *Ethiopian* also printed by the Grammar
School press with the unconcealed hostility of the Europeans. Its
declared aim was hardly calculated to allay the fears of the European missionaries. The Prospectus made it clear that Africans
wished for complete independence.

Even though both sides presented their case fairly, they maintained a relatively sober tone which was not assumed by two other
news media. In May 1868 Benjamin Tregaskis began *The Warder*,
with the expressed purpose of attacking the Native Pastorate and
the Government grant to it. Not only did it go "like hot loaf" but,
according to the Wesleyan Superintendent, it introduced a better
kind of journalism into the Colony than the "namby-pamby para-
graphs and scurrillous [sic] articles"[65] that people were accustomed to
read in other journals. Although he did not soften his opposition
to the Native Pastorate which he called "this great mistake" and
"moonshine",[66] the appearance of another African newspaper, *The
Negro*, with its fire-eating anti-European tone soon drove him to
use the Wesleyan Press against the "depreciation of the Europeans"[67] by Edward Wilmot Blyden, its Editor, and James Johnson,
a close collaborator and sometime Acting Editor. They were lampooned as "conceited, self-sufficient selfish persons, who seek their
own objects"[68] and called the greatest enemies of the true interests
of the Colony.

The Negro, which was founded in 1872 by T. J. Sawyerr, an Aku
of Ijesa origins, and three others, all Johnsonians, minced no
language about its aim—the regeneration of Africa by her own
sons, with Europeans playing at best the part of auxiliaries. By the
end of 1872 the African press had become so popular that it sur-

passed in effect the news media of the Europeans. As one of the
latter observed: "I do see many indications of a desire to be rid
of foreign *supervision of every kind*. I believe there is even a desire
to be without the *co-operation* of white missionaries not only in the
Christian work of all kinds carried on within the Colony, but in
mission work beyond."[69]

All campaigns against the Native Pastorate by Tregaskis and
others failed, as far as the Government grant was concerned. All
the Governors from 1868 to 1874—Blackall, Kennedy and Pope
Hennessy—were of one mind, that the grant should continue
because the institution was in the interest of Africans.[70] In the
Colonial Office, the disestablishment of the Irish Church notwithstanding, there was a determination to retain the Government
support for the Native Pastorate. As an official minuted: "Sierra
Leone is not ripe for any degree of disendowment."[71]

By 1873 the Bishop of Sierra Leone had become so apprehensive
of the Ethiopian movement that he believed that James Johnson
would like to go completely over the brink and found an independent African Church, wholly separated from the Anglican
Communion, comprising all sects and countenancing African
customs with which the Church of England could not compromise.[72]
The Bishop's views of what the Church in Sierra Leone ought to
be were quite orthodox; it was to be nothing more than a projection of the Church of England and he considered it his duty to see
that the movement being led by James Johnson should fail. "I
believe", he wrote, "it would be an untold loss for us not to abide
under the shadow of the Church of the Fatherland, and to keep,
what the Episcopate Church in America and the Church of Ireland
are feeling after, our connecting link with the Archbishop of Canterbury."[73]

According to Bishop Cheetham the only obstacle in James
Johnson's way was the fact that all Church property, including
that of the Native Pastorate, had been registered in the name of
the Church Missionary Society.[74] Therefore he warned that it would
be a great mistake if the Society should ever transfer its property
to the Native Pastorate. As long as he occupied his position, "no
transfer of this property can very well take place without my consent: and that after I shall have ceased to occupy the See, I am
willing to rely that the Society will be faithful to its own principles
and not transfer these Parsonage Houses to any Trust of any Church
which is not in communion with the Reformed Church of England
and desirous of recognition by and maintaining so far as may be
allowed and secured friendly relations with the See of Canterbury."[75]

It should not be imagined that the Bishop was imagining the
dangers. Past experiences in Sierra Leone and other events in

Nigeria in the nineteenth century were to reveal that secession was easier where congregations had become owners of property. The secessionists from the Wesleyan Society of 1821 were able to achieve their aim mainly because they were in legal ownership of their church. It was a lesson the Wesleyans never forgot. Tregaskis even got Hennessy to pass an ordinance vesting Rawdon Street Chapel in himself.[76] In the same manner the rebellion which James Johnson was to lead in 1891 in sympathy with Bishop Crowther was successful because the Church Missionary Society could not claim ownership to the land on which the Mission buildings were erected. In Lagos and Yorubaland, according to missionaries on the spot, the Anglican community would have broken away from the parent body in the years when James Johnson was leader of the Church but for the fact that conveyances had been carried out in the Society's name.[77] Moreover the Bishop's fears should be understood against the fact that in these early years James Johnson's loyalty to the Society had not been put to a severe test, although he exceeded others, European and African, in Anglican opposition to the "Dissenters", as he liked to describe the Wesleyans and the Roman Catholics. James Johnson knew no restraint in language, was inflexible, knew no art of tact and was so extreme in his views that his opponents became frightened.

As will be analysed in the next chapter the feasibility of an independent African Church in the seventies of the last century and of the British withdrawing from their enclaves in West Africa was a wild dream indeed. Even if the British rulers in Church and State had been willing gradually to pull out, the conditions did not exist that would have enabled Africans to govern themselves along Western lines. As the more pragmatic Blyden observed; "if England were to withdraw just at this moment from the constant supervision of these Settlements, there have been no lessons learned during all the past, either by the people in the interior or those on the coast . . . the whole country [will] fall immediately into strife, rapine, bloodshed, and anarchy."[78]

Nevertheless James Johnson and his supporters must not be dismissed as mere day dreamers. The Sierra Leone people could probably have easily governed themselves, at a low level of technical competence perhaps, without the "bloodshed and anarchy" into which Europeans and Blyden would naturally have wished to believe they would lapse. British rule in Church and State seemed to point in the direction of self-government. It was an era when the educated elite in West Africa generally were not feeling any such pangs of discrimination, a time when in both Church and State, educated Africans were offered positions of responsibility and authority. Only a few examples can be cited here. By 1872 the Colonial Chaplaincies of the Gambia and the Gold Coast, which each fetched a salary of £500,—nearly double the salary of a European missionary—were being held by Africans, G. W. Nicol and Thomas Maxwell respectively. In fact in 1874 an African was holding the Colonial Chaplaincy of the Colony of Sierra Leone in an acting capacity. By the same date the only African lawyer in Sierra Leone, Samuel Lewis, was Acting Queen's Advocate, whilst in the same decade Dr. J. B. Horton, the distinguished Military Surgeon, held several high posts in Lagos, the Gambia, Sierra Leone and the Gold Coast. Examples can also be quoted with respect to the Gold Coast and Nigeria. This liberal policy towards the educated Africans, it should be stressed, was not just an expediency owing to the treachery of the African climate. There were officials in Church and State who believed, as a matter of principle, that Africans should be in charge of their affairs. In the Church might be mentioned Henry Venn, in the State Pope Hennessy. Even in the Colonial Office such liberals were not wanting. On the Gold Coast Dr. B. W. Quartey Papafio was appointed on the same scale of salary as his European colleagues. On this point an official minuted as late as 1887: "I would not make any race distinction."[79]

It is natural that people like James Johnson believed that this kind of policy would continue, that the British would soon launch a bold educational programme which would see emerge the technicians, scientists, civil servants, even women authors, and African ecclesiastics who would be at the helm of the Ethiopian state. He was not alone in this expectation. Edward Blyden believed that if the British were serious this could be achieved in a short time; J. B. Horton on the Gold Coast expected the British to grant the rulers of the Colony self-government between 1860 and 1870;[80] and in Abeokuta, in the interior of Yorubaland, "Reversible" G. W. Johnson was dreaming a not dissimilar dream through his Egba Board of Management.[81]

NOTES

1. See article on John Ezzidio by Christopher Fyfe in *Eminent Sierra Leonians* [in the nineteenth century], Freetown, 1961, p. 29.
2. *Industrial Exhibition at Sierra Leone*, London, 1866.
3. *Ibid.*, p. 38.
4. M.M.A. (Box 1868-1874), "Church Missionary Almanack for 1872".
5. C.M.S. CA1/25(e), Bishop Cheetham to H. Wright, 1/2/1873.
6. C.M.S. CA1/0178, James Quaker to H. Venn, 24/12/1871.
7. *Sierra Leone Weekly News*, "Sidelights on Bishop Johnson", 9/6/1917.
8. C.M.S. CA1/0123, James Johnson to Dawes, 20/12/1864; James Johnson to H. Venn, 15/4/1869.

9. *Ibid.*, James Johnson to Henry Venn, 20/12/1864.
10. *Ibid.*, James Johnson, *Journals*, March 1866; James Johnson to Henry Venn, 27/2/1868.
11. 1862, p. 127.
12. C.O. 267/317, Memorial of C.M.S. Native Pastors to Governor-in-Chief, 15/6/1869.
13. *Ibid.*, James Quaker to Hon. G. Phillips, 15/5/1869.
14. C.M.S. CA1/09(a), S. W. Blackall to Native Pastorate, 5/2/1868.
15. C.M.S. CA2/03, J. Hamilton to H. Venn, 14/4/1868.
16. *C.M. Intelligencer*, 1862, p. 127.
17. M.M.A., B. Tregaskis to James Johnson, 1/1/1867.
18. *Ibid.*
19. *Ibid.*, B. Tregaskis to Secretary, 5/6/1868.
20. C.M.S. CA1/0178, B. Tregaskis to an African, 1873.
21. M.M.A., B. Tregaskis to Secretaries, 15/6/1868.
22. C.O. 267/317, James Johnson to J. P. Hennessy, 6/12/1872.
23. C.M.S. CA1/025(e), Bishop Cheetham to H. Wright, 1/2/1873: quotes James Johnson in *The Negro*, 15/1/1873.
24. C.O. 149/3, Legislative Council *Minutes*, 30/10/1890.
25. C.O. 267/317, James Johnson to J. P. Hennessy, 6/12/1872.
26. C.M.S. CA1/0178, James Quaker to Henry Venn, 24/12/1871: quotes James Johnson.
27. *Niger and Yoruba* Notes, London, 1900, p. 15.
28. C.O. 267/317, James Johnson to J. P. Hennessy, 6/12/1872.
29. *Ibid.*
30. *Ibid.*
31. C.M.S. CA1/0123, James Johnson to M. Taylor and others, 19/4/1873.
32. C.O. 267/369, James Johnson to C.O., 26/7/1887.
32a. C.M.S. CA1/09(a), "Text of Sermon preached by the Rev. James Johnson at Trinity Church, Kissy Road on 13 May 1867 on behalf of the Native Pastorate Auxiliary".
33. CA1/0123, James Johnson to T. J. Sawyerr and others, April 1873.
33a. *Ibid.*, James Johnson to M. Taylor and others, 19/4/1873.
34. M.M.A., John Huddlestone to Secretary, 11/6/1821.
35. C.M.S. CA1/0123, James Johnson to M. Taylor and others, 17/4/1873.
36. G. Shepperson and E. Price, *Independent African*, Edinburgh, 1958; G. Shepperson, "Ethiopianism and African Nationalism", *Phylon*, 1953; B. G. M. Sundkler, *Bantu Prophets in South Africa*, London, 1948.
37. C.O. 267/317, "The Fifty-fifth Annual Report of the Sierra Leone Auxiliary Bible Society, 1871" by James Johnson.
38 C.M.S. CA1/0123, James Johnson, *Journals*, March 1867.
39. C.M.S. CA1/09(a), "Text of Sermon preached by the Rev. James Johnson at Trinity Church, Kissy Road on 13 May 1867 on behalf of the Native Pastorate Auxiliary".
40. *Ibid.*
41. C.M.S. CA1/0123, James Johnson, *Journals*, March 1863; *Sierra Leone weekly News*, 3/6/1899 (James Johnson's address at Exeter Hall, 12/4/1899).
42. C.M.S. CA1/0123, James Johnson, *Journals*, March 1867.
43. *Ibid.*

44. C.M.S. CA1/09(a), "Proceedings of the Annual Meeting held at Trinity Church, Kissy Road, June 1870".
45. *The Negro*, 16/4/1873.
46. C.M.S. CA1/0123, James Johnson to G. J. Macaulay, 4/5/1873.
47. C.O. 147/147 James Johnson to J. Chamberlain 27/12/1899.
48. C.O. 149/3, Legislative Council *Minutes*, 12/8/1889.
49. C.O. 267/369, James Johnson to C.O., 26/7/1887.
50. *Ibid*.
51. C.M.S. CA1/02, Minutes on Conference, 2-5 April 1867.
52. M.M.A., B. Tregaskis to Secretary, 14/5/1868.
53. C.M.S. CA1/03, J. Hamilton to H. Venn, 25/4/1868.
54. C.M.S. CA1/L8, H. Venn to G. Nicol, 23/7/1868.
55. C.M.S. CA1/09(a), "Proceedings of the Annual Meeting held at Trinity Church, Kissy Road, June 1870".
56. C.M.S. CA1/025(a), Bishop Cheetham to H. Venn, 1/2/1873.
57. C.M.S. CA1/0178, James Quaker to H. Venn, 24/12/1871.
58. M.M.A., B. Tregaskis to Secretary, 15/6/1868.
59. C.M.S. CA1/09(a), Address from the "Missionary Leaves Association" to the Native Church and Pastorate in West Africa, 4/4/1873.
60. *The Day Spring and Sierra Leone Reporter*, 8 and 15 January 1869.
61. C.O. 270/27, Legislative Council *Minutes*, 20/10/1873. Samuel Lewis was an old pupil of James Johnson in the Grammar School and he was under the spell of Tregaskis; see J. D. Hargreaves, *A Life of Sir Samuel Lewis*, O.U.P., 1958, pp. 17-20. But among opponents of the Wesleyan Superintendent in their support of the Native Pastorate institution were two prominent Wesleyans, John Ezzidio, especially hated by Tregaskis, and the Honourable Syble Boyle, one of the founders of *The Negro*.
62. C.M.S. CA1/09(a), "Correspondence on the Native Pastorate Questions", 4/12/1872 (printed).
63. *Ibid*.
64. C.M.S., CA1/0169, Oldham to Secretary, 15/8/1872.
65. M.M.A., B. Tregaskis to Secretary, 13/1/1869.
66. *Ibid*., same to same, 14/5/1868.
67. C.M.S. CA1/0178, B. Tregaskis to an African, 1873.
68. *Ibid*.
69. C.M.S. CA1/0169, Oldham to Secretary, 15/8/1872.
70. C.O. 267/317, J. P. Hennessy to C.O., 11/12/1872.
71. *Ibid*., Minute on above by J. P. Hennessy.
72. C.M.S. CA1/025(e), Bishop Cheetham to H. Wright, 21/4/1873.
73. *Ibid*., Bishop Cheetham to Secretary, 30/6/1873.
74. *Ibid*.
75. *Ibid*.
76. A. Montagu, *The Ordinances of Sierra Leone*, London, 1857-1881, Vol. V, p. 109.
77. C.M.S. G3/A2/02, J. A. Maser to R. Lang, 1884.
78. C.O. 879/8, E. W. Blyden to G. Berkerley, 12/2/1874.
79. C.O. 147/57, Minute by A. W. Hemming, 2 February 1887, on Jenkins Lumpkins to C.O., 26/12/1886.
80. J. B. Horton, *Letters on the Political Conditions of the Gold Coast*, London, 1870.
81. J. H. Kopytoff, *A Preface to Modern Nigeria*, Wisconsin, 1965, pp. 178-186.

CHAPTER THREE

STORMY PETREL IN SIERRA LEONE II

> In the work of elevating Africans, foreign teachers have always proceeded with their work on the assumption that the Negro or African is in every one of his normal susceptibilities an inferior race, and that it is needful in everything to give him a foreign model to copy; . . . the result has been that we, as a people, . . . have lost our self-respect and our love for our own race, are become a sort of nondescript people . . . and are, in many things, inferior to our brethren in the interior countries. There is evidently a fetter upon our minds even when the body is free, mental weakness, even when there appears fertility.
>
> James Johnson to Pope Hennessy 24/12/1872

JAMES JOHNSON possessed a cutting tongue which he could never curb. Where moral issues and the interest of the Negro Race were concerned, his words were gall and wormwood to all classes of Europeans who would not subscribe to his Ethiopian ideology and to Africans who would not evince fanatical Christian piety and passionate patriotism. Thus whilst the Protestant mission was being confounded by his vision of a monolithic continental African Church, Roman Catholics and their sympathisers in the Colony were having a taste of the vitriol in his tongue and pen.

The re-appearance of Roman Catholicism in the Colony in the early sixties was seen by James Johnson as an act of Satan who wished to use the Catholic Church as his "instrument" to deal a mortal blow to true Christianity and thereby prevent the emergence of Africa as an independent, progressive and modern continent like post-Reformation Europe. For he held the worst view of "Romanism", and he loved to ridicule the Catholic Church. In his judgement "Romanism" was an enemy of progress by its refusal to recognise the Reformation, which he regarded as one of the greatest events in human annals, and the herald of the scientific and technological revolutions of post-sixteenth century Europe.[1] Theologically, according to him, Roman Catholicism was "that system of lies" which had transmogrified true Christianity from its original character to the "vilest heathenism" by enjoining its votaries to be kissing crosses and be "bowing down to the images of holy apostles, martyrs and confessors".[2] Romanism was "the enemy against the Church and the world's peace", because of its authoritarianism which was incompatible with human nature and its denial to the individual of the liberty to approach God directly. Romanism also blasphemed against the Holy Ghost because it claimed to be the repository of all true knowledge, a tactical strategy being employed by the Roman Catholic Church, he said, to prevent its members from having direct access to the Bible, which would have removed the "veil" from the latter's eyes and enabled them to "dispel the darkness of ignorance and sin, convince the people of the corruptness of their faith, lead them to confess Jesus Christ alone, their all-sufficient Saviour, reform their morals (and) give a purity to their Church".[3]

He nursed a special hatred toward Pope Pius IX who in 1870 not only condemned all human progress in science and technology but also re-enacted the doctrine of Papal Infallibility, "at this advanced age", as James Johnson put it.[4] He commiserated with the people of Italy for their "long" imprisonment by the Catholic Church and perceived in the victory of the *Risorgimento* in 1870, which severely curtailed the Pope's territorial jurisdiction, a divine punishment for the usurpation of God's prerogative—Infallibility. He rejoiced that "Rome, the seat of papal power, is no longer a prisoner to her [the Catholic Church]; her gate has been opened. . . . Light is now taken to Rome."[5] Finally his inveterate opposition to the Roman Catholic Church was based upon the belief that Romanism was the greatest enemy of the Negro Race, in the sense that by preventing access to the Bible the thinking faculty of Africans was being emasculated. The African Catholic, he contended, would be too docile, a sort of automaton to be controlled from Rome; Africa would become a spiritual, mental and ecclesiastical colony of the Church of Rome.[6] In other words, for James Johnson the Roman Catholic Church in Africa was an imperialistic agency. Only free access by Africans to the Bible would save them from the clutches of Rome. For, as he declared, the Bible was "the Sacred Word . . . ; the Nation's peace and prosperity and a church's happiness depend most materially upon a prayerful reading of it. Its precepts and premises are holy; its exhortations soul-transforming and elevating."[7]

A man of such extreme views could hardly be expected to notice

in silence the efforts of the Roman Catholic Mission, particularly
when it began to achieve some measure of success, largely among
the few French residents, Jolofs and African repatriates from
Spanish and Portuguese colonial possessions. James Johnson's wish
was that no one in the Colony should countenance the mission's
presence, much less patronise it. Although compared to the Protestant Missions the Roman Catholic Mission had very little success.
yet what little it had he opposed with excessive zeal. In weekly
classes, in monthly lectures, at conferences, in the pulpit and in
the press he attacked the existence in the Colony of these "devour-
ing wolves in sheep's clothing".[8] He went from house to house,
persuading parents who had sent their children to the Catholic
school because of the inclusion of French, Drawing and Music in
the curriculum, to withdraw them.

It was James Johnson's view that the "Romish" system of education was the worst in the world—"the most degrading of degrading
systems"[9]—that would diminish rather than enlarge, damage rather
than improve, the mind of the African child. For recognising the
quality and value of the Catholic school, which was well organised
and better conducted than other schools, the African Editor of *The
Day Spring and Sierra Leone Reporter* became a target of scurrilous
attack. All supporters of Romanism, wrote James Johnson, were
guilty not only of "folly" but of "sinfulness" and should pray to
God to have mercy on them for their error. Little wonder that for
his intolerance he was mauled in an editorial and ridiculed as "the
most righteous of all saints" who "is so just, so holy, so pure, and
so consistent in all things that he needs no mercy—yes, no repentance".[10]

In the meantime James Johnson's anti-Romanism campaign and
the controversy over the Native Pastorate had dissolved into a
wider issue—the effect which the European presence was having
on the inhabitants of the European enclaves on the Atlantic seaboard of West Africa. This issue had a dual aspect: the negative
effect of European contact with Africa and its positive effect, that
is the best way in which Africans could appropriate the formal
Western type of education to the greatest advantage.

In the analysis of this wider issue James Johnson was no more
than one of a trio. No longer was he to enjoy the ascendancy he
had established over the Native Pastorate question and the crusade
against Romanism; no longer was he to monopolise and lead in
ideas; no longer was he to monopolise leadership; no longer was
he to be the lonely virulent critic of European missionaries and the
focus of educated African discontent with the progress that was
being achieved in the interest of Africans in Church and State; no
longer was he to monopolise the limelight and the anger and hos-

tility of aggrieved European missionaries. He became an associate with two other people, an African and a Britisher, themselves stormy petrels in their own right. They were respectively Edward Wilmot Blyden and John Pope Hennessy.

It is not surprising that both Blyden and Hennessy have got their biographers and each has received attention and credit greater than can be sustained by the evidence. Yet who scarcely mentions, how much less recognises, James Johnson's crucial role in the discussion of a West African university and the solvent effects of European contact on West African society.[11] For one thing E. W. Blyden was a gifted scholar, a prolific writer, a phrase-maker, a mesmeriser of audiences and a man with a career so varied that it extended from Liberia to all British West African Colonies, excepting the Gambia, from St. James's Court to the Negro world in America. Then there was John Pope Hennessy, who occupied the highest government position in British West Africa from February 1872 to February 1873, a man too radical and too negrophile for his age both among all classes of Europeans in West Africa and the officials at the Colonial Office.

But neither Blyden, nor Hennessy, nor the Sierra Leonian society of 1868 to 1874 would have pushed James Johnson to the second place or into the oblivion to which he has so far been relegated. In the light of the fact that the attention given to his two other associates has driven James Johnson into obscurity it is of utmost importance to define clearly the relations of these three stormy petrels responsible for what a victim, Bishop Cheetham, called the "Hennessy-Johnson-Blyden fever".[12]

Edward Wilmot Blyden was, perhaps, the only educated African whom James Johnson respected, not as a superior, as many contemporaries affected to believe, but as a colleague and as an African patriot who employed his numerous endowments, many of which James Johnson himself lacked, in the cause of the Negro Race. Both characters require close attention. Blyden was born in the Danish island of St. Thomas in the West Indies in 1832. According to his own evidence he was a pure African, born to Hausa parents. Apprenticed to a tailor in his childhood, he was sent to school by the kindness of missionaries, taking the name Edward from a Wesleyan mentor, Edward Fraser.[13] In spite of his educational background—he was refused admission to an institution in the United States in 1849 on account of his colour—his genius for learning was apparent to the extent that by 1851, when he set foot on Liberian soil, his talent for literary work was already manifest. A self-made man he became the most erudite of the educated elite in the West Africa of his day; no European, missionary, administrator or merchant, was his match in oratorical display. By 1860

Lord Brougham had paid tribute to his literary performance in the House of Lords. With his extensive knowledge of the classics, several European languages and contemporary literature on Africa he did not find it difficult to overwhelm his admirers and several ditties were to be composed about his genius.[14]

James Johnson was not the man who would not appreciate the intellectual superiority of this "prince of *African Literati*", this credit to the Negro Race. But he was not under Blyden's spell. When in 1890 his talents were being extolled to the skies in Lagos at an occasion chaired by James Johnson, the latter had to remind the audience that Blyden was a mere mortal deserving no praise. All praise must go to "the Maker not the instrument".[15] In fact there was never a single occasion when James Johnson quoted Blyden to reinforce an opinion, whilst the latter quoted and cited the former several times.[16]

The true position was that James Johnson was too individualistic to be anybody's disciple. Contrary to the impression which scholars of American Negro activities in Africa have given time and again, namely that manifestation of African patriotism by the educated elite in Africa must be traced to American Negro influence,[17] James Johnson, like many other patriots in West Africa, did not owe his ideas to Blyden or to any American Negro. The Ethiopian programme analysed in the previous chapter was not only unique but a monopoly of James Johnson and of Africans moulded entirely in the West African environment. Blyden had no Ethiopian ideology of a coherent kind or that bore any semblance to James Johnson's, nor did he ever attempt to found an African Church of any kind, much less use such an institution as an instrument for the political unification of the African peoples.

Apart from the peculiar development of James Johnson's mind which has been examined in previous chapters, further testimony of his individuality can be examined. First, there was very little personal association between the two patriots and no letter from one to the other has so far been discovered.[18] Blyden did not pay his first visit to Freetown until 1866, that is three years after James Johnson had begun to show by his behaviour and in journals the stuff of which he was made. In point of fact the evidence is that it was Blyden who first noticed James Johnson. This was at a conference in Freetown on 25 October 1871 at which the latter read a paper described by Blyden to Henry Venn as "an able paper".[19] When shortly after this event Blyden was dismissed from the service of the C.M.S., to which he had been appointed in the previous year, for an alleged act of immorality in Liberia, James Johnson became the leader of a protest group that urged the C.M.S. authorities to re-engage Blyden. So much did James Johnson like Blyden that he obtained evidence from Monrovia which convinced him that the charges levelled against the rising star of African patriotism were *"an entire fabrication"*.[20]

It is essential to examine their similarities and dissimilarities in order to dispose of the notion propagated by European missionary enemies that James Johnson was a disciple of Blyden and that, therefore, on account of this he was unworthy of ecclesiastical promotions. In some ways both had a liberal outlook on Islam, recognising that it had some beneficial effects on Africans, that it was an inferior religion to Christianity and that in the nature of its propagation in Africa its disseminators adopted better and more attractive techniques than Christian missionaries.[21] Time and again, both pioneers of African nationalism stressed, Muslim agents were Africans, with a sense of identity with their potential converts. Of greater importance for them was the fact that from the political and racial viewpoints Islam was doing for Africa more than Christianity "in making itself a religion of the people and country, developing and promoting self-reliance, a capacity for independent life and self-denial".[22] Muslim teachers adopted no attitude of superiority or racial arrogance as Christian missionaries were wont to do, declared James Johnson and Blyden, whilst Muslim teachers practised their faith, particularly with respect to the Koranic injunction about liquor.

Nevertheless their views and attitude to Islam were not entirely identical. Blyden was more tolerant of and more sympathetic towards Islam than James Johnson. Whilst the former believed that Islam was a blessing of some kind, making its votaries virtually half-Christians,[23] James Johnson believed that Islam was a curse, a foreign religion, "that gross and licentious religion",[24] which should be erased from the African continent. The Koran, for which Blyden had a high regard, was for James Johnson "an incongruous mixture of truth and folly, the sacred and the profane".[25]

Both were agreed on what they regarded as the bad behaviour of European missionaries towards their African wards, their racial arrogance and authoritarian tendencies, their habit of devaluing the African; both were concerned about the fissiparous effects of sectarianism on African society, both deplored and denounced the dichotomy between the white man's preaching and his practices whether he was a missionary, a trader, or a government agent.

However there is one respect in which it might be conjectured that James Johnson was influenced by his contact with Blyden. This was in respect to cultural nationalism. For there is no trace of cultural nationalism in James Johnson's letters and journals until 1872, a time when Edward Blyden had been advocating this brand of African nationalism for more than a decade. But whilst the idea may have been imbibed as a result of his contact with Blyden, it should be noted that there were differences in the items of African culture which they wished to be preserved and in the emphasis about the way cultural nationalism should be expressed.[26]

Nevertheless Edward Blyden and James Johnson were different in personality and in ideology in many particulars. James Johnson was a saintly character of a rare kind in West African history who, like the prophets of old, thundered vociferously against the excesses of his age; in contrast was Blyden to whom this attribute was never ascribed and whose life was not free from scandals.[27] Both differed in their attitude towards the institution of polygamy. For James Johnson polygamy was a negation of "Divine Law", the cause of slavery, inter-tribal wars and jihads and a manifestation of human depravity. But for Edward Blyden this African institution was not a sin of any kind but the gift of Providence to Africans to prevent depopulation by the high rate of infantile mortality.[28] In fact he himself lived the life of a polygamist.[29]

Despite all hazards Holy Johnson stuck to his principles, even when his life was threatened; there was no question of sacrificing principle on the altar of expediency. On the other hand Blyden was the master of realism; for him there could be no question of sticking to principles, particularly when his material interest was involved. This is clear from his numerous addresses to various audiences in which he told the people what he knew would please them. It was this characteristic which led to his consistent inconsistencies.[30] For instance in the period 1871 to 1874, with which we are mainly concerned in this chapter, Blyden posed as an exponent of African interests in many respects in the editorial columns of *The Negro*, but in his official and private letters to Salisbury Square and the Colonial Office he urged the British Government to assimilate the Western Sudan to the British Empire and the Church Missionary Society to send white missionaries into the same area as pioneers and masters, with Africans as mere auxiliaries.[31] This, it should be remembered, was at a time when the utterances of James Johnson led missionaries and administrative officers to believe that he did not want white agents in West Africa any longer.

More significant was the varied attitude of both to European intrusion into Africa. Throughout his life James Johnson never approved of European intrusion into the continent and he decried the Scramble in private letters, in memoranda and in public.[32] In contrast Blyden welcomed the Scramble, which he described as an event "ordained of God".[33] James Johnson did not believe that Europeans as a race were endowed with certain talents by divine authority that were denied to other races. Rather, he emphasised throughout his life that the Negro Race was capable of evincing genius in all aspects of human endeavour, "given the opportunity".[34] As early as 1869 he had begun to forecast that before long Africa would begin to boast of female authors. In contrast was the curious doctrine of Blyden's that Europeans were born to be superior to Africans in science, in technology and in ability to dominate other races, particularly the Negro Race and he urged Africans willingly to submit themselves to European rule in obedience to the will of God.[35]

In the light of all that has been said above it is clear that James Johnson and Edward Blyden were more colleagues and collaborators than respectively disciple and master. Both possessed attributes that made them have an instant liking for each other and to combine their talents in the interest of the Negro Race. It was in the short period from February 1872 to about the middle of 1874 that they had the most fruitful opportunity to work together and, for a time, carry with them the educated elite of the Colony of Sierra Leone. Through *The Negro* their ideas were disseminated with a virulence that stirred up bitterness in Africans against European missionaries in a way that the latter were never again to experience in the history of the Colony.

The Hennessy-Johnson-Blyden fever began with the castigation of European missionaries as, in James Johnson's words, "representatives of mistaken benevolence",[36] in a language that was more emotional than rational, more rabid than sober. The fever became more serious than it otherwise might have been when John Pope Hennessy, the Administrator-in-Chief, threw his weight into the scale. Born in 1834 in an Ireland still sighing for deliverance from the grinding heels of John Bull, he was destined to identify himself with the cause of colonial peoples whom he deemed oppressed. He was an unusual kind of governor, the only man in his position in nineteenth century West Africa who gave paramountcy to what he considered African interest at the expense of British imperial, missionary and commercial interests.[37]

The object of British presence in West Africa, reiterated Pope-Hennessy time and again, was not territorial aggrandisement but the "training [of] the natives so as to render them capable of self-government".[38] Students of West African history are likely to be surprised that he went on believing in the early seventies, like James Johnson and J. B. Horton, that the British would consider withdrawing themselves from West Africa in accordance with the recommendation of the Parliamentary Committee of 1865. For events on the Gold Coast between 1866 and 1870 had demonstrated clearly that the British Government had no such intention at all. Nevertheless Pope Hennessy began to behave as if this were the objective

of the British Government and he adopted the maxim that "wherever it can possibly be done I would strongly recommend dispensing
with the services of Europeans in this coast".[39]

It must be stressed that Hennessy's maxim was not based simply
on the fact of the continued hostility of the West African climate—
although he liked to emphasise this to justify his policy of appointing suitable Africans to vacant high posts in Church and State. It
was an article of faith for him. But he also believed that this policy
would make the Administration of West Africa and of the Church
efficient. According to him Africans were the ablest diplomatic
agents in Government relations with traditional rulers, and were
efficient and trustworthy in the public service.[40] Consequently it
was under his administration that Dr. J. B. Horton was offered a
high medical appointment and Samuel Lewis became Acting
Queen's Advocate. When the position of Colonial Chaplain became
vacant in early 1873 Hennessy contended strongly, against the wish
of the Bishop of Sierra Leone, that an African would be better than
any European candidate.[41]

Like James Johnson and Edward Blyden, Pope Hennessy did not
believe in European agency for the spread of the Gospel seed in
Africa. In his judgment supporters of Christian missions in Britain
had misplaced their hope and liberality by investing in European
missionaries. For in the West African climate and circumstances
they were "feeble and ineffective", by no means a match for Muslim
agents. Only African agents possessed the qualities for the Christianisation of Africa and for fighting successfully against Islam:
"The Native Pastors mix with the people, speak their languages,
and understand their habits and customs."[42] He considered it an
injustice that although African agents did the bulk of the work yet
they were put in subordinate places and received a maximum salary
of £82 per annum, whilst their less useful masters were being paid
the triple salary of £250 a year. Nor did he like their authoritarian
attitude and their tendency to emphasise their superior status in
front of Africans. In fact he had to protest at seeing European
missionaries being "dragged about by pairs of negro boys in lieu
of horses".[43]

It is not surprising that James Johnson found an ally in Hennessy,[44] a Roman Catholic, with whom he corresponded on the
above points in a manner that shocked his ecclesiastical superior.
The Johnson-Hennessy correspondence was an idealisation of the
culture and natural endowments of the Negro Race. It was based
entirely on the assumption that Africans were traditionally and
entirely an embodiment of all virtues and completely devoid of
vices. Whatever vices were to be found in West Africa, they said,
were confined to Africans who had exposed themselves to European

contact along the coast. European missionaries saw themselves
lampooned and lambasted by James Johnson as representatives of
a philanthropy that had misdirected its vigour, denationalising
Africans, robbing the latter of their virtues and turning them into
nondescripts. This was well summed up in a part of his correspondence that merits quoting:

> In the work of elevating Africans, foreign teachers have always
> proceeded with their work on the assumption that the Negro or
> African is in every one of his normal susceptibilities an inferior
> race, and that it is needful in everything to give him a foreign
> model to copy; no account has been made of our peculiarities;
> our languages enriched with traditions of centuries; our parables,
> many of them the quintessence of family and national histories;
> our modes of thought, influenced more or less by local circum-
> stances, our poetry and manufactures, which though rude, had
> their own tales to tell. . . . God does not intend to have the races
> confounded, but that the Negro or African should be raised upon
> his own idiosyncracies . . . the result has been that we, as a
> people, . . . have lost our self-respect and our love for our own
> race, are become a sort of nondescript people . . . and are, in
> many things, inferior to our brethren in the interior countries.
> There is evidently a fetter upon our minds even when the body
> is free; mental weakness, even when there appears fertility.[45]

Two other points, neither of them intended to soothe European
feeling, were raised in James Johnson's letters to Hennessy. Firstly
European missionaries were reminded that the climate of West
Africa was a providential warning that their presence in West
Africa should be temporary and that ecclesiastical and administrative efficiency could best be achieved by Africans. Secondly
he emphasised that rather than having Europeans, even tem-
porarily, he would prefer Negroes from the New World, kith
and kin of Africans, who were more likely to identify themselves
with the aspirations and culture of Africa and bring with them to
Church and State the literary and technical talents they had begun
to demonstrate in America.[46]

The Johnson-Hennessy correspondence is significant in two
important ways. First of all it located for the first time in West
Africa a problem which was to receive the attention of colonial
administrators, social anthropologists, educationists and, latterly,
Christian missionaries—the general dislocating effects of Westernism on African society. This is also a phenomenon of current
attention. More significant, perhaps, is its historiographical value.
It recognised that Africans had a culture about which they—particularly the uncontaminated Africans—were proud and in which

the educated Africans should take a pride. This view was contrary to that being expressed by pseudo-anthropologists of the Anthropological Society of London and others like them in the United States, France and Germany, that the Negro Race was not a worthy species of mankind[47] and that their customs and institutions justified no investigation and studies. In fact the historiographical point raised by James Johnson and Pope Hennessy led to a counter-offensive by the Church Missionary Society through its main organ, the *Church Missionary Intelligencer*, in a manner not entirely absent from the present-day academic hemisphere.

Whilst not subscribing to the pro-white "Superior Being" theory of the pseudo-anthropologists, the literary defenders of the Church Missionary Society pontificated that *"the Africa of the negro has no past"*,[48] that she had no culture worth preserving and that in her interest she must be treated as a *tabula rasa* on which completely new material must be written. It declared: "But, it may be asked, Why Europeanize them? The answer might be, What else could ever be done? We have already shown that Africa has no past. How, then, were race instincts to be respected which either had no existence or which were fatal and soul-destroying to the Negro."[49] For, according to Dr. S. W. Koelle, the distinguished German missionary, whose opinion was regarded as gospel truth: "it must be acknowledged that Africa is an uncivilized country, and that consequently many innate talents of its inhabitants have remained for a long time dormant, and can be only gradually aroused by the agency of the Christian religion and a Christian civilization."[50]

However, neither James Johnson nor Pope Hennessy diagnosed to its roots the issue which they raised. The root of the problem was not "mistaken benevolence" as such but the nature of the society that was forced to be in contact with Europeans in the nineteenth century. The Sierra Leone Colony, for instance, like contemporary Liberia and the enclaves of the Atlantic littoral occupied by repatriated Africans, consisted of a polyglot society in which cohesion was very difficult to achieve. As historians of the Colony have clearly demonstrated, and indeed as James Johnson himself observed, each of the over one-hundred ethnic groups represented in the Colony tended to hang together as a social entity *vis-à-vis* other ethnic groups. In fact intense loyalty to the ethnic group was to be found as late as the first decade of this century among the Ijesha to which, it will be remembered, James Johnson belonged on his paternal side.[51] In such a conglomerate society as Sierra Leone's, inter-tribal friction was not unusual. Even when various tribes were represented in organisations like the Church, tribal allegiances and jealousies, such as were to affect James Johnson's fortunes in Yorubaland and in the Niger Delta, were not uncommon. Consequently Sierra Leonians in the years under review tended to be individualistic and in disarray, unable to combine whenever a collective project was on hand. Thus the solidarity that appeared to distinguish the Creoles as a group *vis-à-vis* the indigenous inhabitants of the interior was no more than a façade being corroded underneath by sectional jealousies and lack of confidence in one another.

This is the sociological factor missed by James Johnson, Pope Hennessy and Edward Blyden, and also by contemporary observers, who attempted to explain the lack of collective effort and solidarity in execution of worthy projects by the Creoles in the nineteenth century in moral and racial terms. Bishop Cheetham's observation on this matter is relevant here. According to him the degeneration of the Negro inhabitants of Sierra Leone Colony was chiefly caused by "the fact that in 1841 and many succeeding years, the best men among them were all sent away to the West Indies for soldiers . . . the feebler remained here, the stronger went away: and of course [*sic*]. This could not be without degenerating the offspring, i.e. the present generation."[52] Another cause was "the sins of the people, especially against their own bodies". In subsequent years the spurious explanation which became current was that the liberated Africans were the scum and dregs of their own tribal society which had sold them to Europeans. The Creoles, their offspring, could not be expected to possess virtues which they had never inherited and therefore could hardly be expected to cultivate the habits of self-help and self-sacrifice.[53]

Moreover James Johnson's criticism of the effects of European contact on Africans showed his demonstrating a characteristic that marked his entire career: that of a doctrinaire. He did not perceive that in some ways Christian missions had no alternative to Europeanising their wards in the Colony of Sierra Leone. Take for instance the matter of clothing. Should the liberated Africans not have been clothed at all? What clothing, other than European, should have been adopted by missions and Government who, as philanthropists, had mainly European clothes, generally gifts, to distribute? Or consider the question of language. Which of the babel of tongues in the Colony would be an acceptable and practical *lingua franca*? Which language, other than English, could have been acceptable to all the ethnic groups?

Valid, then, as James Johnson's criticism would be for a later generation, it was invalid for the age and circumstances in which he expressed them. Indeed by expecting from the missions patronage of African culture at this time he showed his lack of pragmatism and an incapacity to understand the situation and circumstances in which Christian missions were working in pre-Scramble Africa.

Moreover he ignored the fact that missionaries were well-intent-ioned, that in the light of their experience they were seeking to make their African wards not only fellow-heirs of their hopes of eternity, but also co-beneficiaries of the human accomplishments in the arts and science by which Europe had become exalted in the eyes of the rest of the world. True in later years James Johnson was to recognise, in other circumstances, the debt which Africa owed to Europe, but however, this awareness came about only after his first visit to England in 1873, when he began to link European material achievements with missionary enterprise.

Furthermore James Johnson and Pope Hennessy were decidedly prejudiced in their attack on Christian missions in these early years. First of all they romanticised African culture, ignoring the unpleas-ing side like human sacrifice, twin-infanticide, slavery and other institutions which in subsequent years James Johnson had to recognise as repugnant to Christian morality. Secondly both of them did not perceive that Westernism generally, the unit, was to blame for signs of disintegration in Africa and not missionary enterprise alone, which was a mere facet of that unit.

Finally in their views and exposition they contradicted each other in one respect. On the one hand they saw in the educated elite the products of "mistaken benevolence", the only hope for the regenera-tion of Africa, the people who were to hold the reins of power in a self-governing Africa. And on the other it was these very people tainted by European contact who were the liars, drunkards, cheats and idlers who were to rule over their superiors, the uncontamin-ated Africans in the interior, who were credited with "a manly bearing, a natural courtesy, a very keen intelligence and a frank and honest disposition".[54]

It was logical that the controversy over the evil effects of Euro-pean contact on Africans should centre on education, the chief agency that introduced Africans to the European mental and cul-tural world, transforming their taste, values and aspirations from the African to the European. The discussion that ensued bore fruit in many respects, leading in 1876 to the affiliation of Fourah Bay Institution to the University of Durham.

Although it is the part played by Blyden in the fanning of the flame of African demand for a West African University that has often been emphasised by scholars,[55] it should be stressed that James Johnson's attention embraced all aspects of education from primary school to university and that with respect to primary edu-cation he was almost alone in presenting the needs of West Africa before the Colonial Office between 1868 and 1874.

In order to place James Johnson's role in the educational develop-ment of British West Africa in its proper perspective it should be borne in mind that he was not an intellectual. Although he had a voracious appetite for gathering information about subjects on Africa and other parts of the world, particularly India and the British Isles, he had no university education. His sentences, which are often too long, are occasionally defective in grammar and structure. He did not have the erudition, the journalistic style and the forceful diction of Edward Blyden; nor was he gifted with the intellectual, introspective and philosophical mind of the distinguished Nigerian educationist, Dr. Henry Carr.

The whole concept of education had been engaging James Johnson's attention before he met Blyden and Hennessy. At Pademba Road he organised a private school, with himself as teacher and with tuition given gratuituously to most of his pupils.[56] In 1869 he had defined his own view of "a solid education" as "a proper training of the mind", that is education as an end in itself rather than as a means to an end.[57] This "solid education", too, must have as its core the Christian religion, through the Bible. As he said, "take it away from a child and you make him a devil." From this time onwards, he abandoned the idea of a purely secular education for the African child for two reasons. Firstly because "education not based upon the religion of the Bible, will be found productive of a race of infidels, atheists, freethinkers, and mere moralists"; it was "the greatest evil that can befall a nation".[58] Secondly, aware that Westernism was having the effect of depriving African children of the healthy moral restraints of tribal life, he wished that Christian morality should fill the vacuum, in order to enable the growing generation to be able to adjust themselves to the strains and stresses of the changing society.

For James Johnson the education given to Africans must be comprehensive, designed to train the Head, the Heart and the Hand, thoughts echoed later by James K. Aggrey of the Gold Coast. Concerning the Hand, he had attempted before 1870 to persuade the local government in the Colony to establish a millinery industry for women as a means to offset bad trade and relieve unemployment among young ladies.[59] In 1874 he emphasised to Lord Knutsford, Secretary of State for the Colonies, the imperativeness of training young men in brick and tile making, "the ordinary pottery work", scientific agriculture, practical engineering "and other like useful and profitable works".[60] There was nothing new in his demands. What made them significant was the timing. For by 1874 the efforts of the Church Missionary Society in the direction of industrial education had virtually ceased to exist. This had previously been inspired by Henry Venn, in concert with the African Native Agency Committee, composed of well-known philanthropists like Sir F. H. Buxton, Lord Shaftesbury and Bishop Wilberforce.

The Native Agency Committee did for several educated elite in West Africa what no colonial government was ever able to do. Between 1851 and 1870 a number of educated Africans were trained *gratis* in Manchester as mechanics, carpenters, clerks and tradesmen. Others were trained in the art of cultivation, cleaning and shipping of cotton and a few were trained in medicine and naval matters. Two individuals stood out distinctly in the discharge of this philanthropic enterprise. These were Thomas Clegg of Manchester under whom most of the trainees passed and who spent more than £7,000 of his own on the programme,[61] and Baroness Burdett Coutts, that noble lady, who gave out more than £2,000.

Several of the beneficiaries of this programme played important roles in West Africa and were to be among the most reliable supporters of James Johnson in Nigeria. There was, for instance, Henry Robbin, a *Saro*, who in his day was the wealthiest man in Abeokuta and whose daughter was later married to Dr. Henry Carr; there were Drs. J. B. Horton, G. T. Manley and W. B. Davies, whose medical skill was of immense value to their society. In the world of business on the Niger might be mentioned Samuel Crowther Junior (a son of the Bishop) who became Agent for the West African Company on board their steamers, and his brother, Josiah Crowther, who became Trading Master for the same Company. Then there was Isaac George, Agent for the same Company in Onitsha and last but not least, one Mr. James Ellis who was married to an English woman, and who bought a house and settled down in Manchester.[62]

However, the liberal generosity of these philanthropists which had raised the hopes of Ethiopians in Church and State was not to last for long. Old age compelled Thomas Clegg to wind up the business and transfer whatever remained of it to Bishop Crowther, whilst one by one members of the African Native Agency Committee died and were not replaced. It was this passing era that James Johnson wished the British Government to revive with the support of the local government of the Colony and, if needs be, with the money of the British tax-payer.[63]

However, James Johnson stressed that training of Africans should be shifted to West Africa, in Sierra Leone. This was because, apart from the supposedly veritable danger of the English climate to the African, he was of the opinion that the Africans trained in Britain would acquire British tastes, traits and habits and indulge in a material living which their earnings might not be able to sustain. Worst of all, contended James Johnson, was the fact that when they returned to Africa they would not mix with their unlettered countrymen or conform to the traditional way of life, whilst at the same time they would have lost the virtues of tradi-

tional African society. In order to have his views put to the Colonial
Office, James Johnson was in 1874 sent to Thomas Clegg in Manchester during which time he had meetings with others who were
willing to take part in the venture.[64]

Once again it is not difficult to perceive the contradiction, indeed
the fallacy, that underlined James Johnson's desire and programme
for an industrial institution situated in West Africa. He himself
and other inhabitants of Sierra Leone Colony who were trained
entirely within the environment of West Africa had little difference
in mental orientation from those trained directly in Britain. James
Johnson and all the Creoles were materially more prosperous than
the unlettered, over whom the elite felt themselves superior. It
was in this tragic dilemma that the educated elite of the colonial
period were to find themselves. The split which Westernism generally created by the emergence of the educated elite was unbridgeable
and still remains with us today.

In the meantime the chief focus of attention in the colony was
the discussion about the necessity for a West African University.
In order to be able to understand the part played by James Johnson
in this matter a brief historical development of Fourah Bay Institution will be of some value.

The history of Fourah Bay Institution since 1827, when the
first student, Edward Jones,[65] signed the Register, was a chequered
one. Although from the start the Institution was no more than a
theological one it drew students of all kinds—mainly C.M.S.
scholars—who became the intellectual leaders of society. But the
founding of the Grammar School in 1845, particularly when it
encompassed education of a general and secular character, reduced
the importance of Fourah Bay in public eyes. The Grammar School
was patronised by people all over West Africa who wished their
children to choose careers other than the Church. Only those who
would definitely become clergymen, invariably C.M.S. scholars,
went to Fourah Bay. Throughout the fifties only ten students were
educated in the Institution, at a cost of nearly £800 a year to the
C.M.S. Evidently it was a waste of money and in 1859 it was
decided to close it down "as a Collegiate Establishment until the
demand for education in the Colony renders its re-opening expedient".[66]

This resolution is worthy of emphasis, as it indicates clearly that
if the C.M.S. could have been sure of obtaining fee paying students
and there had been a real demand for a higher kind of education,
the Church Missionary Society would have been prepared to have
Fourah Bay assume the character of a "Collegiate Establishment".
The Institution re-opened in 1863 and in 1866 it became a subject
of interest for Henry Venn, when it became known that two students

were to be sent by the local government to England to study law and medicine. The Parent Committee began to consider the injurious effects which the training of youths with tender minds in England was likely to have and therefore began to consider opening Fourah Bay to "a class of students to be prepared for medical or legal studies in England: so as not to make Fourah Bay *exclusively* a Theological seminary, though this must remain its chief character".[67] A few months later Henry Venn became concerned about "the omission of a proper provision for a superior education for the ministry and for the learned professions, which ought to have been raised as a superstructure upon the excellent foundation of the Grammar School".[68]

Enough has been said to show that, as far as evidence goes, the concept of the origins of a university in West Africa must be credited to the Church Missionary Society and to Henry Venn. When therefore in 1872 the idea came to the fore in Sierra Leone society it was nothing new. In fact both Blyden and James Johnson had been anticipated by J. B. Horton by about a decade.[69] In his well-known book, *Western Africa, Vindication of the Negro Race*, published in 1868, he had repeated the idea that Fourah Bay be turned to a university. However it should be stressed that Horton used no racial argument in his demand, as James Johnson and Blyden were to do. Horton's University was to be a research laboratory for all disciplines which would make it possible for the mineral and sylvan resources of West Africa to be developed. The disciplines that were to receive the greatest attention in his university were Botany, Mineralogy, Physiology, Chemistry, Engineering and Architecture—reminiscent of the contemporary demand for scientific and technological education in preference to the Humanities and the Social Sciences.

In contrast was the type of university advocated by James Johnson and Edward Blyden. Their demand arose out of their desire to have African culture and racial characteristics preserved, against the supposedly deleterious presence of Europeans. As James Johnson said in the *West African Reporter* of 17 April 1873 it was to be an institution "that will leave undisturbed our peculiarities". The curricula of the university would be African and its teaching staff members of the Negro Race. It was not that Blyden and Johnson agreed in matters of detail. For instance Blyden minced no words that the proposed university should not be under the auspices or control of a missionary body and that all funds for it should come from the colonial chest.[70] In contrast James Johnson could not think of a completely secular university; it must be under the aegis of the Church Missionary Society, though with financial support coming almost entirely from the British Government.[71] So virulent was the language employed by these two advocates, who were being imitated by the *alumni* of Fourah Bay Institution, that the Church Missionary Society became truly alarmed that a secular university in Sierra Leone might become a practical proposition.

It was at this point that the Parent Committee decided to invite James Johnson to England for a discussion with him of all the outstanding issues—the West African Church, education and the university proposal—about which he had given them much anxiety. In fact by this time the atmosphere in Sierra Leone had become charged enough for the C.M.S. to consider it essential to set up in London a sub-committee to study the various measures necessary to meet the challenge posed by the Ethiopian articulations in Church and State by James Johnson. After a careful study of *The Negro* newspaper and the reports from its missionaries the Society observed that "while they would not wish to check the growth of a natural spirit of independence they think there is a tinge of expression which the Committee would deprecate and symptoms that the current of feeling is assuming a direction which requires some intervention on the part of the Committee".[72]

The only way in which the Society felt it could intervene was to summon the "chosen champion" of African aspirations, James Johnson, to England. His role did not receive the approbation of the Society. As they declared: "Appreciating as they do the earnestness, ability and devotion of Mr. James Johnson the Committee regret that he should have seemed to have entertained feelings and opinions of character expressed in the 'Negro'."[73] Nevertheless his character was unsullied. Bishop Cheetham, who was very bitter about the part James Johnson had played in the various controversies, could not refrain from bearing testimony that "he is notwithstanding one of the best of fellows . . . a fine fellow",[74] whilst other missionaries commented on his piety.

The magnanimity of the Parent Society to James Johnson was unusual and was something of a surprise to Bishop Cheetham. James Johnson could have been censured or dismissed from the Society's service, as was to happen to several agents in the Niger Mission ten years later. What weighed much with the Parent Committee was the outstanding quality of his life. The Society believed that he was being hypnotised by Blyden and that the scales would drop from his eyes if only he could be made to perceive the lofty aims and the altruistic purpose of the Church Missionary Society. As he was officially told, "the Committee determined to invite you to this country not only that they might take counsel with you on these questions (the various issues of controversy) but that by intercourse with Christian friends at home, and acquaintance with the labours of earnest men within our parishes your own soul might be

quickened and refreshed, and your judgment matured and
expanded. They had a good hope also that by personal acquaintance with the Committee and their friends, your attachment to
the Society would be strengthened and deepened."[75]

James Johnson's invitation to Salisbury Square became the
centre of attention for all patriots. African members of the Legislative Council, the press and clergymen, put all the burden of their
grievances on him. Churchmen hoped he would work towards the
formation of an African Church, a Church that would possess the
characteristics he was wont to mention; legislators and others
interested in university education expected that he would return
with some agreement that would lead to the founding of the university; all expected that he would succeed in bringing back an
educational package that would preserve African culture and institutions, which would bring about "the formation of a national
intellect from which respect for the race has not been eliminated".
In a long editorial comment *The Negro* of 16 April 1873 expressed
the sentiment of Africans as follows:

> Mr. Johnson will leave for England in few days; and we are
> satisfied that upon all questions relating to the educational
> exigencies of the country—the establishment of the West African
> University—questions of vital importance to the future growth
> of these settlements and to the perpetuity of their political and
> ecclesiastical institutions, Mr. Johnson will be able to give very
> useful information and many valuable hints to the Committee.
> He has, in the recent discussions upon education, borne a very
> prominent and creditable part, and we are sure that his views,
> candidly expressed as they have been, instead of giving offence,
> have met with the most earnest sympathy from enlightened men
> in England and on the coast, who understand the power of race
> instincts.

Rumours of every kind were afloat about what James Johnson
would do, to an extent that astonished the European missionaries.
It was said that he was going to plead for an African Governor
and an African Bishop for Sierra Leone.[76] Bishop Cheetham had
to warn the Parent Committee that although he was "really glad
to be rid of him for a while" no publicity should be given to him,[77]
a warning that was heeded—and that if they were not very careful
James Johnson might be "bribed" with a Roman Catholic Bishopric
of Sierra Leone.[78]

Before an examination of James Johnson's activities in Britain
it is essential to assess the significance of the agitation for a West
African university by James Johnson, Pope Hennessy and Edward
Blyden. Firstly it should be stressed that all of them were quixotic

in their approach and attitude; they were more emotional than rational, more doctrinaire than pragmatic, more prejudiced and sentimental than objective. As has been indicated earlier the Church Missionary Society had never objected to the provision of university education of some kind in Sierra Leone. No scheme for higher education could have been a practical proposition without the support of this missionary organisation upon which the burden of providing education in Sierra Leone had largely depended. But it was a dream for the agitators to hope for a university, or that this expensive experiment would be financed by the British taxpayer. For the Government had never played any considerable role in the provision of even elementary education. A Government grant, and that for specific subjects only, did not begin until 1870, and it was a very small grant. The first government education official, called Director of Public Instruction, one Mr. T. H. Popplestone, was not appointed until 1871. All he could do before death claimed him in 1872 was to conduct examinations in some primary schools three times, at six month intervals. For the next three years his position was vacant; as no candidate would apply for a job of this kind in an unfriendly climate.[79]

It is in the light of this state of affairs that the contempt with which the efforts of James Johnson and Blyden were brushed aside by the officials of the Colonial Office should be understood. Hemming dismissed the university scheme in a sentence: it was a scheme "more easily conceived than established"[80] and J. Lowther: "I don't fancy the idea of carrying out the educational crotchets of these Revd. gentlemen at the expense of the State."[81]

There should be no surprise that the Colonial Office did not examine the merits of the demand of Africans for a university from the viewpoint of the colonial subjects. In Britain herself, where Foster's Education Act had been passed only in 1870 and where free primary education was to wait for another generation, it could hardly be expected that the necessity of giving gratuitous and compulsory education (as Blyden urged)[82] to colonial subjects could have occurred to the Colonial Office. For thinking that university education would be given gratuitously, both James Johnson and Edward Blyden were wishing the Lords of the Treasury to pass through the needle's eye.

Indeed, aware that the question of education was not their business, the officials of the Colonial Office did what neither Blyden nor James Johnson ever considered: they consulted with the Bishop of Sierra Leone. For both James Johnson and Edward Blyden had never thought that their scheme was the concern of the missionaries on the spot, for whom they had some contempt, and they had always deluded themselves that they could appeal to the headquarters above the heads of local administrative officers and the European missionaries.

Nevertheless the African radical opinion, with the threat of secularism, expressed by James Johnson and Blyden had some effect upon the C.M.S. and was clearly reflected in Bishop Cheetham's comprehensive answer to the memoranda of James Johnson and Edward Blyden, copies of which he had received for his opinion.[83] The principle of turning Fourah Bay into a university of some sort, which Bishop Cheetham had accepted since 1871, was gradually put into effect in the following years when the Society resolved "to authorize the principal of the Fourah Bay College to forward through the Finance Committee any application that might be made to him for admission of any youth whose parents were ready to bear the whole expenses of his education".[84] In 1873 the Sub-Committee appointed to study Sierra Leone affairs took a decisive step by recommending: "That the ordinary curriculum of the College shall include instructions in the Holy Scriptures, Latin, Greek, and English, History and Geography, Moral Philosophy and the evidences for the Christian religion, the principles of political economy, Logic, Mathematics and such branches of Natural Science as may be found expedient and practicable."[85] Fees were to be £9 and £36 per annum respectively for tuition and boarding.

With this decision the raising of the status of Fourah Bay to a University College was only a matter of time. The discussion with James Johnson was over details and it dealt with the difficulties being encountered in obtaining men of the right calibre from Oxford.[86] Arrangements were protracted until 1876 when affiliation negotiations with Durham University came through and opportunity of university education was put at the disposal of West Africans of all religious persuasions who could afford the money and could be shown to be people of worthy moral character.

There is no evidence that demand for university education was as popular as James Johnson and Blyden attempted to make out. Blyden's idea that students from all over Western Sudan and from all ethnic groups represented in the Colony would continuously fill places in the proposed university was purely hypothetical;[87] James Johnson's observation that there were eager parents willing to send their children to a university in West Africa[88] was not based on a careful survey of the situation. Only a few parents—and these were exclusively in the enclaves of British West Africa—ever availed themselves of the opportunity. The vast population in the interior was neither consulted, nor did it want to be consulted. As resistance to European intrusion was to show in the last years of the nineteenth century the uncontaminated peoples in the interior did not hanker after connection with the British or their alien system of education. Indeed until the end of the Second World War Fourah Bay continued to be patronised by Christian missions and degrees continued to be taken by scholars who saw teaching as merely a step to the Christian ministry. The majority of them were sponsored by Christian missions.[89]

But the Church Missionary Society need not have been at all alarmed on the question of higher education nor by the Ethiopian movement led by James Johnson. Though James Johnson and Edward Blyden were prolific in suggestions and had an immense capacity for persuasive oratory they could carry the people of the Colony with them only as long and as far as Africans themselves would not be requested to bear any part of the financial burden the scheme would involve. They wanted *everything* done for them by the Government. If this help would not be forthcoming there could be no question of self-help. To advocate this, as James Johnson ultimately had to do, was to touch them at the tenderest spot. Only in 1872, to the chagrin of James Johnson,[90] they had been only too glad to be relieved of the Road and Land Tax by Pope Hennessy, which occasion they went on celebrating for many years to come.[91] Tax or self-help in any form was their bane.

Therefore the moment it appeared that the university of their dream could be had only if they would pay for it, enthusiasm for the scheme died out. Equally astonishing is the manner in which James Johnson was deserted on the African Church question once it became clear that they could have an independent African Church only if they would be willing to tax themselves more. It was a trump card which was adroitly employed by the Church Missionary Society supporters in Britain. The Native Pastorate was written to officially that no more financial help would be forthcoming unless and until the members of the Pastorate withdrew their anti-European and anti-Anglican feelings.[92]

The Native Pastorate's spokesman was its secretary, James Quaker. His language contrasted strongly with that of 1871 which has already been mentioned. He declared that the Pastorate, with its clergy and laity, disowned all that James Johnson had expressed in *The Negro*, that "they could not for a moment anticipate a time —such an event they most cordially deprecate—when there would be a breach of communion between it and the Church of England— when the orthodox doctrines and the Evangelical teachings of the Mother Church so absolutely essential to its permanent stability and vitality would be abandoned as a 'worn out vestment' ".[93] The Native Pastorate surrendered completely to the C.M.S. and was eager to return to its bosom, for it was their eternal prayer that "England may ever continue to befriend benighted Africa, and

Bishop Cheetham be encouraged in his self-sacrificing labours for the good of Ethiopia".[94]

It is an irony that James Johnson began to be deserted just as he was on his way to England. He had been too extremist for the moderates. As Quaker declared: "Mr. Johnson is the great man of the *Race isolation question*."[95] Most of his supporters did not wish racial separation from their European mentors if this would mean an end to European financial grant. For such people James Johnson and Blyden were too much in a hurry, demanding an independence that could not be maintained. It should be stressed that, had financial prospects been excellent and could they have stood alone, James Johnson would not have been isolated. In theory, then, the majority were prepared to go along with him, but not if they had to assume the financial burden. As Quaker again said: "Israel is not to be delivered by killing the Egyptians, otherwise we shall have to wait—a good while in the land of Midian. God's time and mode of operation are the best. Africa still stands in need of all the aid she can get from British philanthropists and British Christians, in order to rise to her proper standard in the scale of humanity."[96] It is a sentiment that many independent African states in Africa today would express.

Thus before he set foot on English soil the African prop for his Ethiopian programme had begun to give way. Nor could he be sure of any further European support. His European collaborators, too, were in 1873 swept off the stage. Henry Venn went to his grave in that year and John Pope Hennessy was transferred to the West Indies. These European collaborators, it should be emphasised, had been willing to recognise the other prop of James Johnson's Ethiopian programme—the conviction that the Negro was biologically the white man's equal and that given the opportunity there was no marvel within the reach of any race that was beyond the attainment of the Negro. But those who succeeded these Europeans both in Church and State did not share these negrophile views. Of particular importance was the idea of the Negro held by doctrinaire pseudo-anthropologists like Winwood Reade and Richard Burton, and which had begun to be imbibed by a few individuals in Salisbury Square. In 1873, within a few months of Venn's death, one of the joint-secretaries declared to a missionary in Sierra Leone that "the Negro is not devoid I think of poetry and metaphysics, finding much difficulty in the higher branches of speculative knowledge and (with rare exceptions) incapable of original philosophic enquiry. He is not I think wanting in conscience; but his conscience is stronger in emotion and feeling than in practical authority".[97]

Nonetheless James Johnson left Freetown on the crest of popularity and arrived in England in a mood of optimism. He was well received by the authorities of the Church Missionary Society with whom he discussed the university scheme and the further development of the Church Organization, both internally for self-support and government, and externally as a Missionary Church. Then he personally met Lord Knutsford, Secretary of State for the Colonies, and discussed with him various matters including higher education, industrial education, the need of a Savings Bank, the necessity for training teachers as professionals, a geological survey for West Africa, in order to discover and exploit its mineral wealth, and the introduction of elective representation to the legislative chamber of British West Africa.[98]

His efforts with the Colonial Office were not entirely a failure. The Governor of Sierra Leone was instructed to introduce a bill at once to create a Savings Bank and some effort was made to introduce the pupil-teacher system into Sierra Leone schools, in order to afford some training to teachers. But on the whole his demands were regarded by the Colonial Office as too idealistic; the idea of elective representation was ridiculed, whilst nothing came out of his programme of industrial education.

With the Church Missionary Society he was more successful. He was assured that Fourah Bay would be raised to the status of a university, with a highly qualified principal, with the Revd. M. Sunter as Vice-Principal and with African lecturers. It was even suggested that one of the latter might be the Reverend Henry Johnson, an Aku of Ilorin ancestry, nicknamed Jerusalem Johnson, whose intellectual powers had been vindicated in translational works and Arabic studies.

Of greater ultimate consequence was the impression this direct knowledge of the C.M.S. and its friends at home made on him. From this time until his death, excepting the period of the Crowther crisis, he learned to make a distinction between the missionaries in West Africa and the Society in Britain. The latter, he believed, would never deviate from its pro-African principles. Whatever anti-African manifestation occurred in West Africa, he contended,[99] was the doing only of the local missionaries which Africans should learn to overlook. This belief in the undiluted philanthropy of the Church Missionary Society was to be reinforced intermittently by invitations with honours to Britain in 1886, 1899 and 1908. In fact from 1874 he had friends, many of them life-long, among his English admirers.

James Johnson was highly impressed by the technological and material advancement of England. On his return he gave a public lecture entitled "England And Its Greatness". From this time on England became in his eyes the exemplar that he would like Africa to imitate, the model that the continent should copy. As he put it, "I envy England its security, greatness and strength. I know how much she owes to Christianity for these things, and therefore ask for the same holy religion, pure and simple, for this country: Its strength is in its purity and simplicity."[100]

The Church Missionary Society also believed that James Johnson's invitation had achieved its purpose, "has brought him more entirely into harmony with the wishes and feelings of the Committee with regard to African matters".[101] On the question of relations with the European missionaries James Johnson believed that the Society had sided with the Africans, that the latter should "forbear" the bad behaviour of missionaries and that should any dispute arise between the races Africans should take their grievances to Salisbury Square directly and accept arbitration.[102]

Indeed so much did the Society become convinced that James Johnson was in its pocket that it was decided to give him a position of responsibility. The situation in Lagos, Nigeria, had become potentially explosive for the C.M.S.; nationalism of some considerable strength was threatening its presence in Lagos. It was believed that James Johnson would be the best person to handle the delicate situation; he it was who would be able "to strengthen the Native Church there as an important step in the direction of calling out and guiding aright the activity and energy of the Lagos Church".[103] In a word he was expected to be the architect of a Native Pastorate, similar to that of Sierra Leone, in which the Venn principles would be clearly observed. His salary was raised from £62 10s to £100 per annum at the transfer.

Although enthusiasm for the university, the African Church and industrial education died out when on his return he urged self-help as the only way out, yet he was still popular in Sierra Leone society. Hence the knowledge of his transfer provoked protestation not only from the African community but from Bishop Cheetham as well.[104] For several years after his transfer to Lagos, demand for his return was made at least three times. For Sierra Leonians after all, he was ever to remain "Wonderful Johnson".

NOTES

1. *The Day Spring and Sierra Leone Reporter*, 8 and 15 January 1869.
2. C.O. 267/317, "The Fifty-fifth Annual Report of the Sierra Leone Auxiliary Bible Society, 1871" by James Johnson.
3. *Ibid.*
4. *Ibid.*
5. *Ibid.*
6. *The Day Spring and Sierra Leone Reporter*, 8 and 15 January 1869.

7. C.O. 267/317, "The Fifty-fifth Annual Report of the Sierra Leone Auxiliary Bible Society, 1871" by James Johnson.
8. *The Day Spring and Sierra Leone Reporter*, 8 and 15 January 1869.
9. *Ibid.*
10. *Ibid.*, Editorials of the issues of 25 December 1868 and 8 and 15 January 1869.
11. Blyden has got of late two biographers, viz. Ruth Holden, *Blyden of Liberia*, New York, 1966, and Hollis Lynch, *Edward Wilmot Blyden, Pan-Negro Patriot 1832-1912*, O.U.P., 1967.
12. C.M.S. CA1/025(e), Bishop Cheetham to C. Fenn, 1/6/1874.
13. M.M.A., B. Tregaskis to Secretaries, 17/4/1872.
14. For example see *The Nigerian Chronicle*, 23/4/1909, and *Lagos Times*, 27/12/1890.
15. *Lagos Times*, 24/1/1891.
16. E. W. Blyden, *The Lagos Training College and Industrial Institute*; Correspondence between Blyden and Carter, Lagos, 1896; E. W. Blyden, *African Life and Customs*, London, 1908.
17. G. Shepperson, "Notes on Negro American Influence on the Emergence of African Nationalism", *The Journal of African History*, Vol. 1, No. 2, 1960, pp. 299-312; R. July, *The Origins of Modern African Thought*, London, 1968, p. 282.
18. Ruth Holden, *op. cit.* See the tributes paid to James Johnson in public on pages 197 and 631.
19. C.M.S. CA1/047, E. W. Blyden to Henry Venn, 28/10/1871.
20. C.M.S. CA1/024, Petition by James Johnson and eight others to H. Venn, December 1871.
21. *The Methodist Herald* (Sierra Leone), 22/2/1888.
22. *Ibid.*
23. C.O. 267/320, "Report on the Timbo Expedition" by E. W. Blyden, Freetown, 1873.
24. C.O. 267/317, "The Fifty-fifth Annual Report of the Sierra Leone Auxiliary Bible Society, 1871" by James Johnson.
25. *Ibid.*
26. See chapter eleven of this book.
27. In 1871 he was accused of having illicit relations with President Roye's wife.
28. E. W. Blyden, *The Significance of Liberia*, Liverpool, 1907, pp 31-33.
29. Ruth Holden, *op. cit.*, pp. 912-14.
30. This writer has read practically all the printed works and many unpublished official letters of Blyden. For similar judgment see C. Fyfe's introduction to the second edition of *Christianity, Islam and the Negro Race*, Edinburgh, 1967, pp. xi-xii.
31. C.M.S. CA1/047, several letters to H. Venn; C.O. 879/8, E. W. Blyden to G. Berkerley, 12/2/1874; C.O. 267/324, E. W. Blyden to Earl of Kimberley, 22/10/1873.
32. A.P.S. G.18, James Johnson to H. R. Fox Bourne, several letters 1891-1894; *African Times*, 1/10/1887.
33. E. W. Blyden, *Africa and the Africans*, London, 1903, p. 45.
34. *Sierra Leone Weekly News*, 3/6/1899: Address by James Johnson at Exeter Hall, 3/6/1899.
35. E. W. Blyden, *Africa and the Africans*, p. 44.
36. *The Negro*, 1/1/1873.

37. Fourah Bay College Library RS 916, J. P. Hennessy, *Papers dealing with John Pope Hennessy's administration of the West African Settlement*, p. 81.
38. C.O. 267/317, J. P. Hennessy to Earl of Kimberley, 28/12/1872.
39. C.O. 267/319, J. P. Hennessy to Earl of Kimberley, 11/10/1872.
40. C.O. 147/24, same to same, 28/12/1872.
41. C.O. 267/320, same to same, 4/1/1873.
42. J. P. Hennessy, *op. cit.*, quotes John Pope Hennessy's Foreword to *Blue Books*, 1871.
43. *Ibid.*, quotes J. P. Hennessy, S. L. 1680 to C.O. in C.O. 267/316.
44. Curiously enough Hennessy merely marked offensive passages of James Johnson's anti-popery writings with exclamations, but no more.
45. *The Negro*, 1/1/1873, containing James Johnson to J. P. Hennessy, 28/12/1872.
46. *Ibid.*
47. Phillip Curtin, *The Image of Africa*, London, 1965.
48. *C.M. Intelligencer*, 1873, p. 228.
49. *Ibid.*, p. 244.
50. *Ibid.*
51. *Sierra Leone Weekly News*, 24/11/1900: see "Activities of the Ijesha Descendants Association" by Dr. William Renner.
52. S.L.A., Confidential Enclosures to Governors' Despatches (Box 1868-1885), Bishop Cheetham's memorandum on James Johnson's letter to Lord Kimberley, labelled "Privileged and Private", 17 April 1874.
53. R. July, *op. cit.*, pp. 298-299.
54. C.O. 267/317, J. P. Hennessy to Lord Kimberley, 28/12/1872.
55. Christopher Fyfe, *op. cit.*, pp. 389-393; p. 405 gives E. W. Blyden the credit.
56. *Sierra Leone Weekly Record*, 9/6/1917: T. S. Johnson's evidence.
57. *The Day Spring and Sierra Leone Reporter*, 8 and 15 January 1869.
58. C.O. 267/317, "The Fifty-fifth Annual Report of the Sierra Leone Auxiliary Bible Society, 1871" by James Johnson.
59. C.M.S. CA1/0123, James Johnson, *Journals*, October 1868.
60. C.O. 879/8, James Johnson to the Colonial Office, 21/1/1873.
61. C.O. 267/325, Thomas Clegg to Lord Kimberley, 21/10/1873 (transmitted by James Johnson in a letter to Lord Kimberley, 3/11/1873).
62. *Ibid.*
63. C.O. 879/8, James Johnson to C.O., 21/1/1874.
64. C.M.S. CA1/023, James Johnson to G. J. Macaulay, 4/5/1874.
65. Not Bishop Ajayi Crowther, as has been popularised by myth. See the Register in the Registry, Fourah Bay College.
66. C.M.S. CA1/L6, Minute of Committee of Correspondence, 18 January 1859.
67. C.M.S. CA1/L7, Henry Venn to G. R. Caiger, 23/5/1866.
68. *Ibid.*, Henry Venn to J. Quaker, 23/8/1866.
69. T. J. Thompson, *The Jubilee and Centenary Volume of Fourah Bay College*, Freetown, 1930, p. 35, chapter XIV.
70. C.O. 267/317, E. W. Blyden to J. P. Hennessy, 11/12/1872.
71. C.O. 879/8, James Johnson to C.O., 21/1/1874.

72. C.M.S. CA1/L8, E. Hutchinson to J. A. Lamb, 11/3/1873.
73. *Ibid.*
74. C.M.S. CA1/05(e), Bishop Cheetham to H. Wright, 1/2/1873.
75. *C.M. Intelligencer*, 1873, p. 262.
76. C.M.S. CA1/025(e), Bishop Cheetham to H. Wright, 21/4/1873
77. *Ibid.*, same to C. Fenn, 9/4/1873.
78. *Ibid.*, Bishop Cheetham to H. Wright, 1/2/1873.
79. C.O. 267/326, A. W. Hemming's minute on the confidential report of Bishop Cheetham on the affairs of Sierra Leone, 4/6/1874.
80. C.O. 267/317, Minutes on J. P. Hennessy to C.O., 28/12/1872.
81. C.O. 267/326, J. Lowther's minute on the confidential report of Bishop Cheetham on the affairs of Sierra Leone, 6/6/1874.
82. C.O. 267/324, E. W. Blyden to Earl of Kimberley, 22/10/1873.
83. S.L.A., Confidential Enclosures to Governor's Despatches (Box 1868-1885); not all of Cheetham's observations in this document were printed in C.O. 879/8.
84. C.O. 879/8, Bishop Cheetham to C.O., 17/4/1874.
85. C.M.S. CA1/L9, "Further Report of Sub-Committee upon matters in Sierra Leone", 1873.
86. C.M.S. CA1/023, James Johnson to G. J. Macaulay, 4/5/1874.
87. C.O. 267/324, E. W. Blyden to Earl of Kimberley, 22/10/1873.
88. C.O. 879/8, James Johnson to C.O., 21/1/1874.
89. This writer scrutinised the Register in the Registry, Fourah Bay College.
90. C.O. 267/317, B. Tregaskis to James Johnson, 9/12/1872.
91. C. Fyfe, *op. cit.*, p. 389.
92. C.M.S. CA1/09(a), Address from the "Missionary Leaves Association" to the Native Church and Pastorate in West Africa, Reading, 1873.
93. *Ibid.*, James Quaker to the Managers and Secretary, "Missionary Leaves Association", 7/5/1873.
94. *Ibid.*
95. C.M.S. CA1/0178, J. Quaker to Henry Venn, 15/4/1873.
96. *Ibid.*
97. C.M.S. CA1/1, C. C. Fenn to M. Sunter, 13/11/1873.
98. C.O. 879/8, James Johnson to C.O., 21/1/1874.
99. *The Negro*, 20/5/1874.
100. *C.M. Intelligencer*, 1875, p. 79.
101. C.M.S. CA2/L4, E. Hutchinson to J. A. Maser, 6/2/1874.
102. *The Negro*, 20/5/1874.
103. C.M.S. CA2/L4, E. Hutchinson to James Johnson, 26/2/1874.
104. C.M.S. CA1/023, G. J. Macaulay and others to the Parent Committee, 7/4/1874; CA1/025(d), Bishop Cheetham to H. Wright, 2/3/1876.

CHAPTER FOUR

PIONEER NATIONALIST IN NIGERIA

God and my country. James Johnson's Motto.

THE isolationist position in which James Johnson found himself in Sierra Leone over the African Church proposal and the West African University scheme was to some extent his own making; he made no conscious effort to organise a followership. It is doubtful whether, had he made an attempt, he could have got a sizeable number of fellow-Creoles to share *in toto* his extremism and views on moral, spiritual and nationalist affairs. It should be stressed that although Holy Johnson had a few life-long friends the basis of his friendship with them was more personal than ideological. As has been noted, for instance, Samuel Lewis, one of these few friends, was opposed to the Native Pastorate grant; G. J. Macaulay (later Archdeacon of Sierra Leone Church) with whom he usually stayed on subsequent visits to the Colony, was never infected with the Johnsonian quixotism in Church and State; T. J. Sawyerr, the publisher of *The Negro*, was attracted to James Johnson partly because of the Ijesha blood they had in common. Even Henry Johnson, nicknamed Jerusalem or Powerful Johnson and who later became an Archdeacon in the Niger Mission, was never ideologically or doctrinally a thorn in the side of the C.M.S. Authorities.

And yet Holy Johnson was at all times popular in every community in which he worked in West Africa. The secret of his popularity is to be found in his selflessness and championship of the interests of his countrymen. An irate British officer, F. Huggins, who deplored his anti-European invectives in Sierra Leone, perceived this fact when he wrote: "I consider him (James Johnson) an intelligent, hardworking, energetic, and honestly zealous labourer in the cause of Christ and of his countrymen and as having great influence amongst them from these qualities, and from the fact of his being one of themselves, endeavouring to do all he can for their advancement."[1]

In Lagos, where he arrived on 9 June 1874, he was to be the most respected, the most popular, the most influential and the greatest patriot for the rest of the century; here there were no Blydens or Hennessys to diminish his influence. In Sierra Leone he had had African colleagues, or rather, seniors in the former teachers—in James Quaker and John Ezzidio, whereas in Lagos he was in age and intellect something like an elder and a patron. In intellect the man who could have outshone him was Henry Carr, one of the best minds of his age, but so junior was Carr to him that James Johnson was instrumental in his being sent to Fourah Bay College in 1877 for a degree course. For the rest of the century the leadership in the Church devolved upon him. Outside the Church he provided both the initiative and the leadership in improvement schemes and in protest movements—whether against the Education Ordinance of 1882 or as chairman of debates about the Berlin West African Conference and the Scramble, or of the petition against Dahomian invasions of Yorubaland, or of pleas that the British should help to put an end to warfare in Yoruba-land.

Some of the positions held and the schemes he initiated in these years may be enumerated. He was for several years Secretary of the Church Committee of the Lagos Native Pastorate, and from 1883 to 1900 the first Secretary of the Lagos Church Missions, the missionary wing of the Native Pastorate; a foundation member of the Board of Education on which he served continuously from 1886 to 1900; a member of the Legislative Council from 1886 to 1894; the convener and chairman of a committee which sought to persuade the British Government to establish industrial education in Nigeria; and the convener of a meeting for the provision of a Poor House "for the weak, helpless and household paupers".[2]

The Lagos in which Wonderful Johnson found himself in June 1874 was politically and socially different from Sierra Leone Colony. In contrast to the latter British intrusion into Lagos was relatively short, violent and incomplete. Occupied by force in 1851 in the name of philanthropy and converted ten years later to a British Colony in the interest of British commerce, it was the land of a homogeneous people, a part of the Yoruba nation, whose customs and institutions were so resilient that they could not be treated as a *tabula rasa* like those of the polyglot newly-planted population of Sierra Leone Colony. It was into this traditional society that the British empire-makers and African repatriates began to intrude from 1852. By 1874 there were about 5,000 African repatriates from Sierra Leone, Cuba and Brazil, out of a total population of about 36,000.

Nevertheless it was the minority intruders who were to determine the political, social and economic life of Lagos for the next hundred years. It was a state of affairs to which the indigenes had not reconciled themselves at the time of Wonderful Johnson's arrival. Politically the British had seized all authority, having compelled Dosunmu, the traditional Eleko, to sign a self-denying ordinance in 1861. Socially the appearance of repatriated Africans was of little advantage to the indigenes. For although these repatriated Africans were mostly of Yoruba stock and a few of them became advisers to the traditional rulers, yet their fatherland lay really in the interior and so far as they were interested in the welfare of the Yoruba nation at all it was the interest of their own sub-ethnic groups in the interior that claimed their attention. Indeed they were in a sense a political danger to the indigenes. For they were more or less protégés of the British rulers, whose mental orientation, tastes, habits and aspirations they seemed to share.[3]

The dissimilarity between Lagos and Sierra Leone Colony struck James Johnson forcibly in favour of the country of his birth. Unlike the Colony of Sierra Leone which was overwhelmingly Christian—30,000 Christians and 8,000 Muslims—Lagos was predominantly 'pagan', consisting of 18,000 'pagans', 8,000 Muslims, 3,958 Protestant Christians and 554 Roman Catholics.[4] Moreover it was much less sophisticated than Freetown; it had not begun to produce a western educated elite of its own, depending largely on Sierra Leone for leaders in the Church and clerks in Government service and in mercantile establishments. Lagos had no newspaper in 1874, the *Anglo-African*, its first newspaper, founded in 1863, having been defunct for nine years; in contrast there were two vigorous newspapers in Freetown, apart from the news media of Christian organisations. Administratively and constitutionally Freetown was well ahead of Lagos. The former was the seat of Government for all British West Africa from 1872 to 1874 and for Sierra Leone and the Gambia in the new arrangement of the latter year; in contrast, rather than being given back an independent administrative status, in 1874 Lagos became an appendage of Accra. In 1874, while Sierra Leone could boast of African representation of eleven years' standing and three members in the current Council, Lagos did not have any African representation, the one nominated in 1872 having been nullified in the new arrangements of that year.

It is against this background that the poor impression which the Lagos of 1874 made on Wonderful Johnson should be understood. In his opinion it was badly located; it was unplanned and overcrowded; its streets were dirty, undrained, narrow, and few and far between; its houses were low, irregular structures, thatched with grass, lacking in ventilation and easily given to flames. Nor was he impressed by its inhabitants, the indigenes and the repatriated

Africans. The latter, he said, were selfish haters of one another, the former debased by the slave trade and liquor to such an extent that they could not appreciate the value of missionary propaganda. He had no doubt that society, generally, was morally weaker than that of Sierra Leone Colony.[5]

Hardly had he landed in Lagos than the leadership in the Church and in the nationalist movement was thrust upon him. He did not have to build his reputation anew; the one he had acquired in Sierra Leone was of sufficient standing to the elite in Lagos who accorded him a warm welcome[6] and was a source of anxiety to the European missionaries who did not like to see him in Nigeria.[7] Leaders of the incipient nationalist movement that had come into existence looked up to him for guidance; the Ijesha Association, whose primary aim was the political liberation of their country from the imperial yoke of Ibadan, gave him its special attention, whilst the Lagos Yoruba Association, an organisation of Oyo Yoruba which hated the Egba and Ijebu whose habit it was to close routes to their fatherland, presented him with money for possible evangelisation of their portion of Yorubaland.[8]

From the beginning James Johnson identified himself with the nationalist movement. Hitherto it has been the fashion among scholars to assume that Nigerian nationalism and constitutional development did not begin vigorously until after 1914.[9] This observation, to say the least, is misleading and not based upon empirical data. Evidence shows that there was a forceful nationalist awakening in Nigeria before 1914; that it was constructive, purposeful, inspiring and fruitful and that it prepared the ground for the better-known post-World War I nationalism. This nationalist movement had three distinct but inter-related strands, viz, the resistance of the Nigerian potentates to British rule, Ethiopianism, and cultural nationalism. These three strands were clearly exemplified in James Johnson's career, as the rest of this book will show.

But it is essential to stress that he did not originate Nigerian nationalism. Therefore in order to put in proper focus his contributions to the early awakening of Nigerian nationalism it is essential to examine the beginnings and nature of the nationalist movement —the "work of the Devil"[10] as the C.M.S. official described it— which James Johnson was expected to guide along a moderate C.M.S. path. By 1870 missionary enterprise had begun to produce inherent nationalism in Lagos and Abeokuta, the two key centres of missionary endeavour in Yorubaland. The educated elite, mainly repatriates from Sierra Leone, had begun to identify themselves with the interest of their fatherland and to protest against specific acts of the British administration they deemed inimical to the interests of Yorubaland. Not only did many of them protest against the violation of the territorial integrity of their country by the conversion of Lagos to a British Colony, but they also deplored the menacing and annexationist tendencies of some of the British rulers in Lagos towards the traditional rulers and peoples in the interior.[11]

From the elite perhaps the most important of these early exponents of nationalism was Captain J. P. L. Davies. Born of Nigerian parentage in Sierra Leone and educated in the C.M.S. Grammar School there, he was trained in naval business through the instrumentation of Henry Venn. By 1856, when he settled permanently in Lagos, he had become a businessman as well, trading between the Gambia and Lagos, and later on the Niger. By 1873 he had become wealthy enough to visit England on holiday and for business. In 1862 his importance was already recognised when he was chosen along with a European missionary, the Rev. J. A. Lamb, to mediate between the Egba and Ibadan at the outbreak of the Ijaye War. In the following year he criticised Governor Henry Stanhope Freeman for his anti-Ijebu and pro-Kosoko policy, which led to the bombardment of Epe by the British navy. As he declared: "The Government of Lagos is a very Despotic one . . . if this is the way to civilize us we should rather be uncivilized. Governor Freeman thinks that we should not be reasoned with at all [but] only obey whatever commands he gives."[12]

Davies could hardly have been expected to tolerate a Freeman in the Lagos Church of which he was a leading layman. But to his surprise the European missionaries in Lagos were Freeman-like in their temper and disposition to their African wards. They saw no necessity to take their converts into partnership. Unlike their counterparts in Sierra Leone they were mainly pioneers who had had to build the Church in Yorubaland from scratch. The Henry Venn scheme of Church government and devolution of authority on the converts had not entered their thinking. They regarded their converts and subordinate African staff as "infants" reclaimed only recently from superstition and barbarism. Their attitude was mainly paternalistic; they looked upon themselves as "Tutors and Governors" and behaved as "little local popes".[13] Had they to wait only for the emergence of locally produced followership their attitude would have been quite in order. But in Lagos their wards were the *Saro* in whom had emerged self-confidence, manliness and assertiveness and who were determined to be treated like men, if not like equals of white men.

In contrast to Sierra Leone, where initiative and leadership were assumed by African agents, it was laymen of the standing of Davies who had to take the initiative in the Lagos Church. For up to the time of James Johnson's arrival all the Anglican churches in Lagos

—five in number—were under the pastoral ministration of European missionaries, Africans merely holding auxiliary positions. Apart from Captain J. P. L. Davies there was J. A. Otunba Payne, destined to become one of the most ardent disciples of James Johnson. A *Saro* with the blood of Ijebu Ode royalty in his veins, he was marked for a long and creditable career in the judiciary of Lagos Colony. In 1874 he was the leading layman in Christ Church in which he was Church Warden. Then there was Charles Foresythe, a lawyer and Government Treasurer, for a time Clerk of the Legislative Council and, together with J. P. L. Davies, leader of laity opinion in Breadfruit Church. Worthy of note, too, is I. H. Willoughby, also a member of Breadfruit Church, an Oyo Yoruba whose tribal loyalty was later to cause anxiety to James Johnson's bid for the episcopate in the eighties.

Since these laymen were not on the payroll of the missionaries they were in a position to challenge the authoritarian tendencies of the European mentors. In 1872 three of them—Davies, Payne and Willoughby—were elected by the laity to the Church Council. Shortly after, to the consternation of their religious guides, they began to take the initiative in certain directions and to spurn the counsels of the European missionaries. Davies' differences with the latter began over an unwarranted interference by them in his business affairs.[14] To his surprise, without having investigated the cause of tension between himself and the European missionaries, Hutchinson, Henry Venn's successor, sided with the missionaries and cold-shouldered Davies when he went to Salisbury Square.[15] For founding the "Lagos Philharmonic Club" with the declared purpose of "enabling young men in Lagos to spend their evenings more profitably than it has been their habit of doing and thus improve their minds in many ways", Charles Foresythe was denounced by the European missionaries for not having consulted with them first.[16] When he presented half of the proceeds of a concert to the Reverend J. A. Maser for use by the Lagos Church his offer was rejected and he was denounced because there was allegedly in the entertainment a "great prevalence of licentiousness which sadly hinders the prosperity of families and churches in this place".[17] In the eyes of the European missionaries Otunba Payne had committed a crime because he attended a ball for Government officials without the prior approval of his religious guides.[18] These laymen could not understand the authoritarian pretensions of the European missionaries. As one of them protested: "do you intend us to be for ever infants in the Church? Are we not to learn to act for and by ourselves, and so get used to move in our social and religious spheres without that ever leaning hopelessly on pastoral guide; too much of which has ever kept us since in a helpless state."[19]

The anxieties of the European missionaries began to increase in 1872 and 1873 as what they regarded as the spirit of African revolt began to infect men of other denominations and their African clerical lieutenants as well. In 1872 the Africans of all denominations, headed by Governor Glover, had the audacity to ask Salisbury Square to send Henry Johnson to the Grammar School in Lagos, in the hope that he would be made principal at some future date.[20] This move, the European missionaries feared, was intended as a subtle plan by the educated Africans to expel them from Lagos. The following year the European missionaries had the extreme pain of seeing John Pope Hennessy, the ultramontane with whom James Johnson corresponded in Sierra Leone, succeed Glover. His popularity, arising out of his encouragement of Africans in Sierra Leone, had preceded him to Lagos and he was enthusiastically welcomed. Characteristically he sought to remove the grievances which the policy of his predecessors had created for the Egba and Ijebu, the two branches of the Yoruba nation for whom British presence in Lagos had been most menacing. He promised to return to them all their slaves who had escaped to Lagos—a thing particularly distasteful to the European missionaries —and also those who had escaped to Ebute Metta, Lekki and Palma, territories claimed by these tribal groups.

Although Hennessy's stay in Lagos was very brief, and to the disappointment of the Africans he was sent to the Bahamas, his policy drove a wedge between the leading educated Africans who agreed with him and the European missionaries who viewed his transfer as a happy riddance. Before he left Hennessy annoyed the European traders and missionaries by nominating J. P. L. Davies to the Legislative Council of the West African Settlements, the first Nigerian to be so appointed.[21]

Hardly had the European missionaries begun to rejoice at the disappearance of Hennessy than the educated elite began to present a united front, combining to found the first supra-tribal organisation in Nigeria with political aims. This was the "Society For the Promotion of Religion and Education in Lagos". Without the prior knowledge of the European missionaries all African clerical agents and prominent laymen, totalling 108, met on 1 October 1873 to found this organisation, which was expected to assume all responsibility for missionary and educational work in Lagos. Their aim, it was said, was to render the European missionaries redundant, so that the C.M.S. might withdraw them.[22] The European mentors, they observed, had not been working in the interest of African independence and this the Africans were committed to achieve. If they organised themselves well, they said, they would realise an average income of £500 a year, that is nearly £200 more than would be required to maintain Church and school establishments. The new society, for which a constitution was provided, it was said, was "a thing ordained of God and a beginning of African Church Missionary Society".[23] £96 9s. 8d. was collected at the inaugural meeting, with the Honourable J. P. L. Davies elected as President, C. B. Macaulay (a trader) as Vice President and C. Foresythe as Secretary.

The "Society for the Promotion of Religion and Education in Lagos" was the first organised collective act of rebellion by the educated elite—the product of Christian missions—against the white man's rule in Nigeria. The hand-writing on the wall was clear, and the European missionaries feared the "serious results" which this "very formidable" movement might have for the Church Missionary Society.[24] Therefore they spared no effort to nip this incipient nationalist movement in the bud. They threatened to dismiss the clerical subordinates if they did not abandon the movement, and sought to prevent concerted effort by appealing to each Church to act independently under their guidance for any improvement they wanted in education.[25] In the face of this opposition by the European missionaries the movement was weakened. But that it had been inspired by the African desire to demonstrate to the disparagers of Africans the virtue of self-help, is clear from the following statement of the Secretary of the movement: "We are generally talked of as being selfish and apathetic and indifferent to public interests and public good; and that unless roused to action we can never think of or do any good for or by ourselves; but whenever anyone of us makes any move with a feeling that we ought to try to do so, he is sure to come into contact with the very clergy who have come to teach the people to do so."[26]

It is clear from the above that James Johnson did not initiate Nigerian nationalist sentiment. Indeed no educated elite did. The real origins of Nigerian nationalism are to be found in the reaction of the shrewd Nigerian rulers in Yorubaland and in Old Calabar to the British imperialism which was just evident during the coming of missionaries to Nigeria in the forties, that is before the European missionaries and educated Africans began to nurse the ideas which Ajayi has dealt with so thoroughly.[27] In Old Calabar and Yorubaland perspicacious chiefs discerned from the beginning the palpable danger of missionary propaganda to the political and cultural independence of Nigeria and spared no efforts to destroy Christianity between 1845 and 1875. This crusade against missionary propaganda on behalf of Nigeria's sovereignty was carried on until the eighties in the Niger Delta by Jaja, by the Ijebus until the expedition against them in 1892 and until the turn of the century by the Fulani Emirs in Northern Nigeria.[28] It is essential to note that less shrewd kings like Eyo Honesty II of Creek Town and the Egba chiefs, who had welcomed missionaries, had by 1875 regretted their zeal in inviting and patronising the religion of the white man which began to threaten their sovereignty in a matter of years and desired to destroy it.

The resistance of illiterate Nigerian potentates to the white man's activity demands, it seems to this writer, greater emphasis than has been accorded to it so far and is not less important than the so-called modern nationalism of the elite. The chiefs were more than watch-dogs of the *status quo* and of their interests. The ideological difference between these traditionalists and the educated elite should certainly not be pressed too far. Apart from the fact that they did not want to embrace Christianity—the logical consequences of which they feared would result in their overthrow and the loss of their sovereignty—many of the kings were in principle as enlightened as the educated Africans. People like Eyo Honesty II and Jaja were not opposed in principle to technological development, nor did the Egba and Ibadan chiefs oppose the idea of railways *per se*; what they feared most were the consequences which might follow the adoption of these "improvements". Moreover if the concept of the nation-state was beyond the ken of the Nigerian traditionalists so its implementation was beyond the reach of the educated Africans. Its achievement was indeed the work of the British administration and it was achieved in the teeth of opposition from the educated Africans, who did not want the various kingdoms and states in what eventually became Nigeria to lose their separate political identities. Indeed only a few of the educated Africans really desired supersession of the Nigerian rulers by the British administration, at least in the period before 1914.

The foundation of the "Society for the Promotion of Religion and Education in Lagos" and the advent of James Johnson should not therefore be emphasised to the exclusion of the "traditional" nationalism of the Nigerian rulers. In fact there was a remarkable degree of co-operation between the "traditional" and the "modern" nationalists, far more than historians and political scientists have hitherto acknowledged. This co-operation can be traced back to 1861—in Lagos and the interior of Yorubaland. A few educated Africans and Dosunmu were never reconciled to the British occupation of Lagos and disseminated anti-British feelings to an extent alarming to the British administration.[29] Because of the danger in Lagos presented by Dosunmu and his educated advisers the administration brought back Kosoko, the man who had been toppled by the British bayonet in 1851 and who, chastened by experience, began to manifest pro-British feelings.[30] Also in the sixties and seventies educated Africans strengthened the intransigence of the

Egba and Ijebu Chiefs to the British, in the name of "Africa for the Africans".[31] In fact in 1873 the "Society for the Promotion of Religion and Education in Lagos" was in a sense part of the seething discontent with British policy since 1861 among both the educated elite and the Yoruba chiefs. Just as the educated Africans wished the white missionaries in Lagos to leave, likewise the Dosunmu party, the Egba and the Ijebu were said to be planning in 1873 a *coup* to expel all white people from Lagos.[32] Anti-British feelings infected the other parts of Yorubaland in 1874, at the destruction of the Ashanti confederacy.[33]

But while all credit for the first stirrings of Nigerian nationalism should not be given to James Johnson and the educated Africans it is beyond doubt that his advent quickened the pulse of nationalist feelings. For the first time the educated Africans in Lagos had a fearless, confident, able and awe-inspiring spokesman who could stand up to the white missionaries whom he did not consider to be superior. He was not the man to respect a white man because of colour, "an accident" as he called it,[34] but would respect a man because of the quality of his mind. As the President of the "Society for the Promotion of Religion and Education in Lagos" remarked to the C.M.S. James Johnson was "one of your best men" from whom "you must expect great things".[35] Within months he had inspired confidence in Africans, showing qualities and capacities which no European missionary had shown in Lagos before. His stature was enlarged by the fact that he was not only the first African to be solely in charge of an Anglican Parish in Lagos but also he was really in control of the most popular and wealthiest church, Breadfruit, on the island. The Society accepted his leadership and guidance at once and within a few months its President, J. P. L. Davies, had said of him: "Mr. Johnson has begun already to improve and organise all connected with our Church and the schools and I must affirm that we have not had a Christian disciplinarian in Lagos for a long time. Mr. J. Johnson I believe is a hard worker and may the Church and your works prosper in his hands."[36]

His superiority to all the Christians in Lagos, both European and African, was recognised by the European missionaries themselves, whose influence began to recede as that of Holy Johnson increased. Perhaps the best testimony is that of Bishop Cheetham, who visited Lagos in 1876 and remarked as follows: "I find him just the same good, earnest fellow that he used to be, greatly improved full of work and not at all sparing himself: and doing very well here. I am afraid there would soon exist far more sympathy between himself and me, than I should feel towards any other man; he mourns over the low tone of spirituality that prevails in missionaries and people alike and while he is doing harm in spreading discontent as to salaries and privileges he is otherwise fulfilling his ministry very satisfactorily."[37]

However, by asking James Johnson to stamp out nationalism in the Lagos Church the Church Missionary Society had misjudged the man. For James Johnson, there was no distinction between a genuine Christian and a true patriot. He was, and was ever to remain for the rest of his life, a dual man—a pious Christian and a passionate African patriot. There was no question of separating the one from the other. Christianity was cause and nationalism effect. Christianity was the creator, the sustainer and *primum mobile* of a nation's existence. The history of Christendom, in his judgment, illustrated this fact.[38] So, he said, Christianity must create an African nation. For him the political salvation of Africans was dependent on their religious and moral growth. For him the association of an independent national Church with an independent national life was an article of faith. It was his belief in the inseparableness of Christianity and the emergence of an African state that was the secret and fountain of his intense passion and apostolic dedication to the cause of the Christianisation of Africa.

The mutual dependence of religion and politics came to have a deeper meaning for James Johnson in subsequent years as he studied the theology of African religion. As he declared: "We Africans in our pure and simple native state know not any distinction between what is secular and what is religious. With us there is nothing secular. Religion enters into every department of life with us, and so it should be with all beings who know that they are responsible to the great Author of their existence and of all creation."[39] It became his practice to read race or African nationalism into practically every matter and to become often unduly hypersensitive in his relations with Europeans. Hence Islam was displacing Christianity in Africa because the former was in the hands of Africans; liquor was being sold in Africa because European races had plotted the extinction of Africans;[40] European missionaries would not visit their African colleagues in the latters' houses because they had a contempt for Africans;[41] the British administration in West Africa would not have Christianity supported in its secular schools because it wanted to destroy the moral and religious fibres of Africans;[42] colonial powers were encouraging Africans to be producers only in order that Africans might not become manufacturers and so on.

The amalgamation of Christianity and nationality in him are discernible in his earliest correspondence. In 1864 he wrote to Henry Venn that he felt himself "called to the discharge of noble duties both to my God and my country";[43] the Church Missionary Society deserved the gratitude of Africans "for giving us both temporal and spiritual liberty"[44] and for vindicating before the rest of the world "the position and the claim of the Negro to the brotherhood of humanity" and proving "that the Negro is not the ape and the brute that he was thought to have been".[45]

Rather than his nationalism being assuaged it was accentuated by the circumstances of the Lagos of 1874. It was in the Lagos Church that he was to have an opportunity to put into practice some of his nationalistic conceptions of the Christian faith. The idea of a Native Pastorate for Lagos had been conceived by the C.M.S. as the only practical way to contain the nationalist energies of, and the struggle for leadership by, the educated Africans. By its prestige and material display Breadfruit Church, the care of which James Johnson assumed, ought to have been the nucleus of the Pastorate institution. It was there that the richest Anglican laity were to be found; but it was also there that the ambitious and nationalism-inclined leaders of African opinion—J. P. L. Davies, Charles Foresythe and R. B. Blaize—were to be found. It was clear to the European missionaries that to start off the Pastorate scheme with Breadfruit would be to encourage anti-European feelings and help achieve the aim of the "Society for the Promotion of Religion and Education in Lagos". Nor was the adulation which the leaders of this organisation were giving to James Johnson welcome to the European missionaries. Therefore within a few months of his advent, that is about a year before the Native Pastorate was inaugurated, the C.M.S. authorities had been advised that they should not start the experiment with James Johnson's church. As Adolphus Mann, a pioneer missionary warned: "Here in Lagos a self-governing Native Church amounts to nothing more than Lagos governed by the Breadfruit Church and by a few members of this large body."[46]

Thus in a sense James Johnson was deprived of the church that would have facilitated the Native Pastorate scheme. But, since he resided in Breadfruit for the rest of the nineteenth century, save for the period from 1877 to 1880, something should be said about his parish and his activities there. In one important way it con-trasted with the Pademba Christ Church District: it was not inhabited by Christians alone. In the Sierra Leone parish there were only "two old Mohammedans" as James Johnson boasted,[47] the rest of the population being professed Christians. But in 1875 there were not more than 1,300 Christians as opposed to 11,000 Muslims and 'pagans' in the Breadfruit parish.[48] The new parish also presented him with another experience. Unlike Sierra Leone where English was the *lingua franca* the majority of the people in his new parish, indeed in all Lagos, understood the Yoruba language only.

Since he looked upon himself as a missionary-pastor and considered the Christianisation of the Muslims and 'pagans' as a primary duty he lost no time in devising means to achieve this aim. First, he began to learn Arabic, in the hope that he would thereby endear himself to Muslims and understand in a better light the standpoint of their religion in relation to Christianity. Then he began to learn Yoruba. By July 1875 he was able to record: "I am now able to conduct Bible classes and give short addresses in Yoruba."[49] From now on James Johnson became impressed with the richness of the Yoruba language and an ardent apostle of its preservation and development for the writing of literature. By 1875 he had become shocked at the contempt with which the educated Africans had begun to hold their native tongue. In order to prevent this attitude from growing further he urged the C.M.S. authorities to introduce the vernacular to its post-primary institutions in Lagos.

Breadfruit Church progressed tremendously under James Johnson's pastoral ministration. Between June 1874 and December 1876, his first tenure in the Church, he was able to collect £772 12s. 11d. for the new building that had been contemplated long before his arrival. It was during his second tenure that the debt on the new Church, which was dedicated in January 1881, was paid off. He conducted no fewer than 1,056 baptisms. Among those children he baptised many were destined to be national figures, people like Lady Oyinka Abayomi, the late Justice Jibowu and Dr. J. O. Lucas, author of the well-known book on Yoruba religion and minister-in-charge of Breadfruit from 1936 to 1965. By 1900 James Johnson's Church was boasting a congregation of 1,400 Christians, 500 of whom were full communicants, with an annual income of more than £1,000.[50]

In his parish, indeed in Lagos as a whole, James Johnson continued to pose as the moral guardian of the people. Concerned that the young men and young women of his parish were not employing their leisure gainfully he began to give them "occasional lectures" on secular subjects, designed to develop in them an interest in reading.[51] In 1885 he declared in an address: "I would recommend to the young men here a steady effort at mental culture, less addictiveness to light amusements which are already too many for Lagos and have a tendency by this abundance to dissipate the mind, and an earnest attention by each one to the claims of religion. I recommend to them the Lagos Mutual Improvement Society and the Young Men's Christian Association."[52]

But although the Breadfruit Church was not part of the Pastorate, founded in 1875 with the Ebute Ero as nucleus, until 25 March 1881, James Johnson remained the Pastorate's leader and inspirer, and his Church its financial backbone. In 1876 alone Breadfruit contributed £137 15s. 7d., which is more than half the total of £254 13s. 7d. realised by the organisation in that year. Against the European missionaries' expressed opposition James Johnson was determined to see that it became a success and, but for the period 1877 to 1880, he was the leader of the Lagos Church. According to him the Native Pastorate came into existence at a time of depression in trade, when almost all prominent African businessmen were in debt to European mercantile houses "and many of the people are scarcely expected to be able to redeem their mortgages".[53] Initially the financing of the institution had to devolve upon women communicants. Nevertheless he was delighted that the people were prepared to endure the sufferings its establishment entailed. It was not long before he began to emphasise, to the indignation of European missionaries, that the aim of the institution was absolute independence from the C.M.S. and the forcing of the European missionaries "up country".

Indeed the institution not only survived but waxed strong in a manner disconcerting to European missionaries. Consisting of only one church in 1875 it took in another in 1878. In 1881 James Johnson added Breadfruit Church and by 1889 the Pastorate had absorbed all the churches but one and to the astonishment of the C.M.S. were demanding other churches outside Lagos. In 1882 the Native Pastorate became a missionary body with its own stations outside Lagos.

It is significant to note that James Johnson seems to have learned a lesson from the bitter controversy about the Native Pastorate institution in Sierra Leone. For in the launching of the scheme in Lagos there was no question of asking for Government assistance, much as he would have wished to see it attached to the British administration for the furtherance of his Ethiopian dream.[54] For one thing the Wesleyans in Lagos were stronger than the Anglican community numerically and financially.[55] In the circumstances it would have been difficult for the British administration to show favour to the Pastorate without feeling obliged to show similar favour to the Wesleyans, an intolerable thing as far as James Johnson was concerned. For, it should be repeated, Wesleyans were for him "the Dissenters". Moreover there was no organic link between Church and State in Lagos—such as there had been for decades in Sierra Leone—which would have provided a means for linking the Native Pastorate with the British administration.[56] For many years he was to advocate that this absence of an established Church in Lagos be remedied and that Africans be appointed as

Colonial Chaplain and as Chaplains in charge of Prisons and the Colonial Hospital.

The creation of the Native Pastorate widened the rift in the social relationship of the white and black missionaries. In the School Board and Church Committee where the two races were represented bitter words were often exchanged and any relationship became purely official.[57] Africans saw in the institution a power agency and a training ground for self-government in Church affairs that would automatically qualify them for self-government in the administration of Nigeria. In the various committees and boards the educated elite began to question the practice of European missionaries in reserving superior positions for members of their own race, as if the grace of God and the operations of the spirit were confined to race or colour. Ousted from power which they had hitherto wielded alone the European missionaries dreaded the direction in which the Pastorate was moving. In an effort to make it indigenous ex-king Dosunmu and his white-cap chiefs[58] were drawn to Breadfruit Church by James Johnson, whilst Muslims and 'pagans' contributed to the erection of the new building of Breadfruit Church, which was opened in 1881.[59] The Prayer Book was revised to exclude prayers for the Queen of England and prayers for the native kings were substituted.

Although administratively the Native Pastorate was a part of Sierra Leone Diocese James Johnson did not regard its Bishop as really being a part of the institution and declared to horrified British officials on one occasion that the Bishop's presence within the Pastorate was tolerated only as "a matter of courtesy".[60] He wanted the institution to become absolutely independent because he believed that the African Church could never attain the necessary moral strength as long as Africans were subjected to the white man; independence would enable the Church to become more adaptable to, and more in accordance with, the native mind. Above all he stressed that only Africans would be able to utilise the rudiments of Christian doctrine found in traditional religion, such as the doctrine of Atonement, the meditation of Christ and the Incarnation in directing the minds of potential African converts to a true conception of the sublime tenets of the Christian faith.[61] In the report of the Pastorate which he wrote in 1883 he defined one of the aims of the Pastorate as follows:

Though our Pastorate is always described as Native it may yet be regarded as aiming at the full attainment of its character rather than as having attained it; for at present the sentiment and language of its prescribed offices used at public services, its rites and ceremonies of worship, the decrees by which it is governed, the chief direction of its affairs, its hymns of prayer and praise and even the tunes to which they are set are not yet its own but those of its foreign teachers. Native Christians breathe not yet those spontaneous native breathings which had marked their devotions in heathenism with the sounds of which the houses of worshippers, the sacred groves, the open fields, the hills and the valleys had very frequently resounded, which though idolatrous bare and bald, ever showed an intensity of feeling and a firmness and vigour of faith not unworthy of man's religious nature. . . . To promote this native character in our Christianity is one of the objects of (our) Pastorate Institution.[62]

Such recognition of the values of traditional religion was blasphemous, as far as European missionaries were concerned, in the last quarter of the nineteenth century. But what incensed them most were James Johnson's speeches and writings, his "vituberations" [sic],[63] at the anniversaries of the Pastorate and in the newspapers. Too often he drew attention to the signal success of the West African Methodist Church into which it will be remembered he was born, from which he reiterated often the Pastorate should draw inspiration. At the inaugural meeting of 1875, at which the Governor, John Dumeresque, was Chairman, James Johnson gave an address that stunned the Governor to such an extent that he compared him to Gordon of Jamaica.[64] In the following year, at the first anniversary of the institution, he spoke in a manner which made a European missionary, the Reverend J. A. Maser, record: "It grated my ears, which are, I confess, always revolting, when the tune 'Africa for the Africans' is struck."[65] A few years later another veteran missionary protested against the "cry for independence from the white man", "this craving for independence from the slightest possible yoke, if yoke it can be called", by James Johnson and feared that what this Ethiopian leader was organising was a "revolt", "a stirring for power against the Church Missionary Society".[66]

Within two years of his arrival in Nigeria the relations between James Johnson and the European missionaries had broken down completely. Every new white arrival in Lagos was warned to regard him as a fanatical hater of the white man.[67] He had not a single friend among them. His opinion of the white missionaries who came to Nigeria for the rest of the century was very low. In his judgment their behaviour was racist and at variance with the teachings of their religious profession. He came to have the conviction that they were neither spiritually nor racially qualified to Christianise Nigerians and that the earlier they left the country for the "regions beyond" the better. He deplored their racial exclusiveness

and unwillingness to accept their African counterparts on the basis of perfect equality. He saw no reason why people of this calibre should desire to see the Negro "hold subordinate positions under the white man and be always ruled by him in his own country".[68] He became implacably contemptuous of the academic and spiritual qualifications of all the white missionaries in West Africa who were, in his words, "men who are not liberally disposed and not ready and willing to demonstrate practically in their own lives their own belief in the brotherhood of our common humanity, the brotherhood that teaches and embraces all races and racial conditions" and wondered why Christian missions could not send to West Africa "men of a higher mental and moral culture and of more liberal views".[69]

So bad had the relations between James Johnson and the European missionaries become that in 1881, without ascertaining the causes of the racial tension in the Lagos Church, Salisbury Square authorities formally accused James Johnson of "manifesting race antipathy" and "hating the white man".[70] These charges he denied emphatically, attributing the source of the charges to his refusal to be subordinated to European missionaries. He declared: "With the missionaries of the present day an independent thought in an African and a clear enunciation of his convictions are a great crime. He has no right to them: he must always see with other people's eyes and swear by other people's opinions: he must not manifest any patriotic sentiments; he must denude himself of manhood and of every vestige of racial feeling and fling away his individuality and distinctiveness to make peaceable existence with them possible and secure favourable recommendations to the Society."[71]

The fear that the Pastorate would secede from the C.M.S. was aroused by James Johnson's persistent demand for a transfer of all Church property, formerly registered in the name of the C.M.S., to the Pastorate. The behaviour and language of James Johnson and of the representatives of the Pastorate on various committees seemed to confirm the suspicion of the Society's missionaries. The laymen of the Church Committee—popularly elected and representing the institution—were "ever to the front and on all committees",[72] complained the Bishop. Such men and James Johnson, it was stated, would "revolt against any control from the bishop", if church property were transferred to the institution.[73] It was even suspected that once independent James Johnson would tolerate polygamy and slavery. After all he could not take orders from a white man. So incorrigible, it seemed to the European missionaries, had the Native Pastorate become that it was being likened to a thorn in the side of Salisbury Square, comparable to the Irish problem in British politics.[74]

The foundation of the Native Pastorate signalled the beginnings of Nigeria towards independence, under the leadership of educated Africans. By marking the beginnings of the displacement of white dominance from Church affairs it removed Nigerian nationalism from the realm of ideology to that of practical achievement. The Wesleyans and Southern American Baptists in Yorubaland and the United Presbyterians in Old Calabar found themselves compelled to devolve power on their converts at a speed astonishing to contemporary observers. Through councils, committees and Native Pastorates, chiefly controlled by the converts, the idea of independence gradually spread throughout Southern Nigeria. Consequently by the end of the century the prestige of the white missionaries had fallen sharply and the days of the all-powerful, paternalistic and patronising missionaries were clearly over. By 1889 James Johnson had concluded that Nigerian converts had vindicated their ability to administer and organise and that they were mature enough to be allowed by the British Government to participate in the administration of their country by the election of representatives to the legislative chamber.[75]

The French priests of the Society of African Missions of Lyons had no illusions about the political implications of the devolution of power on their converts by the Protestant missions. They noticed that by 1879 both the white missionaries and administrators were already regretting the consequences of the education they had given to the Nigerian converts and the nationalist sentiments of the educated Africans.[76] It is not surprising, then, that the French priests rejoiced at the refusal of the C.M.S. to quit Lagos, as the Native Pastorate demanded, and the effective undermining of Bishop Crowther's position in the Niger Mission.[77]

It is remarkable that the Protestant missionaries themselves noticed that the ousting of the white man from the Church would be only a prelude to his ousting from the administration of the country. The C.M.S. Church in Lagos became a hotbed of "contest between the whiteman and the blackman".[78] The effects of the "heaping" of authorities on the Africans in the Church were already becoming manifest by the early eighties. "There is amongst some of the prominent and influential natives of this Coast a strong and frequently expressed feeling that Africa should be for the Africans", regretted a missionary who felt the pangs of Nigerian Ethiopianism. "They desire that Africa should rise in which desire they will have the sympathy and best wishes of every right-thinking person. . . . With such persons the presence of the white man in the country is only partially welcome. They think there is little, if any, need of his assistance in Christianising Africa. . . . Africans should be placed in the most prominent and influential positions, to the performance of the duties of which they are equal. This is the feeling of the equality of races run somewhat to an extreme in favour of Africans."[79] "The Committee have done their best, to bring about a root of Revolting Spirit in the Church": commented another missionary, "The cry 'the native, the native', is simply the worst you can do to them. They cannot bear it. This Spirit of Revolt against the white element is in the Church and will it not go over to politics?"[80]

As in Sierra Leone James Johnson and his ardent followers like Otunba Payne, J. P. L. Davies and Charles Foresythe saw the principle of the Native Pastorate operating in the commercial sphere as well as in the administration. On the Niger, until the advent of Taubman Goldie and his amalgamated company, and in Lagos until the nineties, the big firms left the retail trade largely in the hands of the educated Africans, while many Africans like R. B. Blaize, J. J. Thomas, C. J. George and J. P. Haastrup, to name a few, held their own in the commerce of the Lagos Colony as independent traders. In the civil service educated Africans held positions of responsibility, and in many cases they filled posts which Africans were never to occupy again until the attainment of internal self-government by the former regions of Nigeria during the 1950's. Until 1893 the post of the Chief Clerk in the Secretariat was occupied by Africans; in the eighties an African, Nash H. Williams, B.L., was made Crown Prosecutor and Legal Adviser to the Lagos Administration;[81] Otunba Payne was Registrar of the Supreme Court of Lagos until his retirement in 1899 and was Acting District Commissioner *pro tem*; for many years in the eighties Charles Foresythe was clerk of the Legislative Council and H. S. Willoughby, also an African, the Deputy Sheriff. In fact until 1902 Africans held the post of Postmaster in the Colony of Lagos.

By 1883 the C.M.S. authorities had concluded that James Johnson was becoming too powerful, in a way dangerous to the interest of the Society in Lagos, and that the differences between him and the white missionaries should be resolved. In the Society's words, he had become "an able and influential man . . . the leader of the Native Pastorate head and shoulders above all others", "the head of the party which desires to obtain independent power and control over the finance and general administration of the Church" and the chief cause of the "good deal of friction between the Europeans and natives".[82] In order to contain his nationalism it was suggested that he be made a member of the Finance Committee, the local executive of the Society which also administered funds. It was believed that his anti-European feelings would subside once he was in closer and more confidential relations with the missionaries, whilst at the same time as a sole voice he would not be in a position to influence policy, as all other members would be Europeans.

The European missionaries rejected this proposal. They argued that they would never be able to work with him, that his influence was too strong and adverse to them. As the Secretary of the Finance Committee put it, James Johnson "was considered too much of a partizan [sic] to work with Europeans comfortably";[83] the Reverend J. B. Wood made it clear that "his manner and conduct toward the Society's European missionaries is often very trying"; he would always like to carry out his ideas and "it would be an unfortunate if not a disastrous step to place him on that Committee".[84] Bishop Cheetham who was expected to persuade the missionaries out of their prejudice, had this to say: "I had him out for a walk with me and put many questions to him and the result is that I am afraid of making him even my co-missionary in Lagos. I do not think he is wise. I think his African feelings are dwarfing his catholicity. . . . I think he is trying to hasten an independence of the English Church which cannot be healthy and an independence of C.M.S. control for which in my opinion the Church is not ready."[85]

Although the Society deferred to the unanimous opposition of the European missionaries its disapproval of their attitude was emphatic. "The hesitation to hold out to him [Johnson] the right hand of fellowship and to invite his co-operation," Salisbury Square warned them, "will tend in our opinion to emphasise and increase the difficulty and danger which our brethren evidently feel do exist in consequence of the attitude of independence which characterises the man."[86] In fact the Society was rather over-solicitous to James Johnson. The tactics of 1873 were repeated; in 1884 it was decided to invite him once more to Salisbury Square, to assure him again of the Society's warm friendship and Afrophile policies.

The difference between James Johnson and the European missionaries was both personal and ideological. James Johnson could not genuflex to a white man, although he was by nature very courteous. Once he perceived what he believed to be the truth, personalities did not exist or matter; he became every inch unbending, unwieldy and unreflecting. He could not be moved from his position. Possessed of iron will, fearless and intrepid and plainly outspoken, he would not be companionable to European missionaries who were not disposed to recognise him as an equal or to subscribe to his views on Church and State matters. For the European missionaries the proper attitude which this African agitator ought to have adopted to the Church was one which regarded the Church as entirely international in doctrine and government. But their allegedly universalistic and international conception was narrow and not impartial; they really meant Anglican, that all authority should issue from Lambeth Palace and that no change should be effected in the liturgy and theology of the Church of England. Moreover the personnel that should administer the Church in Nigeria, they believed, must be European. Consequently their attitude to the growth of the spirit of nationality in James Johnson was that he was a rebel trying to revolt against constituted authority. The flaw in their thinking was that their attitude was illogical, that they ought to have perceived that Anglicanism itself was a product of the principle of nationality, against the ecclesiastical imperialism of Rome. In this sense James Johnson was asking for nothing more than that the same principle of nationality that the English had claimed for themselves should be recognised and extended to Nigerians as well.

All that has been said so far about the rise and spread of nationalist ideology in the Christian Church of Nigeria and the partial implementation of this ideology, reveals one fallacy in the belief of scholars, based on their study of the official records of the pre-World War I era. Indeed these records suggest strongly that there was no positive nationalist movement in Nigeria before 1914; that nationalist mumblings about nationhood were merely pious sentiments; that the educated Africans were anything but patriots and spurned with the contempt of ignorance all attempts to devolve responsibility on their shoulders. Nonetheless this impression is misleading. It misrepresents the priority in the thinking of the educated Africans. It does not take into account the fact that for the educated Africans the Church was by far the most important institution in their lives and that it was through the Church that they sought the achievement of their social and political aspirations.

Indeed James Johnson was by no means alone in the belief and hope that Christianity and African patriotism were like cause and effect, although he was the first and the most vigorous exponent of this doctrine in Nigeria. In a broad sense his politico-religious ideas were passionately shared by many educated Africans in Lagos and Old Calabar until the turn of the century. In the thinking of the educated Africans, especially in the last quarter of the nineteenth century, Christianity was not just the pure milk of the gospel but was as well the most potent political instrument that could and should be employed in the creation of a virile, independent, Nigerian nation state. As the newspaper of an ardent disciple of James Johnson put it, Christianity was being zealously patronised in the conviction that "it is the chief instrument that should be employed to promote the advancement of a nation, and that God honours the people that honour Him".[87]

The Church was the only institution in which the educated Africans could give free and unfettered expression to their own personality. Its political possibilities were already clearly understood by the elite in the early seventies and it was mainly because of its political usefulness that the educated Africans zealously patronised Christianity by maintaining their pastors and teachers, by erecting churches and by financing the education of their children, at a time when they were resisting taxation by the secular administration. For the missionary teaching of equality and brotherhood of all men before God, which had been implanted in them, produced in the long run its logical effects. Slowly many Africans began to nurse seedling ambitions for political self-expression and self-government, a corollary to the Christian theory of equality. Missionary education had already begun to stimulate critical faculties and they were becoming familiar with the general notion of British democracy, which all the Protestant missions were compelled to establish as the financial burden devolved on Africans themselves. Consequently the Church became an actual training ground for self-government.

Patriotic Africans came to believe that by practising Christianity they were paving the way for the creation of the Nigerian nation. They could not conceive of a Nigerian state in which 'paganism' would hold its own, inter-tribal wars continue and the economic system remain entirely agrarian. Rather the Nigerian-state of their dream was one in which Christianity would flourish, inter-tribal wars would cease and the industrial, technological and intellectual revolutions which had occurred in Europe would repeat themselves in Nigeria. Only when they were in full control of Church affairs and when Christianity had leavened the society would complete independence follow. Control of the Church would be progressively followed by control of the State. As James Johnson declared: "The people who are incompetent to sit as rulers in their own spiritual affairs can scarcely be said to be qualified to sit as Civil Legislators."[88] In the opinion of the educated Africans, whether in Lagos or Old Calabar[89] or Liberia[90] or Sierra Leone[91] the Christian faith was associated with the emergence of civilised nation-states in contemporary Europe.

Moreover, as James Johnson loved to emphasise, Christianity had another political significance. By encouraging a common consciousness it would reduce to a minimum all other sectional loyalties, such as the many incipient tribal groups that divided Lagos and Sierra Leone in the pre-colonial era. James Johnson was emphatic in his pleas to the Egbas and Ijaws that they should stop thinking in tribal terms but should rather see themselves as units within the organic whole of the Negro Race. He longed for

the time when Christianity would remove from Nigeria "difference
of nationality, language, custom and tribal feuds and warfares" and
produce a feeling of "oneness and common interest".[92] For him
the Negroes in the New World were Africans, "our brothers in
exile", whose repatriation to the land of their fathers he would like
to witness. As he addressed the Ijaw members of the Niger Delta
Church, the Church members of all localities should think of themselves as "only a part of a great whole, a very small section yet of
a very wide and extensive Diocese, a still smaller section of the
Church Catholic, and a comparatively insignificant portion of our
Race, the Negro Race that people the largest portion of the Great
Continent of Africa and that may be found in large and steadily
increasing numbers in exile in foreign lands";[93] the well-being of
the entire race "should be an object of interest and concern to us".

James Johnson himself was an excellent example of the new
concept of nationality that defied tribal frontiers and fostered
cosmopolitanism in Christian adherents. Tribal considerations never
entered his thinking. He became the greatest pioneer of Christianity
in the Ijebu territory not because of his maternal connections with
the people but because the Ijebu combined virtuous characteristics
and patriotism in a way that appealed to him. The christianisation
of the Edo, the Ivbiosakon, the Itsekiri and the Ibo, among many
of whom he was a pioneer, demanded no less attention from him.
In fact he was one of the earliest, if not the earliest, to pioneer
literary work of most of these non-Yoruba tribes.[94]

Indeed James Johnson's Church in Lagos became a dynamo
of nationalist aspirations in the last decades of the nineteenth
century. It was not an accident that the most historic secessions
from the Anglican community which resulted in the founding of
the United Native African Church and the Bethel African Church
respectively in 1891 and 1901—in which as will be examined in a
later chapter he was the key figure—occurred in his Breadfruit
Church. In two ways the atmosphere in his Church bred nationalist
"rebels". Firstly the virtues of independence and of an African
Church were favourite themes of his sermons and addresses.
Secondly the system of government he devised for his church had
developed greater democratic principles than the conventional
administrative system of the other Anglican churches.

For in place of the Parochial Committee, on which the laity's
voice was heard but not decisive, James Johnson introduced, or
rather revived, government by Leaders of classes, all laymen.[95]
Every matter of importance was discussed at the Leaders' Meeting,
the minister himself putting before the Leaders cases of discipline,
admission to Communion and so on. It is not surprising that these
Leaders acquired such confidence that they thought that even in

theological matters majority will must prevail. So bold had they become that his theological stand over the issue of polygamy became a bone of contention between him and the Leaders. At the meeting of 15 December 1884, James Johnson reported the case of a communicant who had given his daughter to another communicant and a well-known polygamist. Opinion was divided on the disciplinary action that should be taken against the father and the daughter. James Johnson ignored the majority opinion, that neither the father nor the daughter could be proved to have committed any basic sin from the Bible. At the meeting held on 12 January 1885 he announced that he had suspended the father from all Communion for six months and that he had dismissed the daughter for allowing herself to be given in marriage to a polygamist, adding that she would be received again when her husband should have reformed his life by dismissing all his wives but one and becoming a full member of a Christian Church.[96]

The grumbling of the Leaders developed into a storm when the polygamists, whom James Johnson had in his usual fashion categorised as an inferior group, decided on a showdown with him. Ten charges, including one that his sermons were often too long, which masked their real grievances, were drawn up. For James Johnson had caused them to be disgraced in a manner they could not have been expected to forget or forgive. At his service in which his church was full to capacity, following the Special Revival Mission conducted there by two ministers from England, the Reverend S. W. Fox and the Reverend F. W. Dodd, James Johnson pronounced unworthy about seven-hundred of his members and turned them back from the Eucharist when they wanted to rededicate themselves to God through the observance of the Holy Communion.[97] On investigation none of the ten charges preferred against Johnson was substantiated. As Bishop Ingham, who would have been only too glad to have James Johnson pilloried, put it, "Mr. Johnson is an autocrat and that is the alpha and omega of his sins against them". They begged the Bishop "to get him [James Johnson] married that he may the better understand their social difficulties".[98]

Indeed Breadfruit Parsonage became the most popular venue for nationalist meetings, partly because James Johnson was invariably chairman of the petition and resolution-makers and partly because it was the most commodious and most convenient place.[99] He was leader of nationalist opinion on various matters ranging from the necessity of the Lagos Government to spend more on education, to the timeliness of bridges being built to connect the island to Ebute-Metta;[100] from the necessity to break up the allegedly secret pact between Lagos thieves and the police to the urgency of devolving political power on the inhabitants of Lagos.

From his advent to Nigeria in 1874 and until his death James Johnson was to become the greatest spokesman for the African peoples in general and for the Nigerian peoples in particular. According to an observer who claimed that he watched him from close quarters, it was his habit to collect data on the political, social and economic conditions of his countrymen and write about these matters in the newspapers at least once a week.[101] More than any other individual, and in most cases single-handed, he persuaded the Colonial Office, directly and indirectly, that the various political, social and economic grievances of the different sections of the Nigerian community were real. Over the Governors' heads he caused to be brought before the British public what he considered to be the misdoings and enormities of British officials and traders in Nigeria, such as the violation of the sanctity of the independence of African states and the erosion of Africa's sovereignty. Both in Church and State he was to advocate the "Africa for the Africans" policy to the exasperation of British administrators, of Salisbury Square and of the European missionaries. He was to become a notorious agitator and *persona non grata* to a succession of governors. Macdonald, the first High Commissioner of the Oil Rivers (later Niger Coast) Protectorate, was to be apprehensive of his influence and plead with Salisbury Square not to transfer him to his area of administration;[102] Governor G. T. Carter, upon whom Johnson was to fall as Edmund Burke fell on Warren Hastings, was to label him a "mischievous patriot".[103] Even as late as 1901 Governor Macgregor favoured his removal from Lagos in preference to the more accommodating Bishop Oluwole.[104]

By 1887 his stature as a nationalist had become West African in dimension, occupying, as a correspondent put it, "a position aloof and alone" in his pre-eminence as an African patriot endowed with rare qualities. He had become a household word in Sierra Leone and in Lagos. As a newspaper published in London eulogised him in October 1887: "It is granted to but few to stand as the Rev. James Johnson does, so endeared to men by noble services and exulted [sic] genius. . . . He illustrates the most admirable type of manhood, and is an example to the rising generation of a life consecrated to the highest uses of humanity."[105]

NOTES

1. C.M.S. CA1/0123, F. Huggins to C.M.S. Secretary, 26/5/1874.
2. *Lagos Weekly Record*, 14/10/1893.

3. S. H. Brown, *A History of the People of Lagos, 1852-1886*, Ph.D. Evanston, Illinois, 1964, p. 41 ff. and p. 173.
4. *C.M. Intelligencer*, 1875, pp. 76-79.
5. C.M.S. CA2/056, James Johnson to E. Hutchinson, 29/4/1875.
6. C.M.S. CA2/033, J. P. L. Davies to E. Hutchinson, 3/8/1874.
7. C.M.S. CA2/096, J. B. Wood to H. Wright, 13/2/1875.
8. C.M.S. CA2/056, James Johnson to H. Wright, 12/10/1874; same to H. Wright, 2/8/1876.
9. J. Wheare, *The Nigerian Legislative Council*, London, 1949; J. S. Coleman, *Nigeria Background to Nationalism*, California, 1956; K. Ezera, *Constitutional Development of Nigeria*, O.U.P., 1960.
10. C.M.S. CA2/L4, E. Hutchinson to J. A. Maser, 27/3/1873.
11. C.M.S. CA2/080, H. Robbin to H. Venn, 7/2/1863; C.O. 147/4, H. S. Freeman to Newcastle, 31/12/1863.
12. C.M.S. CA2/033, J. P. L. Davies to H. Venn, 9/3/1863.
13. *African Times*, 1/4/1878.
14. C.M.S. CA2/03(c), J. A. Maser to E. Hutchinson, 6/2/1873; CA2/033, J. P. L. Davies to E. Hutchinson, 1/9/1873.
15. C.M.S. CA2/033, J. P. L. Davies to Parent Committee, 1/9/1873.
16. C.M.S. CA2/03(c), J. A. Maser to E. Hutchinson, 18/9/1873.
17. C.M.S. CA2/011, J. A. Maser to C. Foresythe, 30/5/1873.
18. C.M.S. CA2/03(c), J. A. Maser to E. Hutchinson, 6/10/1873.
19. C.M.S. CA2/011, C. Foresythe to J. A. Maser, 29/9/1873.
20. C.M.S. CA2/03(c), J. A. Maser to E. Hutchinson, 29/3/1872; Governor J. H. Glover etc. to C.M.S., 14/3/1872.
21. *Ibid.*, L. Nicholson to Secretaries, 6/7/1872.
22. C.M.S. CA2/011, various papers of this society.
23. *Ibid.*, Minutes of Meeting, 3/9/1873.
24. C.M.S. CA2/03(c), J. A. Maser to E. Hutchinson, 19/9/1873.
25. *Ibid.*, same to same 18/9 and 21/10/1873.
26. C.M.S. CA2/011, C. Foresythe to J. A. Maser, 19/9/1873.
27. J. F. Ade Ajayi, "Nineteenth Century Origins of Nigerian Nationalism", *Journal of Historical Society of Nigeria*, Vol. II, No. 1, pp. 196-210.
28. See chapters 1 to 4 in E. A. Ayandele, *The Missionary Impact on Modern Nigeria 1842-1914. A Political and Social Analysis*, Longmans, 1966.
29. C.O. 147/4, H. S. Freeman to Newcastle, 31/12/1863; C.O. 147/6, same to same, 19/4/1864.
30. *Ibid.*
31. *Ibid.*
32. C.M.S. CA2/096, J. B. Wood to E. Hutchinson, 4/11/1872.
33. C.M.S. CA2/049(a), D. Hinderer to H. Wright, 18/5/1875.
34. C.M.S. G3/A2/01, James Johnson to E. Hutchinson, June 1881.
35. C.M.S. CA2/033, J. P. L. Davies to E. Hutchinson, 3/8/1874.
36. *Ibid.*
37. C.M.S. CA1/025(e), Bishop Cheetham to H. Wright, 2/3/1876.
38. *The Day Spring and Sierra Leone Reporter*, 8 and 15 January 1869; *C.M. Intelligencer*, 1875, p. 79.
39. E. W. Blyden, *African Life and Customs*, p. 63: quotes James Johnson.
40. *African Times*, 1/10/1887.
41. C.M.S. G3/A2/01, James Johnson to E. Hutchinson, June 1881.

42. C.M.S. G3/A3/09, "A Report of a Missionary Journey within and beyond the Southern Nigeria British Protectorate", November 1903-July 1904, by James Johnson.
43. C.M.S. CA1/0123, James Johnson to H. Venn, 20/12/1864.
44. *Ibid.*, same to same, 20/12/1867.
45. *Ibid.*, same to same, 15/4/1869.
46. C.M.S. CA2/03(c), A. Mann to H. Wright, 6/9/1874.
47. C.M.S. CA2/056, James Johnson to E. Hutchinson, 29/6/1875.
48. *Ibid.*
49. *Ibid.*, James Johnson to E. Hutchinson, 29/7/1875.
50. For fuller information on James Johnson's ministration at Breadfruit see J. O. Lucas, *Lecture on the History of St. Paul's Church, Breadfruit*, Lagos, 1946, pp. 26-35.
51. C.M.S. CA2/056, James Johnson to E. Hutchinson, 29/7/1875.
52. *The Eagle*, 12 and 26 September 1885.
53. C.M.S. CA2/056, James Johnson to E. Hutchinson, 29/4/1875.
54. *Ibid.*, same to same, 8/7/1875.
55. C.M.S. CA2/03(c), A. Mann to C.M.S. Secretaries, 6/9/1874.
56. See E. A. Ayandele, "The Colonial Church Question in Lagos Politics, 1905-1911", *ODU* (University of Ife Journal of African Studies), January 1968.
57. C.M.S. G3/A2/01, Bishop Cheetham to F. E. Wigram, 3/3/1881.
58. The traditional custodians of lands in Lagos. Their name derives from the white cap they wear, a practice that prevails till this day.
59. *Lagos Times*, 12/1/1881.
60. C.O. 149/1, Legislative Council *Minutes*, 17/10/1888.
61. *Sierra Leone Weekly News*, 28/7/1900.
62. Quoted in *Lagos Weekly Record*, 27 October and 2 November 1917.
63. C.M.S. G3/A2/01, A. Mann to Secretaries, 16/11/1881.
64. *Ibid.*, James Johnson to E. Hutchinson, June 1881.
65. C.M.S. CA2/03(d), J. A. Maser to H. Wright, 9/6/1876.
66. C.M.S. G3/A2/01, A. Mann to Secretaries, 16/6/1882.
67. *Ibid.*, James Johnson to E. Hutchinson, June 1881.
68. *Ibid.*
69. *Ibid.*, James Johnson to J. B. Whiting, 16/11/1881.
70. *Ibid., James Johnson* to E. Hutchinson, June 1881, quotes the latter.
71. *Ibid.*
72. C.M.S. G3/A2/O2, Bishop Cheetham to R. Lang, 29/4/1884.
73. *Ibid.*
74. *Ibid.*, J. Hamilton to F. E. Wigram, 22/2/1884.
75. C.O. 149/3, Legislative Council *Minutes*, 12/8 and 19/8/1889.
76. S.M.A., "Propagande Protestant, 1880" by Père Pagés.
77. *Ibid.*; also J. Poirier to Père Superieur, 6/3/1885.
78. C.M.S. G3/A2/01, A. Mann to Secretaries (undated).
79. *Ibid.*, J. B. Wood to Secretaries, 27/9/1881.
80. *Ibid.*, A. Mann to R. Lang, 9/3/1882.
81. *African Times*, 2/1/1881.
82. C.M.S. G3/1/Ll0, R. Lang to Bishop Cheetham, 30/11/1883.
83. C.M.S. G3/A2/03, J. A. Maser to R. Lang, 17/3/1884.
84. C.M.S. G3/A2/02, J. B. Wood to R. Lang, 13/10/1883.
85. C.M.S. G3/A2/03, Bishop Cheetham to R. Lang, 29/4/1884.

86. C.M.S. G3/A1/L10/ R. Lang to K. Ingham, 19/6/1884.
87. *Lagos Times*, 9/11/1881.
88. *Ibid.*, 14/6/1882.
89. *Ibid.*, 9/11/1881; Esere, *As Seen Through African Eyes*, p. 14.
90. The Gladstone Papers (British Museum), E. W. Blyden to Ewart Gladstone, 25/3/1861.
91. *Sierra Leone Weekly News*, 12/11/1892.
92. C.M.S. G3/A3/011, "Report on the Niger Delta Pastorate Church and Mission work, 1906" by James Johnson.
93. C.M.S. G3/A3/09, Presidential Address by James Johnson to the Third Annual Niger Delta, 25/1/1904.
94. *Nigerian Pioneer*, 20/7/1917.
95. J. O. Lucas, *Lecture on the History of St. Paul's Church, Breadfruit*, p. 31.
96. *Ibid.*, p. 33.
97. *Lagos Weekly Record*, 10 and 24 November 1917.
98. C.M.S. G3/A3/04, Bishop of Sierra Leone to R. Lang, 26/2/1886.
99. *Lagos Times*, 24/1/1891.
100. *Lagos Observer*, 17/1/1884.
101. *Nigerian Pioneer*, 13/7/1917.
102. C.M.S. G3/A3/06, Memo. of interview, 2/3/1893.
103. C.O. 147/95, G. T. Carter to G. F. S. R. Ripon, 19/6/1894.
104. C.M.S. G3/A2/010, H. Tugwell to F. Baylis, 20/3/1901.
105. *African Times*, 1/11/1887.

H

CHAPTER FIVE

SUPERINTENDENT

> You do not see in England that side of Mr. Johnson
> which makes him obnoxious to some extent wherever
> he works. His very excellence is his danger. Conscious
> of rectitude he is unconstitutional, autocratic, impatient,
> inclined to his own way. He will not wait to take people
> on with him.
>
> Bishop K. Ingham to R. Lang 7/9/1887

HARDLY had James Johnson been two years at Breadfruit than, to the grief of his parishioners, he was removed to a higher appointment. He was made Superintendent of all the stations which the C.M.S. had opened in the interior of Yorubaland since 1846. That he had been a success in Lagos can be judged from the fact that, as had been the case with his transfer from Kent to Pademba Road in 1863 and from Freetown to Lagos in 1874, his parishioners petitioned that his position would be difficult to fill.[1] On the morning of 24 February 1877 he left Lagos, with prayers and good wishes and accompanied by several members of the Church and others for part of the sixty-mile route to Abeokuta, the citadel of Christianity in the interior of pre-colonial West Africa that was to be his headquarters. In the judgment of his parishioners, ". . . although your stay in this place has been comparatively short yet the impression of your devotedness to the interests of ourselves and our country, has been so great, that we are now parting with a very dear one with whom we have lived for many years".[2] His importance was acknowledged by Christians of all denominations. On 9 February 1877 a deputation of them had congratulated him on his appointment and presented him with a gift of £25.[3]

The decision to put James Johnson in a position that was to make him bishop *de facto*, though not *de jure*, was not an act of deliberate policy by the Church Missionary Society. There was no

Henry Venn to push the Society to make James Johnson a Bishop, as had been the case with Samuel Ajayi Crowther in 1864. It was the circumstances in Yorubaland in 1875 that persuaded the C.M.S. to transfer control of the churches in the territory to African control. For when they returned to Abeokuta and Ibadan respectively, veteran C.M.S. missionaries Henry Townsend and David Hinderer discovered that the attitude of Yoruba rulers to Europeans was no longer as favourable as it used to be. Gone were the days when the white man was regarded as a prestige symbol and when he could be trusted as a disinterested counsellor and honorary secretary. He was now being suspected as a knight-errant of British imperialism. As Henry Townsend painfully experienced the chiefs had transferred their trust to the *Saros*;[4] in Ibadan the rulers had transferred respect and confidence to a one-time cook of David Hinderer's, Daniel Olubi.[5] Therefore both decided to withdraw to the coast.

It is significant that the instigator of James Johnson's appointment was Henry Townsend, the man who had been most bitterly opposed to Crowther's appointment in 1864. Whatever his prejudices had been in previous years about the white man's superiority and the subordinate role Africans must fulfil, they disappeared after he had seen "a good deal" of James Johnson. He remarked very highly of this Ethiopian's attributes and recommended that he be consecrated Bishop of a diocese that should embrace Abeokuta and Ibadan districts. In addition to his other attributes, said Henry Townsend, James Johnson possessed some qualities which a white man lacked, including "tact" and "practical wisdom" in dealing both with the chiefs and "our native helpers".[6] On being consulted for his views Bishop Crowther gave an excellent account of him as "a pious devoted servant of God, a conscientious Christian, and a zealous worker as a minister of the gospel . . . [with] humble demeanour and unassuming disposition". In the judgment of the Bishop all that James Johnson required was a further experience of two years, when he should automatically be lifted to the episcopate. This step, said Bishop Crowther, would be fulfilling the dream of Henry Venn for Yorubaland.[7]

The task before James Johnson was very formidable indeed. The Yorubaland to which he was posted had a social milieu and a political atmosphere completely different from those he had experienced before; it also posed unusual missionary problems which demanded talents different from those he had displayed either in Sierra Leone or in Lagos. The territory had been in the throes of civil war for most of the century and the last of the major wars, the Kiriji War, broke out only four months after his arrival at Abeokuta. State fought against state, inviting the intervention of foreign powers, both African and European; the misfortunes of one state gave opportunities for others and the people fought each other frenziedly. Sub-tribal interests and allegiance were stronger than loyalty to the interests of the entire Yoruba nation. As James Johnson was to experience, the factiousness of Yoruba politics was accentuated rather than tempered by the educated elite in Lagos, who became wire-pullers, inciting one state in the interior against the other.

Nor was the Abeokuta in which he was to live for most of the time attractive. He found himself in an Egba capital far removed from the romantic description of Mission journals. Socially Abeokuta consisted of an overwhelming majority of Egba 'pagans', numbering about 55,000, a few of whom responded to the appeals of the two alien religions that intruded into their society in the nineteenth century—Islam and Christianity. The 'pagans' were not only traditionalist to the marrow in their attachment to indigenous religion but they had contempt for the religion of Christians. There were the *Saro*, repatriated Africans of Egba affinity who had been returning to Abeokuta since 1839. Up to 1861 the *Saros* had been highly valuable politically because of the influence they had been able to bring to bear on the British Government and this restrained Dahomey, their western neighbour who aimed to subdue the Egba. Although the *Saro* were professed Christians they found the pull of traditional religion and culture so strong that, in the view of James Johnson and other European observers, their Christianity meant nothing. Many of them took 'pagan' titles, had more than one wife, kept several slaves and even returned to traditional religion. It was this class of people that was to give the new Superintendent the greatest difficulty. Not only were they assertive but they also claimed importance for themselves. As Egba by their tribal connection they found it easy to persuade traditional rulers to take particular lines of action in matters relating to the British Government and Christian mission policies.

It was not religion alone that divided the Egba socially. Society was divided according to class—the class of the free and that of the unfree or slaves. The majority of the latter belonged to the Hausa tribe of Northern Nigeria but there were also large numbers of Ijesha and Ekiti Yoruba, victims of the long civil war of the nineteenth century.[8]

Like the rest of the Yoruba country Abeokuta was sovereign and its government was in the hands of 'pagan' rulers deeply attached to traditional religion. Much as James Johnson's Ethiopian programme depended on the foundation of Christianity, he had to work in a predominantly 'pagan' atmosphere and recognise and respect the 'pagan' Egba government. There was no effective co-

ordinated and centralised government for the Egba at the time of
James Johnson's appointment and authority was diffused in a way
that made contemporary observers compare Egbaland to Alsatia
of Germany.[9] Each of the 143 townships that made up Abeokuta
behaved in its own way and each chief in the quarters of the townships behaved according to his own inclinations. The titular head
of the Egba, the Alake, had little authority beyond Ake Quarters.
Since 1869 disagreement over the choice of an Alake between the
civil rulers, the *Ogboni*, and the military men, the *Ologun*, had
worsened the political situation. The division between the civil and
military authorities was well exploited by the *Saro* who, though
divided among themselves, yet constituted a distinct group and
power with a common outlook in several respects. Some of them
became very prominent in Egba politics. Among this class of men
might be mentioned Henry Robbin, the wealthiest man in Abeokuta
in the pre-colonial period and the greatest supporter and protector
of James Johnson in the crisis that later developed in the Egba
capital. Indeed so chaotic was the political situation in Abeokuta
that, it is said, the chiefs lost authority over their subjects and
squandered "the large revenue"[10] of the state; the young men would
not obey anyone, nor respect their elders, whilst husbands were
also losing control over their wives.[11]

The town itself was populous but its streets were very narrow,
and houses were roofed mainly with grass which, as in Lagos and
other Yoruba towns, tended to go up in flames. The town was very
dirty and smallpox used to rage fiercely.[12]

Before leaving for the interior James Johnson was fully aware
of the problems in Yorubaland in general and in Abeokuta in particular, but he was determined to succeed in spite of them. In his
view the credit of the Negro Race was at stake in his appointment.[13]
Moreover he was conscious of the ill-will felt towards him by the
European missionaries in Lagos. None of them wished him well.
Apart from the fact that they could not be persuaded to believe
that the African had the capacity for exercising control of any kind,
they regarded James Johnson's promotion as being too rapid and
a slight upon themselves.[14] For by his new position the Superintendent was expected to exercise powers that exceeded those that
had ever been exercised in Yorubaland by any European missionary.
After all no one had ever been in charge of the entire Yoruba
Mission; hitherto each European missionary had been in charge of
his own station and districts. But apart from the fact that his new
administrative and ecclesiastical functions were not defined, the
instructions given to James Johnson were calculated to make him
a law to himself. He was instructed to extend the missionary
frontier, to improve educational institutions with the aim of

developing a native agency, and to encourage the churches to become self-supporting and self-governing.[15] In other words James Johnson was to carry out the euthanasia of missions expostulated by Henry Venn, a programme that fitted into his Ethiopian dream.

It was a serious and tactical error on the part of the Church Missionary Society that the administrative procedure which he should observe was not clearly defined at the outset. Consequently there developed two interpretations of James Johnson's powers— one by James Johnson himself and the other by the European missionaries. The unconcealed desire of the latter was that the Finance Committee, consisting of European members only and the executive of the C.M.S. in Yorubaland, should have full control over the Superintendent and his activities in the interior and that he should never communicate directly with Salisbury Square.[16] On the other hand James Johnson believed that he was absolutely independent of this body, that he should maintain direct communication with the C.M.S. authorities, and that he should have nothing to do at all with the Finance Committee or with the European missionaries.[17] As things worked out James Johnson discovered that in financial matters, and later in other matters, he was expected to be supervised by the Finance Committee. Thus the seed of inevitable conflict was laid, even before he set out for the interior.

One cardinal objective which the new Superintendent attempted to achieve was the spread of the gospel seed. In this respect he threw himself into his new task with an energy and a zest that was soon to embarrass the European missionaries. Expansion was his watchword and he lost no time in visiting all the existing stations and locating new ones. Had his programme been accepted by his European enemies the missionary frontier would have been pushed northward to Ogbomosho and north-westward to Shaki, embracing all main urban areas in the Egbado country. His journals indicate the unusual missionary problems posed by different areas of Western Yorubaland over which he was Superintendent.

Apart from in Abeokuta, which will be examined in detail later in the chapter, Christianity had hardly achieved any success by 1877. In the Egbado country the inhabitants were demonstrably unresponsive to missionary appeal in spite of over twenty-years' activity in their country. In James Johnson's view the people had become so debased and so demoralised by liquor that they could not perceive the verities of the Christian faith. Then there was what he described as their "stubborn devotedness to idolatory and their excessive worldly-mindedness".[18] He believed that efforts in the towns would yield no fruit and that any attempt made in the territory should be concentrated in the small villages. In Ibadan, next in importance to Abeokuta—with 401 Christian adherents compared to the latter's 2,295 though missionary work was only a few years younger than in Abeokuta—James Johnson attributed the relative failure of Christianity there and in all Oyo Yoruba country to the warfare that had been raging in the area since the second decade of the nineteenth century. Then, he observed, the Ibadan, like all Oyo Yoruba people he visited, had "a faulty sense" that they were important and "respect for the authority of rulers assumes an obstructive form . . . anything that is likely eventually to revolutionize ideas and customs in the country must come from them or have their countenance".[19]

The Superintendent's fleeting visit to Ibadan, Oyo and Oke-Ogun areas did not permit him to penetrate deeply and thereby understand the real causes of the failure of Christianity to impress itself on the people. What he described as "a faulty sense" of importance by the Oyo Yoruba was, in the eyes of the latter, not "faulty". First of all, as "Yoruba Proper",[20] they had contempt for other sections of the Yoruba nation, many of whom in the not distant past had been governed by the Oyo Yoruba through the representatives of the *Alafin*, their paramount ruler. Moreover their sense and conception of dignity was different from that of James Johnson and the educated elite. They did not desire to become Christians because, in their view, traditional religion was in their best interest; they did not wish their children to be educated because this would mean "spoiling" them.[21] Their social system was monolithic and in it they lived, moved and had their being. Above all they were very suspicious of missionaries and their intrusion into their society; they could not identify these intruders with disinterest.

It is against this background of the attitude of the Oyo Yoruba that James Johnson's observations and misjudgments should be understood. In Ibadan he noted: "devil worship is of a very pronounced character: almost every family has its devil-hut in the street."[22] The people relished native beer, a thing offensive to the Superintendent's notion of morality; slaves were being bought and sold and Christians were looked down upon and were being regarded as second class citizens. Indeed apostates were being persecuted severely by members of their families; elementary education was confined to children of converts and the chiefs—many of whom were Muslims—had to be placated by the Mission agents from time to time with "superior gifts". More offensive to the Superintendent's moral and Christian notions was that Ibadan possessed an air of unbounded militarism.

Nevertheless the Superintendent was impressed by the quality of Ibadan Christianity. In order to increase their fervour and spirituality he persuaded the Christians to form themselves into the Ibadan Christian Missionary Society and to adopt a Resolution that would turn them into spies, as in Lagos and in Pademba Road. According to the Resolution: "That the respective congregations of accredited Church members be divided into small classes to be entrusted to the oversight and care of elected Elders and Leaders who shall assist in watching over their spiritual interest by meeting with them weekly at their own residences or some other convenient places for the united reading and study of Scripture, exhortation and prayer; and make cases of want, distress, persecution, sickness and death known to their immediate superintendents: interest themselves in other ways in the people entrusted to them and collect from them weekly class fees and other contributions expected of them."[23]

In Oyo prejudice against Christianity was even stronger than in Ibadan. The soil was so hard that both the C.M.S. and the Southern American Baptists, who had established themselves in the town in the fifties, had abandoned their mission. But after the accession of Adeyemi I, "a young man of a graceful appearance",[24] as James Johnson described him, to the throne in 1875, an agent of the C.M.S. was sent to the town in the following year. At the time of James Johnson's visit there were in Oyo only seventeen communicants without a shepherd but with a self-elected leader, a *Saro* called Thomas, a man "barely able to read and deliver short and simple exhortations". The Superintendent was made to feel that he was not an important man in the Oyo Court. The *Alafin's* officials compelled him and his followers "to uncover our heads long before we came into the portico in which the king received us".[25] He was able to acquire a piece of land for a mission station and to perform an act of kindness by pleading successfully with Adeyemi to commute a death sentence on a Christian woman on the point of being sacrificed by Oro, to a fine of five bags of cowries, the equivalent of 50s. He also baptised three women, a lad of sixteen and three children.

Even more discouraging to missionary propaganda were Ogbomosho, a big town only thirty-two miles beyond Oyo, where sectional rivalry between its 114 townships was rife, and the Oke-Ogun towns of Iseyin, Eruwa, Biolorunpelu, Okeho, Iganna and so on, where there was a clash of authority between the Ibadan and the *Alafin*. James Johnson saw Ibadan agents fleecing these towns, all of whom demanded mission agents. In Iseyin he baptised a boy and a woman. Here he did something he had not done before and was never to repeat: he baptised one of the wives of a polygamist.[26]

Throughout his tour of the interior he lectured the Yoruba on the principles of the British constitution, particularly the law of primogeniture that made the British monarchical system of government free from the rivalry which plagued the Yoruba Monarchy. For the demise of a ruler, if not hastened by ambitious potential candidates, was usually accompanied by disputes among members of the ruling families. It was in Oke-Ogun towns, particularly in Okeho, where he was to witness the inherent weakness of the traditional law of succession. In Oke-ho, a collection of eleven townships, the paramountcy of the Onjo had never been acknowledged by the ten other chiefs. Moreover the Balogun, who commanded the army, often disputed with the paramount ruler and civil war was endemic throughout the nineteenth century. When James Johnson and his party arrived in the town in June 1877 another civil war was about to begin. The Onjo was accused by the Balogun of oppression and conspiracy; war preparations were being made on both sides; arrows were being forged, poisoned and prepared for action. But as long as James Johnson was the guest of the Onjo the opponents of the king pretended to accept peace offers, in order to prevent the Superintendent from interfering in the dispute. Hardly had the Johnson party left for Iganna, a town only eight miles away, than civil war flared up and the king's party was defeated by an overwhelming number. James Johnson was stunned by the way the king met his end. As he recorded it: "he [the king] retreated into his palace which was soon set on fire, repaired into a room, laid himself on the floor, dressed in his richest clothes and with all his jewels and covering himself with a large pile of other valuable cloths. Two of his wives laid themselves beside him and the three were burnt to death."[27]

Apart from the Egbado and Oyo Yoruba areas James Johnson also turned his attention to the Ijebu country, the most anti-missionary part in Yorubaland. In fact the evangelisation of the Ijebu had been one of the main reasons for his transfer to Nigeria in 1874.[28] The Superintendent started with the Remo town of Iperu. It was a hazardous journey there and in order to allay suspicion he had to take off his shoes and conceal his English dress. He literally risked his life; spies followed him; his intentions were misconstrued and the texts of his sermons and addresses understood out of context. Before he was expelled he had an opportunity to address the authorities of the town on the blessings of Christianity for all peoples and the benefits that would accrue to the Ijebu if they accepted it. As a people who were destined to become the most zealous patrons of Christianity in Yorubaland, largely through the unrelenting pioneering efforts of James Johnson, the reaction of the Iperu authorities to the Superintendent's address and visit is worth noting:

The chief who spoke for them began by asking whether we had no ruler in our country and whether we would do anything

without consulting him. Upon my replying that in matters of
religion we do not wait for a sovereign's consent, he answered:
'we have a master without whose consent we can do nothing: we
cannot receive a missionary before the king at Ode and Akarigbo
the first of Iremo kings have received them into their towns. We
do not desire it: we do not want it, we do not feel the want of
safety or comfort. We have been told you threaten the town with
judgment, that you spoke of a 40 days rain to drown all leaving
only two persons and at another time of a fire to consume all
leaving only four persons: it is not long since a portion of the
town was burnt down and we have not yet been able to completely restore it. We have also heard that you poured down
imprecations upon our town and that you made our women
bow down their heads in worship. We do not want this in our
town.'[29]

Dismissed from the Ijebu country James Johnson had no more
opportunity to visit the Oyo Yoruba country. For in the middle
of 1877 the Kiriji war broke out, in which the Egba and Ibadan
fought on opposite sides. The movement of missionaries was
restricted and the routes leading to the Oyo Yoruba country closed.
All that the Superintendent could do was to be in touch with the
agents, a thing he was able to do, as is clearly testified to by his
comprehensive annual reports. In the circumstances it was in
Abeokuta and in the neighbouring Egba settlements that he could
expend most of his energy. Among the Egba, Christianity had produced considerable effects of a kind and on a scale that could not
be found anywhere else in the interior of Africa in the pre-colonial
era. In 1877 there were not less than 2,000 Anglican adherents, six
churches and chapels, six elementary schools and a High School—
all containing 283 scholars.[30] Then there were the farm villages of
Shuren, consisting of 130 Christians out of a population of 400;
Ofada with 120 Christians out of a population of 400, and Afojupa
with 20 Christians out of a population of about 500. In a sense,
too, the churches of Aroloya in Lagos and St. Jude's in Ebute Metta
owed their origins to the Abeokuta Church; for it was Egba
refugees who had left the Egba capital at the *Ifole*[31] of 1867 that
founded these churches.

Christianity had also raised up among the Egba an educated
elite—scripture readers, school-masters, catechists and ministers—
many of whom were serving in other parts of Yorubaland as well; a
measure of self-government had also been introduced in the Church.
For the School Board was made up entirely of natives and both the
Church Council and School Board controlled their own funds.
Materially Christianity had introduced among the Egba a superior

knowledge of brick and tile-making, buildings which recognised the value of light and ventilation, an increased and active cultivation of cotton, preparation of palm oil, and collection of palm kernels and ivory for foreign markets—all of which became a chief source of income for the people. In fact English machines for ginning cotton were "in common use".[32]

From the missionary point of view there can be little doubt that in the circumstances in which he found himself the Superintendent was successful. He manifested many of the virtues of successful missionaries in pre-colonial African society. He had infinite patience. He could tolerate any situation and was always careful not to offend the social laws and customs of the people. Never did he reprove the 'pagans' in a way that might arouse their anger. He disagreed with Henry Townsend that the traditional Egba government should be denounced because it was 'pagan' and that only Christians should be organised and encouraged to seize the government of Egbaland,[33] knowing quite well that the latter end was in the circumstances of Yorubaland unattainable. Indeed James Johnson respected native authorities and he got on very well with the native rulers, many of whom became his effusive friends. According to him he tried to persuade all the rulers in the interior that he knew the British Government did not intend to deprive them of their country and sovereignty. He even got on well with the much feared Are Latosa of Ibadan, who asked him to establish churches throughout the Ibadan empire.[34]

Only in one respect did James Johnson fail to grasp the methods and techniques required for successful missionary work in pre-colonial Africa, particularly where pioneering activities were concerned. This was the necessity to offer gifts to the traditional rulers. Gifts were indispensable to obtain the goodwill and countenance of traditional rulers in the pre-colonial period. Not only must they be given regularly but they should also be of an attractive variety. Hence James Johnson compromised the chances of his success in the Egbado country when he refused to give the Olu of Ilaro, the most important Egbado ruler, the following articles which he demanded before the Superintendent could be allowed a favourable audience and movement within the Egbado country: "a clothes box, nice pairs of English-made shoes and boots, a splendid umbrella, some particular species of duck, all suitable to a king's dignity. The shoes should be superior to my travelling slippers that I had on then as those did not come up to a king's state".[35]

James Johnson laboured under the mistaken belief that unlettered Africans should perceive to the same degree as himself the verities of the Christian faith, should recognise the superiority of Christianity over traditional religion and should appreciate that he was working in their interest for the salvation of their souls. But, as has been indicated with respect to the Oyo Yoruba, uncontaminated African peoples generally saw the white man or his African auxiliary and his new-fangled religion in a different light. The African votary of Christianity was regarded as an inferior person and an outcast. And, as the statement of the Olu of Ilaro shows, James Johnson was himself regarded as a man of lower status than the ruler.

The Superintendent's labours on behalf of the spread of the gospel were of little avail in the face of a hostile Finance Committee which held the purse strings. Not a penny was given towards missionary work, in spite of repeated appeals by the Superintendent for location of agents in many towns including Atadi, Eruwa, Biolorunpelu, Okeho and Iganna.[36] James Johnson's suggestions were brushed aside, his programme was thwarted and his effort stultified. A few issues intended by the C.M.S. for his points of view were answered by the Finance Committee without any reference or intimation being made to him.[37] The Finance Committee claimed the right to promote or even remove teachers under him without any reference to him.

Nevertheless James Johnson was by no means discouraged. In all the churches in the interior he had attempted to persuade the members to choose the honourable path of self-support by encouraging the communicants to raise class fees from one string to five strings. Since the far interior churches were of little significance and the Kiriji War—which hit them harder than the Egba—compelled them to go back to a weekly fee of one string, they raised no apprehension for the European missionaries. But it was a different matter with the Egba who were being encouraged successfully by the Superintendent to become financially and in effect self-governing. The result was the 1879 storm which ultimately swept James Johnson from Abeokuta and the interior.

From the point of view of organisation, purification of the Church, respect for his authority and pecuniary viability, James Johnson's superintendence in the interior, and particularly in Abeokuta, was a success. First, he took—as was ever his practice—the laity into his confidence by having them represented on the School Board, the Church Committee and the Church Council. They were also participants in the annual conference of Egba Christians which he instituted and which brought them in contact with their ministers; then, as was usual with him, he divided each church into classes, under the directorship of Leaders. The clergymen also held a clerical conference every year at which they were free to express views on all matters. There was no question of the

Superintendent imposing any decision on the Abeokuta Church. Free and frank opinion was solicited and appreciated.[38]

The financial success that was achieved by the Abeokuta Church must be attributed to this active participation and control of their affairs by the people themselves. Having assessed the financial capacity of the Christians James Johnson suggested that class fees should be raised from one string per week to seven and a half strings, a suggestion that was approved by a majority vote on 10 October 1877.[39] The result was that in 1878 the sum of £359 15s. 9¼d. was realised. This was more than double the previous year's income of £163 19s. 5d. In 1879 the revenue was even more encouraging, standing at £421 17s. 4½d.

It should also be stressed that these were the years of the Kiriji War. The truth was that the war did not cripple the economy of the Egba, nor did the members ever complain of an incapacity to pay the new rate. The only argument that arose was purely socio-logical. Masters deplored the fact that they were being asked to pay the same fees as their slaves and suggested that the latter should have their dues halved, a demand which James Johnson refused to concede on two grounds. Firstly he contended that since slaves were numerically stronger than masters in the Church, a lowering of their fees would put slave converts in the majority and the latter would be controlling the Church, a situation which the masters would regard as unnatural. Secondly such an action would be un-Christian because it would put slaves into a separate class, as if even in the Church they were not the equals of their masters.[40]

In the light of his experience with the Finance Committee James Johnson decided to set up a Pastorate working capital of £800. Out of the income of 1878 he set aside £200 as the first instalment. It should be stressed again that the Superintendent's action in this respect was fully justified in the light of the instruction he received at the time of his appointment, which instructions were re-affirmed time and again by Salisbury Square. The evil days into which the finances of the C.M.S. began to fall in 1879 further justified the efforts of the Superintendent in the direction of self-support. For by June 1879 the Church Missionary Society had a deficit of £25,000 and clear instructions were sent to Native Churches to depend on their resources as much as possible. Indeed the grant to the Yoruba Mission, as to other missions, was reduced by 15 per cent. James Johnson lost no time in issuing a circular to intimate to the Abeokuta Church the state of affairs. By this date the Abeokuta Church was virtually independent in financial affairs, paying the salaries of all their pastors and teachers. On 7 July 1879 a resolution was adopted at the annual conference of the agents and laymen, to the effect that the Society should be relieved of its expenses. The chairman of this meeting was Henry Robbin and the resolution reads: "That this meeting considers it a Scriptural obligation, an honour and a privilege to a native church founded by a foreign church, as of every individual man, to be self-reliant and to strive to release the Parent from the burden of maintenance to its ministry and other parts of its framework as soon as it may be reasonably expected of it to do so."[41]

At the same time James Johnson tried to improve the moral tone of the Abeokuta Church by denouncing polygamy and slavery. Prior to his appointment the Church had depended on polygamists for its revenue, for they were the wealthiest in the community. In order to eliminate their influence James Johnson believed that if the poorer monogamists could be persuaded to increase their weekly fees to seven and a half strings, a list of communicants could be compiled, polygamists would be excluded and the sanctity of the Church would be regained. He succeeded with the monogamists, particularly among the slave converts, who found in the scheme a recognition of equality denied them in other spheres. Moreover he had never refrained from denouncing from the pulpit the institution of slavery which, as early as 7 November 1877, he had told his clerical lieutenants was "contrary to the genius and spirit of Christianity and the enlightenment of the age".[42]

There is also no doubt that his authority was acknowledged by the laity and agents in the Abeokuta Church. Never was there any occasion of disobedience or flouting of his authority. Perhaps the best testimony of his success in all respects was that of his ecclesiastical master, Bishop Cheetham, who visited the interior of Yorubaland in February 1879, the only time he did so during James Johnson's superintendence, who recorded of him as follows: "He is greatly improved under a sense of weight and responsibility and all sympathy with polygamy, manifest under Blyden's influence in 1873 seems to have vanished under experience of its working. He is acknowledged by other agents as their head."[43]

From all available evidence, then, James Johnson was an immense success, notwithstanding the difficulties with which he had to contend. He did not fail as an administrator; he was able to inspire obedience in his agents; he was implementing the self-support scheme to which the Church Missionary Society had long pledged itself; he never departed from the principles of Anglican worship and on one occasion was prepared to fight sectarian war with the Methodists to the point of shedding blood if necessary;[44] he purged the Church of polygamy; he fought against slavery.

Nevertheless a storm broke over his head in 1879, as a result of the conscious effort of the European missionaries in Lagos and

of the Bishop of the Diocese. The missionaries, it will be remembered, had never approved of his elevation to the post of Superintendent. Their hostility had never been concealed. No African, they
said, could occupy the position to which James Johnson had been
promoted, with a salary of £150 per annum, and an allowance for
keeping a horse. Moreover they could not trust James Johnson
who, it was stated, was bent on being independent of the Finance
Committee and of European supervision. They predicted that he
would end in "failure".[45] It was also believed strongly that the
circumstances in the interior would be favourable to the implementation of his Ethiopian programme; he would "find himself
able without the Bishop . . . appoint to the benefices, whom he
pleases, make his own laws in the Church".[46] Bishop Cheetham,
the man whose opposition had robbed him of consecration as
Bishop in 1876, had never doubted that the Superintendent would
turn the interior churches into an African Church. He was never
able to forget James Johnson's activities in Sierra Leone a few
years earlier. As he warned Salisbury Square even before James
Johnson assumed his office: "I am free to confess, that I should
not myself feel entirely comfortable, that news might not come to
you some day that Bishop Johnson had sanctioned polygamy in
his Church members. He would say, the Archbishop may do as he
likes in his Church and I will do as I like in my [African] Church
. . . he has partly courage and partly stupidity to do it".[47]

The European missionaries were enraged that the Superintendent
began to take decisions without reference to the Finance Committee,
especially over the decision to increase class fees. According to the
Secretary of the Committee he ought to have asked "his brethren
here for advice".[48] They were further incensed that he no longer
applied to the Committee for the salaries of the agents. They
believed that he was in collusion with George William Johnson, the
Saro patriot who had never concealed his anti-missionary feelings
and who since 1865 had been trying to defend Egba's sovereignty
against the menacing threat of the British administration in Lagos.
In fact the Reverend J. A. Maser, the Secretary of the Finance
Committee, took the matter as a personal affront. He began to
communicate secretly with the agents of the Superintendent, inciting
them to rebel against the self-support scheme that James Johnson
was promoting, saying that the Society had never approved a scheme
of that kind.[49]

This last sentiment was openly declared by Bishop Cheetham on
the occasion of his episcopal visit in February 1879. He announced
publicly his regret that the Abeokuta Church had ceased to apply
for C.M.S. Funds, that the Society was rich enough to continue to
finance the Abeokuta Church and that self-government was not a

part of the Society's policy.[50] The effect of this address upon the Egba Christians was electric and James Johnson's scheme, his authority and his popularity collapsed like a house of cards. Capital was made out of the fact that the Superintendent had decided to remove from the list of communicants members who were lax in paying their dues. The Reverend J. A. Maser described the levy of seven and a half strings as "unscriptural" and wondered how the Egba Christians had tolerated for so long the "spiritual Rehoboam",[51] and "tyrant". The Bishop went out of his way to say that the weekly dues of seven and a half strings should be reduced by 200 per cent.[52]

There is little doubt that by removing the names of communicants who had refused to pay the "unscriptural" levy of seven and a half strings a week James Johnson went too far and acted against both the letter and spirit of liberty in religion. Moreover by denying communion privileges to those who would not contribute the levy he was emphasising the material at the expense of the spiritual and he was applying in religious matters a force which he would have been the first to condemn in others as autocratic and tyrannical. But it would not be fair to blame him for being the only one guilty of this offence. For one thing at the very time that he was being charged with this offence a similar step was being taken in a part of the Diocese under the chairmanship of Bishop Cheetham himself.[53] Moreover, as detailed out in his defence, the people who refused to pay their subscriptions were not indigent communicants but people who were wealthy and whose opposition was due to quite different factors.[54]

The real significance of the Bishop's visit was that it provided an excellent occasion for the eruption of bitterness from this group, which had long been building up against the Superintendent since his advent. For one thing it is doubtful whether, given free will, a large number of the wealthy Egba Christians would have liked to give as liberally as James Johnson had persuaded them to do in matters of religion. From all accounts it seems clear that they wished to dispense their pecuniary liberality in other ways—expensive funerals, birthday ceremonies, entertainments and title-taking. Therefore, once they understood that the white man would be prepared to assume their burden they saw nothing unbecoming and undignified about allowing him to draw the chestnut out of the fire for them. There is evidence that not all subscribers appreciated the "self-support and its honour" which the Superintendent constantly emphasised;[55] they did not see themselves losing any liberty.

Thus once an indication was given that the white man, considered a fool who wished to be exploited, would willingly assume their burden, opposition began to build up against James Johnson. Once the grumbling began the detestation of fees became popular. In some of the churches prayers were said to the effect that God might deliver them from the Superintendent and bring back the era of the white man. Meetings upon meetings were held in secret; at prayer meetings God was entreated for success and triumph in their opposition and they invoked Him to look mercifully upon them under a Superintendent whose only cry was *"money! money!"*[56]

Curiously enough the physical demonstration over the class fees was organised and led by women, under the leaderships of Mary Coker, Fanny Fisher, Susannah Lawolu, Lydia Yemowi and Blesy Desola. They were all wealthy traders and slave owners, the last of them having been made the *Iyalode* of the *Parakoyi* (Chambers of Commerce) in 1878.[57]

By 1879 practically all sections of Egba society had been offended by James Johnson. The agents, mostly of the Egba tribe, who had been virtually masters of their churches from 1867 to 1877, found the Superintendent's energy too much for them. Rather than allowing them to be idle during the week James Johnson drove them to undertake evangelistic work to an extent which they considered excessive. Moreover they felt that he was too much of a superior who had a low opinion of their intellectual and professional capacity.

Polygamists, slave holders and several of the converts resented his attempt to lift all of them to his own moral and spiritual plane. For instance several of the converts confessed that their faith in Christianity was weak, that their adherence to the white man's faith was determined by a desire to be relieved of the financial obligations of traditional religion.[58] The polygamists, who were the wielders of influence and power in society, did not relish their being toppled from the power which they had been exercising in the Church even in the days of the white man. Slave owners hated the idea that in the Church they were forced to become the equals of their human property. Nor did they appreciate the frequency and tone in which the Superintendent denounced them as Shylocks for demanding from their slaves a daily fifteen strings ($3\frac{1}{2}$d.), whereas 'pagans' and Muslims were demanding only ten strings (2d.) at most from their slaves. Most of the converts, too, were resentful of his denunciation of drunkenness, for them a new habit and a symbol of an enlarged status in society.

The class fees affair, then, in its own right was a trifle. In fact, much against his wish, James Johnson was prepared to be accommodating and he surrendered to majority opinion by having the fees reduced to two and a half strings a week. But the solution of this issue did not remove opposition to the Superintendent, and there was a demand for his removal early in 1879.

The rallying point for all opposition members was provided by the Minutes on slavery issued in 1879 by the authorities of the Church Missionary Society. It was decided that all employees of the Society who were slave-holders should either dismiss their slaves by January 1880 or relinquish their posts. In Lagos, where British law was in force, this instruction required no application. In the Niger Mission the more experienced Bishop Crowther would not even mention the existence of this instruction to his lieutenants, much less to the chiefs, whose status and prosperity depended on the institution of slavery. Even in Yorubaland other Mission agents were more concerned in informing the C.M.S. about the virtues of this institution, which was so basic to Yoruba society. In fact the Bishop of the Diocese never attempted to be dogmatic about this issue and never questioned the agents about their attitude towards slavery.

James Johnson's attitude was quite different; he alone in Yorubaland took the instruction of the Society seriously. He alone had the daring, if not the foolhardiness, to give priority to dogma over pragmatism. In his letters and journals since assumption of his office he had never spared any words to inform the Church Missionary Society about the cruelties and inhumanities of this institution, giving details of the sufferings of slaves, the prices they fetched from market to market and his hopes that one day these oppressed people would be liberated. A slave, he said, was "a mere thing, a mere slave, a saleable property whose true value is the market place", who could be compelled to share the master's grave "and wait upon him in the other world".[59] Without any reflection—he would not reflect where Christian verities were concerned—he issued a peremptory order to his lieutenants to submit at once a list of the slaves and pawns in their possession. The agents gave a total list of forty-one slaves. At a meeting in Lagos in September 1879, attended by all the agents, they accepted the C.M.S. circular, intended for distribution among Christians. But although they had returned to Abeokuta three days before their Superintendent none of the agents attempted to distribute the circular or mention it.

The Superintendent himself was aware of the serious implications of the circular in Egba society and he moved about it a little cautiously. Knowing the capacity of the agents for mischief James Johnson made some effort to apprise some of the chiefs of the content of the circular and to emphasise that it was intended for Christians only. His contact with the chiefs was achieved through two influential *Saros*—Henry Robbin and Henry Tinney, the Customs Clerk of the Egba Government who was "connected with a leading family".[60]

James Johnson's belief that the slavery circular should affect Christians only was not based upon a thorough knowledge of the law of inheritance in Yorubaland. For the slaves in possession of a Christian were not his property alone, if he had inherited them, or of his offspring after his death. They were a common property of the extended family, which usually consisted of 'pagans' as well. Nor was the Christian's voice necessarily decisive in the disposal of slaves unless he was the eldest man in the family. Indeed African and European observers of Anglo-Egba relations in the second half of the nineteenth century were agreed that fear of the British tampering with their slaves was the major point of the strain in the relationships between the Egba and the British Government in Lagos.[61] Henry Robbin hit the nail on the head when he informed James Johnson that the slavery question was at the heart of the storm that had developed around the Superintendent: "Slave question in Abeokuta is and has always been a very strong matter, so strong that I believe the people of the country would rather go farther away into the interior with such slaves that they can take away with them, than to remain in the country without them."[62]

It is not surprising, then, that the Egba Authorities took a very serious view of the matter. They had never lived down the suspicion that the British authorities in Lagos harboured annexationist intentions against their territory. They looked upon the C.M.S. circular as the thin edge of the wedge which the white man was driving in to demand a general manumission of all their slaves and to take away their country from them. Moreover James Johnson's role as defender and champion of the rights of slaves presented the Egba with a potentially large social danger. It is said that the slaves were fully aware of his championship of their cause and that had the Egba authorities attempted to expel the Superintendent they would have had to contend with a slave revolt. This is probably the explanation for the restraint exercised by the authorities to an astonishing degree even when their orders were ignored by James Johnson.

On 26 October the chiefs met under the chairmanship of the Jagunna of Igbein. The first proposal, it is said, was to the effect that James Johnson was to be waylaid and beheaded. This proposal was rejected because Henry Robbin, who was present at the meeting, reminded them that James Johnson was a British subject and that to touch him would mean to invite the chastisement of the British Government.[63] It was finally decided to expel him from Egbaland. At 8.07 p.m. of the same day the town-crier appeared at the Superintendent's residence at Ake and delivered, as James Johnson recorded it, "in stentorian voice and in authoritarian and menacing language and tone the message of chiefs commanding my flight from the town before 9 a.m. the next day or the house would be plundered and the consequence would be altogether very serious".[64]

James Johnson sat tight. He ignored the order and no harm was done to him, to the surprise of the Reverend J. A. Maser who was alleged to have said that the Egba ought to have stoned him to death.[65] Apart from the fact that his claim to being a British subject was a sufficient protection against physical molestation by the authorities and the fear of a slave rising in favour of the Superintendent, James Johnson was fortunate in having protectors in highly influential *Saros* and Chiefs. Foremost among these was Henry Robbin, who staked his reputation to save Johnson's life, to the extent that he was accused of plotting with the Superintendent against the interests of the Egba.[66] Some of the chiefs were told that James Johnson had been working in Egbaland with the sinister object of making British rule eventually supreme there, that he was a sort of consul and that after the transfer of the country to the British Government had been completed Henry Robbin would accept the office of Governor. He was in fact threatened with the plunder of his goods and the demolition of his house for abetting and harbouring a known enemy of the public weal.[67] Another *Saro* who helped to temper the hostility of the chiefs was Pedro Martins, a member of Breadfruit Church, formerly resident in Abeokuta. The chief who, although he had differed from the Superintendent over the class fees, but nevertheless would not join the opposition, was John Okenla, the Balogun of the Christians whose bravery in various wars was appreciated by the Egba authorities.

Seen against the political situation in Abeokuta and in Yorubaland in general between 1876 and 1880 the surprise is not that James Johnson's authority collapsed but that it was sustained for so long. For the Superintendent was ruling a group larger than that under any chief; he was holding reins of power beyond the grasp of any one chief. So much had authority become diffused, if not decentralised, among the Egba at the time of James Johnson's sojourn among them, that the young men would not obey the elders, the Church members would not obey their pastors and women had broken loose from their husbands' control. Little wonder that some of the women opposed to his authority warned him that he was doing many things that would not have been attempted by an Egba Superintendent.[68]

More important, perhaps, was the tribal element in the crisis that confronted James Johnson. *Vis-à-vis* other Yoruba peoples the Egba had a sense of pride based on the fact that they were far ahead of other groups in the intellectual development of Yorubaland, an ascendancy they were to retain until the end of the Second

World War. The agents in Abeokuta thus found it irritating that an Ijebu man—as they identified James Johnson—should have authority in a land that belonged to the Egba. In their view only an Egba should be made to preside over Egba affairs. Nor did they relish the idea of agents from other tribal groups working in Egba-land.[69] As for the chiefs, who could hardly have forgotten the part played by the Ijebu in their expulsion from their fatherland early in the century, they looked upon James Johnson as someone who had come deliberately to ruin their land. Why, they asked, had he not taken the C.M.S. circular to Ijebuland for distribution if it was such a good thing?

The difficulties which James Johnson met among the Egba would not have discouraged him, and he believed that he would be able to weather the storm. But to his surprise and bitter disappointment the Society whose cause he was maintaining did not back him up. For James Johnson looked upon himself as a reformer and an emancipator. Rather than abandon a cause he believed to be right he was determined to show greater zeal in his opposition to slavery and possibly get himself killed. His greatest criticism was reserved for the Egba whose vices, he said, included dishonesty, in-subordination, irresoluteness, incorrigible selfishness and money-grabbing.[70] As he said: "In a case like this, opposition and dislike are natural but however severe, their duration is often only temporary and I have not been unwilling to face them for the good of the cause."[71]

But instead of the C.M.S. authorities looking upon James John-son as another Wilberforce or Sir Bartle Frere he was charged with "errors in judgment and failure to secure moral influence".[72] Of course these were very vague terms, a veritable avoidance of the issue at stake. In the West Indies and in Britain emancipation champions got credit for a task they performed for a period lasting decades. But in Abeokuta James Johnson attempted almost single-handed to force through emancipation in a very short period. There was no justification for criticising the way in which he carried out the Society's instructions. Because he attempted to encourage self-support he was condemned for showing too much zeal: worse than this he was accused of hating the Egbas.[73]

The fact is that neither on moral grounds nor on the evidence of the facts could the C.M.S. justify their attitude to, and con-demnation of, James Johnson. Privately, of course, in private correspondence with European missionaries, the Society recognised that he had been absolutely loyal and had been very firm.[74] No valid charge was levelled against the Superintendent.

The Society's strange behaviour can only be understood in the light of the events which had been going on behind the scenes since his appointment. In 1876 the Society had been inclined to reprove its missionaries for their prejudice against James Johnson, lecturing them that the latter's appointment was a step "which seems to us one in the right direction [which] may be overruled by God to the advancement and establishment of missionary work in Abeokuta". There could be no question of the Society looking back, it was stressed, and although James Johnson was not a white man, "he has at his back the same influence and support as the white man would have".[75]

A change of attitude began in April 1877, that is barely two months after James Johnson's assumption of his new post. The European missionaries were being reminded that a "new arrangement" was being made for the Niger Mission which involved the injection of white missionaries into a hitherto all-African mission.[76] The implication was that the wisdom of creating another all-African mission in Yorubaland was to be doubted. The European missionaries were encouraged to think that James Johnson's appointment was not permanent, that it was no more than "an experiment" and that he might not be as successful as the Society had thought.[77]

So, whether there had been a crisis or not in Abeokuta, the supersession of James Johnson in the interior would have been merely a question of time. In fact since March 1878, that is nearly a year before the Bishop went to stir up the hornets' nest in Abeokuta, plans to supersede the Superintendent were being made.[78] European missionaries, who began to increase in number, could not be tied down to Lagos or Lekkie indefinitely. No European missionary would go into the interior under an African supervisor. Bishop Cheetham put the current thinking of the European missionaries well when he said that after all James Johnson was only an African and as such could not possess the dignity and prestige of a white man, a view which, as had been shown by Townsend's experience, was not true. "To the great mass of the people," said the Bishop, James Johnson was "only a blackman, and is no wise different from another black man".[79]

James Johnson defended every action and step he had taken in the interior with patience and with facts. But the Society never answered. He was concerned to show that his capability as a Negro was not called into question; he was convinced that his achievements had done credit to the Negro Race. As he protested: "What is my fault. Not moral delinquency: not neglect of duty; not abuse of trust, nor disobedience to orders. . . . My work, I contend has not failed, difficulties nothwithstanding."[80] In their heart of hearts the Society subscribed to James Johnson's verdict. As the Secretaries disclosed to Maser, they "heartily appreciate the firmness and resolution with which Mr. Johnson has endeavoured to carry out their views and put Abeokuta Church on a satisfactory footing".[81] They instructed the white missionary who was asked to succeed James Johnson to work "on Johnson's lines".[82]

Curiously enough, partly because of the assurance and sympathy expressed to him by friends of the C.M.S. in England, James Johnson believed that the local missionaries should be held as being entirely responsible for his troubles in Abeokuta. These missionaries, he said, "do not as a general rule represent the liberal and advanced views of the Society". He even went so far as to sympathise with the C.M.S. "in the difficulty they experience to secure for West Africa the services of a superior stamp of men and thus raise the standard of foreign agency to the necessities of the times".[83] The course that should be taken by the Society, he said, was to improve the educational facilities in West Africa and to raise up a large number of qualified Africans. There never would be a time when European employees of the right calibre, who would interpret and represent the Afrophile policy of the Society, would be produced in any large number. The Reverend J. A. Maser, he said, was already discredited and should be replaced by another person.[84]

To his intense mortification the Society removed him from the interior. He would rather have been killed in Abeokuta than have the Negro Race discredited by his "disratement".[85] He asked: "Why should the Society withdraw me from my position when with a little more help from it, it would have prevented another feather being added to the crown of those who are very fond of preaching up Negro incapacity for independent trust, a doctrine which the Society I believe stands pledged to disprove, and save Negroes, anxious to prove this in themselves or see it proved in others for the good of the native Christianity the country and race from disappointment and despondency?"[86]

By removing James Johnson from the interior the Society discovered again that it had to contend with more than an individual. The Superintendent had become the symbol of the Negro Race. The leading laymen in Lagos memorialised Salisbury Square that the humiliation inflicted on, and the "injustice" committed against, James Johnson were intended for the Negro Race.[87] In its Fifth Annual Report (1880), the Native Pastorate declared that "the whole of the Negro Race is compromised by this removal of confidence". In Abeokuta the patriotic party headed by G. W. Johnson organised opposition against a white successor and attempted to kidnap him.[88] So strong was African feeling on behalf of Holy Johnson that the Church Missionary Society had to announce that his removal from the interior was only "temporary".

NOTES

1. C.M.S. CA2/017, Otunba Payne and others to Secretaries C.M.S., 3/3/1877.
2. *Ibid.*, see copy of memorial to him, 3/2/1877.
3. *Ibid.*, Otunba Payne and others to Secretaries C.M.S., 3/3/1877.
4. C.M.S. CA2/99, H. Townsend to H. Wright, 29/1/1875.
5. C.M.S. CA2/049(a), D. Hinderer to H. Wright, 15/7/1875.
6. C.M.S. CA2/085(a), H. Townsend to H. Wright, 25/11/1875.
7. C.M.S. CA3/04(a), Bishop Crowther to H. Wright, 2/3/1876.
8. C.M.S. CA2/056, James Johnson, Annual Report for 1877.
9. C.O. 147/132, H. Macallum to J. Chamberlain, 5/5/1898.
10. C.M.S. CA2/085(a), H. Townsend to H. Wright, 1/4/1875.
11. *Ibid.*, also CA2/056, James Johnson to H. Wright, 15/9/1879.
12. *Ibid.*, 5/4/1878.
13. *Ibid.*, 9/2/1880.
14. C.M.S. CA2/03(d), A. Maser to H. Wright, 4/8/1876.
15. C.M.S. CA2/L4, H. Wright and E. Hutchinson to James Johnson, 8/12/1876.
16. C.M.S. CA2/03(d), A. Maser to H. Wright, 11/7/1879.
17. C.M.S. CA2/056, James Johnson to H. Wright, 18/1/1877.
18. *Ibid.*, James Johnson, Annual Report for 1877.
19. *Ibid.*
20. Up to the end of the nineteenth century the Oyo Yoruba were referred to in this manner, the rest referring to themselves under distinct names as Egba, Ijebu, Ijesha and so on.
21. S.M.A., J. B. Chausse to Superior General, 1/5/1888.
22. C.M.S. CA2/056, James Johnson, Annual Report for 1877.
23. *Ibid.*, for copy of resolutions.
24. *Ibid.*, "From Ibadan to Oyo and Ogbomosho", 1877.
25. *Ibid.*
26. *Ibid*, "From Ibadan to Oyo and Ogbomosho", 1877.
27. *Ibid.*
28. C.M.S. CA1/025(e), Bishop Cheetham to H. Wright, 18/2/1874.
29. C.M.S. CA2/056, James Johnson to H. Wright, 21/6/1878.
30. *Ibid.*, Report dated 30/1/1878.
31. Yoruba term referring to expulsion of European missionaries and destruction of their property.
32. C.M.S. CA2/056, James Johnson, Report dated 30/1/1878.
33. C.M.S. G/AC 4/2, Henry Townsend to H. Wright, 1/12/1877.
34. C.M.S. CA2/056, James Johnson, *Journals*, "From Ibadan to Oyo and Ogbomosho", 1877.
35. *Ibid.*, James Johnson, *Journals*, "A visit of Inspection to Ilaro and Henerancies", January 1879.
36. *Ibid.*, James Johnson to H. Wright, 5/4/1878.
37. *Ibid.*, James Johnson to H. Wright, 18/1/1878; same to same 2/7/1878.
38. *Ibid.*, Minutes of conferences.
39. *Ibid.*, "Extracts from Minute Book Clerical Conference Abeokuta October 10, 1877".
40. *Ibid.*, James Johnson to H. Wright, 2/8/1879.
41. *Ibid.*, The Minutes of Meeting.
42. *Ibid.*, see Minutes of Meeting of Clerical Conference.

43. C.M.S. CA1/025(e), Bishop Cheetham to H. Wright, 16/5/1879.
44. *Ibid.*, same to same, 2/3/1878.
45. C.M.S. CA2/03(d), J. A. Maser to H. Wright, 1/10/1879.
46. *Ibid.*
47. C.M.S. CA1/025(e), Bishop Cheetham to H. Wright, 2/3/1876.
48. C.M.S. CA2/03(d), J. A. Maser to H. Wright, 11/7/1879.
49. C.M.S. CA2/056, Henry Robbin to James Johnson, 12/9/1879.
50. C.M.S. CA1/025(e), Bishop Cheetham to H. Wright, 16/5/1879;
    CA2/056, James Johnson to H. Wright, 8/2/1879.
51. C.M.S. CA2/03(d), J. A. Maser to Secretary, 3/7/1879.
52. C.M.S. CA1/025(e), Bishop Cheetham to H. Wright, 16/5/1879.
53. C.M.S. G3/A2/01, James Johnson to E. Hutchinson, June 1881.
54. C.M.S. CA2/056, James Johnson to H. Wright, 8/2/1879.
55. *Ibid.*
56. *Ibid.*
57. *Ibid.*
58. *Ibid.*
59. *Ibid.*, James Johnson, Annual Report for 1879.
60. *Ibid.*, James Johnson to H. Wright, 10/11/1879.
61. *C.M. Intelligencer*, 1893, p. 361.
62. C.M.S. CA2/056, Henry Robbin to James Johnson, 12/9/1879.
63. *Ibid.*, James Johnson to H. Wright, 10/11/1879.
64. *Ibid.*
65. C.M.S. G3/A2/02, James Johnson to E. D. Wickham (undated).
66. C.M.S. CA2/056, James Johnson to H. Wright, 10/11/1879.
67. *Ibid.*, same to same.
68. *Ibid.*, 8/2/1879.
69. *Ibid.*, same to same, 18/9/1879.
70. *Ibid*, same to same, 8/2/1879.
71. *Ibid.*, same to same, 9/2/1880.
72. C.M.S. CA2/L4, H. Wright to James Johnson, 19/2/1879.
73. C.M.S. G3/A2/01, James Johnson to E. Hutchinson, 1881,
    quotes the latter.
74. C.M.S. CA2/L4, H. Wright to Bishop Cheetham, 24/10/1879.
75. *Ibid.*, H. Wright and E. Hutchinson to J. A. Maser, 1/12/1876.
76. *Ibid.*, H. Wright to J. A. Maser, 5/4/1877.
77. *Ibid.*
78. C.M.S. CA1/22, H. Wright to Bishop Cheetham, 23/3/1878.
79. C.M.S. CA1/025(e), Bishop Cheetham to H. Wright, 16/5/1879.
80. C.M.S. CA2/056, James Johnson to H. Wright, 9/2/1880.
81. C.M.S. CA2/L4, H. Wright and E. Hutchinson to J. A. Maser,
    19/12/1879.
82. *Ibid.*, H. Wright to V. Faulkner, 19/12/1879.
83. C.M.S. G3/A2/02, James Johnson to Rev. E. D. Wickham
    (undated).
84. *Ibid.*
85. C.M.S. CA2/056, James Johnson to H. Wright, 9/2/1880.
86. *Ibid.*
87. C.M.S. G3/A2/01, dated 25/3/1880.
88. *Ibid.*, J. B. Wood to H. Wright, 28/4/1880.

CHAPTER SIX

EPISCOPATE LOSER

It is rightly esteemed the glory of Mission work in a foreign field that it has been able to call into existence self-supporting Native Pastorate congregations ministered to by Native Pastors. It must be esteemed a greater glory when such Pastorates are like other Churches, self-governing and self-directing, the individual, or the Body representing this collective Government being native. Such a Government is not only a greater proof of missionary success, but it is also an additional and if possible, a stronger pledge of continued existence and natural growth.

James Johnson's Memorandum on Native
Episcopacy 3/2/1887

THE European adversaries who rejoiced that James Johnson was deposed from the pedestal of authority in the interior of Yorubaland were soon to discover that this had not affected his stature in the eyes of the Africans. For his superintendence had not been a failure and in several ways it had enlarged his prestige, vindicated his ability, publicised his qualities and enlarged the circle of his admirers. For never had a European missionary displayed in Lagos and in the interior his kind of ability, spiritual fervour, saintliness and sense of dedication; never had a white missionary such a vast area under his control; never had a missionary performed in effect the duties of a Bishop; never had a missionary's moral and spiritual influence and standard been as perceptibly high as that of James Johnson's in the eyes of native converts; never had any ecclesiastic attempted and succeeded to persuade the Yoruba to take Christianity so seriously and to strain their purse in the manner James Johnson had succeeded in doing between 1877 and 1880.

In fact James Johnson's removal from the interior made him a martyr for the African cause in the eyes of his African admirers and a victim of a conspiracy inspired by envious European missionaries. African resentment at his removal was emphatic. Apart from the protest by the Lagos Christians, his Church, Breadfruit, which had not become part of the Native Pastorate, registered its protest by behaving as if it were "virtually free of the Society".[1] Extremist supporters went as far as trying to prevent his European successor, the Reverend V. Faulkner, from being allowed into Egbaland. In fact, so uneasy was the European successor that he became a virtual prisoner in the Egba capital, fearing that he would not be allowed to return to Abeokuta if he once went down to Lagos. The *Lagos Times*, the first Nigerian-owned newspaper founded in the very year of his deposition by an ardent Johnsonian, R. B. Blaize, lost no time in urging Salisbury Square to reinstate the ex-Superintendent in the name of "Christian justice".[2]

Nor was sympathy for James Johnson confined to Africans. The officials in Salisbury Square admitted to their European agents that James Johnson had been absolutely loyal to the Society, that his attempt to promote self-government in the interior of Yorubaland had been quite in order and that his "firmness" over the slavery matter was right and commendable.[3] Even in their inner thoughts many of the local missionaries recognised that his deposition was unjust and might be "injurious";[4] the Bishop, too, who had made much of the class fee admitted that James Johnson had been "strictly right" in the matter.[5] More important still, as far as Wonderful Johnson was concerned, was that several admirers in Britain sympathised with him and reinforced his confidence in the Afrophile policy of the C.M.S.[6] Once again, he began to say, European missionaries, fearful of being thrown out of job, were the main source of his anxieties and of the reverses being suffered by his Ethiopian programme.[7] He was generously treated by the Society, which allowed him the unusual leave of one year, which he spent in Sierra Leone, before he resumed the pastoral charge of Breadfruit Church.

Consequently, the crisis of 1879-1880 and the unconcealed racial prejudice of Bishop Cheetham and the white missionaries notwithstanding, James Johnson remained a veritable obstacle to the achievement of an end which the Church Missionary Society had had in view since 1872—the constitution of Yorubaland into a diocese under a European Bishop. Had James Johnson been discredited between 1877 and 1880 it would have been easy for Salisbury Square to have superseded him. But as long as he lived, or until the death of Bishop Crowther in 1891, there could be no question of appointing a bishop for Yorubaland, much as the Society would have wished to have done so and much as the interests of the Society dictated taking such a step. The obstacle continued to be James Johnson who had no rival, European or African, in fitness for elevation to the episcopate. This fact, as pointed out in the last chapter, had been recognised and accepted by Henry Townsend, Salisbury Square officials and Bishop Crowther as far back as 1875.

The case for constituting Yorubaland into a diocese was not a matter for controversy. It was a self-evident fact. The Sierra Leone Diocese, of which Yorubaland was a part, was peculiar and unwieldy, embracing at one time or another Madeira, Morocco, Mauritius (in the Indian Ocean) and St. Helena (in the southern Atlantic). Freetown, the seat of the Bishop, was over 1,000 miles away from Lagos. Without taking into account the time lost from fever the Bishop was officially absent from his Diocese for six months in the year. Then, of necessity, the absorbing demands of Sierra Leone claimed most of his attention. Only occasionally could he visit Yorubaland, and that for a few weeks at the most. From 1853 to 1870, a period of seventeen years, there were only four episcopal visits; from 1861 to 1877, sixteen years, there were only seven visits. From 1846 to 1879 Abeokuta was visited five times, Ibadan only twice and Ijaye, before it was destroyed, also twice. Ibadan saw no Bishop between 1859 and 1894; Ode-Ondo, which had been occupied since 1876, had no episcopal visit for seventeen years.

Compared with other mission fields split into dioceses in the seventies in India, China and North America the case for splitting the Sierra Leone Diocese was stronger in many ways. Firstly it was not situated in contiguous territory. Secondly, in statistical achievement Yorubaland alone, with six European missionaries, fifty-one African ministerial auxiliaries, forty-one African teachers, 7,111 Christians and 1,941 scholars in 1887, was greater than the newly created, in 1873 and 1884 respectively, Dioceses of Algoma and Qu' Appelle in Canada; than Lahore and Rangoon in India in 1877 or Mid-China and North China in 1879. Thirdly the Yoruba Mission was older than many other C.M.S. missions which enjoyed accelerated ecclesiastical advancement. In every respect the Yoruba mission was bigger and more developed than, for instance, its eastern neighbour, the Niger Mission.

That making Yorubaland a diocese would promote administrative efficiency, facilitate co-ordination and infuse zeal into the work of the C.M.S. in the territory was beyond dispute; episcopal supervision was, in Anglican missionary areas as in settled Churches, a lubricant to the administrative machine; it would also foster and consolidate spiritual life and develop the missionary zeal and activity of the Church.

The need for making Yorubaland an ecclesiastical division had been perceived in 1872 by the Bishop of the Diocese, who in that year wanted Henry Townsend consecrated Bishop for the territory. But he refrained from making the recommendation because, according to him, Henry Venn would insist on an African Bishop.[8] For the next ten years the urgency of the matter was discussed in Salisbury Square not less than four times and yet on every occasion the issue had to be shelved. As the Archbishop of Canterbury put it, appointing a Bishop for a Yoruba Diocese would raise "practical difficulties".[9] These "practical difficulties" were no more than the fact that James Johnson could not be divorced from a Yoruba Diocese and that no white man would serve under an African Bishop.

Rather than diminishing, events after 1880 emphasised these "practical difficulties" and brought forward the question of the Yoruba episcopate which had been shelved for more than a decade, much to the embarrassment of the Church Missionary Society. First the candidature of James Johnson was progressively strengthened as his attributes received greater and wider recognition, while at the same time the prejudice of the European missionaries became ludicrously pronounced to an extent that could not be approved by the C.M.S. authorities. Secondly between 1880 and 1887 Johnsonians joined in the demand for a separate Yoruba Diocese.

Whilst his energetic activities in the Native Pastorate had made James Johnson a thorn in the side of European missionaries the signal failure of his European successor in Abeokuta provided the Johnsonians with a powerful weapon for a valid chastisement of European denigrators of the Negro Race. For the Reverend Valentine Faulkner discovered that the forces with which James Johnson had to contend were largely impersonal and that the white man did not possess the mysterious prestige for maintaining authority over Africans credited to him by Bishop Cheetham. Faulkner could not raise the issue of the circular on slave-holding among Egba Christians, nor could he maintain law and order. When he attempted to discipline two agents—George and Elliot—for disobedience, both invoked the aid of their chiefs and of their 'pagan' and Muslim townsmen and seized a church—property of the Society—with impunity.[10] Nor had he a good reputation in financial matters. He owed money to a number of Africans and misappropriated the Society's funds.[11]

In Lagos, too, the European missionaries discredited themselves in the eyes of the C.M.S. by their persistent anti-Johnson attitude. It will be remembered that in 1884 all the European missionaries had openly complained that they could neither work with James

Johnson, nor could they tolerate him as a member of the Finance Committee. The man they sponsored was one Frank Hood of Banners & Brothers Company, a European and a Churchwarden of Christ Church. He was recommended highly by Bishop Ingham as "a pillar of the Church and a striking exception to Europeans on the coast in his spiritual endeavours and interests".[12] However the man proved his worth by showing himself a habitual drunkard and a rogue. For, as Treasurer of the Native Pastorate, he ran away with the institution's money, to the tune of more than £1,000, not a penny of which was recoverable from him.[13]

After these events in Abeokuta and Lagos, Salisbury Square relied no longer on the opinion and judgment of its European missionaries in Lagos, nor on that of Bishop Ingham on matters relating to James Johnson. But in the meantime Johnsonians had become more articulate about the ecclesiastical arrangements in the Diocese of Sierra Leone. Demand was two-fold, that either an African successor to the current incumbent, Bishop Cheetham, should be appointed, or that the Diocese should be split into two with one under an African Bishop.[14] It may be noted that Henry Venn had said as early as 1866 that an African should be trained as a Suffragan, but no missionary ever alluded to this wish, much less asked that it be put into practice. Consequently, in order to prevent the racial tension in the Church from developing around the episcopate, successive Bishops refrained, while absent on leave from their Dioceses, from appointing commissaries during the seventies and eighties.

African demand for an African Bishop for the Sierra Leone Diocese was strengthened by the fact that by the eighties the converts were responsible for 75 per cent of the cost of maintaining churches and schools. Moreover many had become convinced that Christianity would not have a permanent existence in Africa unless and until its spread and control had passed completely into African hands. When it became known that Bishop Cheetham would resign his post the *Lagos Times* of 22 February 1882 declared that European supervision of mission work in West Africa should never have exceeded thirty years. In the following year when a European successor, K. Ingham, was appointed, the newspaper asked him to recommend "as soon as possible, . . . a division of the Diocese [and thereby] pay a practical regard to the desire expressed for a Native Episcopate . . . [and] . . . arrange for the raising of sums for Native Bishoprics in the divided Diocese".[15]

The advisability of the C.M.S. turning Yorubaland into a Diocese was further strengthened by two events in 1886. Decentralisation along territorial lines was effected by the Wesleyan Missionary Society and by the British administration. Both bodies, which had been administering the Gold Coast and Yorubaland as a unit, gave each territory a separate identity. The Wesleyans constituted Yorubaland into a distinctive mission under a chairman; in administration Lagos ceased to be an appendage of Accra, the Administrator became a Governor and the Legislative Council for Lagos Colony revived. In May 1886 the C.M.S. had to confess to the Bishop that the creation of a Diocese in Yorubaland "is a question needing very much consideration" and that "more continuous Episcopal superintendence than you are able from the circumstances of the case to provide, would tend much to consolidate and further the work".[16]

More important for Christian missions was the beginning of the return of peace to strife-torn Yorubaland in 1886, following the intervention of the British administration. Prospects for successful Christianisation of the Yoruba improved with the tacit acceptance of British suzerainty by a large portion of Yorubaland. All Christian missions discerned and utilised the opportunity afforded by the return of peace. The Southern American Baptists located Lumbley and Smith in Abeokuta and Ogbomosho respectively; the S.M.A. occupied Oyo and began to make plans to establish themselves in Ibadan and Ijebu Ode. In 1887 the new Chairman of the Wesleyan Mission, the Reverend T. J. Halligey, embarked on a grand missionary tour designed to push his Society's work to Ibadan, Oyo and Iseyin. The C.M.S. in particular, whose missionaries had performed the role of intermediaries in the negotiations leading to the Peace Treaty of 1886, had desired to derive maximum advantage for its work and actually began to consider a strategy for occupying all important places in Yorubaland at the time of the conclusion of peace terms.[17]

Nevertheless the Society could not send white missionaries into the interior until three years after the return of peace. This was because the question of missionary expansion became inextricably involved with the Yoruba episcopate question. Left alone the Society would have liked to continue with its policy of *Quieta non movere* on the matter. The Society forced the issue on itself by the invitation made to James Johnson in 1886 to come over to England.

That James Johnson would force the issue during his visit was apparently perceived by Bishop Ingham. Therefore he offered the African agitator a position that others would have accepted with alacrity, that of Missioner for the whole Diocese, a position that would have made him in effect second-in-command to the Bishop in missionary affairs and that would have more than doubled his salary. To his surprise and chagrin James Johnson rejected the offer with a contempt very painful to his ecclesiastical master.[18]

The atmosphere in which James Johnson found himself when he landed in Britain in 1887 was one calculated to appeal to his patriotic instincts. His stature in Lagos had been enlarged by his appointment as a member of the Legislative Council in the previous year, whilst in the same year he had conducted a successful mission to Sierra Leone. In several ways he received recognition from prominent men in Church and State in England. He became a showpiece of the C.M.S. at the Keswick Convention and the subject of a cartoon over the Liquor Question, with him pointing at a map of Europe with the caption "Africa Rebukes Europe". On this latter issue he also held a meeting with some M.P.s in Room Number 25 in the House of Commons and was a foundation member of the Native Races and Liquor Traffic Committee, an organisation under the chairmanship of the Duke of Westminster, dedicated to agitation for abolition of liquor traffic in Africa.[19] The State gave him the privilege and honour of being present "as an African Representative of West African Colonies and of the Negro Race" at the Jubilee Garden Party of Queen Victoria and he attended the Indian and Colonial Exhibition where he mourned over the exhibits of the West African section because they were "of the poorest and most meagre description".[20]

Of greater significance for us are his views on the decline of Sierra Leone and the necessity for self-government for British West Africa generally which he expressed in a lengthy memorandum submitted to the Colonial Office. He saw the Sierra Leone of his dream passing away, retrogressing rather than progressing. Physiologically, he said, the Creoles had deteriorated and their capacity for increasing the population seriously undermined. The British Government, he said, had failed woefully to fulfil its mission in the Colony; this mission, in his view, was that Britain should make it economically viable, industrialised, a nursery of well-educated elite, possessing modern means of communication and so on. It is worth noting that whilst the inhabitants of the Colony were indulging in panegyrics, looking upon themselves with romantic eyes and beholding their Colony as the beacon on the African continent[21] James Johnson believed that, on the whole, the inhabitants had no cause to rejoice; that no solid progress had been achieved by the British in Sierra Leone.

Particularly significant is the fact that he attributed the problems besetting Sierra Leone Colony and the rest of British West Africa to one main cause—the failure of the British Government to encourage the governed to have a share in the government of their country, a factor which, in his observation, had induced in Africans apathy and a lack of interest and pride in the governments of the colonies. In short, paternalism in the State had been ruinous to

African interest. As he declared: "There is in this [apathy] no security to real progress and no warrant for development on the lines that lead to real greatness. It is desirable that they be lifted up from this if they are to be a strong people, a part of a great and strong nation even though they be of a different race, and be eventually able to govern themselves."[22]

A man who believed that in the State Africans were already ripe for a measure of self-government could hardly be expected to be silent about self-government in the Church which, as has been emphasised, he and educated Africans generally, believed should be the forerunner of political independence. His principles and philosophy of missions are of current interest and demand a detailed attention in this age of division of opinion about the older and younger churches. In two long memoranda[23] he set out in clear language his views on the state of affairs of missionary activity in West Africa, criticising the C.M.S. for killing the spirit of independence in West African countries and working against the evolution of an African Church. With the facts and figures he had marshalled, he made the point that since 1852 the missionary frontier of the Society had been at a standstill, in spite of the relief the Native Pastorates of Sierra Leone and Lagos had given to the Society. He thought the Society's relaxed missionary effort was responsible for the distinct advantage which Islam had gained in spreading southward from the Sudan. The Society should seek to remedy the situation by sending European missionaries with African auxiliaries both to Falaba, a large and strong town in the Sulima country (in the hinterland of Sierra Leone) only recently conquered by a Muslim ruler, and to the western parts of the Sokoto Caliphate. The Colony of Sierra Leone and the whole of Yorubaland, he said, should be abandoned to the Native Pastorates.

As regards Church government the interests of Christianity and the facts of the case demanded that in Sierra Leone "the length of time [of C.M.S. presence there] more than warrants the existence of native supervision long before this time". For the congregations were all African in membership; even St. George Cathedral which was built with the Government's money for its officials had no more than twenty European worshippers, the rest being Africans. In his judgment the churches in the Colony were flourishing because they were in African hands. Had Europeans been in charge of these churches their progress would have been less spectacular. But as long as Europeans retained their presence and control, at any level, the people would never be able to appreciate and acquire the virtue of independence and regard the Church as their property. Already there was no "identity of existence and interest . . . that sense of oneness" between the African members of the Church

K

and their European supervisors. As to the European claim that their presence was necessary to obviate sectional allegiance and jealousy among the clergymen his answer was that "Native African Mohammedan and Heathen communities everywhere rule and govern themselves as independent religious communities without any reference to any foreign religious community, Mohammedan or heathen". James Johnson was surprised that it did not occur to any European Bishop that he should be succeeded by an African. He declared: "There evidently had been retrogression instead of an advance forward in the matter of Native Episcopal Supervision." He refused to accept the view universally expressed and accepted by Europeans, that European presence was indispensable in the West African Church because morality among West African Christians was low and that because of this African supervision and control should be withheld for an indefinite period of time: for "in what Diocese in England or Europe may not faults be found"?

Unlike the historical experience of the Church in other parts of Christendom, contended James Johnson, the Church in West Africa deserved sympathy because she was being born in an age of worldliness and materialism "which affects Christianity everywhere". Moreover Europeans were not a credit to the Church in this part of Africa where they set "evil examples" and thereby contributed to the unsatisfactory state of the Church. In his view the Church in West Africa should not be expected to approach the ideal standard of sanctity overnight; she must be given some time to contend with her particular problems such as Islam, polygamy and traditional religion. Above all James Johnson did not accept the verdict of European commentators that the Church in West Africa had failed or was failing. In fact, in the circumstances the surprise was that she had succeeded so well, both statistically, and in the suppression of inhuman customs and institutions. Whatever the faults which might be found in young churches they were not unique; they were part of the teething troubles not dissimilar in principle to those experienced by all great Churches in Christendom. In any case, concluded Holy Johnson, the imperfections of the Church could not be removed by mortals and should therefore be left to the Author of the Church who in His time would pour out "His spirit largely upon pastors and people".

James Johnson believed that the refusal to create a new diocese out of the Sierra Leone Diocese was motivated by racial discrimination. For instance the North West American Mission which was founded only in 1822, that is eighteen years later than the West African Mission, and whose first episcopate was established in 1849, had by 1887 divided and sub-divided into six episcopates, all filled by Europeans. In India, too, division and sub-division went on without any trouble because the incumbents were all white. It was for the same racial reason, declared the Ethiopian leader, that the Methodist Episcopal Church of America was refusing to admit Negro Pastors to the Bishopric.

The racial law, contended James Johnson, should not operate in Yorubaland, partly because the races were not mixed and partly because the territory was not under British control. Moreover it was a self-revealing fact that Christianity was intended to be racially and culturally neutral, to assume parts of the culture of every people, and he demanded that Church government should be controlled by the peoples among whom the Gospel was being proclaimed. But, unfortunately, observed Holy Johnson: "The idea of an absolute necessity for and desirability of the existence of self-supporting Native Pastorates ministered to by Pastors of their own race as an outcome of missionary labour is certainly an idea that has not yet mastered the mind of the missionary portion of the church." Therefore European missionaries must be written off as a source of weakness, rather than of strength, to the evolution of the African Church.

James Johnson observed further that there was no Scriptural injunction for the Christian missions' desire to establish ecclesiastical imperialism. In fact by the acts of the apostles the New Testament made it clear that churches should be left alone to govern themselves after a few years. There was no question of the slow process of Henry Venn's scheme. West Africa was ripe for independence in Church, as well as in State.

Lastly James Johnson pointed out that the struggle with Islam, about which heated discussion was going on at the time of his visit to England,[24] could only be successful when Africans were in full and complete control of their affairs. The missionary societies should follow the example of Islam, which in Yorubaland "has long ago made itself an indigenous and a native institution. Its foreign teachers and promoters have long ago retired from the position of leaders and teachers and Rulers". The view often paraded by Christian missions to console themselves, that Islam was more readily acceptable to Africans than Christianity because the latter was allegedly more exacting in its tenets, said James Johnson, missed the point: "Is not this difference due to the plan of operation on the part of Christian missions?"

What James Johnson desired was that the Church Missionary Society should have four dioceses: one in Sierra Leone, one in Yorubaland and two in the Niger Mission territories. All, except that in Sierra Leone, should be automatically filled with African Bishops, whilst the fourth one should have an African Suffragan.

In theory none of James Johnson's contentions could be refuted.

Their implementation would bring about the ideal situation. It was certainly in the interest of Christian missions to encourage Native Churches to be thrown onto their own resources, so that the latter might not become weak in character and indisposed to effort; too much dependence on the parents would stunt their energies and destroy any hope of their usefulness. There was another reason why missionary bodies should place overseas Churches in a position of independent and separate existence: to encourage missionary action at home.

However, in the circumstances of West Africa there had to be perpetual conflict between the ideal and the practicable, between theory and practice. The Church in West Africa was not the Church Universal, nor the true invisible Church in Heaven of which the visible Church on the terrestrial globe is a mere copy. The Church in West Africa was created largely by the sweat of European missionaries, with European funds, with European initiative and drive, and not without European interest. The European missionaries could not be expected to behave like Apostle Paul and they had nothing of the vision or liberality of Henry Venn. Henry Venn's name did not occur once in their correspondence. They were convinced that European missionaries were a source of strength to the morality and spread of the Christian Church. Hence when observations were being made by Salisbury Square on the strength of the Native Pastorate in Lagos the Bishop of the Diocese, Ingham, declared that the credit belonged entirely to the European presence. As he declared: "Much of the vigour you notice in Lagos arises from the spirit your own resident missionaries throw into native church work there. They give a high tone to the whole thing and remain behind the scene."[25] The European missionaries did not believe that one generation was enough to produce ideal Christians in West Africa. The idea that at some date—even in the remote future—they would and should leave the Mission field did not occur to them.

As a matter of course they believed further that they had erred by conferring any degree of authority on the converts in Sierra Leone and in Lagos. They found extremely distasteful the scramble for positions in the Church by the Africans and the anti-white feelings that this scramble engendered. By 1884 Salisbury Square had found the African agents in Lagos "full of ambition and conceit" and had declared the following anti-Venn sentiment on the institution being run by Africans under James Johnson's leadership: "It may seem to be inexpedient to set a comparatively infant church prematurely free to shape its own cause to entire independence pecuniarily and materially of the Mission, which represents the Church of England in the Colony."[26] Therefore a plan was made to establish a European link between the Pastorate and the C.M.S. In 1886 J. Hamilton, a man who in the sixties had found James Johnson a bugbear in Sierra Leone and who had just completed an anti-Crowther memorandum in the Niger Mission, was made Archdeacon of Lagos, in the hope that through his ecclesiastical status he could attain some control over the Native Pastorate.

These missionaries who thought differently from James Johnson must not be dismissed as negrophobes. Ironically they loved the people among whom they were working and they believed passionately that only European leadership could provide their African wards with true progress. The Europeans were largely influenced by two concepts. Firstly, that the cultural and technological superiority of the European world was a testimony to the superiority of the white over the African race. Secondly, that Christianity had grown in Europe for over a thousand years and, as products of the cumulative experience of this long period, they had inherited Christian qualities that Africans could not take up overnight. After all, it should be stressed in favour of this latter element in European thinking, there were not many African Christians of James Johnson's calibre in West Africa.

Apart from these concepts held by Europeans it should be observed that James Johnson's demands were ill-timed. In theory he was right, but he failed to consider general opinion and man-made events which must also be taken into consideration. The era of the Scramble reinforced the belief in racial superiority that was being accepted by Europeans in West Africa generally in the last years of the nineteenth century. There was also the fact that in the face of competition by other European powers in Yorubaland British missionaries became patriotic, wishing that no other flag but the Union Jack should fly over the territory. The implication of this was that, contrary to James Johnson's hope, the British would have to impose the British Raj over Yorubaland. There was also the economic interest of Britain which British merchants with the backing of the secular arm wished to see enlarged and which became aggressive as from 1887 onwards. Above all the prospects for evangelisation increased as more and more areas in Yorubaland were being pacified. The romance of going into the interior and sharing in the exhilarating pioneering experience was a most desirable thing for most European missionaries. Nor must it be forgotten that, unlike the pioneers, most of the European missionaries in the Scramble period were better educated than the African agents.

Nevertheless James Johnson's memoranda were not pigeon-holed but were treated with an astonishing seriousness. Officials in Salisbury Square were very much impressed by the memoranda. In their view they were "very able, interesting and important,

dealing with subjects touching the very life of the Native Church".[27]
There was no question about the validity of his views taken on
their merits alone. Nor was there any doubt as to the qualifications
of this African agitator for the episcopate. As a Salisbury Square
official lectured Bishop Ingham: "I confess to feeling that with
such a true man, of power and spirituality and earnest purpose, as
Mr. James Johnson, we should not readily decline an immediate
solution to the question. I believe that he would be enabled under
God as a chief pastor to give considerable impetus to the development and advance of the native Church."[28]

However the memoranda stirred the hornets' nest. The racial
element in the episcopate could not be discountenanced; indeed it
was fundamental and it was to be the rock on which James Johnson's hopes were to founder. The racial problem was highlighted
by the official who extolled James Johnson in the views just quoted.
He declared: "How best to effect the purpose is a matter of extreme
difficulty, but that a solution may be arrived at I personally much
hope and desire. I should think that on the whole a suffragan for
Lagos with Yoruba would be the easiest solution on Archdeacon
Hamilton's withdrawal."[29]

This fundamental racial problem was clearly emphasised in the
views expressed by all the people to whom James Johnson's
memoranda were sent for comments. One of these was David
Hinderer. In the seventies he had observed, like Henry Townsend,
that in Yorubaland "the native teachers of Christianity are acceptable to people and chiefs of this country as whiteman was twenty
years ago" and that it was by African agency that "the extension
as well as the establishment of this work in these parts [Yorubaland]
would be achieved".[30] He had gone further to say that white
missionaries should gracefully agree to serve in the territory under
Bishop Crowther. In 1887, reflecting the pattern of thinking of the
Scramble era among Europeans, David Hinderer began to sing a
new song, jettisoning the views he had so clearly expressed twelve
years earlier. The orthodoxy of 1875 became a heresy in 1887. The
Yoruba churches, he said, were like the Old Testament churches
in the time of the Judges, "wild obstreperious and wanton youth
in the lifetime of a man".[31] To place Europeans under an African
would be "unnatural" and "a dangerous experiment". He spoke
the mind of all the white missionaries when he declared: "A native
Bishop for Yoruba I would at this juncture of the Yoruba mission
deeply regret as tending to thwart the extension of missionary
work in the further interior. For it must of necessity be chiefly
done by European pioneering work, and a native Bishop would
only tend to stop Europeans from entering that field. . . ."[32]

Indeed in the previous year the white missionaries, who were regretting that they were still confined to the coast, had begun to argue that Africans were incompetent for pioneering work. Daniel Olubi, who had been in charge of C.M.S. work in the Ibadan Empire since 1870, was held responsible for the slow growth of Christianity there. He was "of a slow-going and dreamy nature", declared a white missionary.[33] Only white missionaries, it was alleged, could redeem the situation. Moreover the native agents were condemned because of their literary insufficiency. For the first time their biographical sketches became useful. Olubi, it was pointed out, was Hinderer's servant at the age of sixteen; he attended school for a year only. James Okuseinde, another agent in Ibadan, was the same missionary's cook and he could only read his New Testament when he was made a teacher for the lack of any other, whilst Vincent of Ilesha was "a poor worker, a man with no education but barely the ability to read his Yoruba Testament".[34] Even the ability of Samuel Johnson, the historian of the Yoruba, who was transferred from Ibadan to Oyo in 1885 for evangelistic work, was also questioned.

Bishop Ingham's reaction deserves special consideration. He regarded the whole matter as a personal challenge and he used all sorts of arguments that failed to convince the Church Missionary Society. It will be remembered that he had attempted to forestall James Johnson from raising the episcopate issue by offering him the dubious post of Missioner and that the African agitator had spurned this offer contemptuously. The spiritual qualification of James Johnson was not in question. The Church Missionary Society had the highest opinion of his attributes. He was "a man of fine character", "a very remarkable man, peculiarly qualified in many respects to help forward the native Church, a man of great spiritual strength and vigour, as well as of mental and intellectual capacity, of courage and decision".[35]

Ingham could not make any valid case against his African adversary. He made himself look very ridiculous when he went on urging a disregard of the principles that should govern the appointment of a Bishop. It was true, he said, that James Johnson was the *"best"* among the Africans, that the latter admired him and were proud of him. It was also true that the C.M.S. could not "separate the idea of the Yoruba Episcopacy from Mr. James Johnson". Nevertheless, declared Bishop Ingham, the fact that James Johnson possessed the best Christian qualities and that he was too strict an observer of the tenets of the Christian faith should disqualify him for the post of Bishop. As he put it: "this very excellence is his danger. Conscious of rectitude, he is unconstitutional, autocratic, impatient, inclined to his own way. He will not wait to take people on with him."[36] In any case, contended the Bishop, why should the best candidate be offered a job? "It does seem hard," recorded the Bishop, "but does it always follow that the most talented and spiritual man should necessarily be a Bishop? Are there not others with just the qualifications needed who are yet without Mr. Johnson's special gifts?"[37]

The only principle that Bishop Ingham wished to see observed was the racialist one. He argued in favour of a European as his coadjutor in Lagos. Great cuts in all government departments in West Africa were affecting the links between the Church and State; the Colonial Chaplaincy in the Gambia was abolished, the Sierra Leone Chaplaincy virtually so; the axe might fall on the Sierra Leone Diocese after Bishop Ingham's tenure of office, but if a European, and not an African coadjutor, was appointed for Yorubaland before he left office, the Sierra Leone Government would be persuaded to recognise the European coadjutor as his successor. In any case, the Bishop went on, the number of Europeans in West Africa was increasing "as also the races are so mixed here that no one race has a special claim to precedence".[38] Furthermore the C.M.S. would be taking "a SAFE step forward" if they informed the Africans that before they could have an African Bishop they should first raise an Episcopal Fund which would yield an interest of £300 to £500 a year: at a figure they would not be able to reach.[39]

Bishop Ingham was no more than an echo of European missionaries' opinion. The raising of any African to a position of authority higher than their own, was never viewed with approval. In 1878 two Nigerians, "Jerusalem Johnson" and Dandeson Crowther, the youngest son of the Bishop, had been made Archdeacons of the Niger Mission. This placed them ecclesiastically in a position higher than that of any European missionary before the appointment of J. Hamilton as Archdeacon of Lagos. It was not long before both of these educated Africans, particularly the former who was the more able and the better educated, began to come under fire. The decision to make these Africans Archdeacons, declared the Reverend J. B. Wood in his famous report of 1880 on the Niger Mission, was a colossal blunder.[40] The European missionaries had feared that Henry Johnson was only a step away from the episcopate. In 1881 he was constrained to write: "Some have been foolishly supposing that I am looking forward to become a bishop. There is nothing farther from my thoughts. We are all persuaded that Bishop Crowther as he is the first so he will be the last negro Bishop—at any rate for centuries to come."[41]

No European missionary was prepared to imagine an African being elevated to the episcopate at a time when regret was being expressed by several of the missionaries that Samuel Ajayi Crowther was ever made a Bishop. To have James Johnson as a Bishop, a

man who would expect not only Africans but Europeans as well
to observe Christian ethics in a very rigid form and whose attitude
was undisguisedly in favour of Africans, would be for the European
missionaries gall and wormwood. It cannot be surprising, then,
that no stone was left unturned by the white missionaries to discredit
him and neutralise his influence with the C.M.S. To raise James
Johnson to the episcopate, some contended, would set loose tribal
sectionalism;[42] James Johnson, argued others, had become so race-
conscious that he would not subordinate his African feelings to the
objectivity of the highest ecclesiastical office in mission fields. One
of them scoured the records in Abeokuta, and having found that
while James Johnson was Superintendent in the interior he had
imposed an African "heathen" name on a baptismal candidate in
preference to a foreign one, put forward this incident as sufficient
evidence of James Johnson's unsuitability as a candidate for the
post of Bishop,[43] as his action was tantamount to a spiritual crime.
All the missionaries were unanimous in the view that he would
be an "autocrat". One missionary's opinion was short and blatant:
"I sincerely trust the day may be far future which shall see a
native in that post."[44] Lastly they made it plain that "it was well
that the Committee should understand that the appointment of a
native Bishop involved the withdrawal of all European agency".[45]

The last point was the heart of the matter. The issue at stake
was basically racial and it defied a simple solution. As the Society
observed: "we see plainly that we are dealing with a very difficult
and complicated question: that there are distinct objections to any
and every plan that may be proposed and that it is useless to expect
to attain all we could desire by any single step we take."[46]

Bishop Ingham was not satisfied with only having the opinion
of Europeans mobilised against James Johnson. He decided to
mobilise African opinion against him as well, at a time when the
African agitator was away in Britain. It was believed that if it
could be shown that James Johnson was alone in his nationalist
conception of the episcopate issue his undoubted influence in
Salisbury Square would be largely removed. Therefore he took the
unusual step of running post-haste to Lagos. Here he summoned
in April 1887 a Conference of all agents of the Society in Yorubaland and of some laymen to consider the episcopate issue and
polygamy, the latter being a matter that was to be discussed at the
impending Lambeth Conference.

The Conference that took place in April 1887 in Lagos is
important in many ways.[47] That it was summoned at all shows the
extent of James Johnson's influence and of the dread of his influence
in C.M.S. circles in Yorubaland and in Britain. The proceedings
of the Conference are fascinating. In spite of all effort to manipulate

African opinion they reveal clearly the desire of Africans in the Church for independence even in these early years; they reveal the strength of the tribal factor in Yorubaland in the last quarter of the nineteenth century, a matter of current interest; they reveal the form and extent of enmity against James Johnson in Yorubaland in the eighties; they show a highly placed white man, Bishop Ingham, adopting the policy of *divide et impera* in order to achieve his desired result. It was the first time that a large section from so wide an area as Yorubaland had ever gathered together to deliberate upon issues which they regarded as important.

Every effort was made by the Bishop to have an atmosphere appropriate to his mood and a conference that would endorse his preconceived notions and desires. The agents were all employees of the C.M.S. who could not afford the daring of James Johnson nor contradict any opinion ventured by their ecclesiastical master. The laity consisted of people who, though important, were not selected by the people themselves. There was no agenda and no intimation of the subjects that would be debated at the Conference. The Bishop piloted the opinion of the Conference with his opening address which sought to demolish such notions as James Johnson had been propagating from his Sierra Leonian days. He dismissed as a "delusion" Johnson's idea that the Missionary expenditure of life and money on the West African coast was, in part, payment of old scores on behalf of the English people. Ingham opined: "As far as I can make out, the English nation, having paid a certain sum of money, and used its power to clear the coast of trade in human beings, did not and does not retain any particular sense of indebtedness to Western Africa."[48] As for independence, he regretted that the Native Pastorate of Sierra Leone had ever been created—for there, as he complained, he was no more than a chaplain—and he considered the Pastorate an *"illustration of undue haste"*.[49] The delegates, Africans, had overestimated their "capacity and readiness for this or that"; they should be "wise enough and humble enough, thankfully to accept" European help. For the existence in West African society of slavery, polygamy, constant tribal warfare "and other sad circumstances during centuries must necessarily produce a crop of qualities the very reverse of the code of morals that during only forty-six years we have preached in this neighbourhood"; it would be discovered that African brains "under such circumstances" were "more precocious than the moral sense".[50]

Of course no employee of the Society dared say anything contrary to the opinion so clearly put forward by the Bishop. It was reinforced by European speakers. But it is the attitude of the African spokesmen that we should be concerned with; it reveals much of value. There were two clergymen—the Reverend Nathaniel Johnson and the Reverend Isaac Oluwole, and three laymen, viz., J. A. Payne, I. H. Willoughby and Dr. Obadiah Johnson. Nathaniel Johnson, a brother to the last mentioned layman, accepted the principle of an African Bishop as the ideal but concluded that an African would not be able to pay his salary or have money to redeem slaves and "it is money that makes everything".[51] Oluwole declared that the principle of an African Bishop was all right but there were no eligible men yet.[52] Payne, an ardent Johnsonian for more than twelve years and the convener of the Society for the Propagation of Religious Education in Lagos, urged the timeliness and imperativeness of an African Bishop who would be paid by Africans.[53] His reason, he said, was that the African climate deserved a Christianity directed and controlled by Africans. I. H. Willoughby wanted no one but a European, the prestige-maker, and his slogan was "give us a white bishop".[54] Dr. Obadiah Johnson wanted an African Bishop but that his nationality should be determined by the seat of his headquarters.[55]

The speeches of these African spokesmen require closer examination. Their attitude was determined largely by their tribal affinity. As one of them warned the others: "be not moved by clan, race or tribal prejudices."[56] It is difficult to ascertain how far Otunba Payne was influenced by the fact that Ijebu blood ran in his veins, as in that of James Johnson. By the time of the Conference, as will be shown in a later chapter,[57] James Johnson had begun to champion the cause of Ijebuland and both himself and Otunba Payne had begun to co-operate in persuading the Awujale of Ijebuland to accept Christian missionaries. It is also a fact that Otunba Payne had for the previous twenty-five years been a champion of Ijebu interest and that since 1872 there had developed between him and the fanatical leader of Oyo Yoruba opinion, I. H. Willoughby, very bitter relations.[58] Although it is important to bear in mind that Payne had been an advocate of the "Africa for the Africans" cause, yet he was the most dedicated Johnsonian throughout his life.

But there is no doubt that sub-tribal considerations were very strong with the other African spokesmen. Something is known already about the tribal groupings of the educated elite in Lagos in the last quarter of the nineteenth century. They were formed into "Associations" and each had a programme that identified it with the narrower and selfish interests of its tribal group in the interior. In the discussion of the episcopate matter James Johnson became a victim of the tension that developed between these groups. The Oyo Yoruba, for instance, had three spokesmen—I. H. Willoughby, Dr. O. Johnson and Nathaniel Johnson. The cause of the Oyo Yoruba had been articulated unblushingly by I. H. Willoughby since the days of Governor Glover, 1865 to 1872.[59]

This group hated the monopoly of enlightenment by the Egba and of the Anglo-Yoruba commerce jointly by the Egba and the Ijebu, both of whom used their geographical advantage to prevent the Oyo Yoruba from having direct access to the British in Lagos. In order to break the monopoly of these two coastal tribal groups the Oyo Yoruba had used their influence with Governor Glover, who shared their aspirations, to persuade the latter to open the Ondo route in eastern Yorubaland as a channel of communication between Lagos and Oyo Yoruba country. In Glover they had an effusive friend and whenever they had an opportunity to influence the British administrator they advised the latter to adopt decidedly anti-Egba and anti-Ijebu policies.[60] In this group, too, may be mentioned Andrew Hethersett, for a long time a copyist of official despatches and the official interpreter. His Oyo-Yoruba inclinations were made known to the Ijebu several times. These Oyo Yoruba elite did not forget the glory and splendour of the Old Oyo Empire, when their paramount ruler, the *Alafin*, was the most powerful and most influential person in the greater part of Yorubaland, when both power and culture radiated to other parts of Yorubaland from their part of the Yoruba stock. In the hope that the Gospel would do for the Oyo what it had done for the Egba this group, it will be remembered, had given some money to James Johnson in 1875 for the spread of Christianity in their fatherland. Their spokesman at the Conference was Dr. Obadiah Johnson, a prize-winner in medicine at King's College, London in 1885. He was—with Samuel Johnson and Nathaniel Johnson—a great grandson of the illustrious *Alafin* of the eighteenth century, Abiodun. It was his Oyo patriotism that made him demand that the headquarters of the new diocese should be fixed at Oyo and that the Bishop should be an Oyo Yoruba.[61]

Then there was the Egba camp. Not only were they the wealthiest in Lagos but they were also in the vanguard of the intellectual development of Yorubaland. As the centre of Christianity in the interior of West Africa, having at the time of the Conference some fifteen stations, apart from the churches in the capital, with three Egba clergy and several catechists, they naturally looked upon themselves as leaders. One of their spokesmen was S. W. Doherty, the man who, it will be remembered, was used by the Reverend J. A. Maser to organise opposition against James Johnson in 1879. He was not in favour of any other tribe. Moreover there was the Reverend Isaac Oluwole, a rather taciturn but calculating Egba and one of the first graduates of Fourah Bay College. At the time of the Conference he was Principal of the C.M.S. Grammar School, Lagos. He could not have been unconscious of his intellectual attributes when he declared at the Conference that there were no eligible Africans for the post. In subsequent years the popularity of James Johnson in the Lagos Church was to be an embarrassment to this Egba, to the extent that in 1900 he was only too anxious to have James Johnson removed by his consecration to the Niger Delta.

And yet much as the tribal factor was against James Johnson there was no doubt that leaders of opinion were unanimous that only James Johnson was fit to be Bishop. As a European secret investigator discovered: "There was a consensus of opinion that James Johnson qualified and stood *at present* absolutely alone among the Yoruba clergy as one to be thought of for the post." Oluwole might qualify *"in due time"*.[62] But nevertheless for the majority of people James Johnson would be a hard and rigid ecclesiastical director, firm to the verge of obstinacy even on trivial matters. Meticulous and industrious, his eyes would not escape any fault of his lieutenants. It is doubtful whether he could really have had a second-in-command in the Church who would have shared his strictness and dogmatism on all questions. His spiritual and moral standards were so high that he seemed something like a Pope to others, and his spirit was necessarily somewhat dictatorial and domineering. He had impatience, if not contempt, for the opinions of others on moral issues and was hardly ever disposed to be tactful or flexible when carrying out what he considered to be a correct course of action. In some ways his firmness might be described as conscientiousness and not obstinacy. The opposition against him sprang partly from the conviction that James Johnson would—in a way that a European Bishop could not—strenuously endeavour to root out existing evils.

But to return to the Conference. A clerical majority carried the resolution asking for a European Bishop. However, there were rumours that the votes had been rigged, and if carefully examined there can be no doubt that Africans would really have preferred an African Bishop. But carried away by the possibly rigged votes for the resolution Bishop Ingham misrepresented what went on at the Conference. The resolution demanding a white Bishop, he said, was the *"pure African opinion"*;[63] the educated Africans in Lagos, he contended, had declared unequivocally that an African Bishop *"would be disastrous to the Africans themselves"*. He went on: "native episcopacy, at the present, will not lead to *true progress*, but far more likely to endless bickerings and *possibly a schism*." He singled out I. H. Willoughby, inflating his influence, *"Whose opinion has great weight here"*, and urged that no further delay should be tolerated for the location of European missionaries in the interior. One should be located in Ibadan at once. For at the Conference he saw Olubi for the first time, and although he admired the African clergyman for his "evident sincerity" and his influence with the interior chiefs, yet he considered a European guide was necessary to "keep him from making a lot of mistakes".[64]

It is important to stress that the Society did not share the Bishop's illusions as to the authentic desire of the African delegates at the Conference. It was clear that the desire for an African Bishop was very strong among the educated Africans, that they were not enamoured of a European Bishop and that the agents who signed the resolutions at the Conference did so against their conviction. Indeed, with the minutes of the Conference before it, Salisbury Square could not share the Bishop's delusion and correctly measured the barometer of African feelings at the Conference. "It appears to us so far as the Report of the Conference enables us to form any opinion", said the Society, "that these African friends feel that till they can pay a Bishop themselves and till he can have independent position, they would prefer *not* to have a Bishop of their own—not such a Bishop for instance as Bishop Crowther, who they regard merely in name, the puppet so to speak of a foreign Society—and therefore rather a *humiliation* than a glory to their race: but given the means to maintain him and the independent position we do not gather that the Africans would still prefer a European".[65]

In fact African opinion at the Conference would have been more radical than that discerned by the Society had the lay representatives been informed of the subject beforehand. For they would have consulted with the majority of the laity and would have gone to the Conference with a mandate. As the laity later bitterly complained, their mandate would have been emphatic, that an African Bishop should be appointed at once. This was a conviction based on the fact that "the future furtherance of the Gospel in Africa should be under the superintendence of a Native; . . . [that] a European Bishop however energetic cannot be fully acquainted with the idiosyncrasies of the people. . . . That the knowledge of the language of the country is one of the indispensable qualifications required for a Bishop to work up the Yoruba country and which could not be expected of a European".[66]

For the first and only time in the history of C.M.S. work in West Africa the Society jettisoned all recommendations and opinions by its chief representative, the European Bishop, on the Yoruba episcopate issue. After a careful study of all evidence their judgment was "opposed to your own deliberately expressed opinion".[67] First of all the "African opinion elicited at the Conference constitutes one such difficulty", making the problem more difficult. Then all the points marshalled against James Johnson, it was declared, had no intrinsic validity as far as the Society was concerned. "Again Mr. James Johnson himself constitutes a difficulty", it was observed. "He is too strong for them [Africans] they feel that in him they would have a pope. Be it so. . . . May he not have been given to us in this crisis for this very step. It is of course impossible to eliminate the person from the consideration of the question, for if there is to be a bishop who could it be but James Johnson. Would it be possible to pass him by?"[68]

The tribal factor which, as noted already, was operational with the African spokesmen and which was emphasised again and again by the European missionaries, did not impress the Society either. For one thing it was unchristian and it would be unbecoming to pander to it, the Society said.

A Committee called the Corresponding Committee examined the matter in detail. Never before had the Society come nearly to a decision in favour of an African Bishop; not even after Bishop Crowther's death in 1891 was the Society to consider fully and objectively the merits of so pre-eminently qualified a candidate as James Johnson for the highest ecclesiastical post in the C.M.S. mission. An ingenuous solution was devised to dispose of the racial problem. It was recommended that Yorubaland should be divided into two. The western half, comprising of Egba, Egbado and the Oyo Yoruba country should be retained by the Society. This was the area in which the C.M.S. had the most flourishing stations. The other half, comprising the Ijebu and Ekitiparapo countries—largely unevangelised—it was recommended, should be thrown open to the energies and resources of the Native Church. For this area an African Suffragan Bishop should be appointed. He was to be maintained by Africans themselves from the beginning, though depending on the Society for a subvention which would diminish from year to year.[69] The Society was prepared to go as far as hinting, unofficially, to James Johnson that he would soon be elevated to the episcopate.[70]

However the final decision did not rest with either Ingham or James Johnson. Nor did it rest with the Corresponding Committee, which had to report and merely recommend to the supreme Executive, the Parent Committee. This latter body consisted of two power-groups, representing two different shades of opinion that had been developing in Salisbury Square since the demise of Henry Venn. There was the Afrophile group, led by people like Dr. R. N. Cust, Sidney Gedge and J. B. Whiting; then there was the less liberal group led by J. Hamilton and C. Fenn. Confronted with the recommendations of the Corresponding Committee the two groups demonstrated their conflicting views. For the Afrophiles the recommendations did not go far enough. They wanted a full African episcopate, objecting to the resolution that the African Bishop should be a Suffragan. The other group was opposed to any immediate "extension" of the native episcopate. In the judgment of this latter group "it was premature or inconvenient to move at all just at this juncture and in fact that it was too grave a question to express a decided opinion upon".[71] Knowing quite well the feelings of the white missionaries, who had threatened to quit Nigeria if an African Bishop were elected, the Committee concluded that "to place our own missionaries under the independent jurisdiction of a native Bishop would certainly not be acceptable or convenient".[72] Rather than face an eruption of what the Society perceived as potentially volcanic African feelings or a probable *en masse* resignation of its white missionaries in Yorubaland, Salisbury Square challenged and rejected the recommendations of the Corresponding Committee, "not on the merits of the question itself but rather on the question of the ripeness of the case for decision, and the course for procedure to be adopted".[73]

In other words the final decision was to postpone solution to the issue until its revivification by the death of Bishop Crowther. Indeed the whole affair anticipated what was to happen on the occasion of the latter's death, when racial considerations were to override all other factors. It also indicated the strength of African feeling against European domination in the Church, a feeling which reached the verge of rebellion, under the inspiration of James Johnson, when it was ignored in 1892-1894. It also demonstrated the extent and force of James Johnson's influence, making it literally impossible for an influential body like the Church Missionary Society to control the episcopate affair its own way and in its own time.

Hardly had the Parent Committee made its judgment clear before the Society began to give indications that it would not miss any chance to persuade Africans to alter their mind in favour of a European Bishop. On the suggestions of Bishop Cheetham the Society decided to send an important man to undertake a tour of West Africa and speak to all influential members of the Anglican community. It was believed that psychologically this would prepare the minds of Africans for acceptance of a European Bishop. Under the guise of a missioner the Reverend W. Allan, Vicar of St. James Dermonsby, "who is a most constant attendant at our Committees" and whose loyalty to the Society was undoubted, was sent to West Africa. His instructions were clear, to ascertain African opinion on "The need of increased Episcopal superintendence of the Yoruba country and of extending the *Native* Episcopacy".[74]

The Reverend W. Allan did not carry out the instruction of the Society with respect to the episcopate issue. In public, he said, no clergyman would speak against the candidature of the Reverend James Johnson, but in private these clergymen said that although his character was very high and he possessed "acknowledged

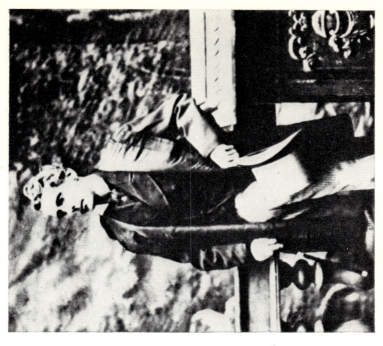

John Pope Hennessy, 1834–1891

Edward Wilmot Blyden, 1832–1912

John A. Otumba Payne, 1839–1906

Captain J. P. L. Davies, 1828–1906

excellences", yet they would not like to have him as their Bishop.[75] He spoke only to a selected few, mainly the clergy and the same lay representatives who were at the Conference of April 1887. He refused to see the large number of representatives of the laity, to the tune of forty-four—who, he said, "mobbed" him and who desired to indicate their views on the episcopate issue and to show that the lay spokesmen at the Conference did not reflect their opinion.[76] W. Allan endorsed all the objections which the anti-Johnsonians had raised before—the tribal factor, James Johnson's autocratic tendencies, the European threat to withdraw *en masse*, James Johnson's refusal to allow baptismal candidates to bear alien names. The records of Breadfruit's contribution to the Pastorate were investigated to discredit him as a Pastor. In his predecessor's time, alleged Allan, Breadfruit Church used to contribute £250 to the Native Pastorate Fund—a blatant lie betrayed by the fact that, as has been mentioned, Breadfruit Church did not become a member of the Pastorate until 1881, that is until James Johnson's resumption of the pastoral charge of the Church—whilst in 1886 the Church contributed only £110 to the Fund. In fact the majority of the people who "mobbed" him were members of James Johnson's Church, a fact that disproves the allegation that by 1887 he was "unpopular" over the foreign name question.[77]

Allan made it clear that a European Bishop should be appointed and condemned James Johnson with a far-fetched reason. He wrote: "In addition to, and apart from, all the foregoing considerations, I must add, although very reluctant to introduce more opinions of my own, that the consecration of the Reverend J. Johnson would be in my judgment a very hazardous step. He seems unfortunately to be so greatly under the influence of Dr. Blyden that it is difficult to foresee how he might develop, if he were in a more independent position."[78]

It appears that the Society did not completely believe the optimism of the Allan Report. For in the following year, 1889, it was felt necessary to test again what the attitude of Africans would be to a possible appointment of a European Bishop. The man chosen was the Reverend Sydney A. Selwyn, Vicar of St. James Church, Hatcham. He was given a big welcome in Lagos and this was taken by the C.M.S. as a sign that the episcopate crisis was over. Indeed it was considered to propose him for the post of Bishop for the proposed Diocese of Yorubaland.[79] Unfortunately the indiscreet words he uttered at a party given in his honour on his return to Britain, and which were published in the *Kentish Mercury*, when he referred to Africans as "monkeys", inflamed African opinion against him.[80]

James Johnson, who had been led to expect that he would be

made Bishop, took the non-fulfilment of his expectation very calmly and gracefully. In 1888 he was appointed a member of the Finance Committee, without any objection on the part of the European missionaries. He did not believe that in the opinion of Africans he was an objectionable candidate for the episcopate. There was no visible sign of any African opposition against him. The impression he had was that an African was actually desired but that financially the Africans were not fully ready yet to be able to pay his salary, which alone would consume anything between a third and half of the total income of £900 of the Native Church in 1887.[81] Money, then, it seemed to him was the rock on which the episcopate dream foundered as it had been the rock on which his Ethiopian continental Church had foundered in 1873-1874 in Sierra Leone.

But for Johnson money need not have been the obstacle; he thought that Nigerian converts should be able to tax themselves to any extent necessary, and to bear their own burden and enjoy the consolations of independence. As early as 1887 he had declared that direct taxation should be introduced into Nigeria.[82] On this matter James Johnson was alone, singularly alone, throughout his life. The strength of the nationalism of the agents at the Conference of April 1887 notwithstanding, the minutes revealed a fundamental difference in the attitudes of James Johnson and most of his contemporaries to nationalist issues. With the possible exception of the most devoted Johnsonians like R. B. Blaize, J. A. Payne and Dr. Obadiah Johnson, few educated Africans shared in 1890 James Johnson's faith in the timeliness and practicability of a self-governing African Church from which the white man's money and therefore rule would be completely excluded. In principle few would question the desirability of such a goal but in practice very few believed that the Nigerian converts had the financial resources which the achievement of such a goal would demand. This lack of financial strength on self-government matters was for a long time to be a retarding factor to the concrete achievements of Nigerian nationalism until the birth of nation-wide political parties after the Second World War. It prevented the nationalists from translating their ideas into practice both in Church and State. As has been shown in the last chapter, it was not that financial resources were lacking. But they preferred to spend their money on drinks, festivities and social functions, like naming ceremonies, funerals and so on. Thus the crux of the matter, then as now, seems to lie in the unwillingness to make the sacrifice to bear one's own burden of development and thus diminish the extent of their dependence on Government or outside aids.

The difference between James Johnson and most of his contemporaries therefore lay in the fact that until his death he was an idealist with no practical sense. For instance James Johnson was fanatically idealistic when he wanted the converts to become independent and finance the evangelisation of Nigeria at a time when they were not financially in a position to do so; Holy Johnson was more doctrinaire than his contemporaries when he advocated absolute prohibition of the liquor traffic and imposition of heavy direct taxation at a time when any form of taxation was baneful to the masses and when no other sources of revenue were available for the administration of the country. As will be clear from the next chapter James Johnson was to be alone in 1889 in his vision of self-government for Lagos, a cause he was to advocate with zeal in the Legislative Council and which was to be opposed to a man by all sections of the island's community.

Indeed there is no evidence that James Johnson would have been supported over the episcopate affair had his disposition been otherwise and had he been determined on a showdown with the Church Missionary Society. The West African press was not only very mild in its criticism of the decision of the 1887 April Conference about the colour of the proposed Bishop, but judged wrongly that "the idea of race entered less into determination of the question than the feeling that the European by his antecedents and connexions would naturally enjoy greater facilities for carrying on the work than a Native".[83] Moreover there was the fact that many of the vocal educated Africans were more concerned about their own interests—the question of polygamy, to which they wished the C.M.S. Lambeth Conference to give a favourable attention—rather than about the elevation of Holy Johnson to the episcopate. From experience the polygamists were fully aware that for the stone that the Church Missionary Society had given them, a Bishop such as James Johnson would give them a scorpion. Consequently it was the issue of polygamy, rather than that of an African episcopate, with which they were concerned, publishing their views in a pamphlet.[84]

By 1890, then, James Johnson had become the Episcopate Loser. The idea that this African agitator might be a Bishop for Yorubaland had ceased to be nightmare to the European missionaries. Thomas Harding, who had been unable to move into the interior for years, went to Ibadan. Well could the Reverend J. B. Wood rejoice and recommend that, pending the nomination of a European Bishop, the superintendence of Yorubaland should be shared among the European missionaries in the following manner. He was to be in charge of Abeokuta district, T. Harding of Ibadan area and either J. Brayne or R. Kidd, to be located in Ilesha, to supervise the Ondo mission.[85]

NOTES

1. C.M.S. G3/A2/01, J. B. Wood to H. Wright, 17/7/1880.
2. *Lagos Times*, 12/1/1881.
3. C.M.S. CA2/L4, H. Wright to Bishop Cheetham, 24/10/1879.
4. *Ibid.*
5. C.M.S. G3/A2/01, Bishop's Report of Visit to Abeokuta, p. 23.
6. C.M.S. CA2/L4, C. Fenn to James Johnson, 24/10/1879.
7. C.M.S. LA2/L5 J. B. Whiting to James Johnson, 16/8/1881.
8. C.M.S. CA1/025(e), Bishop Cheetham to H. Wright, 2/3/1879.
9. C.M.S. CA1/22, F. E. Wigram to Archbishop of Canterbury, 27/10/1881, quotes the Archbishop.
10. C.M.S. G3/A2/01, James Johnson to Rev. E. D. Wickham (undated).
11. C.M.S. G3/A2/02, J. A. Lamb to R. Lang, 8/5/1883.
12. C.M.S. G3/A2/03, K. Ingham to R. Lang, 29/4/1884.
13. C.M.S. G3/A2/L6, R. Lang to J. Hamilton, 13/7/1886.
14. *Lagos Times*, 22/2/1882.
15. *Ibid.*, 25/4/1883.
16. C.M.S. G3/A1/L10, R. Lang to K. Ingham, 14/5/1886.
17. C.M.S. G3/A2/04, D. Hinderer to R. Lang, 22/11/1886.
18. C.M.S. G3A2/L6, R. Lang to J. Hamilton, 26/11/1886.
19. *African Times*, 1/10/1887.
20. C.O. 267/369, James Johnson to Sir H. Holland, 26/7/1887.
21. *Memorial of the Celebration of Her Majesty's Reign and of the Centenary of Sierra Leone*, London, 1887.
22. C.O. 267/369, J. Johnson to Sir H. Holland, 26/7/1887.
23. C.M.S. G3/A2/04, "A Memorandum on matters affecting the interest of the Lagos Native Church, the interior Yoruba Mission and the West African Church and Mission generally and suggestions in regard to them for the Committee of the C.M. Society"; also "A Memorandum on the West African Native Church and Mission and Native Episcopacy."
24. Blyden's book, *Christianity, Islam and the Negro Race*, had just come out and Canon Taylor wrote an article, "Our Foreign Missions a Failure", in *Fortnightly Review*, October 1887. James Johnson contributed to the debate in a long article in *The Methodist Herald*, 22/2/1888.
25. C.M.S. G3/A1/02, K. Ingham to R. Lang, 7/9/1887.
26. C.M.S. G3/A1/L10, R. Lang to K. Ingham, 19/6/1884.
27. C.M.S. G3/A1/L11, R. Lang to K. Ingham, 11/3/1887.
28. *Ibid.*, 21/4/1887.
29. *Ibid.*
30. C.M.S. CA2/049(a), D. Hinderer to H. Wright, 15/7/1875.
31. C.M.S. G3/A2/04, D. Hinderer to R. Lang, 18/7/1887.
32. *Ibid.*
33. *Ibid.*, D. Hinderer to R. Lang, 22/11/1886.
34. *Ibid.*, same to same, 22/11/1886.
35. C.M.S. G3/A1/L11, R. Lang to K. Ingham, 29/7/1887.
36. C.M.S. G3/A1/02, Bishop Ingham to R. Lang, 7/9/1887.
37. *Ibid.*
38. *Ibid.*
39. *Ibid.*

40. See copy in papers released in early 1963 in C.M.S. Archives.
41. C.M.S. G3/A2/01, Henry Johnson to E. Hutchinson, 31/3/1881.
42. C.M.S. G3/A2/05, Revd. W. Allan's Report, April and May 1888, on his visits to Lagos.
43. *Ibid.*
44. C.M.S. G3/A2/04, J. Vernal to R. Lang, 20/8/1887.
45. C.M.S. G3/A2/05, Rev. W. Allan's Report, April and May 1888.
46. C.M.S. G3/A1/L11, R. Lang to Bishop Cheetham, 29/7/1887.
47. The proceedings published as *The Church in the Yoruba Country Its Needs and Its Difficulties,* C.M.S. Library.
48. *The Church in the Yoruba et seq.,* p. 5.
49. *Ibid.,* p. 26.
50. *Ibid.,* p. 16.
51. *Ibid.,* p. 23.
52. *Ibid.,* p. 24 .
53. *Ibid.,* p. 22.
54. *Ibid.,* p. 24.
55. *Ibid.,* pp. 24-25.
56. *Ibid.,* p. 22.
57. Chapter Eight.
58. C.O. 147/24, Enclosures in J. P. Hennessy to Lord Kimberley, 14/10/1872.
59. The Glover Papers (Royal Commonwealth Library, London), Bundle 5 for I. H. Willoughby's letters to J. H. Glover.
60. *Ibid.,* Unlabelled bundle, The Yoruba National Association of Lagos to Pope Hennessy, 26/5/1872.
61. *The Church in the Yoruba Country et. seq.,* pp. 24-25.
62. C.M.S. G3/A2/05, Rev. W. Allan's Report, April and May 1888.
63. C.M.S. G3/A1/02, K. Ingham to R. Lang, 29/4/1887.
64. *Ibid.*
65. C.M.S. G3/A1/L11, R. Lang to K. Ingham, 29/11/1887.
66. C.M.S. G3/A2/05, Memorandum dated 20 March 1888 presented to the Rev. W. Allan by the laity.
67. C.M.S. G3/A1/L11, R. Lang to K. Ingham, 29/7/1887.
68. *Ibid.,* same to same, 29/7/1887.
69. *Ibid.,* "Extracts from Minutes of Committee of Correspondence", 19 July 1887.
70. C.M.S. G3/A2/L6, R. Lang to James Johnson, 20/9/1887.
71. C.M.S. G3/A1/L11, R. Lang to K. Ingham, 11/8/1887.
72. *Ibid.,* same to same, 29/7/1887.
73. *Ibid.,* same to same, 11/8/1887.
74. *Ibid.*
75. C.M.S. G3/A2/05, Rev. W. Allan's Report, April and May 1888.
76. *Ibid.*
77. See Memorandum to him dated 20 March 1888.
78. *Ibid.,* Rev. W. Allan's Report, April and May 1888.
79. C.M.S. G3/A2/L6, R. Lang to T. Harding, 15/11/1889.
80. C.M.S. G3/A2/06, J. A. Payne to R. Lang, 23/7/1890.
81. G/AL 4/30, James Johnson to S. W. Fox, 14/2/1900.
82. C.O. 147/62, James Johnson to E. Stanhope, 4/1/1887.
83. *Sierra Leone Weekly News,* 10/9/1887.
84. Keyinde Okoro (ed.), *Views of Some Native Christians of West Africa on the subject of Polygamy etc., Lagos,* December 1887.
85. C.M.S. G3/A2/06, J. B. Wood to R. Lang, 31/7/1890.

CHAPTER SEVEN

LEGISLATOR

> The good Mr. Johnson has done by his presence in the
> Council-Board cannot be over-estimated; he has the
> courage of his conviction, and it seems that he is to
> suffer for such sterling gifts which we are trying to
> stimulate and which should he be allowed to lose his
> seat will be a deathblow to all educated and patriotic
> Africans.
>
> R. B. Blaize to Aborigines
> Protection Society 22/3/1894

WHILST James Johnson's enemies, European and Africans, were
denying him the opportunity to utilise his undoubted talent for the
ecclesiastical organisation and Christian spiritual directorship of
Yorubaland, his capacity for statesmanship was being recognised
and employed by the Lagos Government. For in 1886, when Lagos
ceased to be constitutionally an appendage of the Gold Coast, a
Legislative Council was established, composed of four official and
three unofficial members. It was decided by the first governor under
the new arrangement, A. C. Moloney, to nominate two African
representatives as unofficial members. And James Johnson was
one of these, the other being C. J. George, J.P., a prominent
Wesleyan of the Egba tribal group and a trader.

The appointment of James Johnson is significant in two respects.
Firstly, he was the first African clergyman to sit on the Legislative
Council in British colonial Africa. For, according to the regulations
governing this appointment, a clergyman was by his profession
disqualified. However, this regulation had to be waived in James
Johnson's favour.[1] Secondly, his appointment was an unequivocal
testimony of his position as the foremost African patriot in Lagos.
In the words of the governor: "The first native in the place [Lagos]
for consideration in justice to his abilities and interest in his race,
is the Reverend James Johnson of the Church of England."[2]

By the time of his appointment Holy Johnson was expressing ideas on African representation and participation in the Governments established by the British in their enclaves in West Africa. Whilst it should be noted that there were others in Lagos who demanded not only elective representation but also had a vision of Nigeria as an independent parliamentary democracy, yet James Johnson's ideas were unique in two ways. Firstly, he wished democratic principles and African participation to reach a wider circle of people, through municipal councils, in order to "give the people real interest in their towns, lead them to take care of them and help to make them self-reliant".[3] Secondly, he was the singular advocate of the view that African representation should not be the exclusive preserve of the educated elite but that the illiterate rulers and masses should also be taken into partnership in the government of Nigeria.[4]

James Johnson's plea on behalf of this unlettered majority for representation on the Legislative Council was based on his observation of the traditional system of government in the interior of Yorubaland. He had been struck by the manner in which issues were resolved, how law and order was maintained and how harmony was achieved in society. He had come to the conclusion that in several ways traditional Yoruba government was better than the British establishment in Lagos. For instance, he said, Lagosians were less law-abiding and more prone to crimes than the unlettered inhabitants of the hinterland.[5] In Lagos there was a police force which was finding it difficult to apprehend offenders; in contrast, in the interior where there was no standing police force, murders were few and rarely went unpunished. Therefore in 1884 when the question of a Legislative Council was publicly discussed James Johnson urged that the illiterate people in the interior should be made partners in government, and that they should be given the opportunity to elect representatives; he was convinced that they could offer "sound advice on both political and internal economy"[6] to the Lagos Government.

In recognising the virtues of the traditional system of government in Yorubaland and in wishing that the unlettered Africans should be taken into partnership in the administration of Nigeria—as equals—James Johnson was more than half a century ahead of his age. The educated Africans tended to look down on the unlettered and, as the history of nationalism in Africa generally shows, literacy became the *sine qua non* for leadership; literacy became a status symbol; only the educated were allowed to sit on legislative councils and it was more the interests of the educated elite that African representatives looked after; the educated elite agitated for emancipation from colonial rule, in the hope that power would be transferred to them. The illiterate were ignored in Nigeria until after the Second World War, when universal adult suffrage superseded literacy as a qualification for voting.

Out of his whole career, the years 1886 to 1894, when he was a member of the Legislative Council, were the most eventful and the most fruitful. The legislative chamber created an atmosphere which elicited his talent and gave him the opportunity to serve his country. In the chamber he became a man of action, not just the inspirer and theorist that he largely was, or was constrained to be, in the Anglican communion. As a legislator he was notable for two things—his lack of concern for himself and his constant concern for the African and his interests. He brought before the British Government the grievances and hopes of all classes of the Nigerian population—of the chiefs, the oppressed, prisoners, traders, the poor, the educated elite, and tax-payers. As a nominated unofficial member it would have been wiser for him to have ignored the claims of these various sections of society, particularly when these clashed with the wishes of the British administration. For he was expected to be a "yesman", like his colleague, C. J. George. This was the only way by which his membership could have been prolonged, as happened in the case of C. J. George, who was allowed to retain his seat till his death in 1906. But James Johnson had to be removed in 1894 because he refused to see himself and behave as a government nominee who should endorse the policies and acts of the British Government at all times. Rather he looked on himself as an elected member, with obligations to his constituents. No other nominated unofficial African member in British West Africa before the First World War saw himself as the spokesman of Africans to the extent of offending the British administration;[7] no other African nominee wished to relinquish his seat at the expense of his convictions and African interests; none of them was sacked as a result of opposition to official policies. Neither Sir Samuel Lewis of Sierra Leone, nor J. M. Sarbah of the Gold Coast, nor any subsequent legislator in Nigeria before the First World War, was ever to be as independent-minded, as aggressive, as refractory to, and as consistently critical of, the British Government, voting alone against official opinion, as James Johnson was and did in his eight years in the Legislative Council of the Lagos Colony.

The Legislative Council of the Lagos Colony was in the early years, particularly during the administration of Governor A. C. Moloney, an effective engine of legislation, giving the fullest possible scope to African members and respecting the latter's opinion. The atmosphere that prevailed in its chamber encouraged African initiative and a free and frank opinion, rather than a meek and docile submissiveness to official whims and caprices. The man responsible for this atmosphere so healthy to the growth of unfettered African opinion was the Governor himself. Of all Lagos administrations before 1914, the Moloney administration of 1886 to 1890 was certainly the most considerate towards the wishes of the Africans. Moloney used to consult James Johnson on questions affecting the Yoruba hinterland,[8] he made avoidance of conflicts with the interior kingdoms the cornerstone of his policy, and he paid deference to the kings and chiefs in a manner none of his successors was ever to do.[9] In 1887 the Moloney administration passed an Education Ordinance which was considerably in advance of that of 1882, making government grants to schools dependent upon results, according recognition to the vernacular, and encouraging industrial education.

To James Johnson the Moloney administration was the best the Lagos Colony ever had and was a veritable demonstration of his conviction that the British were in Nigeria to carry out his Ethiopian programme.[10] In the economic sphere, as middlemen, Africans were beneficiaries. The years of aggressive European commercial effort which was destined to undermine their middlemen position had not yet begun. Politically, save on the coast, the danger of Britain's seizure of the sovereignty of the states in the interior was not yet a reality. In the Moloney era the Egba could still dream of regaining Ebute Metta, while Ijebu sovereignty was real. Well could James Johnson envisage a British administration confined to the Colony of Lagos and only in "friendly alliance" with the "independent" states in the interior.[11] Thus could David B. Vincent, later Mojola Agbebi, compose a dirge on Henry Robbin, the ardent Johnsonian, and be presented a financial award for his patriotic efforts by Alfred Moloney.[12] And so could J. A. Otunba Payne have his ability officially recognised and himself described to the Colonial Office as "an efficient and zealous officer".[13] Indeed there was much to stimulate African hopes in an administration that sent two Nigerians to Jamaica for a course in tropical horticulture and granted a scholarship award to a promising surveyor and grandson of Bishop Crowther, Herbert Macaulay, with the hope that he would be of "benefit" to his country.[14]

It is against this background that the role and the achievement of James Johnson as a legislator should be understood. In these years the Legislative Council effectively controlled the finances of the Colony. Votes and budgets were discussed item by item. This provided James Johnson with an excellent opportunity to play the role of the watchdog of the people in matters of finance, condemning extravagance in any form. He deplored the costliness of the passages and leave being enjoyed by European civil servants.[15] On 25 June 1888 he accused the government of paying the sum of £8,000 for a building, intended to house the Treasury, for which the owners, the Banners Brothers, had indicated they would take £6,000.[16] On 17 October of the same year he dubbed as extravagance the appointment of two secretaries in the Secretariat for work that could be done by one person.[17] On 16 June 1893 he opposed and voted alone against the vote of £92 6s. 2d. as a gratuity for the family of the late Reverend M. Sunter, Inspector of Education, as a misuse of public funds, on the grounds that in his life-time the Reverend M. Sunter had been paid "a good salary", besides passages to and from England.[18]

James Johnson, who never missed a single meeting except when he was away from the Colony, was jealous of the power of the Council over financial matters. When Moloney's successor, Sir G. T. Carter, with whom Johnson clashed repeatedly, began to sidetrack the Legislative Council by using the all-white, all-official Executive Council to make some grants, James Johnson was the only member who protested against this extraordinary and illegal procedure, forcing the Governor to defend his action on every occasion. On 6 June 1893, James Johnson protested against Carter's "habit" of applying to the Legislative Council for votes after the money had been actually spent—as in the case of £4,637 spent on the military expedition against the Ijebu in the previous year.[19]

In the way James Johnson saw the constitution of the Colony after 1886 the Governor was not the impeccable officer above criticism, nor the final arbiter and authority, nor the medium through whom all grievances of the Nigerian peoples should pass. He alone had the temerity to challenge Governor Carter's right and power to unilaterally issue ordinances to prohibit the sale of ammunition to the Ijebu on the eve of the expedition against the latter;[20] he alone it was who questioned Carter's right to refer to the Executive Council, rather than to the Legislative Council, a Bill for the increase of the Constabulary;[21] he alone in these years communicated directly to the Colonial Office on matters affecting the Lagos Colony, without any prior intimation to the Governor;[22] he alone dragged the Governor to the tribunal of British public opinion, accusing the highest British official in Nigeria of telling lies;[23] he alone before 1914 dared to threaten to take legal action against a Governor if the latter did not apologise or retract some statements;[24] he alone before the First World War publicly compared a Governor to the notorious Governor Eyre of Jamaica.[25]

A man who entertained these views of the Governor could hardly be expected to be deferential to the official and ex-officio members of the Legislative Council. The representatives of the European merchants, whose interests were so often diametrically opposed to those of Africans, found themselves lambasted as leeches and as a bad moral influence on their African customers.[26] No head of department escaped the venom of his tongue, whether he be the Chief Justice, J. Smalthian Smith, with whom James Johnson engaged in duels on more than three occasions; or the Queen's Advocate, who was literally confounded as James Johnson "alarmed" the chamber with details of the incompetence of his department to apprehend murderers;[27] or the head of the Public Work Department whom he accused of employing too many work-men for too little work and of not exercising sufficient supervision over his department.[28]

The cause of the poor and oppressed was championed by James Johnson with unabated zeal. It is significant to note that his maiden speech, made on 31 July 1886, was to the effect that the lot of the common people should be considered. To this effect he urged that corrugated iron sheets should be allowed into the country duty free, so that the common people might be in a position to purchase them. But the issue that concerned the majority of people was the fraudulent practice of European merchants who began to supply African producers with cloths of shorter length and of an inferior quality. The European traders used to deal in pieces of so many yard folds. But as time went on there was introduced the practice of importing finished pieces made up into the same number of folds, but having each fold a few inches less than thirty-six. More-over the quality of the cotton goods was of little value to the West African. Little cotton was used and there was too much chalk and starch. The result was that once washed the materials became transparent and useless as clothing.

The natives answered back by adulterating palm oil and by soaking palm kernels in water in order to increase their weight before they were taken to market. In the Legislative Council, where the spokesmen for the European merchants were completely oblivious of the grievances of the Africans, Thomas Welsh alone sought for a redress of the European grievances. James Johnson counter-attacked by asking for a full-scale simultaneous inquiry into the grievances of both sides.[29] It was largely because of his relentless pressure on both the Lagos Government and the Colonial Office that a new Ordinance protecting African interests came into existence. For the existing Ordinances up to 1888 had no provision that would compel importers to affix the number of yards contained in a piece of cloth. It was difficult for any dissatisfied buyer to bring before the Court any of the merchants and traders guilty of this fraudulent practice or for the Court to convict and punish any of them. James Johnson succeeded in getting the Government to regulate and define proper measures.

In the legislative chamber James Johnson also brought before the Government the necessity to look after prisoners and the sick. The former, he said, should not just be punished but their character improved, whilst the latter deserved Government solicitude. To this end, he said, African ministers should be appointed as Chaplains to give the two classes of people the consolation of religion and the benefit of regular visits.[30]

Another class of oppressed people whose cause was championed by James Johnson both inside and outside the Council chamber were a group of Nigerians who became victims of the atrocities being committed by Leopold's Government in the Congo.[31] In the month of August 1890 alone, 390 people from the Colony of Lagos offered themselves to work as labourers, carpenters, bricklayers and blacksmiths. Agreements to this end were signed on 16 August in Lagos. But hardly had they been deposited in the Congo than they began to regret that they had ever gone there. At Matadi, a group of them said, they were exposed to sun and rain and when six of them had the audacity to ask the Chief Agent there for shelter they were flung into prison and subsequently chained and led as a gang to work. Many of the labourers were beaten to death. Moreover, they complained against ill-treatment by white officers and were severely dealt with for declaring the wish to return to Nigeria. Then the terms of August 1890 were altered to convert them into soldiers and their pay was withheld. When some of them insisted on returning to Nigeria the Agents who had employed them paid only a portion of the return passage of ten of their number, refusing to pay even a part of the fare of others. Whilst in the Congo, they alleged, their letters to Nigeria were frequently intercepted, thus preventing their complaints reaching Lagos earlier than the middle of 1891. Of those flogged to death James Johnson was able to ascertain four, viz., Oto (alias Samuel Vincent), Ogidan, Adebiyi and Egunleti.

According to his own reports, James Johnson did not just accept the version of the labourers who came to him but conducted an independent inquiry to ascertain the authenticity of their allegations.[32] Both in the Legislative Council and in a letter to the Colonial Office he appealed to the British Government for "a full inquiry on the fact . . . on behalf of its subjects and in the interest both of justice and humanity".[33] His appeal did not fall on deaf ears, for the British Government took prompt action.[34]

James Johnson also exerted himself on the liquor question, a matter which was of interest to all. Liquor, which European traders exchanged for African produce, was generally believed by the people to be harmful to African interest, both physically and materially. In the Legislative Council James Johnson was a member of a committee set up to study and report on the liquor trade in the Western District of the Colony, with the idea of extending the Spirit Licence Ordinance there. In the Report James Johnson took the hardest line, declaring that "from his experience the Western District was the most debased morally and physically. The inhabitants were known to be excessive drinkers, and if this was not noticeable, it was because they were quite inured to it. Education made no progress with them—they did not want it; they were so degraded by drink."[35] He wanted trade in liquor to be "entirely abolished", a view very unpleasant to both the Administration (which derived its revenue almost entirely from duties on liquor) and the European traders who found it a suitable means for fraud.

As a Legislator James Johnson was also the champion of the sanctity of the dignity of the traditional rulers and the defender of the territorial integrity of the "independent" kingdoms in the interior. Although he was aware of the economic dependence of the island of Lagos on the interior suppliers and wished harmonious relations to exist between the British and the traditional rulers, he did not want the British to extend their sovereignty to the neighbouring states. Hence he protested bitterly against the unfurling of the British flag at Ilaro, calling it a rape of the Egba.[36] For, as Superintendent in the interior, he knew the historical connection between Ilaro and Abeokuta, knew the latter's authority over the former had been a reality for more than a generation, and knew Egba authority had never been questioned by the inhabitants of Ilaro. There was no question of nursing any prejudice against the Egba for the treatment he had received from them in 1879.

James Johnson would not allow any traditional ruler, however minor his position, to be maltreated by the British with impunity. This was why he was so embittered against the Lagos Government by their rough treatment of Ashade, the king of Ado, a small independent kingdom situated north-west of Lagos. On 11 March 1891 this paramount ruler was apprehended by a detachment of armed police and forcibly removed from his territory to Lagos. The crimes allegedly committed by this natural ruler were the murder of a certain woman, Falubi, said to be a British subject resident at Badagry; the seizure of three persons, relatives of another British subject; the seizure of a canoe from some traders of Agiliti, another Ado village, on its way to Badagry market; the seizure of the wife and child of a certain British subject at Ibikun, a British Protectorate; and the blocking of the trade route between Ado and Badagry. Although Ashade offered no resistance his hands were at first bound very tightly behind his back, and then brought forward and kept in irons. He was led almost naked to the ship, having been dragged out of his house. His house was pillaged by the Hausa troops and money and valuable cloths were taken away. When this case came before the Legislative Council, hurriedly summoned to consider an ordinance that would legalise the action of the Government and deport him to some other place, James Johnson fought on behalf of Ashade and disputed the legality of the Bill.[37] He contended that as Ado was an independent African state the British authorities had no right to enter the territory. What right had the Lagos Government to challenge the indisputable claim of the king to close his routes to trade? Furthermore, he declared, Ashade had been right about all his seizures of persons, who owed him debts. For Ashade was a Yoruba, not an English man, and according to traditional law he was perfectly right. What right had the British over Ibikun, a part of Ado state? When the British made Ibikun a part of the Lagos Protectorate was the king of Ado informed? Also, said Johnson, what evidence was there that the king actually committed the murder he was being charged with?

Thanks to this championship of the cause of Ashade, the proceedings of which were published in the local newspapers, the chiefs and people added to James Johnson's effort. After a while Ashade was "pardoned" and allowed to return to his kingdom, after a fine of £50 paid by the Lagos Chiefs.[38] In fact James Johnson was never at a loss to find principles to invoke to prevent natural rulers from being humiliated. Thus when on 3 October 1892 Governor Carter brought before the Council an Ordinance "to legalise the detention and deportation of a certain political prisoner Abaku of Moshi [Mushin]" who, according to the Government, had been making himself "extremely troublesome, and had gone so far as to prohibit any produce being brought down to the Ejinrin market from his district", the Chief Justice, Smalthian Smith, was horrified to hear James Johnson putting forward "so unequivocal a defence" of traditional religion in order to justify Abaku's action. For in this case James Johnson could no longer defend Abaku on the platform of territorial integrity, as Ijebuland had been annexed by the British. Therefore he argued that Abaku's offence was religious, not political. Abaku's behaviour, he said, was in obedience to the instruction of "the Fetish of his country" and that since Abaku believed that this "Fetish" existed for the good of his country he should not be challenged, for was the British Government not neutral in religious matters?[39]

Perhaps the greatest beneficiary of James Johnson's exertion on behalf of Nigerian potentates was Oyekan, Oba of Lagos from 1884 to 1901. For the tragedy that befell Dosunmu, Oyekan's father, in 1861 was not just the termination of his sovereignty over the island of Lagos. By the treaty, too, he signed away the birthright of his family for the sum of £1,000 annual grant for the duration of his life. It was made clear by the British administration that with his end would also end the Oba for Lagos. But by the time Dosunmu died in 1884 the ethics and legality of the British action in 1861 were already being questioned by educated Africans like James Johnson. According to James Johnson the king himself cried aloud before he breathed his last that he did not sign the so-called treaty of cession out of free-will, nor did he understand the severe terms of the termination of the Obaship for Lagos.[40] Nor did the royal family wish to admit that the so-called treaty existed. Therefore Oyekan was picked by the family and crowned in the traditional manner. Hardly had this event occurred than an attempt to receive the recognition of the British administration began, a recognition that would include the continuation of the annual allowance of £1,000.

Fortunately for the royal family it was the king who knew Joseph, A. C. Moloney, that was on the throne. Moved by the ethics of the family's demand he allowed Oyekan to be made an *Oba*. But this did not imply recognition of him as traditional ruler of Lagos by the British administration. As A. C. Moloney declared: "While every consideration and courtesy have been extended to Oyekan and his family the policy that has been pursued by the Government has been to discourage anything which might raise hopes, the realization of which it is not intended nor expedient to allow. H.M. Government have decided definitely that there shall be no successor to the late Docemo."[41]

It was at this juncture that James Johnson took up the cause of the royal family. He had never regarded British presence in Lagos as legally or morally valid, although at the same time he never desired that the British should withdraw their presence. All he wanted was a reconciliation of both British and traditional interests. It was not in the interest of the British, he said, to scrap or devalue the Lagos monarchy. In fact it would yield great dividends if the wound that had been inflicted by the seizure of Lagos was healed by a policy of reconciliation with the monarchy. In this respect, he said, Oyekan should not only be recognised but sufficient annual allowance made to him for the upkeep of royalty. Such a step would go a long way towards winning for the British the affection of the other Yoruba rulers who had never reconciled themselves to the British occupation of any part of Yorubaland.[42] Furthermore, contended James Johnson, a reconciled *Oba* of Lagos would be an invaluable intermediary between the British Government and the "independent" states in the interior. He therefore called on the British Government to grant Oyekan more than a moiety of what Dosunmu had enjoyed.

James Johnson alone was solely responsible for raising the matter in the Legislative Council. His language was very unrestrained. The treaty of 1861, he declared, was a cheat and by it the British discriminated against Africans. For in India, where similar treaties had been signed with potentates, so opprobrious a clause, denying the potentate's successors recognition and a financial grant, was never suggested.[43] On this matter he was supported by C. J. George. He demanded nothing lower than £500 for Oyekan. Opposed to him were the official members of the Council, who not only denounced the monarchy but were adamant that not a penny should be added to the grant of £120 per annum. Finally in 1889 the *modus vivendi* evolved was a grant of £200. It was not until January 1894 that further pressure by James Johnson made the Council agree to an increase of £100. But even then the increase was made on the understanding that no allowance from the Government would ever be made to Oyekan's successors.[44]

The part played by James Johnson in the Oyekan affair should not be underestimated. But for his exertions the monarchy of Lagos would have been abolished in law if not in practice. But as it was, *de facto* recognition was given to Oyekan and the royal family, the legal state of affairs notwithstanding. Thus by the time that Herbert Macaulay entered politics and began to champion the cause of the monarchy of Lagos the problem he had to tackle was much less difficult than it otherwise would have been. In a sense, then, James Johnson prepared the way for, and anticipated, the activities of Herbert Macaulay on behalf of the institution of *Obaship* in Lagos.

By far the greatest single question that occupied the attention of James Johnson in the Council chamber was the disparity that existed in the terms of services of Europeans and Africans. A firm believer in the equality of the races, James Johnson advocated Africanisation of all posts for which there were competent Africans. Africanisation, he held, was in the best interest of Africa for two reasons, partly because Africans would not be as expensive as Europeans and partly because he felt that the former would identify themselves more than the latter, or any foreigners, with an institution that belonged to their country. But as long as there were Europeans in the civil service of West Africa James Johnson believed that merits, rather than pigmentation of the skin, should determine status, salaries and promotions. He failed to take into consideration such facts as the European officer having a higher standard of living than his African colleague and having to maintain two homes through his wife remaining in Europe.

There were many things in the civil service of British West Africa offensive to James Johnson's notions of justice. First of all there

Dr. Obadiah Johnson, 1849–1920

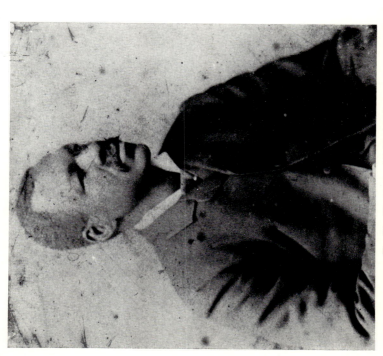

R. B. Blaize, 1845–1904

James Johnson in his later years

were different scales of salaries for Africans and Europeans, the most highly paid African coming just short of the initial salary of the lowest paid European. The maximum salary of the best paid Africans rose from £175 to £350 per annum between 1889 and 1900, while the minimum for a European rose from £220 to £450, apart from paid leave and "overseas allowances" in the same period. In contrast Africans were not entitled to quarters, could not enjoy leave at all or, if grudgingly given, it was unpaid. For instance J. A. Payne had a leave of absence in 1886 for the first time since 1863.[45] The official explanation for this disparity was that Africans were as a rule inferior to Europeans, a view that was being universally accepted by all classes of Europeans in the era of the Scramble. As an officer in the civil service of the Lagos Colony put it:

I do not believe (and I speak without Racial prejudice) that the African, however well educated, of the West Coast has undergone for a sufficiently long period the gradual process of brain development which is necessary towards the higher intellectual functions and without which a human being cannot apply the knowledge which he may have acquired by aid of memory from books—a facility which the savage emerging from barbarism enjoys much in the same way as the European child also acquires readily by heart (i.e. by memory) a more or less parrot-like knowledge of the deep meaning of which or the mode in which to utilize it, it is entirely ignorant.[46]

This prejudice was reinforced as time went on by the *Pax Britannica* which put the white man in the position of unquestioned authority and generated the idea that the acquired territories of West Africa were the possessions of the British Crown. The civil service was not regarded as Nigerian or Sierra Leonian but British. In such circumstances it was natural that white officers should believe that the higher positions in the civil service were their prescriptive rights. "As long as this is the case", contended an official in the Colonial Office complacently in 1909, "no native African can expect to be appointed to any but subordinate posts".[47]

In the Moloney era, when things were on the whole fair for the educated Africans, the point of interest for James Johnson was not salaries but how to get Africans appointed to some high posts in the service. The particular positions for which he fought deserve some attention. He was instrumental in the appointment of Henry Carr as sub-inspector of schools and clerk to the Board of Education. The appointment of Henry Carr, a graduate of the University of Durham, was announced in the Legislative Council in August 1889. He combined this post with that of Chief Clerk in the Secretariat at a salary of £150, rising by an annual increment of £5 to £175. Not only did James Johnson secure the appointment of this able African to a post in education but he followed Carr's treatment with detailed interest. Carr's status, James Johnson reminded the Government time and again, must be given due recognition and his office accommodation must be one of dignity.[48] As an educationist Henry Carr was to have no equal in West Africa for the next fifty years.

One jealously guarded department in the civil service of Lagos Colony which Europeans wished to retain for themselves was the Medical Department. Since the death of Dr. N. T. King, the first Nigerian medical doctor, who had once been appointed Assistant Colonial Surgeon, the Medical Department had been closed to Africans. In 1884 an African, Jenkins Lumpkin, had qualified in England and had applied for a post in the civil service. He had been fobbed off with the reply that there were no vacancies and that he would be informed whenever positions were available. In the next three years three appointments, all European, were made in the Colonial Hospital.[49] The official view in Lagos was that the "large European community" in Lagos should be served by European doctors only, that Europeans had no confidence in the skill of Africans for medical science and that African doctors who wished to join the civil service should be advised to go to the Gold Coast, where they could be located in several Government outstations.[50] It should be stressed that apart from diplomas from the Royal College of Surgeons (Edinburgh) Dr. Lumpkin was also a Doctor of Medicine (University of Brussels) and a Licentiate (double) in midwifery from both colleges.

Indeed he was far better qualified than Dr. C. S. Grant, the Colonial Surgeon in Lagos. When the latter in 1887 was asked to comment on the renewed application by Lumpkin (who had settled in Lagos and was having a fair practice among Africans and the French Firm of Regis Aine) for the post of Assistant Colonial Surgeon, he had the following to say *inter alia*: "I have no personal acquaintance with Dr. Lumpkin, but I believe him to be well qualified in respect to diplomas and degrees in medicine and surgery. . . . European officers have a great aversion to the attendance on them in sickness of Native medical men and they have not that confidence in their skill, judgment, experience, resources, sympathy of interest in the cases which ought to exist and are of the greatest importance between patients and their physicians."[51] More serious, he said, was that a person of Dr. Lumpkin's type, who was only a step removed from "complete or nearly complete parental barbarism", could not have his intellectual powers forced in a few years "to an equality in cerebral development" with those of a European. Never should West Africans be appointed as medical men, he advised very strongly, because:

These men have spent their childhood and youth amidst uncivilized or very partially civilized surroundings in their daily lives. They have had no chance of intuitively imbibing in the domestic family circle that abstract regard and admiration for all that is implied in the word honour (truth, honesty, loyalty) in which a gentleman should be imbued and which as a rule becomes a part of an English gentleman's nature through the training and unconsciously acting influences of his childhood and youth. Among West Africans there is no real contempt or dislike for falsehood, for underhand dealing, for petty malice or trickery. On the contrary they constitute the natural and, in his opinion, the legitimate weapons and artifices in the daily life of an African and he only dreads the blunder of being found out in their practice.[52]

Nevertheless within a year educated Africans had to be admitted into this preserve of Europeans, thanks to the agitation led by James Johnson and others. For although there was no segregation in the Colonial Hospital there were not wanting individual European medical officers who were prone to deny adequate attention to Africans. It was this state of things that culminated in the Adeola affair in June 1888. On 4 June that year a lady stranger by the name of Adeola was found in a helpless condition by the police at Ebute Ero market and thence taken to the Colonial Hospital. According to the diagnosis of Dr. Cecil Digby, an Assistant Colonial Surgeon already notorious for his hatred of Africans, she was suffering from "incurable elephantiasis". She was kept in hospital without prescriptions until 20 June when Dr. Digby ordered her discharge on the ground that no good could be done to her by treatment. She was removed to the bush near the hospital where she lay overnight till the following evening, when she had to be re-admitted to the Colonial Hospital through the intervention of James Johnson and the police. In the meantime the patient contracted diarrhoea.

James Johnson led an agitation against the "cruel and revolting"[53] affair and the Governor, A. C. Moloney, ordered a commission of inquiry. On 29 June the patient died and was hurriedly buried. Her body had to be exhumed and the all-white commission found Dr. Cecil Digby, Dr. Mattei and the African dispenser, William, guilty of manslaughter. On 5 July the Governor interdicted Digby. But the Coroner, Haddon Smith—whom James Johnson declared was unqualified to perform the duty of Coroner[54]—described as a "mess mate" of Dr. Digby's, pronounced death by natural causes on Adeola. All three persons involved were consequently acquitted

and reinstated. So horrified by the affair were the officials in the
Colonial Office that they ordered the instant dismissal and trial of
Digby.[55]

It was this convenient atmosphere that James Johnson seized
to press for the appointment of Africans as Assistant Colonial
Surgeons. He conducted a personal investigation, outlining cases of
ill-treatment of African patients by European medical officers in
the Colonial Hospital over a period of two years. On his recommendation Governor Moloney resolved to appoint African Assistant
Colonial Surgeons.[56] The first two appointees were Dr. Obadiah
Johnson and Dr. J. K. Randle, each on a salary of £240 per annum,
a house allowance of £40 and a horse allowance. They were the first
educated Africans to receive so high a salary in the civil service
of Nigeria. These two men were to play a significant role in the
nationalist movement in Nigeria, the one (O. Johnson) as a legislator and the greatest critic of European economic imperialism in
Nigeria and the other (J. K. Randle) as one of the founders of the
People's Union, the first distinctly political organisation in Nigeria.

On the whole James Johnson was successful in getting Nigerians
appointed to the higher positions in the civil service during the
Moloney era. But when Moloney finally left the Colony in 1889
and was subsequently succeeded in the following year by George
Thomas Carter, James Johnson had to deal with a king that knew
not Joseph. Discrimination against Africans increased under Carter;
there was no question of getting one single high appointment for
Africans, whilst even where it was clear that capable Africans were
available they were passed over in favour of Europeans. No two
personalities presented a greater contrast than James Johnson and
the new Governor. Carter nursed contempt towards educated
Africans with their pretensions to learning and their irrational
imitation of European culture.[57] Unlike James Johnson he did not
see the Legislative Council as a forum where nominated unofficial
members should ventilate African feelings, but rather looked to
such members to be grateful "beni oui oui" people; nor did he,
again unlike James Johnson, see the Legislative Council as the
precursor of a popularly elected Parliament in a free Nigeria.
When time and again James Johnson pressed him on many issues
he began to summon the Legislative Council less frequently and
transferred matters to the Executive Council on which Africans
were not represented. Carter saw no reason why he should treat the
Native rulers as equals, much less be deferential to them. Rather,
he believed, they should be overawed by the physical capacity of the white man whose peremptory orders must be promptly
obeyed.[58]

It was inevitable that the two personalities should quarrel in the

Legislative chamber over the new trends the civil service began to assume. Under Carter certain offices which had been held by Africans became the monopoly of the whites whilst the salaries attached to them were at the same time increased. For instance Henry Carr, the accomplished scholar whose abilities were acknowledged by the Colonial Office, it will be remembered, had been appointed in 1889 to the traditionally-held African post of Chief Clerk, at a salary of £150 rising to £175. In 1893 he was relieved of his post which was removed to the white monopoly list. A European was appointed to the post on a salary of £200 rising to £250 per annum. And although Henry Carr held the post of Inspector of Schools almost continuously from 1891, he was dropped in 1909 when the headship of the Education Department was considered too high for an African. Although he held the M.A. degree of Durham University and a B.C.L., and although according to a Colonial Office spokesman, Carr was a man of "exceptional ability", yet he was passed over in the appointment of a Director of Education for one Mr. E. G. Rowden whose experience and academic qualifications were less than Carr's.[59]

The treatment meted out to Henry Carr was a matter of special concern to James Johnson. There was no questioning of his ability —hence his holding the two important offices of Chief Clerk and Inspector of Schools—and yet his salary was much less than that of a European holding a single post. In the Legislative chamber James Johnson pressed that Henry Carr should be offered a salary that would reflect his ability and duties. Carter had no answer to give other than that he considered the salary being paid to the African civil servant as "adequate".[60] So much did James Johnson feel convinced that injustice had been done that he and another Johnsonian, R. B. Blaize, wrote "profusely" to an influential man in England, Bosworth Smith, about the necessity to increase Henry Carr's salary, a step that incensed Carter further.[61]

In the Legislative Council James Johnson challenged Carter over the discriminatory treatment that people like Pratt, Oke, Macaulay and Dr. Johnson, were subjected to by the Carter administration. Pratt had succeeded A C. Willoughby, an African, as Superintendent Pay and Quarter-Master in an Acting capacity. But to James Johnson's surprise, rather than making him the substantive holder of this post—hitherto always an African post—a white man, one Mr. Harding, was appointed in his place. E. H. Oke had been working in the Prison Department before he was sent to Britain for further experience. His additional qualification had no effect on his salary of £6 a month. On the other hand there was a less experienced European gaoler who was being paid £250 per annum. More glaring was the case of Herbert Macaulay who, it will be remembered, was sent to Britain by Moloney in 1890 to qualify as an engineer. He qualified duly as a civil engineer with credit, but on his return was put on the scale of £90, to rise to £150 by £10 annual increment, as Surveyor of Crown Lands. In the same department were European foremen earning £250 a year. It was only after much agitation by James Johnson that Herbert Macaulay's initial salary was raised to £120 per annum.[62]

One more example, out of many, may be offered. Obadiah Johnson, it will be recalled, had been appointed Assistant Colonial Surgeon in 1889, following the agitation over the Adeola affair led by James Johnson. Obadiah Johnson had graduated as B.A. (Duneld) in 1879, when he left for England where he studied at King's College, London and the University of Edinburgh. In 1884 he achieved M.R.C.S., England and L.S.A., London. The following year he was elected an Associate of King's College and graduated M.B.C.M., Edinburgh. Early in 1888 he was appointed Assistant Colonial Surgeon at Sherbro, Sierra Leone, where he served until he was appointed in Lagos in 1889 as Second Assistant Colonial Surgeon. Before the end of the year he obtained the M.D. of Edinburgh University. Not only was his skill appreciated by Africans but European firms patronised him. In the meantime, however, a European by the name of J. W. Rowland was appointed and became his senior in the administration and in terms of salary too. Naturally the relations between the two became strained. Rowland took the opportunity to discredit O. Johnson when the latter protested against the new order and asked for an increase of salary. In his Confidential Report, Dr. Rowland wrote: "I have the poorest opinion of Dr. Johnson's professional ability, as in addition to other qualifications he is indifferent as to the result of treatment. He is singularly disqualified for the post of a public medical officer, as he is idle, indifferent, and has never displayed any business capacity."[63]

And this was the very man whose qualifications—academic and practical—were extolled in 1901 by Sir William Macgregor, himself an experienced medical practitioner. The latter asked the Colonial Office to nominate O. Johnson to the Legislative Council, so that he might help the Lagos Colony with his opinion and knowledge on sanitary questions. In fact Carter himself admitted that Rowland's view of O. Johnson was incorrect; that the former had a grudge against the latter and that O. Johnson was "more intelligent than the majority of Africans who are educated in England",[64] but he, a layman, added: "I fear he is unable to make practical application of his knowledge".[65] Carter's view, that the academic superiority of a few distinguished Africans over their white colleagues should not be taken into account for appointment and promotions, was by no means unique, but was universally held by Europeans in West Africa for the rest of James Johnson's life. A spokesman in the Colonial Office remarked in 1909 that qualification must not be judged by academic attainment, for an African "is rarely if ever so well 'qualified'—using the word in a wide sense— . . . as an Englishman to fill a post involving the exercise of authority".[66]

Perhaps the most important single Bill that came before the Legislative Council not only during James Johnson's membership but throughout the first phase, 1886-1913, of the existence of this legislative body was the Municipalities Bill, the first reading of which was made on 12 August 1889. As far as the Lagos Government was concerned it arose purely out of financial considerations —to persuade Lagosians to increase the revenue of the Government.[67] There was no question of desiring to teach the people how to become self-reliant or to introduce them to the art of self-government. The primary object of the Bill was that all matters that concerned Lagos should be left to its inhabitants. This principle itself would have been all right had the Bill ended there, or had it stated further that all the financial involvements implied by this Bill would be paid for by the Lagos Government. But the Bill went further than that, emphasising that the Town Council would have to consider measures it deemed fit to be in the interest of the people and to levy rates. Every house which had an annual value of £2 and upwards was to subscribe to the rates.

The latter part of this Bill was most objectionable to a majority of Lagos people. The idea of any form of direct taxation was most reprehensible to them and no pretext was ever given to the British Government to encourage it to impose this direct taxation. Consequently no section of Lagos community ever agitated for social amenities. The Lagos community was divided broadly into two— the educated immigrants and the indigenous, largely illiterate, people. The former would not object to having piped water, electricity, education and even self-government, provided they were not required to pay a penny towards the provision of these amenities. Moreover they were aware that whatever form of direct taxation was launched would be a tax on wealth, and as virtual monopolists of the retail trade they would have to bear the brunt of such tax. From the material viewpoint they—and not the indigenes—were the beneficiaries of commercial contact with the European world.[68] Their relative affluence was reflected in the superior quality of their houses, their patronage of sophisticated European manufactured goods and their imitation of Victorian tastes and manners. Moreover these educated immigrants had their grievances against the European community. The Europeans, it was often said, were the real beneficiaries of the social amenities introduced with Government funds.

This class of elite never found it difficult to carry along with them the unlettered indigenes. For one thing the latter were very poor and literally dreaded any speculation that Government would wish to take money from them. Secondly they still relished their customs and traditions and were convinced that these were better suited to their aspirations and well-being than the alien ones being introduced by the European community and the educated immigrants. They could hardly be expected to be enamoured of innovations like electric light, pipe-borne water and so on. Even self-government could hardly have any meaning for them. Self-government for Africans would mean self-government for and by the educated immigrants who, in view of the indigenes, had joined the white man in robbing them of their sovereignty.[69] It is against this background that the potentially violent reaction of both educated immigrants and the indigenes to all suggestions of direct taxation until the First World War should be understood.

In the Legislative Council the Government was very cautious. C. J. George and Hammond represented the European merchants who had had a preview of the Bill and who knew the extent of the unmistakably and potentially violent temper of the people. They lost no time in opposing it and warning the Government of the acts of civil disobedience that might result from the introduction of the financial aspect of the Bill.[70] Even the Acting Governor, Captain D. C. Denton, saw the futility of pressing the claim of the Bill at the very first Reading. As he said, a deputation of 850, "a fully native representative assembly of every quarter of the town" had met him a few days before. "Spokesmen of each party were heard. Their words were identical and short. All they said was that the Bill would tax them and for this reason they objected to it in toto."[71]

In British West Africa, Governments of pre-World War I knew when and how to stop in order to prevent eruption by the governed. In the Gold Coast in the early sixties and in Sierra Leone in the early seventies they had withdrawn tax measures or a Bill of this kind. But James Johnson would not be moved by popular opinion, as long as that opinion was against what he believed was intrinsically right. In the Legislative Council he declared a wholehearted support for the proposed measure which, he said, "had been wanted a long time".[72] Opposition to the Bill should be discountenanced, for had it not emanated mainly from the selfish, privileged classes? Moreover, he contended, the masses did not know what was really in their interest. In the circumstances it was the duty of Government to do what was right, irrespective of the wishes of the governed.

With the lapse of time, he declared, the scales would drop off the eyes of the people and they would appreciate and be grateful that their intrinsic interest had been given paramountcy by the omniscient Government. Furthermore the laying out of streets in Lagos had been opposed to such an extent, and feelings ran so high that it was not safe for supporters of the scheme to walk out at night. The licensing of canoes, which had been opposed, was now being appreciated; the laying out of streets, too, would soon produce a similar result. He was sure that this attempt to devolve self-government on the people would yield gratitude for the government in the future.

James Johnson was more of a statesman than a politician. There was no question of dabbling in expediencies; he considered the overall, ultimate interest of the people and country; he was concerned entirely with measures and not at all with men. The Municipalities Bill would inoculate the Lagosians with the virtue of self-reliance; this was a sublime objective for which, he believed, every African should be prepared to make any sacrifice. In his assessment the Bill provided the people of Lagos with a golden opportunity; it was a godsend and should never be spurned. For, as will be recalled, it was James Johnson's view that the peoples inhabiting the enclaves where the British had established their rule had been ripe for municipal self-government as early as 1874. He denounced the British administration for having delayed a measure of this kind until 1889; the British had been guilty of "over-paternal government". But for the effect of this he could not understand why the people of Lagos would not grasp with ecstacy and alacrity the opportunity to govern themselves. After all, "Lagos before the cession was independent, and the people managed their own affairs, perhaps not quite in the right way but yet the system had its advantages, the people thought and acted for themselves and they had by themselves paid taxes towards maintaining the Government of their country, even as their countrymen in the Independent Native States pay tolls and other taxes to keep up the Government of their several countries."[73]

In spite of the strong opposition mounted against the Bill, both inside and outside the Legislative Council, James Johnson was inveterately opposed to its withdrawal. He would not budge; he had never budged in a matter of this kind; he had never budged over the Native Pastorate question in Sierra Leone, repeating as late as 1913 the opinion he had held nearly fifty years earlier;[74] he had never budged over the slavery question in Abeokuta, the parochialism of the inhabitants of which he never failed to denounce for the rest of his life; he had never budged an inch with the members of his Church in Breadfruit over the issue of polygamy and they had to accept his views without rebellion for the rest of his Pastoral ministration among them.[75] It cannot be surprising, then, that he did not budge in the Legislative chamber on a matter in which he felt the credit of the Negro Race was at stake. He made it plain that the Bill was "a good means of educating the people". The only concession he was prepared to make was that in order to make the Bill palatable the rates could be reduced at the beginning and the British Government subsidise the Municipal Council until the people became educated to appreciate its value. For a start, too, he said, rates should be paid by the educated, the wealthy and the influential section of the community only.[76] He believed that it would not be long before the unlettered section of the community would be educated on the voting system and on how to elect their representatives, as Christians had begun to do in their periodical elections.

Outside the Legislative chamber only a minority supported James Johnson, but even those did not want to go as far as James Johnson had desired. He was once more alone in his conviction of the salutariness and timeliness of a self-government "with honour" and with the financial incubus attached to it. He was more than fifty years ahead of his time and his expectations were in some ways very quixotic. Consider, for instance, the fact that in Lagos barely more than 4,000 of the 42,000 inhabitants could be said to be English-speaking. How could the non-English speaking mass be made to understand the complicated provisions of the Municipality Bill, or the deliberations on the Municipality Council? How could they be made to intelligently elect representatives to the Council?

Scarcely twenty-five people supported James Johnson and, it is said, never had his popularity and prestige reached the nadir of 1889. As he himself admitted there were threats to kill him.[77] Two Johnsonians who supported him were J. O. Payne and R. B. Blaize, but ranged against him were men of substance and influence in society. Incidentally the most outspoken of his opponents was I. H. Willoughby, the man who, as was noted in the last chapter, had been the greatest tool in the hands of the European adversaries of James Johnson during the discussion whether to make the latter a Bishop. No stone was left unturned by James Johnson's enemies to draw for the Lagos Government a macabre picture of what would be the consequences of any attempt by the British administration to impose the Bill on them. The Bill, they declared, would drive the Yoruba states into the arms of the French; the interior people would sever commercial relations with Lagos and starve the latter; loyalty to the Queen would disappear and utter ruin attend the trade of Lagos. The Bill, they said, was "jesuitical", "oppressive", "the most cruel and tormenting Ordinance" which they had ever heard of. In I. H. Willoughby's words: "we hate it, we detest it, we abhor it, it is cruel; we beg most humbly that it be removed from the archives of this government."[78]

The opposition to James Johnson was strengthened by the fact that by 1889 the newspaper of his ardent supporter, R. B. Blaize, had ceased to exist, whilst that owned by a prominent Wesleyan, J. B. Benjamin, The *Lagos Observer*, was still flourishing. In an editorial of 13/7/1889, that is before the Bill came for the first reading in the Legislative Council, the newspaper had declared: "We say that the general tendency of the Bill is evil, that if forcibly introduced for generations to come, it will be found impracticable and that it implies an exchange of existing order for general chaos ... we emphatically assert that the new measure would be uncalled for since the Colony is rich enough for any necessary improvements that might be desired." Wesleyan leaders like C. J. George and J. P. Haastrup, who had an axe to grind against the sectarian tendencies of James Johnson, all used The *Lagos Observer* as the main medium of their agitation. James Johnson, the newspaper declared, had ceased to be the authentic representative of Africans for he was not echoing *vox populi*. Independence such as James Johnson was hankering after, they pronounced, was beyond their dream; they were perfectly satisfied to remain under British rule. "The reign of our present Gracious Queen is all peaceful", a spokesman declared before Acting Governor Denton, "surely she wishes us no unhappiness. This House Taxation will make the present misery most miserable, and the misery there is now in the community cannot be guessed."[79]

Over the Municipality issue James Johnson's *vox clamantis in deserto* persistently preached to deaf ears. The unsplendid isolation in which he found himself in 1889—by no means for the first time in his career—requires a brief observation. Significant as his ideas were he lacked one quality, the will and temperament to appeal to the masses, which might have aided the cause to which he was dedicated. But he was a rugged individualist and he never organised a followership as such. Those who admired him and subscribed to his Ethiopian programme did so purely out of patriotism. They were in the main a very small group among the educated Africans, people who were in a position to appreciate his disinterested and passionate patriotism and to whom his programme was both intelligible and inspiring. There is no evidence that even this small group was ever organised. The three most devoted were Captain J. P. L. Davies, R. B. Blaize and J. A. Payne. And yet, ironically, James Johnson had expected support from the masses who, he assumed, would perceive issues in exactly the way his own intellectual advantages and African patriotism enabled him. In the

Municipality Bill matter James Johnson with his small group of followers lost the support of the masses and were lambasted as "a clique, whose pretensions to self-government could only be read through a glass darkly. They forget that it is not the rule of the government to make hasty and capricious laws nor indeed is it also to defy the masses even at the up-push of a mere handful of men."[80]

Since his membership in the Legislative Council depended upon the good will of the colonial governor James Johnson could hardly have been expected to get on with Carter. Indeed had James Johnson's first term in the Legislative Council continued into the beginning of Carter's tenure of office it is probable that Carter would not have caused to be renewed the African patriot's membership for another term. For both clashed at the very first meeting of the Council under Carter's governorship, over discrimination against Africans in the civil service.[81] Moreover it was not long before their conflict broke out in the open over the Ijebu Expedition, in which they took different sides. Carter and Johnson never saw eye to eye. James Johnson attached the greatest importance to Christian virtues and ethics and judged politics, events and people from the Olympian height of a Christian idealist and a passionate African nationalist. Carter on the other hand was neither a strong Churchman nor a moralist, but a man of great practical sense who looked upon British administration in Nigeria mainly from the interest of the imperial power. Their battle of words resulted in uncomplimentary comments about each other. James Johnson likened Carter to Warren Hastings of Indian atrocities fame and Governor Eyre of Jamaican brutality fame. Carter saw in Johnson a "mischievous patriot".[82] At a time when over 95 per cent of the revenue of the Lagos Government derived from duties on liquor James Johnson asked Carter to "abolish entirely" the traffic or tax it out of existence on moral grounds. Whilst Johnson wanted to see the eventual Christianisation of Nigeria through the instrumentality of the educated Africans Carter preferred practising Muslims to Christian hypocrites.[83] Carter's hatred for James Johnson was intensified by the legal action which Johnsonians threatened to take against Carter for misrepresenting the facts of the events that culminated in the Ijebu Expedition and for misrepresenting Johnson in his reply to the latter's allegations against him. It is essential to emphasise that Carter consequently apologised to Johnson, an apology which the latter accepted with the significant regret that historians of the Ijebu Expedition were likely to use the official records by Carter to his, Johnson's, discredit.[84]

Carter found James Johnson increasingly aggressive and was resolved on having his pound of flesh. He attempted to get rid of Johnson prematurely, by asking him to resign from the Legislative

Council before his term had expired, a demand the African patriot refused to grant.[85] Anticipating Johnson's resignation Carter had appointed in his place a docile African, James John Thomas, who would not offer "any factious opposition to the Government when dealing with General Legislation business".[86] Indeed the Governor was apprehensive of James Johnson's danger to his administration. For instance, when in 1894 Ogedemgbe, the veteran military leader of the Ekitiparapo, was arrested, not only did Carter treat him generously and give the full facts of the case—corroborated by African sources—but he also warned the Colonial Office to be on its guard against a possible "petition" by James Johnson to the Aborigines Protection Society, who might interpret Ogedemgbe's arrest as "interference with 'Native Customs' ".[87]

The termination of James Johnson's membership in the Legislative Council did not evoke popular protest. Only Johnsonians made any positive effort to influence the Colonial Office to reinstate him. He himself never indicated that he had lost a remunerative post nor did he regret that he had maintained a sturdy defence of the cause of Africans. His opinion on the various issues he had attempted to tackle as a legislator never changed; nor did he cease to air his views and to inform the British Government, over the heads of the Governors, of the grievances of the peoples of West Africa generally.

There can be no doubt that in the Legislative Council of Nigeria James Johnson was "the right man in the right place",[88] far more radical and far more determined to give African interests a priority over British interests than all other nominated African members of the Legislative Council in subsequent years. Even judging from the account of Wheare[89] his performance in the earlier Council was more impressive than that of most of the elected members between 1923 and 1946. With his removal from the Council chamber the debates became less exciting than before. Although the number of nominated Africans in the Council increased from two to four the latter, in the main, performed the part of conventional nominated unofficial members. As far as the Legislative Council was concerned the British had no longer a thorn in its side until the institution of the elective principle in the reconstructed Council of 1922.

It is essential to put James Johnson's performance as a legislator in proper focus. His skill as a debater is difficult to assess because the proceedings of the Council were rarely reported verbatim. However the evidence that exists indicates that he spoke more often than any other member on both important and trivial matters. On three major issues, viz. The Oyekan affair, the Ijebu Crisis and the Municipalities Bill, he was well informed and was able to stand up to the officials in his mastery of detail, based on a careful study of data. For purposes of debate on political, material and social affairs he informed himself about the conditions and achievements of the British in India and in Britain, in order to assess British achievements in Nigeria. In terms of literary quality he was to be excelled before 1914 by Dr. O. Johnson and Sapara Williams. He showed little literary skill, never used imagery, and his language lacked adornments; he was concerned and satisfied mainly with laying bare facts before the Council. But because he spoke with emotion, reinforced by sincerity of purpose, and was often censorious, his language possessed considerable acerbity and was often irritating to officials.

One major way in which James Johnson's exit from the Legislative Council was felt by the educated Africans was with respect to the fate of civil servants. The lot of these people was not once raised by the African nominated unofficial members from 1895 to the dissolution of the Council in 1913; not one of the African members was prepared to lose his seat on the platform of crusade on behalf of African civil servants. The latter's lot was worse than ever. The few educated Africans whose appointments to higher positions had been secured through James Johnson's exertions found the situation more and more unbearable. Three of them—Dr. O. Johnson, Dr. J. K. Randle and Herbert Macaulay—were forced to resign their appointments by 1900 and to enter private practice. The only one who remained was Henry Carr, a thoroughly Europeanised African and an unassertive man as far as Europeans were concerned. And yet his experience was a mental agony for him, as is clear from the following privately recorded brooding of his:

> There are European officials who will resent the idea of an African native occupying the position I have the honour to fill and will do all in their power to disparage and depreciate his qualities. . . . I am as it were a permanent understudy and have the mortification of seeing younger men with defective knowledge of local conditions constantly placed over me to disparage me and depreciate my labours, simply to exalt what they want the authorities to believe is their superior knowledge. I stand damned because the policy seems to be that I am not to go further than I am. This places me at a great disadvantage. The presumption is against my fitness and capacity, and is not flattering to my self-respect. In every other department, the rule is that men already in the civil service must be promoted. The Education Department stands an exception. This is wounding to my own self-respect.[90]

Indeed the only man who paid attention to the fate of Africans in the civil service after 1894 continued to be ex-legislator James

Johnson. In 1899, on the occasion of a visit to Britain, he held discussions with the men of the Colonial Office about the plight of this class of Africans. He had collected data "from an important French official source from which I had sought for information",[91] that in French colonial possessions Frenchmen willingly served under their African superiors. Why, he asked, should this not be the case in Nigeria? Why did the element of colour enter the civil service? As he commented: "it yet remains that the distribution of its offices by the Government among both its white and coloured subjects should be such as to impress the people generally with the idea that the same privileges are at all times conceded to all British subjects of whatever colour alike, and that the only test the Government requires for the employment in its offices is intellectual capacity, a good character and general fitness, and that natives possessing and manifesting these are as much open to employment in its service as their English fellow subjects, and that there is no other barrier than the lack of this to a native to any very important office that may be in its gift."[92]

But the situation in which European dominance in all spheres in West Africa had to be accepted was already fixed. Eleven years earlier there had been Afrophile officers in the Colonial Office who were prepared to record the view that there should be no racial discrimination in the distribution and remuneration of positions in the civil service of British West Africa. But at the turn of the century the view that the African was biologically inferior to the white man had become a maxim. Such a view, as we saw in the last chapter, had robbed James Johnson of the episcopate. It was in the spirit of the age that Reginald L. Antrobus minuted on the representations of this African agitator on civil service conditions in Nigeria: "Generally speaking, the highest education fails to impart to the African something which the European possesses, and which makes him competent to administer and to occupy positions of trust. . . . It would be impossible to explain this to Mr. Johnson but I don't think his appeal on this score need cause us much searching of heart."[93]

Perhaps the greatest achievement of James Johnson in the Legislative Council is the fact that throughout his eight years' membership he fulfilled a constitutional role, showing that in some respects he was the Peter Wentworth of the Nigerian Legislative Council, which was to evolve into the modern House of Representatives. Like the Tudor radical he asserted his right to freedom of speech and of the Legislative Council to be the tribune of the people and the centre of power to check the authoritarian tendency of the all-powerful colonial governor.

NOTES

1. C.O. 147/55, A. C. Moloney to Earl of Granville, 19/4/1886.
2. *Ibid.*
3. P.P. C.4477, *Further Correspondence Respecting the Affairs of the Gold Coast*, Enclosure 2 in No. 16.
4. *Ibid.*
5. *Ibid.*
6. *Ibid.*
7. M. Wright, *The Gold Coast Legislative Council*, London, 1946; E. W. Blyden III, *Sierra Leone: The Pattern of Constitutional Change (1924-1951)*, Harvard Ph.D., 1959.
8. A.P.S., James Johnson to H. R. Fox Bourne, 5/4/1893.
9. A. B. Aderibigbe, *The Expansion of the Lagos Protectorate 1861-1900*, Ph.D. London, 1959, pp. 123-187 for details about Moloney.
10. C.O. 149/3, Legislative Council *Minutes*, 13/3/1889.
11. C.O. 149/3, Legislative Council *Minutes*, 13/3/1889.
12. *Anglo-African Who's Who*, 1910, p. 4.
13. C.O. 147/57, A. C. Moloney to C.O., 10/9/1886.
14. 147/73, A. C. Moloney to Bellamy, 4/12/1889.
15. C.O. 149/4, Legislative Council *Minutes*, 16/6/1893.
16. C.O. 149/1, Legislative Council *Minutes*, 25/6/1888.
17. *Ibid.*, 17/10/1888.
18. C.O. 149/4, Legislative Council *Minutes*, 16/6/1893.
19. *Ibid.*
20. *Ibid.*, 19/4/1892.
21. *Ibid.*
22. C.O. 147/62, James Johnson to E. Stanhope, 4/1/1887; James Johnson to H. Holland, 18/3/1887.
23. A.P.S., James Johnson to H. R. Fox Bourne, 5/4/1893.
24. *Ibid.*, R. B. Blaize to A.P.S., 29/8/1893 (forwarded money for legal action on behalf of James Johnson against Carter).
25. *Ibid.*, James Johnson to H. R. Fox Bourne, 28/6/1894.
26. C.O. 149/1, Legislative Council *Minutes*, 6/11/1888.
27. C.O. 149/4, Legislative Council *Minutes*, 14/10/1893.
28. *Ibid.*
29. C.O. 149/3, Legislative Council *Minutes*, 13/4/1891.
30. *Ibid.*, 29/10/1889.
31. *Ibid.*, 18/9/1891.
32. N.A. Ibadan (C.S.O. 12/10) 913/1891, James Johnson to D. C. Denton, 24/4/1891.
33. *Ibid.*
34. C.O. 149/3, Legislative Council *Minutes*, 18/9/1891.
35. *Ibid.*, 10/2/1891.
36. *Ibid.*, 24/8/1891.
37. *Ibid.*, 14/3/1891.
38. *Ibid.*, 27/5/1890.
39. *Ibid.*, 3/10/1892.
40. C.O. 149/1, Legislative Council *Minutes*, 17/2/1888.
41. C.O. 147/62, Minute by A. C. Moloney, 10/5/1887, on James Johnson to H. Holland, 18/3/1887.
42. C.O. 147/62, James Johnson to H. Holland, 18/3/1887.
43. C.O. 149/1, Legislative Council *Minutes*, 17/2/1888.

44. C.O. 149/4, Legislative Council *Minutes*, 25/1/1894.
45. C.O. 147/57, J. A. Payne to C.O., 19/8/1886.
46. C.O. 147/58, Dr. Grant to Ag. Colonial Secretary, 16/3/1887.
47. C.O. 520/87, Memorandum by C. Stratchey, 10/12/1909.
48. C.O. 149/4, Legislative Council *Minutes*, 9/10/1893.
49. C.O. 147/57, Jenkins Lumpkin to C.O., 26/12/1886.
50. C.O. 147/58, Ag. Administrator to H. Holland, 6/4/1887.
51. *Ibid.*, Dr. Grant to Ag. Colonial Secretary, 16/3/1887.
52. *Ibid.*
53. C.O. 147/65, A. C. Moloney to H. T. H. Knutsford, 31/8/1888.
54. *Ibid.*, James Johnson to A. C. Moloney, 21/6/1888.
55. *Ibid.*, C.O. to A. C. Moloney, 14/11/1888.
56. *Ibid.*, A. C. Moloney to H. T. H. Knutsford, 31/8/1888.
57. C.O. 147/85, G. T. Carter to G. F. S. R. Ripon, 21/11/1892.
58. C.O. 149/2, Executive Council *Minutes*, 16/3/1892.
59. C.O. 520/87, Memorandum by C. Stratchey, 10/12/1909.
60. C.O. 149/3, Legislative Council *Minutes*, 23/10/1891.
61. C.O. 149/4, Legislative Council *Minutes*, 7/7/1893.
62. *Ibid.*, 9/10/1893 and 14/10/1893.
63. C.O. 147/95, G. T. Carter to G. F. S. R. Ripon, 20/6/1894: quotes J. W. Rowland.
64. C.O. 147/155, W. Macgregor to J. Chamberlain, 26/5/1901.
65. C.O. 147/95, G. T. Carter to G. F. S. R. Ripon, 20/6/1894.
66. C.O. 520/87, Memorandum by C. Stratchey, 10/12/1909.
67. C.O. 149/3, Legislative Council *Minutes*, 12/8/1899.
68. J. H. Kopytoff, *op. cit.*, pp. 101-102.
69. *Ibid.*, pp. 129-130.
70. C.O. 149/3, Legislative Council *Minutes*, 12/8/1889.
71. *Ibid.*
72. *Ibid.*
73. *Ibid.*
74. *Jubilee Volume of the Sierra Leone Native Church*, London, 1917, pp. 207-208 (Jubilee Sermon February 1913 by James Johnson).
75. J. O. Lucas, *op. cit.*, pp. 33-34.
76. C.O. 149/3, Legislative Council *Minutes*, 19/8/1889.
77. A.P.S., James Johnson to H. R. Fox Bourne, 5/4/1893.
78. *Lagos Observer*, 24 and 31 August 1889: Report of the Deputation.
79. *Ibid.*, 24 and 31 August 1889.
80. *Ibid.*, Editorial.
81. C.O. 149/3, Legislative Council *Minutes*, 23/10/1891.
82. C.O. 147/95, G. T. Carter to G. F. S. R. Ripon, 19/6/1894.
83. *Lagos Weekly Record*, 7/7/1894.
84. A.P.S., James Johnson to H. R. Fox Bourne, 27/12/1893.
85. C.O. 147/91, Conf. G. T. Carter to G. F. S. R. Ripon, 23/6/1894.
86. *Ibid.*, same to same, 7/3/1894.
87. 147/95, same to same, 19/6/1894.
88. A.P.S., R. B. Blaize to A.P.S., 22/3/1894.
89. Wheare, *The Nigerian Legislative Council*, London, 1949.
90. Ibadan University Library, Henry Carr Papers, Car V5.
91. C.O. 147/147, James Johnson to J. Chamberlain, 27/12/1899.
92. *Ibid.*
93. *Ibid.*, Minutes on above dated 17/1/1900.

N

CHAPTER EIGHT

POLITICIAN

Egypt is a part of Africa, Ethiopia is the land of the
Negro people, the land to which I belong . . . the European Governments have parted that Continent among
themselves—by what law, by what right, I know not.
Yes, but they have done it. It is undoubtedly the right
of might over right, for they have a stronger power.

James Johnson, addressing a S.U.M.V.
Conference in London in January 1900

JAMES JOHNSON'S performance as a Legislator shows clearly that
he was not just the "Pope" of Nigeria, wrapped up in spiritual
contemplation and living far away from the madding crowd. He
was not only in but of society. Unlike St. Augustine he did not
regard human society as evil or secular. Ideally it was Christian
and an agency for the fulfilment of the divine purpose. Nor was
James Johnson's society just the one in which he lived physically.
Rather it was that of mankind on the terrestrial globe. Hence the
affairs of men in Europe, in Russia, in Japan, in India and in the
New World came under his observation,[1] though—as should be
expected—not as much as that of Africa in general and of West
Africa in particular. Not that he felt he was a citizen of the world
in the sense of the Stoics of Ancient Greece. But from his theological
belief arose the idea that Man had a basic immutable nature which
could not be altered by geography and accidents of history, that the
human species constituted a family and that what happened to
one people should be the concern of others.

His concern for peoples outside the African continent was not
over political matters as such but over the foibles of their human
nature—a nature that could, like that of Africans, make them love
and hate, virtuous and vicious, spiritual and mundane, ascetic and
sensual. Hence he was incessant in denouncing the war element in
European peoples. As in national politics James Johnson wished

that Christian principles governed international relations. He denounced war generally, whether between professed Christian nations or between a Christian and a non-Christian state, although he never denied that war might fulfil the divine purpose. He denounced the Franco-Prussian war of 1870 and commiserated with its victims.[2] He was shocked by the Russo-Japanese war of 1904-5, believing that as a Christian nation Russia ought to have taught Japan, a "pagan" country, the art of peace.[3] As a continent in which Christianity had flourished for centuries James Johnson believed that the peoples of Europe ought to have become completely saturated with Christianity to the point of beating their swords into ploughshares and their spears into pruninghooks.

But not only was James Johnson astounded by the failure of the European powers to keep the peace and allow Christian ethics to determine the pattern of relations among themselves. He was scandalised by the nature of their contact with, and their attitude to, the African continent. The Europeans, he said, failed to exhibit Christian virtues in their dealings with Africans. They were first and foremost plunderers. For centuries they had plundered Africa of millions of her inhabitants, thereby making her history "dark" and debasing her peoples. As he put it in 1873: "Centuries upon centuries have found and left us an ill-used people. The land has been denuded of its inhabitants; . . . the intellect has been oppressed and the body enslaved."[4] Even after the cessation of the trans-Atlantic slave trade Europeans continued to plunder Africa, first of her sylvan products and then of her enormous mineral resources. This act of plunder, he said, continued into the colonial era; the desire to plunder was responsible for the Scramble; never had altruism, pure and simple (excepting British repression of the slave trade), determined Europe's contact with Africa. The result, he observed, was that "No nation or people on the earth now occupy the unfortunate and wretched position we occupy. We have too long been a prey to the cruel force of the greed after gain that has marked commerce by Europe with Africa".[5]

In his observation the pattern of economic relations between Europe and Africa was unsatisfactory and inimical to the latter's interest in several ways. Firstly it was not based on the principle of equality. This was glaringly so in the pre-colonial period when European traders along the coast denounced the middleman's system, that is the pattern of trade in which African intermediaries stood between European traders and the producers in the interior. Selfish to their finger-tips these merchants used to invoke the aid of the gunboat with the slogan of Free Trade and were responsible for many of the military expeditions against African peoples in the two last decades of the nineteenth century. These traders, contended James Johnson, were themselves middlemen; they were intermediaries between the manufacturers in Europe and African buyers. Therefore they had no right to point an accusing hand at the African middlemen.[6] Worse still was the fact that they were monopolists, denying African traders equal opportunities. For he had found out, in Manchester, as early as 1873, that it was impossible for African traders to buy directly from manufacturers.[7] It became the rule among manufacturers to sell their wares through commission agents, that is the metropolitan headquarters of the firms operating in West Africa. In the light of this state of affairs James Johnson took the position that the middleman system should continue to operate in the continent until European merchants were prepared to revise their attitude and allow African colleagues to compete with them on equal terms. Not only did he keep a constant watch on the selfishness of Europeans in matters of trade but he collected data from many educated African merchants in Lagos in the last quarter of the nineteenth century. Among those were J. S. Leigh, later his father-in-law, a prosperous trader with six factories on the Niger who was squeezed out of the territory's trade by the Royal Niger Company; J. J. Thomas, who succeeded him on the Legislative Council, but who in later years found European competition so adverse to his business that he retired to Sierra Leone, and R. B. Blaize, the arch-Johnsonian who enjoyed the reputation of being the wealthiest educated African in West Africa in the last quarter of the nineteenth century.

Secondly, James Johnson deplored the fact that in the Afro-European commercial contact Africans were no more than incidental beneficiaries. Railways, roads, telegraphs and other facilities that improved communication and transportation, he declared, were not introduced for the convenience of Africans but for the development of European trade. He saw no reason why the minerals in the bowels of Africa should be "disgorged" by aliens and carried away by the Europeans for their own benefit.[8] He was very critical of the policy of colonial governments because they did not encourage the creative and inventive genius of Africans in regard to traditional industries and because they persuaded Africans to be merely producers instead of manufacturers of the type and variety of contemporary Europeans.[9]

Thirdly, James Johnson considered that Africans were being cheated by Europeans, in the sense that in return for the rich commodities the latter were receiving from Africa and which were helping to "promote wealth and comfort in Europe"[10] Africans were being given in return largely the poisonous, vile and debasing gin.

That James Johnson's three basic criticisms of European commercial relations up to the era of colonial rule are historically valid cannot be denied. Contemporaries like Mary Kingsley and Edmund Morel, popular defenders of British rule in West Africa, emphasised clearly that commerce was the primary determinant of the British presence in West Africa;[11] European traders like John Holt and educated Africans like Dr. Obadiah Johnson recognised that Africans were no more than incidental beneficiaries,[12] whilst the debasement of Africans and the economic unsoundness (from the African viewpoint) of drenching Africa with gin was admitted by empire-makers like F. D. Lugard and Taubman Goldie.[13] The amateurish criticism, by James Johnson, of Afro-European commercial relations to some extent would still apply today.

More disturbing to James Johnson were the political implications of the European presence for Africa. For him the European powers were intruders who had no right whatsoever, "except that of might", to instal themselves in any part of the continent, thereby violating the territorial integrity of Africa and depriving traditional authorities of their sovereignty.[14] Never did he approve of any such violation, although he was in some instances accommodating in his attitude, accepting the *fait accompli* in the cases of Sierra Leone and Lagos.

James Johnson's views on the political implications for Africa of European activity may be examined in three phases, viz., the pre-Scramble period, the Scramble era and the time of colonial rule. In the first phase he watched carefully the relations between the British in their enclaves and the Africans in the hinterland. His attitude as to the relations that should subsist between the British and the "independent" states in the interior was very ambivalent. On the one hand he recognised the benefits that might accrue to the people of the interior by their associating themselves with the British. He wished the latter to introduce technological marvels such as roads, railways and telegraphs; to help in opening up rivers to commerce. The British should also seek to industrialise the hinterland. They had specific political functions too. They were to pacify the interior in a convincingly disinterested manner by putting an end to inter-tribal wars and by locating in the interior "residents" who could persuade the people of the benefits of a sophisticated economy and of the virtues of peaceful co-existence.[15]

Some observation should be made about James Johnson's attitude to relations between the British and interior African kingdoms in the pre-Scramble era. Firstly it implied that the myriads of independent African kingdoms should be left alone to preserve their separate identity, rather than having their separate existence effaced in favour of the continental state which, as analysed in an earlier chapter, James Johnson expected to logically follow his continental African Church. For in practical terms there was no formula in his conception that would forge the innumerable "independent" African states or kingdoms into one monolithic African State. Moreover, it should be stressed again that it is an implication of his Ethiopian programme, that by backing up Christianity the British would be a major factor in the evolution of such an African state. He was, then, contradicting his theory when he asserted that the British should be content with clinging to the coast and that they should not seek to exercise any political influence, other than that outlined above on the "independent" kingdoms in the interior. This conflict between theory and practice can be easily explained. James Johnson could not afford to be logical in a situation in which, in the Hegelian manner, every Thesis must have its Antithesis. The Thesis was the theory of an African State, the Antithesis the instrumentality of the British, through the backing of the Ethiopian Church. James Johnson rejected the Synthesis which would have produced a British Colony rather than an African State. Certainly the Church in such a Colony would not be Ethiopian; it would, as analysed in an earlier chapter, be thoroughly Anglican and therefore imperialistic.

It was this impracticability of his ideology that made James Johnson patently illogical. His theory was determined by African interests alone. He was suffering from a myopia which made him misconstrue the purpose of British Administration and of Christian missions in West Africa. To his thinking, the British were to behave like an inanimate tool in the hands of Africans; they were to draw the chestnut out of the fire for the latter. For example in Nigeria they were to help in the maintenance of law and order. But James Johnson could not conceive that the presence of the British in Lagos and the performance of the functions he expected of them must logically, if gradually, lead to the assimilation of Yorubaland into the British empire. Johnson was naïve to think that the only reward the British should expect from all their exertions on behalf of the Yoruba was commercial privileges, which the building of roads and railways by the British would give to British traders.[16]

Secondly, he was hardly consistent in the role he cast for the British, suggesting on the one hand that force against one state would be justified, whilst in the case of another it would not be justified. He was in a sense being an opportunist. It will be recalled that in the Legislative Council and in correspondence with the Colonial Office he denounced the Treaty of Cession of 1861 as being legally and ethically invalid, because it was based on force rather than on consent.[17] But he was prepared to invoke this very treaty against another African state, Dahomey, of which he entertained the worst views. According to a Clause of this treaty the British bound themselves to curb the unbridled militarism of Dahomey and put an end to the ravages being committed by that State in western Yorubaland. As far as this Clause was concerned, said James Johnson, this treaty was valid.[18] Therefore he charged the British with faithlessness, declaring that they should be held responsible for the acts of devastation being perpetrated against the Yoruba by that State. He was prepared to say that force should be deployed by the British to tame Dahomey. Consequently James Johnson became the most vigorous and most vocal advocate of the use of force against Dahomey among the educated elite in Lagos in the last quarter of the nineteenth century. In 1887 he urged the British to use "English troops", whilst three years later he was chairman of a committee that sent a memorandum to the British Government, drawing the attention of the latter to the non-fulfilment of the obligations it had undertaken in 1861.[19] Indeed in order to persuade the British to do something about the perennial Dahomian invasion of Yorubaland he sent his own personal appeal to both the Church Missionary Society and the Aborigines Protection Society to use their good offices to obtain the desired end.[20]

James Johnson's prejudice against Dahomey *vis-à-vis* the Ijebu further illustrates the inconsistency of his doctrine regarding the relations that should subsist between the British and the interior kingdoms. Although, as will be analysed presently, the Ijebu were in the view of the British as reactionary, as bloodthirsty, as selfish and as barbarous as Dahomey, James Johnson desired that preferential treatment should be given Ijebuland. For instance he would not object to force being used against Dahomey in order to compel the latter to accept the Gospel, but he would not like force to be used against the Ijebu to achieve a similar end, even when there was a treaty by the Ijebu with the British in 1852 according to which the Ijebu pledged themselves to allow missionary propaganda in their country. All he wanted the British to do with the Ijebu was to use "its moral influence to encourage the spread of the Christian religion among non-Christian peoples", even when he admitted that human sacrifice still prevailed among the Ijebu in the last decade of the nineteenth century.[21]

But it should be stressed that for James Johnson the Ijebu were not quite on the same level as the Fon of Dahomey. For one thing, unlike the kings of Dahomey who had made it plain that they would not have missionaries of any description in Abomey, the rulers of Ijebuland were not beyond persuasion over the matter of having Christianity introduced into their country. Given time, James Johnson was convinced, the Ijebu would accept the Gospel.[22] But had James Johnson taken the trouble to find out he would have discovered and approved the reason behind Dahomey's rejection of the missionary and his doctrine, the reason being essentially the same as that of the anti-missionary leaders of opinion in contemporary Ijebuland. For like several rulers in the Ijebu country before the 1892 conquest, the kings of Dahomey believed that the missionary was not just a disseminator of a new-fangled faith but also the knight-errant of the European soldier and ruler. Having familiarised himself with the popular versions of the origins and course of Dahomey's history James Johnson, by nature very credulous, became convinced that Dahomey "was founded in blood and ever since his [sic] whole course had been marked by blood" and wondered why Providence should have tolerated the existence of a state "so destructive, so useless for constructive purposes, so murderous and so vile".[23]

The important point to grasp about James Johnson's inconsistency and illogicality concerning the relations that in his view should exist between the British and the "independent" African states in the interior is that it was the product of a conflict of loyalties, viz., loyalty to Christianity and loyalty to African nationality. Much as he would have liked the continent to become Christianised and transformed to the technological and material standards of contemporary Europe he would not have wished this at the expense of the independence and sovereignty of African States. Whenever there was a conflict between the two loyalties he invariably resolved it in favour of loyalty to African nationality.

This point cannot be overstressed. He became the most dedicated and most sturdy defender of the territorial integrity and sovereignty of West African states in the era of the Scramble. The Yoruba, the Ashanti, the Timnes and Mendes, the Edo and the Ibo, which are the largest ethnic groups in the forest belt of West Africa, were all defended in petitions, correspondence to the Colonial Office, and in news conferences in Britain. James Johnson was primarily concerned with doing what the historian of Africa in the post Second World War period has been doing—of presenting the African side of Afro-European relations in the last quarter of the nineteenth century. From James Johnson's records and protests it is clear that the African viewpoint was entirely different from the European side of the story which the European *dramatis personae* put down for the consumption of the British public and students of Imperial History. All the major expeditions in West Africa, he said, were never provoked by Africans. They were wars of aggression by the British, who undertook them for reasons other than humanitarian. Several expeditions that claimed his attention explained the different motives of the British intruders. In the case of the expedition against Benin, for instance, he said the blame lay squarely on the heads of the British officials who were arrogant and who deliberately flouted the authority of the *Oba* of Benin who had advised them that he was not in a position to receive them until after completion of the customs in which he was then engaged.[24] James Johnson went so far as to conduct his own research as to the feelings of the Edo and the circumstances leading to the expedition against them. His conclusion was that the Edo deserved neither the "vengeful, destructive and desolating sword of the British" nor the loss of their independence.[25]

The Ashanti of the Gold Coast and the Timnes of Sierra Leone, he said, were justified in resisting the British as the expeditions against them were completely unjustifiable. In the case of the Ashanti, he pointed out, they had never enjoyed the British presence and had always made it clear that they would never like to become part of a British Protectorate.[26] As regards the Timnes their paramount rulers were right to resist the Hut Tax, for what right had the British to impose a tax on a people who had never indicated willingness to come under British rule?[27] In the case of the Ijebu Expedition several factors were at work. There were British soldiers hunting for medals who therefore did everything to provoke the Ijebu; there were also British commercial interests and British arrogance.[28] In all these circumstances, he stressed, the recalcitrant African peoples, upon whose heads the British caused fire and sword to descend, were fighting against the imposition of an undesired foreign rule. As he declared to a British audience in 1900, Africans were not hankering after the white man's rule and were fighting in order "to retain their own independence, the ownership of their own land, which they have received from their own ancestors, which they believe to have been given them by God".[29]

In West Africa there were two peoples whose physical subjugation he either positively desired or never regretted. These were the Fon of Dahomey and the Ibo of Eastern Nigeria. The latter, whom he claimed to have studied at close quarters, were extremely detestable to him in several ways. First of all, he said, they were the most degraded of all the African peoples he had ever come across. As he wrote: "The people are generally barbarous, wild and savage and scantily clothed." They had no respect for human life: "Assaults with the use of deadly weapons and murders are very common. A young man [sic] must, in order to get himself recognised as having attained manhood in society, have cut off the heads of at least two persons, men or women, and exposed them to public view."[30] Furthermore he found the terrorising activities of the Aro with their military arm, the Abams, inimical to the interest of Eastern Nigeria. But the most revolting habit that horrified him beyond description was their cannibalism. He observed: "Cannibalism appears to have sprung up among them from a desire on the part of aggrieved persons to revenge themselves upon their enemies and satisfy themselves as to the completeness of their triumph over them, and also to testify their cruel joy over it by eating them up. . . . The frequency of the practice adopted by Ibos has led to an acquisition of a liking for human flesh which has come to be preferred often to the flesh of beasts. To gratify this taste, not only are living persons frequently fallen upon and put to death; not only are the bodies on the battlefield dragged into the camp when possible and distributed; and not only is the butcher's knife frequently made to take the place of care and attention to a sick person, but dead bodies are also dug out of their graves for the purpose of being fed upon."[31] It is not surprising that he did not protest against British invasion of Iboland, as he did with respect to the invasions of Benin, Yorubaland, Ashanti and the interior of Sierra Leone. Indeed he was grateful to the British for the effort being made to suppress cannibalism in the country. In fact James Johnson went out of his way by urging the Ibo to accept British rule with good grace and "reconcile" with the alien rulers.[32]

James Johnson's various protests did not deter the British. Expedition followed expedition until the first decade of the twentieth century. Therefore he accepted establishment of colonial administration as a *fait accompli*, against which it would be futile to fulminate. In fact he appreciated and acknowledged the beneficial effects of British colonial rule, though without enthusiasm and without the emotionalism with which he had denounced the loss of African sovereignty. Railways, telegraphs, roads, maintenance of law and order, termination of chronic inter-tribal and intra-tribal warfare and establishment of schools—were all regarded by him as gains for Africans in the colonial establishment.[33] There was no question of inciting Africans against British rule. Curiously enough he was very loyal to the British and he regarded them as the most benevolent colonial power in Africa. This view was a conviction based upon his experience. A tour to the Spanish Island of Fernando Po convinced him of the relative benefit of British colonial rule. For here not only did the Spanish refuse to raise up an educated African elite but they began to suppress the latter to the extent that Africans who qualified as medical doctors were not allowed to practise their profession in urban areas. He believed that the Bubi, the indigenes of the island, would have preferred to be under British rule.[34] In the same manner he observed in the German territory of the Cameroons that the colonial power was very unpopular and that the natives desired to come under the British.[35]

Loyal as he was to the British he did not desire that their suzerainty over the territories which their fire and sword had conquered should be more than formal. Therefore all the opportunity he had at the beginning of this century was employed in advocating the doctrine of Indirect Rule, as the only practical and sensible system of administration that should be established in British West Africa. This system should be adopted, he said, because it was the only means of alleviating the bitterness which African peoples were nursing against the British for the loss of their sovereignty. The traditional rulers, he declared, must be the pillar of such a system and African customs and institutions which were not incompatible with humanity should not only be retained but studied. His view on Indirect Rule was succinctly expressed thus to a British newspaper in 1901:

> Let Great Britain rule them [Africans] through their
> own rulers, and their own native councils, and let the
> soil remain their soil, their own. In that way they will
> be conciliated, and in that way and along those lines
> they may eventually become loyal subjects of the
> British Empire.[36]

James Johnson found it difficult to believe that the British would ever establish an elaborate system of administration in the conquered territories. For instance he did not think that the British claim over Yorubaland involved nullification of the existence and authority of the "independent" states in the interior. In his judgment, as late as 1903, Yorubaland was no more than a British "sphere of influence".[37] In 1903 he defended the sovereignty of the Egba Government against the assault upon it by the British traders who moved in to the Egba country at the establishment of the *Pax Britannica*. The traders, who viewed themselves now as rulers, protested to the British Government against payment of tolls to the Egba and Ibadan authorities, tolls that they had hitherto paid. In their protest they had the support of the powerful pen of E. D. Morel, founder and editor of the influential *West African* [later *African*] *Mail*.

With some effect James Johnson demolished the arguments of the traders and was supported by the Governor, Sir William Macgregor.[38] He emphasised that the European traders were liars when they claimed that toll collecting was a recent imposition in Yorubaland. As his research revealed to him: "Toll collecting is not a new thing with Abeokuta and other Yoruba Native States. Its origin goes back hundreds of years for besides the fact that tolls had been always collected by the people long before the great disruption occasioned by the trans Atlantic slave trade, there is a tradition as long as the Yoruba Nation almost, in its heathen religious system, of Orunmila, the Divine Son of God, appearing on earth in human form, travelling about from place to place in

it for the purpose of correcting the evil practices that had well
nigh swamped it—or were prevalent in it and paying upon the
demand of the Quibade (Onibode) the toll gate Collector, the toll
demanded at the gate of him also of others."[39] As far as he was
concerned Ibadan and Egba Governments were equals with the
British Government in Lagos, and as long as the latter arrogated
to itself the right to collect customs as a source of revenue the
independent states in the interior had the right to do the same.
Since the European merchants would not object to the claim of the
British Government to the right to collect customs, James Johnson
believed that the European traders were manifesting contempt for
African Governments by denying the latter's right to tax them; the
objection of the white man in the interior to paying customs to
African Governments "savours so much of a despisal of the
Native". Were they not intruders in the interior? Who invited them
to go there?

More serious, from James Johnson's point of view, was the fact
that the attitude of the European traders was a "menace to and an
indirect attack upon the independence of their [Egba] position as
a Native Government and an effect to get Abeokuta annexed to
Lagos". For by the Treaty of 1893 the independence of the Egba
had been guaranteed by the British Government. The eyes of these
British traders were clearly on the termination of Egba independence, for "these Merchants are simply playing the role of the late
Cecil Rhodes and his confrères in South Africa".[40] The way in
which these traders would like to see Egba independence eroded,
he said, was clear from their suggestion that in place of their
traditional tolls, the Egba should be paid annual subsidies. In
his vigorous protest he declared this would be a breach of the treaty
of 1893 and a travesty of the British sense of justice and right.

Outside British West Africa James Johnson paid attention to the
fate befalling Africans in German and Spanish territories, in
Leopold's Congo and in South Africa. In all these countries, he
observed, Africans were being oppressed. The people under German
rule in the Cameroons, he said, were groaning under the colonial
rule. On the inhabitants of Fernando Po he observed: "The people
impress me as being patriotic and anxious for the independence
of Africa and the African and the Institutions of foreign origins
among them. It is a feeling shared by all classes of the native
population, rich and poor alike and it is of an intelligent
character."[41] He used the worst epithets for Leopold's "accursed
rule" in the Congo where "cruel and devilish misdeeds" were being
perpetrated on Africans by "miscreants", where "a large number
of towns and villages" were being depopulated and where men,
women and children were being "murdered in cold blood" in the

exploitation of the territory "for the support of European Commerce".[42] He hated the Afrikaners of South Africa, to the point that he wished that Africans in West Africa had been recruited by the British to fight against them in the South African War.[43] He was concerned about the plight of African miners in South Africa.

The plight of the Negroes in the New World did not escape his attention. He regarded them as Africans in exile and because of their vicissitudes in America which "closes the doors of many institutions against us for the fault, crime and sin of colour", he wanted them to return to Africa.[44] In 1890 he was a member of the Reception Committee that invited Edward Blyden, his colleague in the stormy days in Sierra Leone, to Lagos, for the expressed purpose of prospecting for a suitable area in Yorubaland where immigrants might settle down.[45] He was embittered by the racial discrimination that accompanied the establishment of colonial rule in Africa—what he described as "a recrudescence here and there of that colour prejudice which had in the past often affected to dissociate the Negro from the human family, all which suggest a slavery like to and even worse than that from which the Negro peoples in European colonial possessions on the coast and in America have been liberated".[46]

But it was in Yorubaland that James Johnson was able to interest himself most in political affairs, where he was not just an observer but an active participant and a spokesman for the Yoruba *vis-à-vis* alien peoples, both African and British. Concerning the British James Johnson did not believe that they had the intention of taking over the Yoruba country or that they constituted an enemy to Yoruba interests. Like several educated elite he believed that the traditional authorities should draw nearer to Lagos rather than move away from it; that the British would be favourably disposed towards them if they patronised Christian missions and maintained mutually beneficial economic contact with Europeans along the coast. Throughout his stay in the interior he impressed on the chiefs that their fear of the British having an eye on their sovereignty had no foundation.[47]

His interest in the affairs of Yorubaland had been active since his Sierra Leone days. Here, though far away from their fatherland, many of the Yoruba recaptives continued to be concerned about the warfare that had been responsible for their forcible exile. They used to deliberate on measures that might ameliorate the condition of their country. Such meetings James Johnson had attended as far back as 1863.[48] He diagnosed the disease of the Yoruba country correctly. Though culturally and linguistically the most homogeneous ethnic group in the forest belt of West Africa, no nation could be more divided than they were. Section fought against section, as if they were not members of the same stock, to the extent of inviting outsiders to fight against themselves. As James Johnson put it, "their own private piques and envies" were so strong with them that they would never abandon their "incorrigible selfishness" and "unite forces together" to fight against the most determined foe of Yorubaland in the nineteenth century, the Kingdom of Dahomey.[49] His analysis of Dahomian relations was anything but objective. Without investigating the causes of the unending Dahomian attack on Yorubaland throughout the century, he concluded that Dahomey was in the wrong, was "the ferocious lion of the forest", founded and thriving on blood, and incapable of any virtue. His prejudices against Dahomey were basically those manifested by contemporary missionaries and British officers like Burton, Duncan and Forbes. But had he made the attempt to ascertain the causes of the strained Yoruba-Dahomey relations he would have discovered that the Yoruba, particularly the Oyo and Egba Yoruba, had provoked Dahomey in very many ways in the past and that all that Dahomey was doing in the nineteenth century was to exact its pound of flesh.

James Johnson had prejudices in favour and against groups within the Yoruba country. He was favourably disposed to the Ijesha, the Egba and the Ijebu and undisguisedly hostile to the Ibadan. As an Ijesha by his paternal connection he could not be indifferent to the tale of wrongs and oppression which the Ijesha in Lagos used to relate to him against Ibadan, the state that became so powerful that by the outbreak of the Kiriji War in 1877 it had established an empire that covered the Ijesha and Ekiti countries in eastern Yorubaland. Breadfruit Church became the rendezvous of fomenters of rebellion against the imperial yoke of Ibadan, and was known as the Ijesha Association. Its origin is said to have dated from 1852 but its "mover and leader"[50] was Phillip Jose Meffre, an immigrant from Brazil who had been converted from Ifa to Christianity.

The avowed object of the organisation was the promotion of the welfare of the Ijesha country, socially, economically and politically. At first it consisted of Christians only but under the pretence of a wish to Christianise Muslim and "pagan" Ijesha, the latter religious groups were dragged in and the body became a sort of Benefit Society. They met at Breadfruit Church every Sunday and at every meeting a portion of the Bible was read and explained to non-Christians. But the primary aim was to achieve independence for their fatherland. Recording a meeting he had with an illiterate Ijesha woman, James Johnson said that her words on "her native home, its present subjection to the Ibadans and the independence and happiness of past days moved me with her words and tears:

the fact that her country is a subject country cuts like a dagger into her soul and would, if it were possible, place her at the head of an army".[51] James Johnson sympathised with the cause of the Ijesha, attended some of the meetings of the Ijesha Association in his early days in Nigeria and "was delighted by the spirit manifested by all".[52] Consequently at the outbreak of the Kiriji War, which broke out just a few months after he arrived in Abeokuta as Superintendent, he saw the Ijesha as fighting a war of independence.[53] But there is no evidence that he ever joined the Ekitiparapo or subscribed to the programme of the Ijesha Association, many of whose members transferred themselves physically to the Mahin country (south of Ondo) where they arranged the supply of ammunition to the warriors at Kiriji.

James Johnson nursed deep-seated hostility against Ibadan, which he labelled as the Dahomey of Yorubaland and the source of all warfare in the country. First of all he found distasteful Ibadan's unbridled militarism which enabled it to establish an empire over other Yoruba groups. Secondly he heard tales of Ibadan's *Ajeles* (consuls) in the Ijesha country and witnessed the oppressive activities of Ibadan's emissaries in the Oke Ogun areas. Moreover he was convinced that Ibadan's imperial ambition was insatiable, that she was harbouring the intention of assimilating the coastal kingdoms of the Egba and Ijebu to her empire. Thirdly he was disappointed that little or no interest was being evinced in Christianity by men of substance in Ibadan. The disease of Ibadan, he said, was warfare and he held them up as the real cause of all wars, eternal trigger-pullers:

> Occupation is various, but war is the principal one followed by not a few: it is that which promises prominence and important social position. All less exciting employments are subordinated to this and sometimes despised. . . . Everything around them helps to develop and strengthen the war element. War and the battlefield and the exploits therein and captives of enemies are daily topics of conversation. There are annual expeditions. A *causa belli* is easily found. The wars waged are I am afraid more offensive and aggressive than defensive.[54]

In contrast to the Ibadan warmongers were the supposedly peace-loving Egba, according to James Johnson. With regards to the Egba he was being guided more by fancy than by facts. He declared, like several missionary observers before him, that in the various wars that had honeycombed the Yoruba country since the beginning of the century the Egba had been blameless, had been peace-loving, had been thirsty after Christianity and were primarily concerned with agriculture.[55] The true position was certainly different from that imagined by James Johnson and the missionary observers. The Egba had their due share of blame for the wars that engulfed Yorubaland in the nineteenth century. Since their settlement in Abeokuta around 1830 they had fought aggressive wars, spreading themselves westward on land that belonged to the Egbado and displacing the authority of the *Alafin* in that part of Yorubaland. In the Ijaye War of 1860 to 1865 warmongers among the Egba were dreaming of driving away the Oyo Yoruba from the Egba home-steads which the latter had occupied in the last days of the Old Oyo Empire. The Egba consistently provoked Dahomey by harbour-ing refugees from Dahomey and by involving themselves in the politics of Ado and Porto Novo, areas within the orbit of Dahomey's authority.[56] Even in the Kiriji War in some ways the Egba might be described as the aggressors. According to an account by James Johnson himself the Ibadan caravan from Porto Novo that was alleged to be carrying arms in May 1877 took care to avoid Egba territory but was fired upon by the Egba, a provocative act that the Ibadan took coolly.[57] In fact so anxious were the Ibadan for peace that they asked the Ijebu at once to mediate. But the Egba followed their act of provocation with another—expulsion of all Ibadan people from the Egba country.[58] The fact that the Egba did not participate very actively in the Kiriji War after 1879 can be explained: their territorial integrity was no longer menaced after that date when the Ibadan had to deal with the rebellion of the Ekitiparapo who were being aided by the Muslim army of Ilorin.

There is no truth whatsoever in the statement by James Johnson, that the Egba were anxious to become Christians or had eagerly embraced Christianity. The true position was that only one chief—John Okenla—became a Christian, even though many of the chiefs were far more accommodating to Christianity than in other parts of the interior of West Africa. For they perceived the political and military advantages which the Egba derived from the presence of missionaries and their wards in the Yoruba country. Toleration of missionary propaganda by the Egba, on a scale without parallel in, for example, Ashanti and Dahomey, affected the judgment of James Johnson, as of other missionaries. But the Egba were surely far remote from the following picture of them painted by James John-son during the Kiriji War:

> Egbas are not disposed to war: they do not generally care for it—agriculture and commerce are what they care for. Since the determination to fight with Ibadan I have often heard them say—'since white men [missionaries chiefly] told us it is better to betake ourselves to trade and agriculture than pursue war, we have given it up and have turned farmers and traders. We do not want war'. Heathens and Christians alike have thus

spoken. There is [a] force already created: it is the force of Christianity, of legitimate commerce, of agricultural industry and of native experience of their superior advantages.[59]

Indeed he was so much carried away by sentiment that he came to see the Kiriji War in terms of Christianity versus traditional religion, the former being represented by the Egba and the latter by Ibadan. Victories by the Egba in skirmishes were lauded out of their value and those by Ibadan underwritten. The achievements of the Egba in the war, James Johnson affected to believe, were owed to Christianity. As he said, "true Christianity inspires its professor with courage and boldness".[60] The grounds for this conviction were that the brunt of fighting fell on the Christian party in Abeokuta, under the leadership of Balogun John Owolatan Okenla. It was Christians who led the Egba army in the war and in a public meeting their leader was reported to have boasted of his Christianity as follows: "which of you, which of the Baloguns of Abeokuta has been able to show on the battlefield the courage it has been my privilege to show? None, no one can gainsay this. What has made the difference? Christianity the religion I now profess and which I took up in the full manhood of my life."[61] James Johnson was intensely proud of the military prowess of the Christians and was immensely delighted that this military capacity increased the prestige and the influence of the Christian party in Egbaland. The result was that by 1879 they had constituted a power to be reckoned with even in the selection of Oyekan, the Alake. It was already patent that they could not be persecuted again with impunity or treated like second class citizens as in the period before 1875.

But James Johnson must not be dismissed just as a partial observer of the power-politics of Yorubaland. As a man deeply interested in Yoruba affairs he was aware that the economic interpretation of Yoruba warfare in the nineteenth century, which coloured the official despatches and which has been reiterated by present day historians, was incorrect. The efforts of the Ijebu and the Egba to prevent the Oyo Yoruba and the Ijesha from having unrestricted access to the coast, he recorded, was not primarily motivated by the desire to monopolise the trade with Europeans. It was political considerations that determined the attitude of the Ijebu and the Egba to the routes, and not because they found economic contact with the Europeans so advantageous to the point that they would like the routes to be controlled for economic purposes regardless of the hazards. It was the fear that Ibadan would use the routes for military purposes against the Ijebu and the Egba that persuaded these tribal groups to close them against the Oyo Yoruba.[62]

So deep was James Johnson's interest in Yoruba politics that

o

his papers are the best source for an understanding of the economic effects of the Kiriji War on the Egba and Oyo Yoruba peoples. In Ibadan, he observed, so serious was the effect of the war that in 1879 people began to pawn themselves for ten shillings.[63] The price of food like meat and corn went up more than fourfold. By April 1878 the price of salt in Ibadan had risen from 1s. 6d. per lb. to 10s. per lb. and provision prices rocketed by 600 per cent. The Ijebu and the Egba, who were in a position to trade with Lagos, did not feel the pinch as did the peoples in the interior.

However, after 1880 James Johnson was not visibly partisan in Yoruba politics and in spite of his sentiments in favour of some parties his chief objective for the Yoruba was the achievement of peace. In 1882, 1883 and 1889 he presided over meetings of Lagosians and educated elite which resulted in sending deputations to the Lagos Government and the Awujale for mediation in the Kiriji War. In these years he was consulted by the Lagos Government on the interior problems and he received the commendation of Sir Samuel Rowe and Sir Alfred Moloney.[64] It should be stressed that it was expected that the aid being sought from the British would be given by the latter *gratis*; it was not expected that it should be a convenient pretext or excuse for the instalment of British suzerainty in the Yoruba country, which British aid eventually became.

In a sense, then, wittingly or unwittingly James Johnson and others like him contributed to the establishment of the British Raj in Nigeria. By advocating the Christian religion as best for Africa a cornerstone in the cohesion of traditional society was being threatened; by advocating contact between the white man and the adoption of his language, his material tastes and technological know-how, it ought to have occurred to him that the more powerful white man would eventually lord it over weak Africa. Educated elite of the kind of James Johnson were in themselves, ironically, a potential threat to the cultural and political systems of Africa and unconscious, but effective, mental collaborators with the white man with whom they shared a common ideology and mental attitude. It is important to bear in mind this point in any analysis of the exertions of this African patriot, or of any African patriot for that matter, towards the preservation of the territorial integrity and cultural heritage of Africa and Africans.

Throughout his career and in Yorubaland the people whose political fortunes attracted his attention most and for whom he staked all his talents were the Ijebu, with whom it will be recalled, he was connected by his mother. The British found the Ijebu very difficult to deal with. For the British were able to engage in some form of dialogue with other Yoruba groups either through Euro-

pean missionaries or African agents or associations. In other parts
of Yorubaland there was no question of the complete dominance
of British influence commercially or otherwise, to the extent the
British wished. But this was not the case with the Ijebu, whose
proximity to Lagos should have made British influence strongest.
The dialogue that existed between the Ijebu and the British was
formal and enforced, rather like that between two independent
states. There were no missionaries who could indirectly, though
effectually, keep the British informed of internal happenings; no
educated elite whose cultural and mental attachment to Britain
could make them potential collaborators and fifth columnists whenever the British were to come into the Ijebu country; no semblance
of British influence in any way. Indeed the wall between Lagos
and Ijebu Ode was strong and seemed unscalable.

Between 1852 and 1856 all efforts made by the C.M.S. to
establish stations on Ijebu soil failed. And yet the Christianisation
of Ijebuland was desirable from the point of view of Christian
missions in several ways. First of all it was noticed that the Ijebu
were more intelligent than their neighbours. Secondly Ijebuland
was compact and geographically strategic, as the natural gateway
to the Oyo Yoruba country in the interior; for routes through the
territory would reduce both time and expense by more than 40
per cent. Thirdly the demographic pattern seemed to be favourable
to missionary expansion. Largely village communities, it was
thickly populated with villages and towns situated within fifteen
miles of each other. Fourthly Ijebuland was relatively peaceful,
having been untouched by the civil war that transformed the demographic pattern of the northern half of the Yoruba country in the
nineteenth century.

The desire to Christianise this people had consumed James
Johnson in his Sierra Leonian days and it will be recalled that the
hope that he would achieve this end was one of the main reasons
for his transfer to Nigeria. Hardly had he landed in Lagos than he
began to study and learn to understand the attitude of the Ijebu
to British intruders generally. In his judgment the Ijebu were a
very remarkable people, the acme of what Africans ought to be.
In principle they were not opposed to Christianity as such; what
they feared like the plague were the political implications which,
they perceived, would accompany the introduction of the Gospel
into their country. In James Johnson's view the Ijebu were endowed
with rare attributes, many of which were not only absent in Lagos
but in contemporary European society. Intelligent, shrewd, intensely
patriotic and cautiously conservative, they were fanatically jealous
not only of their independence but also of the territorial integrity
of all Yorubaland. Unlike other peoples, declared James Johnson,

the Ijebu were never liars and were strict observers of international agreements.[65] Unlike so-called Christians from Lagos the Ijebu were not "thieves" and in their commercial relations with Lagos integrity was their watchword. Then, unlike all their neighbours, they were peace-lovers. As he wrote of them in 1878: "Whatever might have been their predilections for war before they hate it now with intense hatred."[66] Also they were an industrious people, excellent traders and able agriculturists. It was in Ijebuland, too, that the institution of slavery was not only the most humane but also where slave labour was not employed on the farm. Above all, from James Johnson's point of view, they were passionately proud of their customs and institutions which they believed were best for themselves and which they would not like to see modified or replaced by alien customs. Consequently, of all the tribal groups in Yorubaland, they were the most sensitive to the imperialistic designs of the Lagos Government and were unceasing in trying to persuade the Ibadan, the Egba and the Ondo to withdraw their patronage of missionaries whom the Ijebu regarded as heralds of British imperialism.[67]

These attributes, which James Johnson believed were the unique possession of the Ijebu, virtually hypnotised him to the extent that whatever defects existed in their society paled into insignificance. They were attributes of African patriots and sturdy defenders of African culture and sovereignty. Therefore, he said, the Ijebu should be given a different treatment as far as missionary enterprise was concerned. Slavery, traditional religion, human sacrifice, their "self conceit and extra-strong conservatism" should not provide any excuse for forcible evangelisation of their country;[68] their qualities were so priceless that infinite patience should be exercised. But he believed that if they could be convinced that acceptance of Christianity would eliminate, rather than confirm, their fears they would eagerly embrace it. As he wrote: "What excellent qualities they possess cannot fail sanctified by God to be an advantage to the cause of Christianity if they possess it."[69] To this end he was extremely patient in his missionary effort in the Ijebu country. As mentioned in an earlier chapter it was the Remo section of Ijebu-land to which he devoted attention in the seventies. The humiliation he suffered notwithstanding he went back to Iperu again and again and he should be held responsible for the untimely death of the paramount ruler of that town whose life was taken from him by his chiefs because he had shown hospitality to this intruding and importunate James Johnson.[70] In 1882 he went to see the Akarigbo of Remo and secured a plot of land for a mission station after James Johnson had given the assurance that patronage of Christianity would ward off, rather than aid, British imperialism in the country.[71] In 1889 he and Otunba Payne had begun to be personally responsible for two agents whom they had persuaded the Awujale to receive.

But most missionaries and British officials saw the Ijebu, particularly those under the immediate eyes of the Awujale, in a different light. Ijebu's cautious conservatism was misconstrued as reactionary traditionalism and their patriotism and love for their customs and institutions as anti-British behaviour and barbarism. For the Ijebu people refused to allow white people to enter their territory and study their customs and institutions. Even the movements of other Yorubas in their kingdom were strictly regulated. Missionaries were particularly hated by the Ijebu, partly because they had learned through Kosoko the role which these professors of a new religion had played in the British occupation of Lagos,[72] partly because they were convinced that their traditional religion was the best for them, and partly because they associated missionaries with social and political subversion. But they also nursed implacable contempt for the white man, from whom they did not believe anything worth learning could emanate. For the Ijebu believed that the white man was an inferior being, a "peeled" man and descendant of a legendary albino, whom an unkind Providence had condemned to live beyond the sea after Man had been created at Ile Ife.[73] The Ijebu believed that their national guardian, *Obanta*, had decreed that they should have nothing to do with the white man. This was why the Awujale swore never to defile himself by shaking hand with a white man and why the unwelcome presence of any white man in the Ijebu territory used to arouse horror and was always followed by sacrifices to appease the gods.[74]

None of the intruders—missionaries, traders and administrators—ever appreciated the Ijebu viewpoint. They all described the Ijebu as selfish middle-men sharks who exploited both people in the interior and the European traders alike. They failed to understand the fact that trade was not paramount in Ijebu thinking, that the Ijebu restricted the commercial frontiers of the European traders to the markets of Ikosi, Ejinrin and Ikorodu, primarily because they feared that unrestricted European movements in Yorubaland would result ultimately in the political subjugation of the territory. So jealous were the Ijebu of their independence that, it is said, the Awujale made a law to the effect that no Ijebu should owe any Lagos man any debt, lest the Lagos Government made that a pretext for attacking their territory.[75] It was the same fear of loss of their territory and independence that made the Ijebu refuse to allow missionaries to establish themselves in their country. The intruders replied to the Ijebu's love of independence with undisguised hostility and stigmatised Ijebu country as the nursery of slaves and Ijebu's frequent closure of roads as the main cause of the eternal civil war in the Yoruba country.[76]

From the point of view of James Johnson the effort he and others were making through the Ijebu Society were already producing favourable results by 1890. The Awujale was indeed anxious to see Christianity strongly established in his country. Even in matters of trade the Ijebu Society began to persuade the Awujale to understand the principle of Free Trade. Under the belief that in England the restrictions hitherto placed on Africans to buy directly had been removed, the educated Ijebu elite wrote to the paramount ruler in August 1890: "We would like you to understand that there is a great change in the world now. The principle of free trade rules generally . . . we would respectfully advise you to remove every difficulty to travelling through your country to the interior or to Lagos, and to Lagos people also. Ijebu will not lose by this; it will gain much, only the benefits will be more generally distributed. . . . Missionaries are not traders. Their mission is one of love, they seek to do good to men's souls and bodies. Allow them free access to you and through the country, and make no charge whatsoever on their journey."[77] It is significant to note that Moloney conceded the fact that the Ijebu were becoming pervious to enlightenment and that he encouraged James Johnson and Payne to be unrelaxing in their worthy efforts.[78] Indeed, since Moloney had no intention of annexing the Ijebu territory, he found the Awujale very co-operative and friendly, and emphasised to the Colonial Office the cordiality of Anglo-Ijebu relations at a time that Anglo-Egba relations were nearing a breaking point.[79]

Anglo-Ijebu relations could improve to a *détente* at James Johnson's pace only as long as Moloney was Governor. As was the case in his fortune in the Legislative Council a change in his relations with administrators began with the termination of the Moloney era. Hardly had Moloney left Lagos than the Acting Governor, Captain Denton, tactlessly, and according to the Ijebu sources intentionally, awakened Ijebu's suspicions about British intentions towards the Ijebu country. Ijebu sources indicate that Denton, himself son of an Anglican minister, egged on by war-disposed traders, was determined on a showdown which would eventuate in the conquest of Ijebuland by "Christian England".[80] In the Legislative Council where Denton gave a lurid picture of the "insult" that had been inflicted on him and the British Empire, James Johnson refused to accept the Denton version of that affair, but blamed the Acting Governor for provoking the Ijebu deliberately by his "surprise" visit with a military entourage and by his attempt to purchase Ijebu sovereignty with money.[81] In Ijebu Ode, contended James Johnson, Denton had behaved in an anti-Ijebu manner in spite of the civility which the Ijebu had returned for his tactlessness and threatening behaviour. When in June 1891 the Egba reiterated their claim to Ebute Metta, Denton readily ascribed the Egba claim to supposed Ijebu instigation.[82]

It was at this stage that George Thomas Carter arrived. The intractable nationalist Johnson and the imperious imperialist Carter could hardly be expected to see eye to eye. It may be said that Carter was to Johnson like an irresistible force being applied to an irremovable object. Their bitterest duel was over the Ijebu crisis. Within a week of his arrival in September 1891 Carter unleashed his hostility towards the Ijebu in bitter words which he repeated often for six years. Without any first-hand knowledge of them he announced that the Ijebu were absolutely bereft of all virtues, were the embodiment of all conceivable vices, "every vice a native race could have", including the worst form of slavery, human sacrifice and "fetishism". They were "extremely conservative, averse to change, and intractable to the last degree".[83] James Johnson could hardly believe his ears when on 14 December 1891 Carter declared in the Legislative chamber: "All who have followed the past history of Jebu in reference to this Colony will admit that the time for talking has gone by and the period for decisive action come." They were a "bar to the development of the rich country beyond".[84]

The records make it clear that Carter was bent on war, even at times when the Colonial Office gave him emphatic instructions to work for peace. There is no evidence, except his own, that the Colonial Office instructed him to demand an "apology" for the alleged insult the Ijebu had inflicted on Denton. The official records reveal clearly that over the Denton affair the Colonial Office was divided into hawks and doves. There was in fact only one hawk, A. W. Hemming, who on 27 October 1891 minuted that some "decided action should be taken against the Jebus and to punish them" and that the opportunity should be seized to break down "the middle wall of partition, which they have set up between the trade of the interior and Lagos".[85] He represented the view of the traders, who were execrated by James Johnson and the other members of the "Jebu Descendants" who sent their version of the Ijebu crisis to the Aborigines Protection Society. R. H. Meade, another official, and Lord H. T. H. Knutsford, Secretary of State for the Colonies, made it plain that no war should be waged against the Ijebu, that a blockade might be considered and that the Egba, rather than the Ijebu, qualified for punishment.[86] Indeed Carter had made up his mind to destroy the Ijebu kingdom on the grounds of their supposed backwardness and "vices" alone. As he confessed in later years: "In view of these facts I could not but feel that a service would be done to humanity, and a wholesome impetus given civilisation, by the breaking of this baneful and oppressive organisation known as the Jebu Kingdom."[87]

By December 1891 relations between Carter and Johnson were so strained that altercations were exchanged in the Legislative Council. For the next four months James Johnson and other patriots exerted themselves to see that the crisis did not develop into an armed conflict. The Ijebu were pressed to give no cause whatsoever for British wrath. Hence when Carter sent a message to the Ijebu authorities, demanding that a high-powered delegation should be dispatched to "apologise" for the alleged insult on Denton and to discuss the question of routes no time was lost to answer Carter's summons. But James Johnson was distressed at the methods and attitude being employed by Carter at every stage. Rather than treat the delegates as ambassadors of a respectable government, in every respect equal to that of the British Government, Carter treated them with contempt, as if they were a conquered people. Before any formal meeting took place the military capacity of the British was displayed in a parade to convey to the Ijebu delegates the message that fire and sword awaited their country if they refused to do the bidding of the Lagos Government. At the meeting, where the delegates were very meek but firmly uncompromising about Ijebu's sovereignty, Carter's manners were brusque, menacing, haughty and blustering.[88] The delegates "apologised" for the alleged insult, declared the routes open and then urged the Governor to bring Ibadan warriors back to their country from the battlefront at Offa.

Carter's answer was to attempt to decoy the delegates to sign a treaty that would have compromised Ijebu sovereignty severely. However, though unlettered the delegates were equal to the occasion. They perceived in the "treaty", a death warrant and so they refused to sign it because they had no mandate for such an undertaking. They declared that as they "knew no book" and such "book" was contrary to their religion they would have nothing to do with it, all the threats notwithstanding. In the circumstances, as far as James Johnson was concerned, Carter added one indiscretion after another by causing the violation of a Yoruba custom, kolanut splitting.[89] The Governor asked two educated Ijebu—Payne and one Jacob Williams—to 'sign' the treaty on behalf of the Ijebu and asked Otunba Payne to perform the custom of splitting kolanut.

James Johnson was enraged at the treatment meted out to the delegates, a treatment of which he was at every stage an eye witness. For him the so-called treaty upon which Carter was to base his action for military subjugation of the Ijebu was null and void. By civilised standards, he declared, "parties to a compact are expected to agree together upon its terms".[90] But the so-called treaty of

21 January 1892 was never signed or ratified by the Ijebu Government, and they disclaimed any connection with it. Nor did the delegates have anything to do with it; they dared not take a copy of the so-called treaty to Ijebuland. As James Johnson protested after the expedition mounted against the Ijebu in the name of the "treaty": "If the deputies refused to sign the treaty, as indeed they did—if the splitting of the kolanuts was not their own act, as it would have been had they approved of the proceeding—if the Ijebu Government refused, as indeed it did, to accept and ratify the treaty and disclaimed any responsibility in connection with the signing of the treaty and the kolanut splitting said to have been had over it, where, I ask was the treaty, for an alleged breach of which an army was marched to Ijebu, hundreds of its people driven to eternity, its Government broken up, and its independence taken away from it or placed in a very uncertain and doubtful position."[91]

It is not surprising that James Johnson saw Carter as an "Iconoclast" who came to destroy his achievements in Ijebuland. He and other educated Africans exerted every effort to see that the so-called treaty of 21 January 1892, notwithstanding the Ijebu, should give no cause for war. Even after the outrageous and overbearing behaviour of the missionaries, who deliberately worked for war, made the Ijebu "break" the so-called treaty, James Johnson still believed that the crisis could be peacefully resolved; he did all he could to persuade the Ijebu to remain calm. Johnson and other educated Africans, the white cap chiefs and the Ogboni of Lagos, took steps that they believed would settle the crisis in a peaceful manner. On 16 April 1892 a strong delegation was sent to Ijebu Ode to ascertain the facts, as the Ijebu saw them, and persuade the Ijebu to grant Carter all he wanted.[92] It was believed by the Africans that if the Ijebu authorities were allowed thirty days to resolve the internal tension that had been created by the series of provocative acts by the Lagos Government and missionaries there would be no war.

But Carter had no intention of a peaceful solution to the Ijebu crisis. While he assured James Johnson that in principle he was not against the peace efforts of the Africans in Lagos he was busy manœuvring the all-white Executive Council and the Colonial Office into war against the Ijebu. For up until 10 March 1892 both the Executive Council and the Colonial Office sanctioned only a blockade of the Ijebu and the Egba, the latter having closed their routes in protest against British annexation of Ilaro. As the minutes of the Executive Council testify, Carter fathered the idea of a military expedition on its members and went as far as saying that the authorisation of the Colonial Office for war need not be awaited. On 19 March, say the Minutes, "he [Carter] was strongly of opinion that an expedition to Jebu Ode would be far more satisfactory than instituting blockade, and would have a more permanent effect. His Excellency therefore asked Council whether they agreed that this was the best thing to do and whether they were of the opinion that the Expedition ought to be undertaken."[93] On 4 April he declared that his opinion "was that the British flag should be hoisted at Jebu Ode and other places: as it appeared to him useless expense undertaking this expedition unless some portion of the Jebu territory were taken possession of".[94]

There is no doubt that Carter had begun to act clandestinely, outside the Legislative Council, because he would have had to put up with the diatribes of James Johnson in the legislative chamber. Moreover a revelation of his military plan and his determination to destroy the Ijebu Kingdom would have provided James Johnson with a weapon with which to whip up public opinion against Carter, with reverberations in the British press and the House of Commons, as actually happened after the expedition. Carter's bellicosity was unabated; he was beyond persuasion. On the eve of the expedition Carter boasted that he would wipe out the Ijebu from existence and repeople their country with their erstwhile foes, the Ibadan.[95]

James Johnson was intensely mortified by the expedition launched against the Ijebu in May 1892 in which, in his language, thousands of Ijebu people were "murdered" by the British.[96] To his surprise Carter found himself dragged before the tribunal of British public opinion, through the numerous, impassioned and lengthy accounts which James Johnson sent to Travers Buxton, the energetic Secretary of the Aborigines Protection Society. Never before in Nigeria had a British Governor been so attacked by an African in the unrestrained manner in which James Johnson attacked Carter and revealed facts which differed from the official reports. Never before had the British Government been so virulently criticised in the manner of James Johnson in his letters, a few of which ultimately were put before the House of Commons.[97] In fact the Colonial Office had to ask Carter to offer explanation for his deeds. In effect Carter's administration was put on trial. The Governor found himself cornered into the defensive by James Johnson's exposure of his activities. Slurring over the issue he defended his actions on purely humanitarian grounds.[98] Every argument advanced by the Governor in the official dispatches, which were shown to James Johnson by the Aborigines Protection Society, was demolished by him in detail.

James Johnson's letters are of undoubted historiographical significance, a hint to historians that the official despatches should not be regarded as being free from distortion. For James Johnson disputed every fact in the official despatches and Johnsonians threatened to take legal action against the Governor for misrepresenting James Johnson's role in the Ijebu crisis.[99] It should also be remarked that the Johnsonians were restrained from taking legal action by the Aborigines Protection Society after Carter had apologised to James Johnson. The latter accepted the apology but, as noted earlier, with the significant regret that historians of the Ijebu expedition were likely to use the official records by Carter to his (Johnson's) discredit.[100] Also worthy of note is the fact that the Johnsonians regrettably allowed themselves to be persuaded by the Aborigines Protection Society to destroy the papers containing the African views, which they had threatened to publish in order to reveal further Carter's distortion of facts in the official dispatches.

A character like James Johnson, for whom veracity was of the utmost importance, found it impossible to believe that a Governor pontificating on a people he had never seen before should be trusted. What right and what experience, he asked, had Carter to write on the Ijebu crisis, a matter which went back to the middle of the nineteenth century? In his judgment: "The Governor might have allowed natives, who have followed with interest the march of events in their country, have lived long among the people and acquired information from them, to be as much acquainted with the history of important affairs in it as himself, if not more so. It so happens that I have been brought much into contact with the question of the chronic interior warfare and the road-closing connected with it by both Abeokuta and Ijebu against Ibadan."[101]

The Ijebu expedition removed the illusions he had been entertaining since his Sierra Leone days about the purpose of British presence in West Africa. He found it difficult to understand why the British Government should have approved of an action which, in his opinion, was extremely reprehensible and in many ways unbecoming of "a rich, great, powerful and professedly Christian nation".[102] An expedition against the Ijebu or against any Yoruba state was the last thing he ever expected. In many ways the Ijebu expedition contravened the ethical and national principles to which he dedicated his life. First of all the commercial explanation offered by traders and supported by the Governor and the British press, he contended, had no ethical validity and was a demonstration of the fact that in commercial transactions Europe would not deal with Africa on the basis of equality. For, as stated earlier in this chapter, the British traders in West Africa and in particular those who engineered the Ijebu expedition, were middlemen. "Since this is the case," declared James Johnson, "I ask by what law do they demand, as a thing to which they have a right, that Ijebu should surrender its position as a middleman to them in order to increase their trade profit? and how can the British Government justify the war it has waged with it in support of this demand?"[103]

The events which culminated in the expedition against the Ijebu revealed to James Johnson in bold relief that for the British there was no question of sanctity for African States; that they did not recognise the existence of the "independent" Yoruba States and that, therefore, there could be no question of treating them as sovereign states and equals with the Lagos Government. Nor were the British concerned with ethics, as their behaviour in respect to the so-called treaty showed. He was equally disappointed with the role played by the British missionaries, particularly Herbert Tugwell, and the way in which this missionary insulted the Ijebu authorities, laws and customs. He could discern that British occupation of the Ijebu country might be only a prelude to the annexation of Yorubaland. As he protested: "The British Government has begun with Ijebu. We know not where and when it will cease the work of destruction to which it now addresses itself."[104] He was henceforth apprehensive that the British aim was "to reduce native kings and princes and princesses and chiefs to the position of common subjects, and to a condition of abject dependence upon it—poverty and beggary".[105] As his vision of a sovereign Yorubaland collapsed before him he wrote like a defeated man: "The British Government may break up and even efface Ijebu. It may smash up Abeokuta and otherwise injure and weaken the Yoruba country. It may, for the benefit of its own trade, deprive the interior countries of their independence. It may succeed to get itself feared by all around. But I fear it has lost no small measure of the respect, affection and interest and confidence had for and in it before and its prestige with the whole interior country generally."[106]

James Johnson's championship of the cause of Ijebuland was undertaken at a high price. Henceforth he was regarded as a dangerous agitator in the Colonial Office. Representations by him on social, moral and political issues were accepted with courtesy, but were often pigeon-holed or treated with casualness.

Nevertheless from the missionary viewpoint and the interests of the Ijebu that he had so much at heart the Ijebu Expedition was a blessing in disguise and gave him his chief task for the remaining part of the nineteenth century. This opportunity would not have arisen through the slow and uncertain process of evangelisation and enlightenment in which he had so much faith. It was largely the Remo section of Ijebuland that occupied his attention. His dual position in the Lagos Church Mission, the missionary wing of the Lagos Native Pastorate, was of advantage to the Remo. In his capacity as Secretary to this body he compiled reports annually; as Superintendent of the Remo District the political events in the area, particularly the nature of British colonial rule, received his attention. In his characteristic fashion he threw himself into the task as the chief co-ordinator, once more behaving more or less like a Bishop,

as in the period 1877 to 1880. During his superintendence stations
grew from three in 1892 to eleven in 1900, with an average of 500
adherents. In 1898 when the C.M.S., who had been in charge of the
Ijebu Ode district, transferred this area to the Lagos Church
Mission, James Johnson had to add this area also to his task. His
reports, which were printed, are not only comprehensive but form
the main source for a study of the growth of C.M.S. work in the
Remo District.[107]

The point that should concern us here is James Johnson's attitude
to the political implication of missionary work in the Ijebu country.
Before the expedition he had laboured to convince chiefs in the
Remo District that acceptance of Christianity would enhance rather
than endanger their prestige, that it would deter rather than hasten
the British advent. It was in this belief that in 1890 the Akarigbo,
the paramount ruler of the Remo, had granted land for missionary
purposes;[108] it was also for this reason that Remo chiefs had shown
their enthusiasm for Christianity at the time of the expedition,
thinking that their escape from the exemplary punishment which the
Ijebu Ode people had suffered was due to their pro-missionary
attitude. But within two years, to their consternation, they discovered that patronage of missionary enterprise did not absolve
them from British rule and in very many ways eroded away their
sovereignty. For in 1894 the Remo country was declared part of
the British Protectorate and soldiers and administrative officers
were posted in their midst. Panic-stricken the Akarigbo urged
James Johnson to help arrange with the Lagos Government the sort
of independence being enjoyed by the Egba according to the Anglo-
Egba treaty of 1893.[109]

But not only did the chiefs begin to regret that they had lost
their sovereignty to the British, they also regretted that the presence
of the agents located in their domains by the Lagos Church
Missions had encouraged their subjects to flout their authority. For
their subjects who had embraced the white man's religion became
disobedient, believing that conversion had absolved them from
tribal duties and loyalties to their chiefs. Nor could the chiefs
appreciate the fact that immemorial customs and institutions had
begun to lose their force and sanctity. In some areas the chiefs
became incensed that Mission agents did not check the excesses of
the "wild" Hausa troops stationed in the country; others were
annoyed that the agents began to assume an air of superiority over
traditional rulers, posing as agents of British rule. Many chiefs did
not like the idea that mission agents did nothing to prevent slaves
from running away from their masters. These were some of the
problems to which James Johnson had to address himself in the
last decade of the nineteenth century.[110] He did not approve of

the disloyalty of the converts to the traditional authorities, but as he lived in Lagos there was little he could do about the endless conflicts, between them and the natural rulers, which featured so much in his annual reports.

Few people were aware of the bold fight put forward by James Johnson on behalf of the sovereignty of Ijebuland before the expedition; the chiefs, too, were mostly unaware of the feeble attempts he made to persuade the converts to behave themselves and respect traditional authority after 1892. But by 1916 James Johnson's exertions on behalf of Ijebu's interests had become widely known and acclaimed by the Ijebu people. For in that year he performed what was to the masses of the Ijebu country a miracle: he caused a deposed rightful Awujale to be reinstated by the British Government.

The story of the miracle is simply stated. In the middle of November 1915 the Awujale, Fusigboye, died. The choice of a new Awujale was the prerogative of a special kind of court officers known as the *Odis*, subject to specific laws among which the following were of the greatest importance. First of all the successor must be taken from the family whose turn it was by rotation to provide an Awujale. By 1916 there were only three royal families left. Secondly the candidate selected must possess the following qualifications. He must be an *Abidagba*, that is a person (male) born at the time when his father was on the throne; he must be a freeborn and his mother must not be a slave; he must have no physical deformity. Lastly he must be a man of integrity. In November 1915 it was the turn of the Tunwashe family to present a candidate but the only qualified candidate, Adenuga, was too young. Therefore the *Odis* decided to ask the next Ruling House to present a candidate, with the understanding that by the time of this candidate's death Adenuga would be old enough to wear the crown. Consequently Ademolu of the Anikilaya family was selected by the *Odis*, was duly recommended to the chiefs and was duly crowned as Awujale. It is significant to note that James Johnson was not only consulted by the Ijebu kingmakers but that he participated in the selection and was "the principal eyewitness of the nomination, election and coronation" of the new king.[111] The legality of this decision was not disputed by the British Government.

Matters would have rested there but for the extremely indiscreet, rash, injudicious and unwarranted intervention of the Resident of Abeokuta Province, Commissioner P. V. Young. On 27 August 1916 this white officer, who was in control of Abeokuta at the time of the Ijemo revolt of 1914, peremptorily deposed Ademolu on the ground that he was a "weak" man, in favour of a younger member of the same family, by the name of Adekoya. In fairness to the British officer it should be stated that he was trying to be a modernist, preferring a young and literate man to Ademolu, who had no other asset than that he qualified according to traditional laws. For in age he was already seventy-six and from all account he was demonstrably physically unfit to perform the functions of his office. In the words of another administrative officer, he was "so decrepit and feeble a personality" that he could neither reign nor rule.[112] Commissioner Young believed that the laws of succession that had placed such a misfit on the throne had become outdated, and that they should be modified to serve the changing society of the Ijebu. Moreover he believed that, as the chief officer of His Majesty's Government in Abeokuta Province, British sense of right and authority should be final, rather than such laws which, as it seemed to Young, had ceased to justify the reason for their existence.

However, Commissioner Young did not fully appreciate the force of tradition and the fact that a theoretically right viewpoint and excellent intentions were one thing, whilst what was administratively expedient another. The Ijebu could not have understood his excellent intentions at the expense of the immemorial laws and customs which the application of Young's ideas involved. For Adekoya, the man unilaterally selected by the Resident, was singularly unqualified. He was not an *Abidagba*; his mother was a slave; he was an ex-convict and one of his toes was missing. In other words Adekoya violated all the rules. In spite of the opposition registered by the people of Ijebuland about the deposition of Ademolu, Young installed Adekoya before the palace and he was acclaimed Awujale by policemen and prisoners. Needless to say it was a mock installation, a big joke, as the traditional kingmakers would not perform the rituals and ceremonies which by tradition used to last months.

The whole affair was extremely offensive to James Johnson's conception of right and justice. From the nationalistic point of view Young's behaviour was a clear demonstration of British authoritarianism, a humiliation being inflicted upon a conquered people. Since 1892 the Ijebu had been smarting under the humiliation of British jurisdiction, the Awujale being reduced to the position of a cypher. It was one thing to deprive a people of their sovereignty and devalue the institution of monarchy, but it was quite a different thing to treat with contempt the laws and institutions of a people, which laws and institutions the people believed were the determinants of their cohesion, their prosperity, their pride, their solidarity and their future, and which determined the essence of their soul. It is against this background of wounded pride and feelings, this fear for their future bliss being thrown into jeopardy, that the reaction of the Ijebu people to the actions of Commissioner Young should be understood.

Rather than be under the rule of a "usurper", several people left the area under the Awujale's immediate control. For the Ijebu people Adekoya, who resorted to persecution of the hostile population, was an instrument of British oppression. The "usurper" and his supporters further enraged the people by deliberate distortion of, and misinformation about, Ijebu laws of succession which they expected the British to countenance.

The problem that confronted the kingmakers and chiefs and the people generally was how to put before the British Government the facts of the case, how to represent the wounded feelings of the masses and to obtain a complete redress of their grievances. This was the problem, the burden, which the legitimist party placed on James Johnson's shoulders. The kingmakers and chiefs left Ijebuland for Lagos and throughout their stay, lasting several months, put up in the residence of James Johnson, to the latter's great personal inconvenience.[113] According to eye-witness accounts James Johnson never doubted that Ademolu would be reinstated. He made it clear to them that if only they would believe in the Christian's God Ademolu would be restored to his throne by the British. So much did the elders disbelieve that they and Ademolu promised that if matters were put right they would become Christians. For months James Johnson regularly attended the Acting Lieutenant Governor, Colonel H. C. Moorhouse, and subsequently of the Lieutenant Governor, A. G. Boyle. The importunity and pleadings of this ecclesiastic were not in vain. In less than five months Ademolu was back on his throne. The Lieutenant Governor decided to go to Ijebu Ode to ascertain the facts. From 2 January to 5 January he investigated the matter personally, gave forty-eight hours notice to the "usurper" to vacate the palace and declared Ademolu restored.[114]

The Ijebu could hardly believe the outcome. Among the religious traditionists who fulfilled their pledge to abandon traditional religion if James Johnson succeeded in the Ademolu case was Adebule, an elder uncle of Bishop S. O. Odutola, through whom in turn the latter was converted to Christianity.[115] Under the impression that the miracle had been performed by the Christian's God Ademolu was crowned in St. Saviour's Church, Ijebu Ode, on 14 February 1917, by which time James Johnson had begun an episcopal tour of the Niger Delta. In Lagos Ademolu himself had been under "the careful and systematic teaching of Bishop Johnson".[116] He accepted the gift of a Bible. Henceforth, although he did not renounce traditional religion, Ademolu with his chiefs became regular Church-goers and his palace a prayer-meeting venue for women.

James Johnson took no self-glory for himself on the reinstatement of Ademolu. Rather, in his last sermon to the people for whom he had done so much, he was concerned that they might see in Christianity no more than an agency for worldly achievements. It is largely because of his role in the Ademolu affair that he is today largely remembered. Well it was that on 8 January 1940 a portrait of Bishop James Johnson was unveiled by an Awujale and the memory of his achievements have ever since lingered on as the greatest son of Ijebuland.[117]

NOTES

1. See his presidential addresses to the Niger Delta Board which met in February every year (1901-1917) in C.M.S. G3/A3/0 series.
2. C.O. 267/317, "The Fifty-fifth Annual Report of the Sierra Leone Auxiliary Bible Society, 1871" by James Johnson.
3. C.M.S. G3/A3/010, Presidential Address to Delta Church Conference, 20/2/1905.
4. C.M.S. CA1/0123, James Johnson to M. Taylor and others, 19/4/1873.
5. *African Times*, 1/10/1887.
6. A.P.S., James Johnson to H. R. Fox Bourne, 17/6/1893.
7. *Ibid.*, same to same, 9/5/1893.
8. C.M.S. G3/A3/09, James Johnson's Presidential Address to the third Annual Delta Church Conference, 25/1/1904.
9. C.O. 267/369, James Johnson to H. Holland, 26/7/1887; *Sierra Leone Weekly News*, 25/8/1900.
10. *African Times*, 1/10/1887.
11. M.P., *The Aborigines Friend*, July 1901, p. 54.
12. M.P., J. Holt to De Wille, 2/1/1901; Herbert Macaulay Papers, Mss. IV, Dr. O. Johnson to E. Morel, 18/12/1912.
13. E. A. Ayandele, *op. cit.*, pp. 310-12.
14. *Niger and Yoruba Notes*, London, July 1900, p. 15.
15. C.O. 149/3, Legislative Council *Minutes*, 3/3/1889; 267/369, James Johnson to H. Holland, 26/7/1887.
16. C.O. 149/3, Legislative Council *Minutes*, 13/3/1889.
17. C.O. 147/62, James Johnson to H. Holland, 18/3/1887.
18. *Ibid.*, James Johnson to E. Stanhope, 4/1/1887.
19. A.P.S., Copy of Memo. enclosed in James Johnson to H. R. Fox Bourne, 14/3/1891.
20. A.P.S., James Johnson to H. R. Fox Bourne, 14/3/1891.
21. *Ibid.*, 30/5/1892.
22. C.M.S. CA2/056, James Johnson to H. Wright, 2/7/1878.
23. *Ibid.*, same to same, January 1880.
24. A.P.S., James Johnson to Buxton, 17/6/1893.
25. C.M.S. G3/A3/09, James Johnson to F. Baylis, 24/9/1904.
26. C.O. 147/153, James Johnson to J. Chamberlain, 28/6/1900.
27. *Ibid.*
28. A.P.S., James Johnson to H. R. Fox Bourne, 9/5/1893.
29. *Niger and Yoruba Notes*, July 1900, p. 15.
30. C.M.S. G3/A3/09, "Report of a Missionary Journey into Interior Iboland, Southern Nigeria, from February 24-April 8 1903" by James Johnson.
31. *Ibid.*

P

32. *Ibid.*
33. C.M.S. G3/A3/010, "Bishop Johnson's Journal Report, December 1904-July 1905".
34. C.M.S. G3/A3/09, "A Report of a Missionary Journey Within and beyond the Southern Nigeria, British Protectorate from February 24-April 8 1903" by James Johnson.
35. *Ibid.*
36. *Sierra Leone Weekly News*, 28/7/1900.
37. C.O. 147/166, James Johnson to W. Macgregor, 23/7/1903, enclosed in Macgregor to Chamberlain, 25/7/1903.
38. *Ibid.*, W. Macgregor to J. Chamberlain, 25/7/1903.
39. *Ibid.*, James Johnson to W. Macgregor, 23/7/1903, enclosed in Macgregor to Chamberlain, 25/7/1903.
40. *Ibid.*
41. C.M.S. G3/A3/09, "A Report of a Missionary Journey within and beyond the Southern Nigeria British Protectorate from November 1903 to July 1904" by James Johnson.
42. C.M.S. G3/A3/010, Presidential Address to Delta Church conference, 20/5/1905, by James Johnson.
43. C.M.S. G3/A3/09, James Johnson's Presidential Address at Niger Delta Church Conference, 25/1/1904.
44. *Sierra Leone Weekly News*, 23/1/1915.
45. *Lagos Times*, 21/2/1891.
46. C.M.S. G3/A3/09, James Johnson's Presidential Address, 25/1/1904, to the Third Annual Delta Church Conference.
47. C.O. 149/3, Legislative Council *Minutes*, 24/8/1891. A.P.S., James Johnson to H. R. Fox Bourne, 5/4/1893.
48. A.P.S., James Johnson to H. R. Fox Bourne, 5/4/1893.
49. C.M.S. CA2/011, James Johnson to J. A. Maser, 12/5/1879. C.M.S. CA2/056, James Johnson to H. Wright, January 1880.
50. C.M.S. CA2/056, James Johnson, Annual Letter, 1874.
51. *Ibid.*
52. *Ibid.*
53. *Ibid.*, 1878.
54. *Ibid.*, James Johnson to J. A. Maser, 16/7/1877.
55. *Ibid.*
56. *Ibid.*, James Johnson to H. Wright, January 1879.
57. A.P.S., James Johnson to H. R. Fox Bourne, 5/4/1893.
58. *Ibid.*
59. C.M.S. CA2/056, James Johnson to J. A. Maser, 16/7/1877.
60. *Ibid.*, James Johnson to H. Wright, January 1879.
61. *Ibid.*
62. A.P.S., James Johnson to H. R. Fox Bourne, 5/4/1893.
63. C.M.S. CA2/056, James Johnson, Annual Letter, 1879.
64. A.P.S., James Johnson to H. R. Fox Bourne, 5/4/1893.
65. C.M.S. CA2/056, James Johnson to H. Wright, 2/7/1878.
66. *Ibid.*
67. E. A. Ayandele, *op. cit.*, p. 57.
68. C.M.S. CA2/056, James Johnson to H. Wright, 2/7/1878.
69. *Ibid.*
70. *Sierra Leone Weekly News*, 16/1/1915.
71. C.M.S. G3/A2/010, James Johnson to F. Baylis, February 1902.
72. C.M.S. CA2/049, D. Hinderer, *Journals*, 26/12/1854.
73. A.P.S., J. P. Haastrup, "Report of the Deputation of the Native Inhabitants of Lagos to Ijebu Ode", Asipa Ilu's Speech.

74. C.M.S. CA2/056, James Johnson to H. Wright, 21/6/1878.
75. P. A. Talbot, *The Peoples of Southern Nigeria*, 4 vols., O.U.P., 1926, vol. 1, p. 221. Reprinted Frank Cass, 1969.
76. C.M.S. G3/A2/01, J. B. Wood to Secretaries, 17/3/1882; C. Phillips to Governor, 29/8/1881.
77. A.P.S., quoted in James Johnson to H. R. Fox Bourne, 9/5/1893.
78. *Ibid.*
79. C.O. 147/63, A. C. Moloney to H. Holland, 21/8/1888.
80. A.P.S., "The Jebu Matters" by James Johnson, Payne and others, which gives a different version of the Denton affair.
81. C.O. 149/3, Legislative Council *Minutes*, 10/7/1891.
82. C.O. 149/2, Executive Council *Minutes*, 12/6/1892.
83. *Report of Proceedings at a Banquet—to Sir Gilbert Carter, 16 June 1893*, Liverpool, 1893, p. 10.
84. C.O. 149/3, Legislative Council *Minutes*.
85. C.O. 147/84.
86. *Ibid.*, dated 14 March 1892.
87. *Lagos Weekly Record*, 19/6/1897, quotes from a paper read by Carter before the Royal Colonial Institute.
88. C.O. 147/84, G. T. Carter to H. T. H. Knutsford, 25/1/1892.
89. Kolanut is a symbol of goodwill and friendship. It is used for entertainment. If eaten together—it can be easily split to pieces—it cements friendship; it can form part of an oath.
90. A.P.S., James Johnson to H. R. Fox Bourne, 18/4/1893.
91. *Ibid.*
92. J. P. Haastrup, *op. cit.*
93. C.O. 149/2, Executive Council *Minutes*.
94. *Ibid.*
95. C.O. 806/357, James Johnson to H. R. Fox Bourne, 30/5/1892.
96. A.P.S., James Johnson to H. R. Fox Bourne, 18/4/1893.
97. Printed in C.O. 806/357.
98. C.O. 806/357, G. T. Carter to H. T. H. Knutsford, 17/8/1892.
99. A.P.S., R. B. Blaize to A.P.S., 29/8/1893.
100. *Ibid.*, James Johnson to H. R. Fox Bourne, 27/12/1893.
101. *Ibid.*, same to same, 5/4/1893.
102. *Ibid.*, same to same, 9/5/1893.
103. *Ibid.*
104. *Ibid.*, same to same, 30/5/1893.
105. *Ibid.*
106. *Ibid.*
107. Ibadan University Library, *The Annual Reports of the Lagos Church Missions 1879-1917*.
108. C.M.S. G3/A2/010, James Johnson to F. Baylis, February 1902.
109. *Ibid.*
110. *The Annual Reports of the Lagos Church Missions 1879-1917*. See Reports for 1893, 1896 and 1897-98.
111. *Lagos Weekly Record*, 6 and 13 January 1917.
112. N. A. Ibadan Ije Prof. 3 J. 6/1922, "Memorandum on Ijebu Native Administration" by W. B. Smith, 10/5/1922.
113. C.M.S. G3/A2/017, H. Tugwell to G. T. Manley, 30/5/1917.
114. *Lagos Weekly Record*, 6 and 13 January 1917.
115. Interview, 7/3/1967.
116. *Western Equatorial Diocesan Magazine*, April 1917, p. 112.
117. Now in the Reading Room, Ijebu Ode.

CHAPTER NINE

REBEL

> This is terrible . . . Bishop Crowther is in the opinion of
> all natives of West African coast and elsewhere a
> nonentity, and a mere figure in the Mission. This insult
> to him not to speak of others had incensed the whole
> native Christian community everywhere irrespective of
> Denominational distinctions . . . there is a limit to
> patience.
>
> James Johnson to J. B. Whiting 24/9/1890

IN a broad sense the year 1890 may be taken as the watershed
in James Johnson's career. Up to now the ethereal Ethiopian programme he had announced since his Sierra Leone days had
prospects of being implemented ultimately, if not immediately. In
the Church, African leadership in local matters became an
orthodoxy with all Protestant missions. In the Anglican Communion, the reactionary racism of the local missionaries notwithstanding, the principle of African episcopacy was still to be
jettisoned. The liberal spirit of the age was exemplified in the fact
that by 1890 Africans were holding the principalship of the three
Protestant secondary schools in the Colony of Lagos. In the State
the Moloney atmosphere excited hopes of African leadership in the
civil service, in which Africans controlled the police, filled the posts
of Treasurer and Crown Prosecutor and acted as Queen's Advocate.
In commerce and in the professions, such as law, medicine, printing
and journalism the capacity of the Negro Race to master the white
man's skill was being vindicated. On the whole, although the
progress being achieved in all these institutions and walks of life
did not go as far and as fast as James Johnson had hoped, yet it
was in a spirit of elation and gratification that on 13 March 1889
he paid warm tributes to A. C. Moloney as the ideal governor whose
administration "entitles itself to the gratitude of the people".[1]

But by the end of 1891 he perceived the dawn of a new era, for

the worse, in Afro-European relations. The implication of this new
state of affairs for his Ethiopian programme was clear and emphatic;
his vision and hopes began to collapse like a house of cards. This
was why he bellowed so much when he saw the Sword of Damocles
hanging over the territorial integrity and sovereignty of Africa. The
"vengeful, destructive and desolating sword of the British", which
had begun in the legislative chamber with Carter was the clear
sign that African leadership in various departments of public
life was becoming a thing of the past, a heresy in the Scramble
era.

However, there was one quarter where he did not expect his
hopes and vision for Africa to be falsified or affected by the
unpleasant change in Afro-European relations—Salisbury Square.
Up to 1889 it was an article of his faith that the spirit of Henry
Venn pervaded the headquarters of the Church Missionary Society,
that the non-application of the Venn principles, which would have
eventuated in the emergence of an all-African non-sectarian Church
controlled by Africans, was the evil design of the local missionaries.
But by the end of 1891 he discovered to his intense mortification
that the spirit of Henry Venn had been completely exorcised in
Salisbury Square and replaced by that of the Scramble era. For by
this date not only had Bishop Samuel Ajayi Crowther been toppled
from the episcopate by a new breed of missionaries, the eldest of
whom was younger than the African Bishop's youngest child, but
their behaviour was fully and unblushingly endorsed by the directors
of the Church Missionary Society. The shock this knowledge and
experience gave him was terrific, transforming him into the inspirer
and leader of a rebellion judged by the official historian of the
Society as the most serious of its kind in its missionary experience.[2]
In fact for the first and only time in his career James Johnson
made an attempt to opt out of the Anglican Communion and
amalgamate all Protestant Churches in Nigeria, a step that implied
a casting off of the ecclesiastical yoke of Lambeth Palace and a
repudiation of C.M.S. directorship.

That James Johnson raised the standard of revolt in a matter that
did not directly and potently affect him as a person is a clear
illustration of one cardinal virtue of his—selflessness. On the two
occasions in the past, 1880 and 1887, when his interest was involved
in the Yoruba episcopate issue, he had refused to stir or organise
African opinion, as he might have done in 1880 against his "disratement" by the Church Missionary Society. Why then did he work
for a restoration of the authority of Bishop Samuel Ajayi Crowther?
Why did he throw himself into the crisis in the Niger Mission
with such zest, such phrenetic energy? Why did he choose to stake
and exhaust his credit with the C.M.S. directors, just as he had

staked to his personal disadvantage his membership of the Legislative Council over the Ijebu expedition?

The answer to these questions is simple. The Niger crisis posed for James Johnson a challenge of the gravest kind. It challenged his grand conception of the Niger Mission as a uniquely African possession; it was a challenge to African patriotism, genuine Christianity and humanity; it was a rape of justice to Bishop Crowther, and was to hasten him to his grave. For James Johnson Bishop Crowther, the most romantic figure in a romantic age, was the most perfect symbol of the hopes of the Ethiopians of West Africa. Liberated by the British in 1821 he was the second and the first African student of Fourah Bay College and the first ordained African missionary in Yorubaland. It was on the Niger Mission that he was to use the best of his talents and to spend the greater part of his life. This Mission he had founded in 1857 and he was its director until 1864 when he became the cynosure of the world of missions as the first Negro Bishop in modern times. From this time onwards Crowther symbolised the capacity of the Negro Race to learn and master Western ways of life, to understand and live according to the sublime tenets of the Christian religion, to found, organise and direct a mission to an extent staggering to all the alien-founded alien-controlled Protestant missions that gathered themselves together in the Gabon in 1876.[3] In no other part of the Negro World did an African possess such vast powers as Crowther had, over a limitless diocese which, as he defined it, covered an area nearly half the size of India. Until 1880 he ruled his vast mission single-handed, gathering in his hands ecclesiastical, financial and administrative powers, without any advisers or committees, such as were to be found in all other missions of the Church Missionary Society. Little wonder that its uniqueness made the Ethiopians believe that the Niger Mission was the nucleus of the African Church of their dream.

The meaning the Niger Mission had for James Johnson can hardly be imagined. Since his Sierra Leone days it had been "that important Mission".[4] During his pastoral charge of Christ Church Pademba, not less than three members were recruited for service in the Mission. One of them was the Reverend J. During on whom the axe of the C.M.S. was to descend eventually. Whenever these three agents came to Sierra Leone on furlough their accounts were found thrilling.[5] Indeed James Johnson wrote a pamphlet on the Niger Mission the proceeds of which he contributed to the Niger Bishopric Fund.[6] His transfer to Lagos brought him nearer to the Mission and it became his habit to invite the Bishop to give an address at Breadfruit and receive donations from his Church.[7]

The statistical success and the apparently genuine piety and financial liberality of the Delta Christians, eagerly published in C.M.S. journals, filled him with unmeasured delight. The humanising effects of missionary activity like the abolition of twin-murder, human sacrifice, worship of God through the media of totem animals, and the successful introduction of literacy among the peoples were all for James Johnson, as well as for Salisbury Square, enormous achievements without parallel in contemporary Africa.[8] And this was a field worked by an African agency alone, though with funds replenished from time to time largely by the Mission's admirers in Britain and Canada. Much as he was prepared to admit that the quality of Christianity in the Niger Mission was not what it ought to be and much as he recognised that many of the agents were a discredit to Christianity—observations which, he said, would be valid of any contemporary Christian society—he was convinced that the Niger Mission was a marvellous indication of African capacities to succeed, to rule and be ruled by members of their own race, to organise, to administer, to respond to Christian appeal and to demonstrate the virtues of self-reliance, self-discipline and liberality.[9] The necessity to develop to the full these virtues became his concern in the eighties, to the point that three times he suggested to Henry Johnson, Archdeacon of Upper Niger, the timeliness and imperativeness of constituting the Delta churches into a self-supporting body,[10] as he had attempted to do in the interior of Yorubaland from 1877 to 1880.

But his Ethiopian conception of the Niger Mission apart, James Johnson had a very deep respect for Bishop Crowther, whom he regarded as a sort of ecclesiastical sire. A traditionalist in matters of etiquette, he could not but he filial to a man whose youngest child, Dandeson Coates Crowther, was born in 1840, that is within the same age-range as his own. Consequently, at least up till 1877, James Johnson used to consult with and take advice from the Bishop on ecclesiastical and other matters.[11] The Bishop, in turn, admired him for his virtues and looked upon him as his potentially worthy successor. Although the two did not see eye to eye on all issues there was the greatest cordiality in their relations. The differences between them were basic and consequent on differences in the circumstances of their birth, age and upbringing. Much as he lauded and would like to see implemented in Nigeria the Venn principles Bishop Crowther was never prepared to see the Church as a vehicle for African nationalism, nor did he see Christianity and African nationality in the cause and effect manner of the Johnsonians. A recaptive, he was bound to be deferential to the white man in a manner revolting to a Colony-born man like James Johnson. The Bishop was first and foremost a pragmatist, cautious in speech, consciously refraining from language that would harm anyone; his emotions were stable and he would never speak rashly as the emotional, tactless and loud-mouthed James Johnson was wont to do.

Bishop Crowther's dark days began in 1877, that is the very year that James Johnson's vicissitudes as Superintendent began, when the Church Missionary Society decided to dilute the Negro Race blood of the Niger Mission with that of the white man. This was the origin of the Niger Mission crisis, the full story of which is still to be told in spite of the effort already made by several scholars.[12] The crisis can be reduced to one denominator, race consciousness, and this was the veritable determinant of the relations between Europeans and educated Africans in the last quarter of the nineteenth century. Race consciousness was at the bottom of James Johnson's removal from the interior of Yorubaland in 1880; race consciousness was dominant in the thinking of the majority of speakers at the April 1887 conference on the Yoruba episcopate issue; race consciousness was decisive in the judgment of the Parent Committee on the same issue; and race consciousness influenced the attitude of Carter to the supersession of Africans by white men in the civil service.

Nor was it a one-sided affair, a monopoly of the representatives of the white race. The consciousness of being an African and of defending African interests at all hazards dominated the thinking of the educated elite generally and of James Johnson in particular. Racial feeling in favour of Africans, as has been shown, made him over-sensitive in his dealings with Europeans; he saw race in everything. Race consciousness had consumed him since the sixties and had determined his activity up to now.

That Europeans and Africans imbued with race consciousness should come to conflict was inevitable. But it was not until the eighties that the conflict assumed a serious dimension. By now the Europeans were on the offensive, the Africans on the defensive. Race consciousness had to assume this form because the conflict was taking place on African soil. As it appeared race consciousness in Europeans became aggressive and was transformed into a race superiority doctrine. Applied to the West African situation the race superiority doctrine demanded a reinterpretation, or fresh analysis, of facts, a revision of formerly held doctrines, a restatement of policies, the announcement of new doctrines and principles to explain and justify the new order of European leadership in all departments of life.

No one man was responsible for the new state of affairs; no one institution or body, no one country or nation, should be thought of as initiating it. As a doctrine racism was nothing new in human history. The anti-Negro aspect received the widest propaganda in Europe and the New World around the middle of the nineteenth century.[13] As a belief it had adherents among Europeans in West Africa before the Scramble era, but these adherents were few and far between. It was from the eighties onwards—as witnessed by the arguments that robbed James Johnson of the Yoruba episcopate —that racism became an article of faith of virtually all classes of Europeans.

It was not the product of literary protagonists as had been the case a generation earlier, but that of the Scramble era. It was a veritable era of conquest. The continent was conquered; African customs and institutions began to be battered, if not conquered; the mind of the African began to be suppressed, if not conquered. The African began to be compelled to learn the white man's rules of government, of economics, of thinking, of acquiring knowledge and of behaviour. It was an era when Europeans began to flock into West Africa in very large numbers, to dominate and rule and to ram into the African the superiority of their race. This sense of racial superiority was a natural one, derived from the marvels achieved by the white man in material culture, in technology and in literacy.

The Christian Church could not have been immune to the new doctrine. After all, it was logical that as members of the race that introduced the new and superior religion—a point never disputed by the educated Africans themselves until the time of the nationalist agitation after the First World War—the European missionaries should regard it as a prescriptive right to be the sole directors of Church affairs.

It is in the context of this atmosphere that the behaviour of the European missionaries, which was so passionately execrated by James Johnson and which toppled Bishop Crowther from the episcopate, should be understood. In other words they should not be seen as individuals shaping the course of history as such. Rather they should be viewed as the products and symbols of the general feeling of the Scramble era.

It was quite logical that in the eighties the achievements in the Niger Mission came to be believed in C.M.S. circles as being apparent rather than real. A Church based on sound Christian principles and progress by consolidation, it came to be contended, could not be having the bewildering statistical success of the Niger Mission. The universal belief of all classes of Europeans—missionaries, traders and administrators—was that Africans were inherently incapable of comprehending the eternal principles of the Christian faith, or that it would be in the distant future before genuine Christian converts could be made. If it took Christianity centuries to find roots in Europe, it seemed to them, how could it be expected that Christianity would be implanted in primitive Africa in a matter of years or decades? The implication of this belief was that the spiritual fitness of the African missionaries who were spreading Christianity, not merely as auxiliaries but in many ways as pioneers, had been too much exaggerated; that by allowing Africans to disseminate Christianity without the physical supervision of white missionaries, a grievous harm had been done to genuine Christianity in Nigeria. In order to correct the regrettable mistake that had been inadvertently made, it was being argued, it was absolutely necessary for the white missionaries to resume all control of existing mission establishments and pioneer all new openings.[14] In Yorubaland, it has been shown, white missionaries of the C.M.S. refused to go into the interior unless they superseded the African agents who had been the torchbearers of Christianity since the disaster of the sixties, and all threatened to quit the Mission if the episcopate of Yorubaland was given to James Johnson. The Wesleyan Missionary Society posted white missionaries in Ibadan and Oyo, while the Reverend W. J. David lectured the Foreign Board of the Southern American Baptist Mission on the virtues of Africans serving "under the superintendence and assistance of *white man*".[15]

It can at this point be appreciated that Bishop Crowther was not the only victim of the prevalent race superiority doctrine of the eighties, but that attention came to be focussed on him by James Johnson because he was its greatest victim in Nigeria. The point has to be made here that from the very beginning Henry Venn's vision of an African Church, controlled entirely by Africans, was never shared wholeheartedly by either the Church Missionary Society or Lambeth Palace. Their reluctant approval of Ajayi Crowther's consecration as Missionary Bishop of the Niger had been given only after the deadliness of the Niger Delta to white missionaries had been emphasised by Venn.[16] It was only to be expected that whenever the territory ceased to be pestilential to white people some pretext for entry into, and control of, the Niger Mission would be sought by some white missionaries. An excellent opportunity was provided by the victory of quinine over the mosquito. From 1875 onwards white traders began to return to the Niger and they began to plan to throw out educated African traders altogether.[17]

In fact by 1879 many white missionaries were itching to go to the Niger basin. In that year John Milum, Chairman of the Wesleyan Mission and Society, went up the Niger, pronounced the Niger Mission a failure and recommended strongly to the executive of the Foreign Mission in London that the highlands north and south of the Niger should be occupied by the Society's white missionaries.[18] The French Catholic priests of the Society of African Church Missions, who had always looked upon the Niger Mission experiment as the work of the devil, reconnoitred the Lower Niger and reported sanguinely that in a matter of years the tares which Crowther had been sowing would be pulled out and the genuine seeds planted.[19] Apart from the officials of the National African Company, who appealed to some C.M.S. missionaries to replace African with European agents, the C.M.S. had a spokesman in Edward Hutchinson, the Lay Secretary who had succeeded Venn in 1873. By 1879 he had become fully convinced that all talk of the treachery of the African climate was rubbish, and he encouraged white missionaries to get themselves ready to go to areas that had been hitherto dreaded.[20] In 1878 he had the chance of introducing a European into the Niger Mission, when, on Bishop Crowther's appeal, a steamer named *Henry Venn* was given to the Bishop by his admirers in England for his missionary needs. The steamer was put under the command of a white captain.

First through a lay agent, J. H. Ashcroft, and subsequently through successive General Secretaries, Bishop Crowther's authority in the Niger Mission was eroded until by 1890 all authority, including the ecclesiastical power to dismiss agents, had been assumed by the European Secretaries and missionaries. As one of the latter put it, Bishop Crowther had by 1890 been reduced to a "sort of ordaining and confirming machine".[21] In 1883 when some missionaries had begun to suspect his integrity in the financial affairs of the Mission, Crowther was given specific instruction to halt the territorial expansion because the Niger Bishopric Fund was "English" money.[22] In the same year the European General Secretary of the Mission, J. Hamilton, was given the power to dismiss any agent irrespective of the wish of the Bishop. The white missionaries who were injected into the Mission resolved that as long as Crowther was at the head of affairs, rather than expand, the Niger Mission should contract to the territory south of Onitsha. The Niger Mission came to be progressively discredited; memorandum followed memorandum as one European succeeded another as General Secretary, all pronouncing the Niger Mission a monumental failure that could be transformed into success only by white leadership and control.

Up to now investigations on the Niger crisis have concentrated almost entirely on the question of whether the Niger Mission was a success or a failure and have tried to interpret the behaviour of the European missionaries and the C.M.S. on the basis of the data relevant to that point alone. As has been mentioned earlier, the real root of the crisis was race consciousness. The question of whether the Niger Mission was a success or a failure is irrelevant and very subjective. It all depends on the yardstick by which success or failure is to be measured. There was no mission-field or contemporary Christian community that did not consist of the wheat and the tares, as did the Niger Mission. As far as James Johnson was concerned the Mission was an enormous, though not an unqualified, success. Statistically it was far more successful than any other Mission in West Africa, in the sense that its four thousand converts were indigenes rather than *Saros* as in Yorubaland; in terms of humanisation Christianity put an end to the cannibalistic propensities of the Ijaw and stopped infanticide and twin-murder in the Ibo area; it improved the conditions of slaves; in terms of piety the Niger Mission had its martyrs. In other respects, however, the Niger Mission was a failure. As observed by James Johnson it failed to encourage the converts—many of whom displayed wealth —along the path of self-support; nor was there any question of making the Church indigenous in the Niger Delta. Perhaps the most glaring failure which James Johnson did not perceive and which in subsequent years was to lead to a schism under his directorship, was the absence of a policy for the Ibolisation and Ijawlisation of the Niger Mission.

That James Johnson and Africans were not alone in the observation that the Niger Mission was on the whole a success may be judged from the views of Europeans who knew the Niger area well. According to John Milum, head of the Wesleyan Mission in Nigeria for a decade, the Niger Mission was "a work so creditably done by Africans".[23] Captain R. D. Boler, an ardent Christian whose experience of the delta area covered a period of more than thirty years, judged that Crowther's achievement amounted to "wonders".[24] Of particular importance was the judgment of one of the missionaries responsible for the deposition of the Bishop, the Reverend J. A. Robinson, namely that the Bishop had given a "long and arduous service".[25]

Racism of the Scramble era was to be exemplified by the missionaries who constituted themselves into the Sudan Party. Twelve in number they were on the whole young, zealous, well-educated men from Cambridge and Oxford. They must not be dismissed as mere negrophobists. Many of them believed that they were working in the real interest of the Niger inhabitants with whom the African agents, "black Englishmen", had failed to identify themselves. Except for one of them, the Reverend J. A. Robinson, who seems inconsistent and an hypocrite, they were people of conviction and dedication and some of them manifested signs of deep spiritual impulses. And although they were over-idealistic, perhaps quixotic, in their attitude towards evangelisation in Africa the cultural aspect of their programme, which emphasised the adoption of African clothing, architecture, a Church based upon agricultural economy and vernacular teaching, was commendable and ought to have been appreciated by James Johnson and Bishop Crowther. Nor can one argue against their advocacy of the Ibolisation and Ijawlisation of the Niger Mission.

But however grand their ideas stood on paper and however genuine the altruism they professed, the arguments they adduced to justify their anti-Crowther behaviour and the way and manner in which they literally destroyed within a week the edifice which the African Bishop, with his African agents, had been erecting before they were born, were calculated to unleash all the venom James Johnson was capable of. No set of Europeans—not even Benjamin Tregaskis in Sierra Leone, nor J. A. Maser in Yorubaland, nor even Carter in the Legislative Council—trampled with undisguised delight all the principles to which he had dedicated himself. Hardly had the new missionaries set foot on African soil than they began to issue sensational statements. All Christian missions that had ever operated in Africa, they declared, had been building on sand;[26] their methods were wrong, their messages were wrong, their agency, the African, was wrong. Not a single Christian, they said, had ever been produced in West Africa, a view they were to modify only in respect of James Johnson after they had come to know him.[27] But the greatest error that had been committed by Christian missions, they alleged, was the spread of the gospel through the instrumentality of the *Saro*, that is people of James Johnson's type, through whom he was seeking to have his Ethiopian dream translated to a reality. The worst place in the West African mission field, they said, was the Niger Delta which was being worked entirely by the *Saro*. For this class of educated African was the worst, consisting of "swarms of ragamuffins".[28] The Niger Mission was a charnel house; it possessed no redeeming features. As one of them said, "The beloved and much lauded Niger Mission had from first to last presented an almost uninterrupted history of swindling."[29] The Church Missionary Society, they contended, must bear the blame for ever putting Crowther at the head of the Niger Mission "in the face of the warnings of those who could best judge", "elevating to the episcopate Samuel Crowther prepared for a manhood of rule by a boyhood of slavery".[30] The maxim that should not only be perceived but implemented at once by the Society was that in the Niger Mission "work must be initiated and controlled by European missionaries".

By far the most outspoken of this new breed of racist missionaries was their youngest member, Graham Wilmot Brooke. Born in 1865, he was a freelance individualist crusader in the conversion of the Muslims of the Sudan. Since 1881 when he had met Gordon of Khartoum the conversion of these people had been his obsession. All the zeal and abundant energy that had for five years failed to bear fruit in his crusade in several directions came to be directed against Bishop Crowther and the Niger Mission. It is rather strange that although Salisbury Square officials knew that some of his doctrinal views were heteredox,[31] yet he was not only employed but made head of the Sudan Mission. This young man had planned the fall of Bishop Crowther a year earlier than is usually believed. In the latter half of 1889 Robinson had asked the C.M.S. to request Bishop Crowther, believed to lack the calibre of an "organiser and ruler", to "retire honourably on a good pension".[32] From his diaries it is plain that since April 1889 Brooke had concluded that Bishop Crowther must go, although he had nothing but praise for the character and person of the Bishop himself. On 17 April 1889, when he met the Bishop for the first time, he recorded the view that he "is a delightfully simple, guileless old gentleman, full of endless fund of anecdote from a most eventful life; far too simple and passive in temperament for dealing with the hard cunning men who from time to time are under him".[33] On his way back to England he occupied himself with sorting out the allegiance of all the members of the Parent Committee, condemning the Africanist members who were not likely to countenance the idea of having the Bishop removed from the episcopate. His objective and determination were clear: "The Bishop must go as counsellor to the [proposed] Bishop of Yoruba."[34]

His hatred for the *Saro* was very great indeed. In his judgment only James Johnson was a genuine Christian. J. A. Payne, the ardent Johnsonian, was like other *Saros,* a "humbug".[35] On 1 April 1889 he had the following dialogue with Nevill, Principal of Fourah Bay College:

Brooke: Do the clergy here have walks with their wives?
Nevill: No.
Brooke: Are the clergy here of the typical West coast kind, like Lagos ones for instance?
Nevill: Yes, just the same.
Brooke: Is there any one of them who stands out and apart like James Johnson for instance?
Nevill: No there is no one like that here.
Brooke: Sierra Leone is become a den of thieves.[36]

By April 1889 both Brooke and Robinson had provoked the *Saro* agents of the Niger Mission to such an extent that they had begun to fear that these "black Englishmen" would poison them.[37]

James Johnson's reaction to the formation of the Sudan Party was one of mixed feelings. On the one hand he was elated that the methods of evangelisation which the racists had been boasting would yield phenomenal results would be learned by him and others. But on the other hand he was put in a state of anxiety because these new methods would be tried in the territory occupied by the Niger Mission. As he said: "We do not object to learn the way of God more perfectly from any Aquila and Priscilla who have learnt more of it from the Holy Spirit and are willing to teach us." But "from the very first time that I learnt of the Society's plan and arrangement with Messrs. Robinson and Brooke", he was convinced that "it would be better for the new method of work to be tried in a new field . . . rather than violently disturb existing state of things for it".[38]

Apart from the "utterances" of the members of the Sudan Party, particularly those of Brooke, the true purpose and aim of the new missionaries were discernible in their doings in the Niger Mission. For the hatred of the *Saro* that had been building up was expressed in ways that James Johnson found revolting and unchristian. The first to be humiliated was the Bishop. At the historic meetings that took place in the last third of August in 1890 at Onitsha the octogenarian Bishop was put on trial.[39] His Mission, he was told, was the work of the devil because it was being financed from "polluted sources", that is subscriptions from European and African liquor dealers. He was lectured that he did not know how to convert souls to Christianity. But the other agents had a much rougher deal. The Muslims in the Nupe Kingdom, including their Emir of Bida, were told that all the African agents that had worked in the Niger Mission were liars and *Kafiris*, that they should unlearn all that the Africans had been teaching them, and that contrary to the teaching of the Africans they should believe in the existence and potency of witchcraft.[40] In order to discredit the African agents the Christian adherents were asked to prefer allegations against their former teachers, as the only condition for their being received back into the Church.

As the news of the treatment of the Bishop and the disconnection of most of the agents reached Lagos and the atmosphere became filled with the tales of the wrongs and humiliations that had been so signally inflicted upon the Negro Race by Brooke and others, James Johnson was aggrieved but he did not immediately contemplate rebellion. In the belief that the members of the Sudan Party "who did not know existence when Bishop Crowther began the Niger work and were children when Archdeacon Johnson and others in that mission were called to the sacred ministry" had behaved as they did without the knowledge of the Church Missionary Society, James Johnson presented the African case to the C.M.S. officials.[41] He was the only African who did so. He asked for an impartial commission of inquiry. His only source of information was the African one, supplemented by the public utterances of the new missionaries, labelled as "young purifiers".[42] They were racists first and foremost, declared James Johnson. The desire to dislodge the African in favour of the European, and not the evangelization of the Sudan, was their objective. "The charges upon which most of these grave actions have been taken seem so very light that one is forced against his own will to the conclusion that concurrently with the expressed desire to attempt the evangelization of the Mohammedan section of the Niger and of the Sudan by means of a new method of work, was a desire practically to shelve the founder of the Niger Mission if possible, and rid it of many of its other native labourers against whom it is impossible for anyone to urge age, infirmity, defective learning, indolence and the like, and who have not to my knowledge or to the knowledge of anyone in the River been openly and formally accused of any serious moral faults."[43] It should be added that the automatic confidence James Johnson had in the agents of the Niger Mission was not due only to the fact that he had the greatest belief in the dogma of Africa for the Africans, but also to the fact that he had infinite trust in African agents in the interior, even when they were not under immediate supervision.[44]

In spite of the propaganda of the Church Missionary Society and its news media about Brooke and others James Johnson saw no evidence of virtue in Brooke and his colleagues. Rather they were, in his view, unabashed hypocrites, "tremendous fanning denunciators" and fanatical haters of Africans. In his eyes they were a strange sort of people, inexperienced and anything but Christian in their lives and behaviour. They were people who "seem to delight in the ruin of others, in hearing and retailing slanders, receive *ex parte* statements and act upon them, condemn others unheard, set themselves to the dirty work of ferreting faults against fellow Christians; invite and encourage others in the absence of the victims of their ill-will in malice to inform against them. . . . Yet all this information from different and accredited persons represent Messrs Brooke, Robinson and Eden as having done. Men who are always ready to believe and are always suspecting evil things of others do not shew that their own minds are pure."[45]

For James Johnson the argument of these missionaries, who "entertain such an overweening confidence in themselves and such a strong sense of the incapacity of native Christian missionaries for the work of evangelizing their own countrymen", that the disconnected agents were spiritually unfit, was a farrago of nonsense. "Who has been the judge of this unfitness?" he asked. For had they not shown themselves as "Men who whilst they profess to attain to a higher degree of spirituality and to be anxious to lead others to it, think they can make truer and sounder converts and do the work more speedily . . . have failed to such an extent to impress others with their own Christ-likeness"?[46]

But whilst he was prepared to exercise patience, waiting for the directors of the Church Missionary Society to do "simple justice" and set up "a fair and impartial enquiry" with whose results he would abide, he did not have to wait long to withdraw suspension of judgment. For one thing neither the Niger Delta Christians nor the educated Africans were interested in presenting any case to anybody; the reaction of Africans was one of anger and outraged feelings, a conviction that they were victims of racial prejudice. Secondly the Church Missionary Society had ceased to be the one of his previous experience, playing the role of the impartial arbiter between the races, as it had done in 1873-74 in Sierra Leone and in 1884 to 1887 in Lagos. In the past not only was James Johnson invited to Salisbury Square but he was patted on the back as if the Africans had obtained a favourable judgment over the local missionaries.

There was no mistaking the nationalist fervour evoked in the Africans by the behaviour of the "young purifiers". It was spontaneous and it infected the unlettered Africans as well. Even the Emir of Bida resented the humiliation meted out to his African friend, the Reverend Charles Paul, and asked the Royal Niger Company to remove the missionaries from his Kingdom.[47] The African population in Lokoja, their chief seat, became so hostile that the missionaries there began to fear that they might be poisoned. In the Delta support for Bishop Crowther by the Christian adherents and the 'pagan' chiefs was complete, the African agents making the best use of the occasion by lecturing the converts on negrophobism in Britain and the United States.[48] The Bishop himself became a very pathetic figure. For days he sat speechless in the piazza of his residence in Bonny, gazing into the vacant air. All effort by his children to arouse him was of no avail. In Lagos the white man became an object of hissing and jeers.[49]

It was in this tense atmosphere that the idea of a West African Church, such a conglomerate African Church that James Johnson had advocated from time to time, began to be seriously discussed in the press. It is significant that the leader of the "young purifiers", Brooke, established contact with James Johnson, recognising the latter as a man of strong influence who could make the creation of an African Church possible. Therefore he appealed to Holy Johnson to consider only the spiritual aspect of the programme of the Sudan Party, to disbelieve the idea that they hated Africans and to "reserve" his judgment and any contemplated action until their missionary effort in the Sudan should have yielded abundant fruits.[50]

Q

It was at this stage that Edward Blyden, collaborator with James Johnson in Sierra Leone in earlier years, accepted the invitation which James Johnson and a number of the educated elite, who were called the Reception Committee, had given him. To the displeasure of the European missionaries James Johnson was alone among African clergymen who welcomed this erudite and prolific orator, and he took the most prominent part and allowed the schoolhall of his parsonage to be the venue of most of the meetings that resulted in sensational anti-European addresses.[51] At the official welcome meeting it was James Johnson who read the address he had written. In it he prayed that Blyden's visit to Lagos "may please God . . . to inspire in us and in our people generally, a greater interest in ourselves as a people; a greater love for and devotion to our country; a greater desire to labour each one in his own measure to promote its advancement".[52]

Blyden's visit to Lagos had a great impact on the educated elite and his pronouncements, in which he stressed the urgency and timeliness of establishing an African Church, added force to the conviction of several people who had been nursing the idea of an African Church. Blyden's visit was designed to produce effects on the educated elite in another way. According to James Johnson the main purpose for inviting Blyden was in connection with African Colonization, the desire to encourage Negroes in the New World to migrate back to Africa. Blyden was expected to choose "empty" areas in Yorubaland where emigrants of Yoruba origin would be settled.[53]

Nevertheless the racial tone of the West African press and Blyden's speech notwithstanding, James Johnson would not have been disposed to organise rebellion against the Church Missionary Society. But to his chagrin and horror, apart from the undisguisedly anti-African tone of the Society's news-media in Britain the Sub-Committee urged to look into the matter was dominated by men imbued with the Scramble ideology. One looks in vain for evidence to show that the Society played the role of the honest broker in the dispute between Europeans and Africans. James Johnson's representations, and the protests of other educated Africans and chiefs, were treated with impolite disdain. The racists in the Sub-Committee, who outnumbered the negrophiles by more than three to one, carried the day. They believed everything contained in the reports of the European missionaries, upheld the principles underlining the recommendations of the nihilists and confirmed the nominal position of Bishop Crowther. Only one thing they could not do; they could not remove the Bishop, although as one of the "young purifiers" had boasted, it was already known to the world that Bishop Crowther was no more than a nondescript and "whether he retains

office or not, the Bishop has been deprived of the honour due to
his age and office. He has been publicly shown to be a mere
figurehead, without power and almost without influence in his
own diocese, of which but a few years ago he was the absolute
ruler".[54]

African opinion was not only ignored but was considered "illegitimate" by the Society. The Africans were regarded as no more
than mere children who could not know what was in their best
interest—white spiritual and physical guidance. It behoved the
Africans to accept the well-intentioned chiding of the Society with
good grace. Apart from the Society's journals, in an open letter
addressed to them the Africans were urged to accept it as a fact
that the West African Church was like the Church of Corinth
condemned by Paul. The Africans were wallowing unabashed in
immorality, hypocrisy, showiness and mouth religion. The only
prophylactic for all these spiritual diseases and "false pride" was
white rule. The Society declared:

> Englishmen have had the benefit of a Christian Civilization for
> many centuries; and we do most sincerely believe that those who
> have had this blessing have certain gifts and talents to use in
> the Master's service which you do not possess, and by which we
> may in a very important manner help and serve you. We cannot
> but trust and we must say that the considerations just named point
> to the great desirableness of your having European advice con-
> stantly near at hand, and your availing yourselves, for the instruc-
> tion and training of spiritual agents of that particular kind of
> ripened Christianity, learning and experience, which can scarcely
> be looked for except in European teachers.[55]

This language of the Scramble era was different from that which
James Johnson had heard from Salisbury Square in the days of
Henry Venn. It was like Carter's language of threat to the Ijebu
and James Johnson was stunned by it. His faith in the Church
Missionary Society was profoundly shaken. It was the most serious
blow he had ever suffered in the hands of the Church; his Ethiopian
vision was irrevocably doomed. His reaction was twofold. Firstly
he made it possible for the Delta part of the Niger Mission to
repudiate C.M.S. control and become an independent organisation.
Secondly he attempted to take away all other churches of the C.M.S.
in Lagos and amalgamate them with other Protestant bodies into a
West African Church.

It is surprising that the C.M.S. expected James Johnson to remain
absolutely loyal and accept the measures being taken to destroy
the principle of Africa for the Africans. That he was respected is
clear from the fact that it was to him alone that the Society cared

to write, offering an explanation to persuade him to accept the *fait accompli*.[56] There was no question of taking the points he had brought before the Society one by one; these were never considered. The Society's answer was an appeal as well as an admonition that he should recognise the principle of the white man's supremacy. As the Secretary wrote: "I do earnestly ask that you will now unite with us. . . . May I add one word which perhaps may seem to you to savour of remonstrance. I cannot but feel that you do not apprehend the motives which have actuated us in the proposals which we have recently made for the future work in the Delta. . . . We have been very far from being influenced by any racial feeling. . . . But we do think that experience in the past, not on the Niger or in West Africa only but in India and elsewhere, has taught us that the co-operation of Europeans is needful."[57]

This letter of January 1891 was a red rag to the Gallic Bull. James Johnson decided that the Delta churches should combine and immediately assert their independence from the Church Missionary Society. The significance of James Johnson lies in the fact that he was the central figure of the rebellion. It is possible that but for his inspiration and efforts, "the element of race feeling which the Reverend James Johnson has encouraged",[58] the Delta Church, which was founded on 29 April 1892 under the name of Niger Delta Pastorate, would not have become independent. It was commonly known that the enthusiasm of most of the educated Africans for desirable schemes cooled off whenever such schemes affected their purse. This it has been shown had been James Johnson's experience with such desirable schemes as the independent African Church in Sierra Leone in 1874, as the Yoruba episcopate for the African in 1887-8 and as a municipal council for Lagos in 1889. This was why the European missionaries ridiculed the much-discussed West African Church, which they believed would be but another project in the air.[59] In fact, but for the positive steps taken by James Johnson, the independent Church movement for the Delta would indeed have remained in the air. For in the final analysis only three educated Africans were prepared to subscribe generously to the founding of the Church. These were Dr. O. Johnson, J. A. Payne and Z. A. Williams, subsequently editor of the *Lagos Standard*. Although the Delta converts and chiefs were potentially strong financially, they were not yet aware of their financial viability, having never before maintained any agent of their own. They therefore looked to Lagos and Sierra Leone for financial assistance.

James Johnson's Breadfruit Parsonage became the rendezvous of important educated Africans such as J. A. Payne, Dr. O. Johnson, J. P. L. Davies, Z. A. Williams, N. H. Williams and J. A. Savage.

It was in his Parsonage that the two resolutions of 17 April 1891, which he drafted, were adopted, advising Bishop Crowther to set up an independent Delta Pastorate and promising an annual grant of £500 for five years or until the new independent Church was able to stand on its own feet.[60] In fact all that the Delta Christians needed was inspiration. For within a year the Church commanded resources greater than it had previously contemplated. All the financial assistance that the thrasonical nationalists in Lagos ever gave to the Pastorate was £100.

The Johnson resolutions had a decisive effect on Bishop Crowther. Hitherto the old Bishop had accepted, though sorrowfully, the decision of the Church Missionary Society. The resolutions not only convinced him that Africans would not leave him in the lurch, but also made him bold, adamant and defiant. The most submissive Bishop in the C.M.S. experience, who had before obeyed "orders", associated himself with the greatest rebellion against the C.M.S. and asked twice that the Society relieve him of his position if it wished.[61] James Johnson had the greatest influence on the Bishop. On his return to Lagos in November 1891, afer the paralytic stroke that he had suffered in the Delta two months before, James Johnson led a delegation who encouraged him by showing him the pride with which Africa regarded him.[62] The effect of this African support for the Bishop was the complete failure of the C.M.S. to wean him from his nationalist programme of an independent Delta Church.

The Bishop appreciated James Johnson's exertion on his behalf and he requited it. With the idea that he was breaking with the Church Missionary Society, though not with the Anglican Communion, Bishop Crowther asked the Archbishop of Canterbury to consecrate James Johnson as his suffragan in the proposed independent diocese, with the hope that the latter would succeed him at his death.[63] So much did James Johnson endear himself to the hearts of the Delta Christians that after the Bishop's death they asked Lambeth Palace to consecrate him as their "independent African Bishop".[64] So much was Johnson's role in the Crowther crisis appreciated that Archdeacon D. C. Crowther, the Bishop's youngest son and compeer of James Johnson, rather than push himself forward for candidature to the episcopate, conceded the position to Johnson. For many years he hardly took any decision without first consulting with James Johnson.

The quiet founding of the United Native African Church in August 1891 and the idealistic resolutions adopted by its founders, have obscured the immense significance and achievements of the independent Niger Delta Pastorate. In a sense this organisation was an African Church, not only because it was the creation of African nationalism but because it possessed similarities with the other so-called African Churches. Up till James Johnson's death, at least, the personnel of the Pastorate was entirely African, just as was the personnel of the other "African" Churches. In initiative, in capacity for organisation and administration, territorial expansion and statistical success the Niger Delta Pastorate achieved more than any other African Church in Nigeria before the First World War. It was the only "independent" African Church that had secondary schools for boys and girls in this period. However, like the other so-called African Churches, the Niger Delta Pastorate was un-African in its retention, except for marriage regulations, of the Anglican form of worship. The liturgy and forms and formularies of worship continued to be largely Anglican. Like the other African Churches the Niger Delta pastorate adopted a rational attitude towards the secret societies, particularly the *Owu Ogbo*, which Christians were encouraged to join in order to reform it.[65] The Niger Delta Pastorate remained an entity, and not a part of the C.M.S. organisation until after the First World War.

Just as he never regretted his break with the State over the Ijebu Expedition and the autocratic tendencies of Governor Carter, James Johnson never regretted that he organised rebellion against Salisbury Square over the Niger Mission Crisis. His actions were based on motives of Christian ethics, African nationality and sheer humanity. By not giving Africans the chance to know the reasons for their disconnection and defend themselves before an impartial commission of inquiry, he felt, the C.M.S. had behaved contrary to explicit Scriptural injunctions. As he lectured Salisbury Square, the latter's behaviour "is to me contrary to I Timothy 5:19 which says 'Against an Elder receive not an accusation, but before two or three witnesses' and to the spirit of our Lord's teaching in Matthew 18:15-18 and throws open the door for slander in which, I confess with shame, my country-people are very fond of indulging".[66] He considered it inhuman for the Society to dismiss people who had served in the Niger Mission all their lives, were too old to learn new trades and who by the action of the C.M.S. were disqualified morally to be employed in any other walk of life. For him, too, it was a maxim that in a field like the Niger basin racial co-operation was impossible and it was the Europeans, not the Africans, who should go to the "regions beyond". As he declared: "Experience has shown that after a Mission amongst natives has attained a certain stage of advancement, it is often extremely difficult to maintain always or for any very long time perfect harmony and true and sweet brotherly relations between European missionaries and native agents thrown together and working together as parts and parcels each of it. Prejudices seem to rise more easily on both sides; temptations to distrust one's motives become on both sides stronger; a want of confidence becomes mutual; relations are strained."[67]

James Johnson could not forgive the Church Missionary Society for not apologising for the insults (acknowledged by the Society privately) which the "young purifiers" had hurled at the old Bishop. "There has been no apology made by the missionaries since", he wrote, "or by the Committee to him on their behalf. This has caused many to ask, whether such a conduct would have been tolerated by the Society if it had been exhibited towards a European missionary Bishop . . . and whether if exhibited, it would have been treated with a similar silence."[68] Also James Johnson saw the Niger crisis as a crisis for Africa. It was Africa that was being put on trial and it behoved all Africans, Christian, Muslim and 'pagan', to rally round the Bishop in the rebellion against the Church Missionary Society. For James Johnson had the apprehension that the bungling of the Niger Mission in favour of the European racists indicated that no African successor to Ajayi Crowther would be appointed when he died. "This is considered a very clear and very strong public sentence against Native Agency," protested James Johnson, "as a throwing back of its advancement for ages to come; and also an arrangement that will not be truly helpful to the Native Churches or to the people of the country generally."[69]

James Johnson made it clear further that in order to prevent the C.M.S. and the racists from having all the Niger Mission under their control under the new dispensation it was his considered opinion that Africans should seize the Delta area and put it under the exclusive control of Africans under an African Bishop. The African view in this respect was put as follows to Salisbury Square: "The people do not subscribe to the generally unfavourable opinion entertained of them, though they are not insensible of faults of themselves: and they do not desire to see Bishop Crowther succeeded by any other than a Native. Whilst they do not expect that any European missionary labouring in the Niger Mission would be really willing to submit to the supervision of a Native Bishop, or accord to him any other than constrained respect. They think that self-support by and general provisional native help to the Delta Churches would enable these Churches in case of Bishop Crowther's resignation or death, to secure if it please God for themselves what they and the whole Native African Church community in the West Coast fear from the events of the last two years, they must entertain no hope, at present at least of getting from the Society."[70]

At the same time that the standard or revolt was being upheld by Bishop Crowther and the Delta converts and James Johnson was providing it with a reinforcement, he was making an attempt, the only attempt of his life, to found an independent African Church.

The details of the scheme are still to be discovered but it is clear that James Johnson was the central figure in the movement. Meetings of ministers and laymen of all Protestant denominations in Lagos took place in his Parsonage under his Chairmanship.[71] He with Henry Johnson, who had been dismissed from his Niger Mission post, drew up the Basis of Union and he was to give the signal that would inaugurate the new African Church in March 1891.[72] The scheme involved repudiation of alien control and was still under consideration months after the founding of the Niger Delta Pastorate. The scheme involved as well the setting up of a seminary and a secondary school, with a department of technical education. There was a move to purchase the premises of the Southern American Baptist Mission in Lagos for a sum of £1,000, which the educated Africans were prepared to pay in cash at once.[73] According to James Johnson the scheme failed because of an unexplained "unfortunate incident".[74] But according to other sources the non-sectarian African Church failed to emerge because the theology and the forms of worship on which James Johnson insisted were basically Anglican.[75]

This latter view would seem to have some validity. James Johnson was always an Anglican. He never succeeded in purging himself of sectarianism. Unknown to the supporters of the Niger Delta Pastorate, even at the height of the crisis, James Johnson's mind was not only Anglican but never really abandoned the Church Missionary Society to which it had become glued. For in his private letters he continued to declare that the Niger Delta Pastorate did not really constitute a "severance" from the Society, that Bishop Crowther's relationship with the Society would not be affected in any way, that European missionaries of "acknowledged piety and experience" should still be allowed to work with the institution and that the Church Missionary Society would "continue to exercise parental interest and control" over the Pastorate Churches.[76]

Of course the Church Missionary Society was not deceived as to the real nature and consequences of the rebellion. Certainly though his heart continued to be with the Society, to which he felt Africans should be eternally grateful, the language Johnson was using in public and the group he organised in his Parsonage provided the necessary inspiration which produced the actual rebellion. Henceforward he became a *persona non grata* with Salisbury Square which minced no words that it held him squarely responsible for the rebellion.[77] Consequently his claims to be considered as Crowther's successor were completely ignored by the Society, although the West African press, African opinion in Sierra Leone, Lagos and the Niger Delta and Lambeth Palace regarded James Johnson as the central figure in the succession problem.[78]

Months before Bishop Crowther died Bishop Ingham had suspected that the independent movement in the Niger Delta could not be under the declining Bishop's control, that for the movement to receive the blessings of Lambeth Palace would be throwing the episcopate into James Johnson's lap. In order to prevent such a dreaded eventuality he advised that a European Bishop should be sent to Yorubaland at once, so that the Delta area could be said to merge into *"my Diocese"*, according to the charter under which he was appointed which, he claimed, was to embrace all areas under the British Flag 20 degrees north and south. Since in August 1891 the British were establishing the Oil Rivers Protectorate, embracing the Delta region, he felt he could claim the area.[79]

The C.M.S. could hardly have entertained a suggestion of this kind as long as Bishop Crowther was alive. It was felt necessary to wrench him from the clutches of the nationalists by persuading him to abandon the independent movement. To this end J. Hamilton, who had in the eighties been a General Secretary, and W. Allan, the man who had been sent to Lagos in 1888 to wean Africans from the idea of an independent African Bishop for Yorubaland, were sent to Sierra Leone and Lagos. According to them James Johnson's influence over the Bishop was decisive.[80] Perhaps to placate James Johnson Allan told him that the idea of an African succeeding Bishop Crowther in the Niger Delta could be entertained,[81] but privately he advised Salisbury Square in unmistakable terms that never would he ever consider this African agitator for the episcopate.[82]

Bishop Crowther would not be dissuaded from the nationalist scheme, the efforts of the C.M.S. emissaries notwithstanding. It was as a nationalist that he breathed his last in the last hours of the last day of the last month of 1891. It was a mark of James Johnson's position that it was he who delivered the funeral oration the text of which has not survived but which was judged by European listeners as being "too racial".[83] Bishop Crowther's death revived an issue bigger than that of the Yoruba episcopate. Without any heartsearching the Society decided to appoint a European Bishop who would be in charge of all the C.M.S. stations in Nigeria and the Gold Coast, all of which would constitute a new Diocese of Western Equatorial Africa. In spite of the strength of African opinion James Johnson's claims were completely ignored. In 1887 Bishop Crowther had reminded the Parent Committee that James Johnson was due for the episcopate. Before he left Bonny in September 1891 he had confessed to the Archbishop of Canterbury a physical inability to discharge the duties of his office and had named James Johnson as his Suffragan. On 25 July 1892 the new Niger Delta Pastorate formally requested Lambeth Palace to consecrate "our beloved James Johnson" as successor, declaring that his salary would be paid by Lagos and Sierra Leone Christians.[84]

The opinion of European and African observers about the fitness and qualifications of James Johnson for the episcopate had not changed at all. The Reverend Herbert Tugwell, who was to be consecrated Bishop of the new diocese in 1894, declared: "As to the Reverend James Johnson's intellectual ability no man can doubt: as such I highly regard him. . . . If by God's grace he could be set at liberty and could deal impartially alike with the African and European I should indeed rejoice to see his undoubted abilities receive full recognition and am convinced that working on Scriptural lines he would be a great power."[85] In distant Bonny one Annie Jombo, who had the worst opinion of the Crowther family and wished to see a European Bishop in the Niger Mission wrote: "I think that the Yoruba Mission should have a native Bishop of whom the Reverend James Johnson is the only fit man in Western Africa, and I hope the date is not distant when you shall call him to England for his consecration for he is a God-fearing man and possessed with the power of The Holy Ghost."[86]

But neither the Tugwells nor the Annie Jombos were the king-makers. In Salisbury Square the kingmakers voted in favour of a European successor, without any strong opposition from the Afro-philes, such as had been encountered over the Yoruba episcopate issue four years before. The man on whom the lot fell was the Reverend J. S. Hill, who from 1876 to 1878 had been pushed to work on the pestiferous island of Lekie during the time James Johnson assumed the superintendence of the interior. Only the refusal of the Archbishop of Canterbury to consecrate Hill, unless two Africans were consecrated with him as Assistant Bishops, obviated a total defeat for James Johnson and his followers. To this end the Bishop Designate was sent to West Africa to report back to Lambeth Palace on the state of African opinion.

J. S. Hill was not the ideal man for the task committed to him. He had been one of the dissentient voices against the appointment of James Johnson as Superintendent in 1876. In ideas and character he was the opposite of the African patriot. By getting in touch with the Church Missionary Society and taking along with him all the adverse reports against the Africans in the Niger Mission from 1880 onwards Hill did not conceal the fact that he was not going to West Africa with an open mind. It was an article of his faith that an African could never be a credit in a position of authority; for him the slogan Africa for the Africans was the crudest of nonsense; Africans could only be made to behave themselves under the guidance of the white man. His views were orthodox for the Scramble era. As he declared: "The natives left to themselves, without the influence of a few ambitious leaders, I believe would seldom seek native supervision in preference to Europeans. The business matters moreover under native régime, are not as a rule conducted with that much regularity, and delicacy of feelings usually found in Englishmen. . . . Socially the domestic customs do not improve without the influence of the English home life. Few of our native clergymen eat, for instance, with their wives. I know of many that do not except when at our houses. These last facts have a very real influence upon the minds of many thoughtful natives, and are important when the question of their governing themselves without any supervision whatever, is under consideration."[87]

His orthodox Scramble era views on the African apart, J. S. Hill could not have been unhurt by the response given him by James Johnson when he offered the latter the post of Assistant Bishop. James Johnson was reported to have retorted sharply: "Half Bishop to whom?" In fact so much did Hill feel this rebuff that he refused to report to Lambeth Palace that he ever made Johnson an offer.[88] As James Johnson explained it, the suggestion was revolting in two ways. Firstly it was not the ideal, which was the independent African episcopate he had sought all his life to obtain and from the achievement of which he would not be dissuaded. Secondly the position of a "Half Bishop" was inferior to that of the Superintendent that he had occupied from 1877 to 1880.[89]

In the circumstances one cannot be surprised that Hill adopted an undisguisedly anti-Johnson attitude. For the rest of his stay in Nigeria he indulged in activities intended to deflate this African patriot. In his report to the Archbishop he misrepresented the position of James Johnson in African eyes and enlarged the importance and influence of the protégés of the European missionaries. James Johnson, declared the Hill Report, should never be offered the post of Assistant Bishop because to do so would be bribing him to make him keep quiet. Moreover, said Hill, James Johnson "is not liked; he would not be acceptable to the Lagos clergy".[90] The two Africans he recommended were Isaac Oluwole and Charles Phillips. The latter, he said, was an excellent evangelist and "the most spiritual man we have"; the former "is the clergyman most beloved by the clergy and laity".

Hill's assessment of the three Africans was not based on any independent investigation but on the data provided him by the European kingmakers in Lagos and Abeokuta. Fortunately the private papers of one of the Africans, Charles Phillips, exist.[91] These two sources throw some light on the degree of acceptability of the three Africans to the clergy and laity. According to Phillips' account he was approached by J. S. Hill on 2 November 1892. The

offer was both a surprise and an embarrassment to him in three
ways. Firstly he felt that he was unqualified for the post because
of "want of extended experience". Secondly he was aware of the
inadequacy of his education, as he had never had secondary or
collegiate training. Thirdly, "there are eligible seniors whose
presence makes my selection very invidious and uncomfortable."
However he was chosen by the Europeans "in preference to others",
six "seniors" of whom James Johnson was foremost.[92]

In fact the European missionary whose opinion carried the
greatest weight was J. B. Wood, who had been consistently opposed
to all attempts to put James Johnson in a position of responsibility
since the seventies. In recommending Oluwole and Phillips, Wood
made it plain that they would know their position in relation to
Europeans. But James Johnson would never fulfil this function. Of
him Wood wrote: "Undoubtedly the foremost man among the
native clergy is J. Johnson and he has some qualifications which
would make him a very useful man in the higher office. But unfortunately he holds views and adopts methods in carrying them out
which would, I fear, not seldom be the cause of serious, not
improbably, very serious embarrassment. . . . I am sure he is a
thoroughly good man, and both an earnest and efficient worker.
Personally, I should be glad for several reasons to see him a Bishop.
But my fears of him in the higher office are greater than my
hopes."[93]

In the Niger Delta Hill indulged in an anti-Johnson campaign.
He attempted to browbeat the people there to free themselves from
James Johnson's influence.[94] His attitude to the Delta Christians
was that they were rebels, but he thought it would be easy to persuade them to return to the bosom of the Church Missionary
Society. To this end he urged them to accept a constitution. But
both Archdeacon D. C. Crowther and James Boyle, who were in
the Delta area and whom he had thought were the real directors
of affairs, told him that they must consult first with James Johnson.[95] Hill made every effort to persuade the Delta to drop James
Johnson as the person they would like as Bishop on the grounds
that he was already "an old man"[96]—that is at the age of fifty-five!
The answer he received was most unpalatable to him. They would
not have anybody else except James Johnson, and he must be made
a full Bishop. They were fully prepared to pay his salary. They
would never have an Assistant Bishop, for this would be "a retro-
gressive step, as there are natives competent to fill with credit and
honour the post now vacant . . . to accept any other than a Native
Independent Bishop in succession to him, is tacitly to admit his
work among us a failure, and this will be the greatest piece of
injustice and ingratitude shewn to one who all his life laboured

at so much personal sacrifice and with so much success to raise us from the depth of misery in which we are sunk".[97]

It was not long before events belied the claims made by Hill for Oluwole and Phillips. For by allowing themselves to be consecrated as "second rate bishops", as the West African press ridiculed the docile Africans,[98] they stood in African opinion as betrayers of the Negro Race. By refusing this position of "Half Bishop" James Johnson reflected the climate of opinion of Africans all along the coast. The reception accorded to Hill and the Assistant Bishops in Lagos was very cool and hostile. Bishop Hill was hoisted with his own petard and was swept into his grave in a state of nervous tension and paroxysm. Both Oluwole and Phillips found Lagos so hostile that they disappeared into the interior.[99] For several years to come Oluwole, who was supposed to be the ecclesiastical boss in Lagos, second only to Bishop Herbert Tugwell, paid the price of appearing to be a traitor to the African cause in 1894. In the opinion of one of the "young purifiers" of 1890: "In Lagos we Europeans are not wanted, in this sense, as heads and directors of Church work. The reception of Bishop Hill and his colleagues was markedly cold and indifferent, and so, why should we any longer continue to force ourselves on an unwilling people?"[100]

The official attitude of the C.M.S. to the rebellion of 1892-94 was a very negative one. Having obtained the Hill Report Lambeth Palace adopted a similar attitude, optimistic that it would soon collapse.[101] For the first time since 1863 there was a complete break in communications between James Johnson and the Church Missionary Society which was to last for several years. Not a letter passed between him and the C.M.S. headquarters. For James Johnson, who since 1881 had been receiving his salary from the Lagos Native Pastorate, the remaining years of the nineteenth century were eventful and singularly free from contentions with Church and State. His attention was almost entirely absorbed by the excitement and challenge of evangelising the Ijebu country, Oluwole noticeably refraining from visiting the Remo District, which was regarded as distinctly James Johnson's preserve.[102]

In fact James Johnson married in April 1895, having found a lady of the type he had been looking for for nearly thirty years before. She was a daughter of J. S. Leigh, a wealthy educated Egba. Sabina A. Johnson was reported to be a very pious lady. She had been trained in England for five years, loved to write in the newspapers, became an ardent advocate of hobbies for women, liked to weave African cloths and baskets, was a lover of music, and played the piano. For the short time that she was James Johnson's wife she was a jewel to him, "a most affectionate, devoted, and truly Christian and pious wife".[103]

In 1896 he led his admirers, including J. A. Payne, J. S. Leigh, J. A. Savage and Henry Johnson, in forming *The Lagos Literary and Industrial Institute*, a body aimed at fostering the intellectual life of Nigeria by establishing an embryo university where technical education and the arts would both be taught. A building was to be erected at Ebute Metta by public contributions; promising Nigerian youths were to be sent there on scholarships, in preference to institutions in foreign countries, in order to preserve Nigerian culture, a high standard of Christian morality, "Racial integrity and instincts of our youth".[104] It was no more than another attempt to revive the university education programme he had announced in the stormy days at Sierra Leone. And once again Blyden was in Lagos. Since 1895 he had taken up a civil service appointment there and he was connected with the scheme. It was expected that the Lagos administration would offer some financial help. The scheme fell through, however, partly because the Lagos Government was financially unresponsive and partly because the scheme was beyond the financial ability of the educated Africans themselves. They had enough financial responsibility in the elementary and secondary schools which they had to maintain in an age when the British administration did not consider the education of the people as its responsibility.

In the meantime the rebellion that James Johnson had led was proving a much greater success than the most sanguine promoters had expected. The only outside money which the Delta Christians received from the nationalists in Lagos and Sierra Leone was £200. For at the end of 1892 it became clear that with a balance of £495 19s. 6d. the Delta Christians controlled funds larger than that of Sierra Leone and had a surplus greater than that of the Lagos Pastorate. This was apart from the £200 grant for industrial education by the Oil Rivers' Protectorate Government. Henceforth the Delta Church stood financially independent and the following figures are worth noting.

Year	Income			Expenditure		
	£	s.	d.	£	s.	d.
1892	828	2	10	332	3	4
1893	1,238	7	8	748	3	4
1894	1,969	5	0	1,570	11	9
1895	1,210	5	5	1,086	13	7

The Pastorate undertook heavy building expenses, and boasted of a secondary school for boys and the first Grammar School for girls in Eastern Nigeria. Moreover the Pastorate evangelised the hinterland as far as fifty miles, and established Mission stations at the

important markets of Akwete, Ohambele and Azumini. By 1897
it had as many as twenty-one chapels.

In the opinion of Sir Claude Macdonald, the first High Commissioner of the Oil Rivers' Protectorate, the institution was an
asset to the Niger Delta peoples. Its clergymen were doing "most
excellent work in these Rivers".[105] To the chagrin of the Church
Missionary Society the Pastorate received moral and material support from Macdonald and his officials from the beginning. They
donated generously to it. One of the first acts of the British
administration was to convert the Pastorate's Theological School
into a Government institution, which gave the Pastorate's students
theological training *gratis*. Then A. L. Jones, the Chairman of
Elder Dempster Shipping Lines, voted ten pounds to the Pastorate
annually, apart from free passage for Archdeacon Crowther on the
coast and to and from England whenever he was doing business
for the Pastorate, a privilege not accorded to the European
missionaries of what remained of the Niger Mission.[106]

Left to the Church Missionary Society the Niger Delta Pastorate
would have remained a separate entity indefinitely. Pressure that
Salisbury Square should recognise the success of the rebellion and
come to terms with it came from two quarters—the Oil Rivers'
Protectorate Government and two of its European missionaries.
For after the 1890 purge and the rebellion it had provoked those
that remained of the nihilists discovered that the much condemned
and much vilified *Saro* were, after all, the prop of the Mission
and that without them "the Niger Mission will fall to the ground".[107]
The two stations of Brass and Abonema which had been persuaded
by the European missionaries to remain loyal to the C.M.S. so that
the latter might win back for them their markets which the Royal
Niger Company had taken away, were completely neglected for
lack of staff. In Abonema the chiefs threatened to massacre all
Christians and but for the timely intervention of the secular
administration the Society would have lost both the station and
Brass. It was at this stage that Macdonald cabled the Colonial
Office that the C.M.S. should be urged to "settle all dissensions"
existing with the Pastorate,[108] so that the Society's two stations in
the Delta might be brought to the same level of care and supervision
as that of the Pastorate's churches.

Two European missionaries observed the disparity in the prosperity and success of the Pastorate and the poverty and failure of
the Society in Brass and Abonema. One was H. H. Dobinson, one
of the nihilists of 1890. He urged the C.M.S. to swallow its pride
and come to terms with the nationalists who had after all found
"their liberty" and *"won the battle"*.[109] But the man who initiated
the steps that led to resumption of links between Salisbury Square

and the Pastorate was Herbert Tugwell, Bishop of Western Equatorial Africa from 1894 to 1920. He had witnessed the rebellion and was convinced that Africans had their grievances, that to some extent the rebellion had some justification. As has been indicated he had even been prepared to see James Johnson succeed Bishop Crowther. He did not want to preside over a diocese in which the independent Niger Delta Pastorate area would jostle with his own. Moreover he noticed that the rebellion had been a success and that it was better to integrate the institution within his diocese at a time when there was not yet any doctrinal or liturgical difference with the Anglican Church.

After a wooing visit to Bonny, the Pastorate's headquarters, Bishop Tugwell commented on the "good order, organisation and good discipline" that characterised the Pastorate work in all its branches and pronounced the following verdict on the C.M.S. station: "The contrast between the work at Bonny and the work in Brass is painful and is not to the credit of the great Society we represent. I should say at every point the contrast is in favour of the work at Bonny. Financially, educationally, morally and spiritually. At Bonny a spirit of enthusiasm and aggression is manifest, in Brass apathy, defection, discontent prevail."[110] Not only did Tugwell strive to restore amity between Salisbury Square and the Pastorate but he promised the latter to obtain from the "great society" an apology to Africans about the treatment of Bishop Crowther. This, Tugwell impressed upon the Society, should be done in order "to establish that spirit of unity and affection and love so much to be desired".[111] Bishop Tugwell was certainly statesmanlike and immediately after his consecration he was prepared to condemn some of the behaviour of the nihilists of 1890. Against the wish of the Church Missionary Society Tugwell and Dobinson made statements acceptable to the Ethiopians of West Africa, indicating that the society had shown "remorse" for the events of 1890-1892. In March 1896 Dobinson announced publicly in Freetown to a crowded audience: *we deplore some of the events which occurred in 1890 by which some men were misjudged and suffered much.*"[112]

It is against this background that the decision of the Africans to respond to the wooing of Herbert Tugwell should be understood. Salisbury Square and the Niger Delta Pastorate negotiated as equals. James Johnson was the leader of the African negotiators, the others being D. C. Crowther and James Boyle. The Draft Constitution was finally reviewed "clause by clause" by Tugwell and James Johnson for ten days at stretches of three hours each.[113] Then it was sent to Sir Samuel Lewis of Sierra Leone to obtain the opinion of this leading African lawyer and supporter of the "rebellion".

Contrary to general opinion the Constitution, which was finally adopted in 1897, did not integrate the Niger Delta Pastorate organically with the Church Missionary Society.[114] Rather it reflected in bold relief the salient principles that James Johnson had always stood for and which had inspired the rebellion. The Constitution upheld the principle of African episcopate and throughout the negotiations Bishop Tugwell gave the African negotiators every assurance that Africans would be given an independent African Bishop who would not be subordinate to himself.[115] In the preamble the rebellion was officially sanctioned by recognising the existence of the institution as from 29 April 1892, when it was established "in humble dependence upon God". The African made it clear that Church property was not negotiable. In many ways the Constitution was different from that which had been given to Lagos or Sierra Leone. Firstly although the Constitution assimilated the Pastorate to the Anglican Communion, it was completely silent over its relations with the Church Missionary Society. Consequently its personnel from the beginning to the end, for as long as James Johnson was alive, continued to be African. Secondly, unlike that of Lagos or Sierra Leone, the Constitution was not an imposition.

Well did James Johnson rejoice at the success of the rebellion he had done so much to inspire and lead. His report of the visit he made to the Delta for the constitution negotiations sounded a note of victory and triumph for the Africans. It should be emphasised that, after all, the Pastorate had negotiated on the basis of perfect equality. The success already achieved was a clear demonstration of "the capacity of the Negro for self-government", he declared. "If anything else", he informed the public through the press, "the Delta Pastorate has belied the statement of many an English Churchman that our Native clergy are disqualified to hold the position of head of a spiritual institution and I feel bound to confess that the nature of the work done within quite a brief period of the organization of the Delta Pastorate institution, has certainly corroborated the fact that if Africa will ever be Christianized it must be by her sons."[116]

Nevertheless all was not as well with the Niger Delta Pastorate as James Johnson persuaded himself to think. Just as he himself was never completely a rebel—still retaining sentimental loyalty for the C.M.S.—so the formal absorption of the Niger Delta Pastorate into the Anglican Communion was a victory for the English culture and national characteristics that pure Christianity had acquired in the English atmosphere. As long as the Pastorate was not prepared to diverge liturgically, theologically and doctrinally from the Anglican Church its independence was really compromised. As the Constitution made it plain the Niger Delta

Pastorate, like all C.M.S. churches in West Africa, recognised the ecclesiastical leadership of Lambeth Palace, declared its adherence to the rituals, the ceremonies, the accoutrements, and the doctrine of the orders of Deacons, Priests and Bishops—indeed to all the trappings of Anglicanism.

NOTES

1. C.O. 149/3, Legislative Council *Minutes*, 13/3/1889.
2. Eugene Stock, *The History of the Church Missionary Society*, London, 1899, Vol. III, pp. 392-397.
3. *Conference of West African Missionaries*, Gabon, 1876.
4. C.M.S. CA1/0123, James Johnson, Annual Letter, 1871.
5. *Ibid*.
6. *Lagos Weekly Record*, 9/1/1892.
7. C.M.S. CA2/056, James Johnson to E. Hutchinson, 8/7/1875.
8. C.M.S. G3/A2/L2, R. Lang to E. T. Phillips, 26/1/1883.
9. C.M.S. G3/A2/01, James Johnson to J. B. Whiting, 16/11/1881.
10. C.M.S. (Papers released in 1963), James Johnson to J. B. Whiting, 24/9/1890.
11. C.M.S. CA3/040, Bishop Crowther to H. Wright, 2/3/1876.
12. J. F. A. Ajayi, *Christian Missions in Nigeria*, 1841-1891, Longmans, 1955, pp. 250-5; E. A. Ayandele, *op. cit.*, pp. 205-26.
13. Philip Curtin, *The Image of Africa*, p. 363ff.
14. M.M.A. T. J. Halligey to Osborne, 26/2/1888; C.M.S. G3/A3/05, P. A. Bennett to R. Lang, 5/2/1890.
15. *Foreign Mission Journal*, January 1881.
16. Lambeth Palace Archives, *The Tait Papers*, H. Venn to Bishop of London, 20/5/1864.
17. F.O. 84/1541, F. Easton to F.O., 3/11/1879.
18. M.M.A., John Milum to J. Kilner, 11/10/1879; same to same, 5/4/1880.
19. S.M.A., J. Poirier to Père Superieur, 6/3/1885.
20. E. Hutchinson, *The Lost Continent: Its Rediscovery and Recovery*, London, 1879, pp. 58-60.
21. C.M.S. G3/A3/05, C. F. H. Battersby to R. Lang, 23/10/1890.
22. C.M.S. G3/A3/L2, The Secretaries to Bishop Crowther, 18/7/1883.
23. C.M.S. G3/A3/05, John Milum to Dr. R. N. Cust, 21/1/1891.
24. *Ibid.*, Captain R. D. Boler to C.M.S. Secretary, 24/1/1891.
25. *Ibid.*, J. A. Robinson to R. Lang, 14/2/1891.
26. *Sierra Leone Weekly News*, 16/8/1890.
27. C.M.S., G. W. Brooke's Diary in F4/7, Entry 1/4/1889.
28. *Ibid*, 4/1/1889.
29. C.M.S. G3/A3/05, G. W. Brooke to R. Lang, 28/5/1891.
30. *Ibid.*, Niger Missionaries to Committee of C.M.S., 28/10/1891.
31. C.M.S. G3/A3/04, G. W. Brooke to R. Lang, 17/12/1888.
32. *Ibid.*, J. A. Robinson to R. Lang, 9/7/1889.
33. C.M.S., G. W. Brooke's Diary in F4/7, Entry 17/4/1889.
34. *Ibid.*, Entry 10/10/1889.
35. *Ibid.*, Entry 11/4/1889.
36. *Ibid.*, Entry 1/4/1889.
37. *Ibid.*, Entry 16/4/1889.

38. C.M.S. G3/A3/05, James Johnson to F. E. Wigram, 25/9/1891.
39. Copy of Minutes of Finance Committee in C.M.S. G3/A3/05.
40. C.M.S. (Papers released in 1963), James Johnson to J. B. Whiting, 24/9/1890.
41. *Ibid.*
42. *Lagos Weekly Record*, 9/1/1892.
43. C.M.S. (Papers released in 1963), James Johnson to J. B. Whiting, 24/9/1890.
44. *Ibid.*
45. *Ibid.*
46. *Ibid.*
47. C.M.S., *Sudan Leaflet*, Entry 19/7/1890.
48. C.M.S. G3/A3/05, Annie Jombo to C.M.S., December 1891.
49. C. C. Newton to H. M. Tupper, 12/4/1892, in *Foreign Missions Journal*, Vol. XXIII, July 1892.
50. C.M.S. G3/A3/04, G. W. Brooke to James Johnson, 20/12/1890.
51. *Lagos Times*, 24/1/1890.
52. E. W. Blyden, *The Return of the Exiles and the West African Church*, London, 1891, Appendix, p. 35.
53. *Lagos Times*, 21/2/1891.
54. C.M.S. G3/A3/05, J. A. Robinson to R. Lang, 14/2/1891.
55. C.M.S. G3/A2/L6, Printed Paper entitled "To the West African Christians connected with the Church Missionary Society", 4/9/1891.
56. C.M.S. G3/A3/L3, K. Ingham to James Johnson, 15/1/1891.
57. *Ibid.*
58. C.M.S. G3/A3/05, G. W. Brooke to F. E. Wigram, 1/8/1891.
59. C.M.S. G3/A3/04, G. W. Brooke to F. E. Wigram, 24/12/1890.
60. See Appendix A.
61. C.M.S. G3/A3/05, Minutes of Finance Committee, Onitsha, August 1890; Bishop Crowther to R. Lang, 10/8/1891.
62. *Lagos Weekly Record*, 14/11/1891.
63. C.M.S. G3/A3/05, Bishop Crowther to R. Lang, 1/12/1891.
64. *Ibid.*, Memorial of Pastorate sent with D. C. Crowther to Archbishop Benson, 6/9/1892.
65. *The Delta Pastorate Chronicle*, 1897, p. 35.
66. C.M.S. G3/A3/05, James Johnson to F. E. Wigram, 25/9/1891.
67. *Ibid.*
68. *Ibid.*
69. *Ibid.*
70. *Ibid.*
71. J. B. Webster, *The African Churches Among the Yoruba 1888-1922*, Oxford, 1964, p. 66.
72. *Ibid.*
73. N. A. Ibadan, H. Johnson, *Diary*; H. Johnson to H. M. Trupper, 9/6/1891.
74. C.M.S. G3/A2/010, James Johnson to F. Baylis, February 1902.
75. *Lagos Weekly Record*, 27 October and 3 November 1917.
76. C.M.S. G3/A3/05, James Johnson to K. Ingham, 25/9/1891.
77. C.M.S. G3/A3/L3, F. E. Wigram to James Johnson, 15/6/1891.
78. *Sierra Leone Weekly News*, 4/1/1892.
79. C.M.S. G3/A3/05, Ingham to K. Ingham, 7/8/1891.
80. *Ibid.*, W. Allan to K. Ingham, 8/12/1891.
81. *Ibid.*, same to same, 22/12/1891.

82. *Ibid.*
83. *Ibid.*, same to same, 1/1/1892.
84. *Ibid.*, Memorial sent by D. C. Crowther to Archbishop Benson, 6/9/1892.
85. *Ibid.*, H. Tugwell to R. Lang, 23/5/1892.
86. *Ibid.*, Annie Jombo to C.M.S., 14/4/1892.
87. C.M.S. G3/A3/06, J. S. Hill to Archbishop, 20/12/1892.
88. *Ibid.*
89. C.M.S. G3/A3/08, James Johnson to H. Tugwell, 5/10/1899.
90. C.M.S. G3/A3/05, J. S. Hill to Archbishop, 20/12/1892.
91. *Phillip's Papers* (N.A.1), *Diary*, Entry 24/11/1892.
92. *Ibid.*
93. C.M.S. G3/A3/05, J. B. Wood to J. S. Hill, 19/10/1892.
94. C.M.S. G3/A3/06, "The Congregation and Members of the Delta Pastorate Church Bonny—to Archbishop of Canterbury, 29/7/1893".
95. *Ibid.*
96. *Ibid.*
97. *Ibid.*
98. *Lagos Weekly Record*, 12/8/1893.
99. C.M.S. G3/A2/07, H. Tugwell to F. Baylis, 8/1/1894.
100. C.M.S. G3/A3/06, H. H. Dobinson to F. Baylis, 5/2/1894.
101. *Ibid.*, "Memorandum by Edward Cantuar", 6/3/1893.
102. Oluwole and E. Stock, "A Notable African Bishop", *The Church Missionary Review*, 1917.
103. C.M.S. G3/A3/09, James Johnson to F. Baylis, February 1902.
104. Egba Archives, Ake, Abeokuta, paper dated 28/5/1896.
105. C.M.S. G3/A3/06, Sir C. Macdonald to C.M.S., 10/3/1894.
106. E.M.T., Sepelle, *The Church in the Niger Delta*, P. Harcourt, 1955, p. 124.
107. C.M.S. G3/A3/05, H. H. Dobinson to R. Lang, 7/6/1894.
108. C.M.S. G3/A3/06, Sir C. Macdonald to C.M.S., 10/3/1894.
109. C.M.S. G3/A3/05, H. H. Dobinson to R. Lang, 13/7/1892.
110. C.M.S. G3/A3/06, H. Tugwell to F. Baylis, 26/6/1899.
111. *Ibid.*, same to same, 2/7/1895.
112. C.M.S. G3/A3/09, H. H. Dobinson to F. Baylis, 24/7/1896.
113. C.M.S. G3/A3/06, H. Tugwell to Dr. Smith, 3/10/1895.
114. See copy in G3/A3/07.
115. C.M.S. G3/A3/06, H. Tugwell to F. Baylis, 9/11/1894.
116. *Lagos Echo*, 15/1/1898.

CHAPTER TEN

HALF BISHOP

I have declined to accept the kind invitation of the late
Bishop Hill to be an Assistant Bishop. . . . My opinion
and feelings regarding the position have undergone no
alteration, but on account of the circumstances of the
present situation upon the condition that with your
consent, sympathy and co-operation and of those of the
C.M.S. Committee and others in authority in connection
with the matter I should be at liberty and as soon as I
possibly can work to promote the independent Bishopric
of the Delta.

James Johnson to Herbert Tugwell 5/10/1899

HAD he so desired James Johnson could have been consecrated
Assistant Bishop of Western Equatorial Africa in 1893. His rejection of the post, which Oluwole and Phillips accepted with alacrity
and eternal gratitude to the white man, revealed a particular
characteristic of his nature, which prevented him from realising
what was possible. It hardly ever occurred to him that in the affairs
of men, as individuals or as communities, there is perpetual conflict
between the actual and the ideal, between the attainable and the
vision. Official after official in the Colonial Office was kept amused
by his memoranda on the social and the political welfare of the
peoples of West Africa which showed how little could this African
agitator perceive the distinction between the desirable and the
feasible.[1] For, James Johnson, more than most men, lived in the
realm of dogmas. Obsession with dogmas in turn blurred his perception of the realities of a situation. Thus in 1893 the dogma of
Africa for the Africans which should see an independent African
Bishop succeed Samuel Ajayi Crowther was of greater weight with
him than the fact that Lambeth Palace had announced unequivocally that Africans should not expect anything higher than a
subordinate position; the Christian dogma that God is no respector

of race or colour appealed to him more than the realities of the Scramble era that accorded paramountcy to human and racial considerations in the directorship of Church and State.

Little wonder that in spite of the realities of colonial rule, in which the white man was the undisputed lord in Church and State, James Johnson continued to live in hopes for, and in the vision of, the Ethiopian programme he had conceived in Sierra Leone. Thus only four years before he was swept into his grave he declared in his longest and most memorable address, that he was still looking forward to the emergence of "an independent and self-governing African Church in communion with other Churches like itself, with its Ministry including its episcopacy, its liturgical service and other ecclesiastical arrangements bearing the distinctive hallmark of Africa, even as our negro colour distinguishes us from other peoples, although we and they are members of one and the same human family".[2] During the First World War, at a time when the European economic stranglehold of Africa was virtually complete, James Johnson still saw the economic emancipation of Africa at the corner, through the agency of the African Movement,[3] an organisation of Negroes in the New World dedicated to the objectives of settling Negroes in West Africa and economic self-determination for the Negro Race.

Nevertheless, whilst never abandoning his dogmas James Johnson was constrained to seek to achieve the ideal by first accepting the inevitable—the *fait accompli* of British colonial rule. Therefore his tactics continued to be protests and petitions about specific grievances of the Nigerian peoples to the Colonial Office either directly or indirectly, through the Aborigines Protection Society. In the Church the situation was different. Unlike the State the white lords had to recognise the ideal, and had to say so from time to time. Consequently James Johnson had the opportunity to manœuvre and continue to press that the ideal should be put into effect.

It was because the Church continued to parade the theory of the ideal that James Johnson and the Niger Delta Pastorate Christians refused to accept the decision of 1893, by which a European succeeded Crowther, as final. Just as James Johnson pooh-poohed the idea of a second-rate Bishop so the Delta Christians were resolved that, rather than have a European Bishop or an African Assistant Bishop, they were better left alone. They were adamant about an "independent African Bishop", in the person of James Johnson, and, as they affirmed, they were able and ready to pay his salary. Indeed although Lambeth Palace would never grant this wish it was an ideal against which the Church could not argue. Therefore on 12 December 1893 the Delta Christians were informed by Archbishop Benson: "It is my heartfelt desire ultimately to appoint an independent native Bishop and I am ready to take the necessary steps so soon as the development and organization of your Church justify such an appointment."[4] For the next five years the Pastorate held on unyieldingly to this ideal. As is clear from the preceding chapter it was from a position of strength that the Pastorate negotiated the Constitution of 1897; it was in an ecstatic mood that James Johnson reported to the press on the purpose and achievements of the Institution after his visit to the Niger Delta in 1896. The confidence and hopes of the Pastorate rested on its financial buoyancy. Contrary to the expectation and prediction of the C.M.S. and Lambeth Palace the Pastorate was able to bear its burden and push the missionary frontier into the interior.

But the Pastorate's confidence was illusory. The independence in Church affairs, which its members began to parade and James Johnson began to extol, was premature and out of tune with the state of affairs in the political and economic spheres. The white man's indisputable overlordship in these two spheres could spell doom to independence in religious affairs. This was precisely what happened. For when the white man's Government decided to super-impose its metropolitan monetary system on the traditional one and determine the rate at which traditional currency would be driven out of existence the Delta Christians had no choice but to accept the situation. Hitherto twelve manillas, the traditional currency in the Niger Delta, were equivalent to one shilling. But from 1896 onwards twenty manillas were demanded for the same amount of British coin. In other words the replacement of traditional currency with silver currency meant a depreciation of the former by 67 per cent. For a long time to come the 4,000 Delta Christians had to pay their subscriptions in manillas. The result was that although the institution was in a position to continue to pay its staff the hope of being able to pay the high salary of a Bishop— £350 per annum—disappeared. After 1896 the institution had hardly credit of £100 each year. The deteriorating financial situation will be understood from the following facts. In 1897 income was £959 5s. 11d. whilst expenditure was £1,047 16s. 7d., leaving a debt of £88 10s. 8d. So penurious was the institution that it began to resort to begging from the Church Missionary Society. In 1897 D. C. Crowther begged for facilities and funds for the training of agents for the Pastorate and in 1898 submitted ceremonially to the authority of Bishop Herbert Tugwell. In May of that year, in the presence of representatives of converts in Bonny, he resigned his Archdeaconry and was formally again appointed by Bishop Tugwell as Archdeacon and his Commissary in the Niger Delta.[5]

Indeed the tide was turning against James Johnson. Not only did church after church in the Niger Delta make it plain in 1898 that in the circumstances in which they now found themselves they could not pay for an independent African Bishop; not only did church after church ask that the Church Missionary Society give them an Assistant Bishop and pay for him, but a number of prominent laymen began to say that it was Archdeacon D. C. Crowther, the man who after all had been connected with the Delta Church for more than twenty-five years, that they wanted and not James Johnson.[6] Not that they had anything in particular against James Johnson, but it was the former who had been dealing with the day to day problems of the institution since its inception. But D. C. Crowther would not accept the honour; he felt that it belonged to James Johnson.

But the man who deserves the greatest credit for the consecration of James Johnson as "Half Bishop" of the Niger Delta was Bishop Tugwell. The part played by James Johnson in apparently bringing the Delta Church back to the C.M.S. bosom impressed the Bishop. Perhaps he felt that Johnson's nationalist inclinations were on the wane. After all he had not been boisterous since 1894, except over the liquor question, an issue on which both Tugwell and the C.M.S. agreed *in toto* with the African agitator. Then in 1899 James Johnson accepted gratefully an invitation from the C.M.S. to attend the Society's centennial celebration. Tugwell decided that Johnson had suffered enough for his African feelings and that his spiritual and administrative abilities should be employed by the Society.[7] To this end he decided to make James Johnson an Assistant Bishop of the Niger Delta Church Pastorate. A very clever tactician, Tugwell, who since 1893 had been persuading the Delta Church to abandon the ideal of an independent African Bishop, exploited the financial incapacity of the institution to the full.

James Johnson's stature in African eyes was by no means diminished, in spite of the fact that his ecclesiastical status was inferior to that of both Oluwole and Phillips. Nor was his excellence unacknowledged by the Society. For in Nigeria both Assistant Bishops were ignored in 1899 by the Society when it invited James Johnson alone to its centennial celebration. As a newspaper commented on the invitation:

We are glad that Mr. Johnson has promptly responded to their [C.M.S.] call. He is far and away the greatest native clergyman that the C.M.S. Missions have yet produced in West Africa (excepting always Bishop Crowther) and his visits to England have always helped the Society's work. But there are reminiscences in connection with his past labours which will not readily fade from his or our memories. He has not been wafted to the present position on 'flowery beds on ease'. True greatness is never reached by means of so luxurious instrumentality. We are sure, however, that the Reverend gentleman would have been pleased if he could have gone this time as the representative of an independent native Church, the outgrowth of the Society's labours. Such a Church has been the object of his most earnest aspirations for more than a quarter of a century. We trust he will be more successful than on his two previous visits in getting the Society to move in directions which the actual conditions and exigencies of the work demand.[8]

In England James Johnson was the cynosure of Church Missionary Society supporters as on the two previous visits. On 12 April he gave an address in Exeter Hall. The theme remained constant, what it had always been. The Mission world, he declared, had been failing in its duty to help achieve the Ethiopian programme which, he said, was ordained of God. The Cross should bestride the African continent, chase out the Crescent, put an end to the liquor traffic and raise up an African agency if the Church was to escape the fate of the North African Church and of the Congo experiment of the sixteenth and seventeenth centuries. Would the Mission world allow this to happen? "When you have before you in God's own word the prophecy and promise that Ethiopia the land of the sun-burnt people, shall stretch out her hands unto God?"[9] The Church Missionary Society was singled out for commendation, not because of its large role in the Christianisation of Africa but because of its upholding of the dignity of the Negro Race in the face of increasing negrophobia in the white man's world. He declared: "The Church Missionary Society has vindicated the position and the claim of the Negro to the brotherhood of humanity. The Church Missionary Society has proved to the hilt that the Negro is capable of being taught the Gospel of Christ and that he can give his heart to Him who has died for him. The Church Missionary Society has also proved that the Negro is not the ape and the brute that he was thought to have been but that he is a man, an intellectual being and, that, given the opportunity, given the advantages, he can hold his own as almost any other person in the world."

By this time James Johnson had no idea of Tugwell's plan for him. Unknown to him was the fact that the Society in which he reposed so much faith did not really forgive his past in the Crowther rebellion and was deaf to Tugwell's idea of elevating him to the position of Assistant Bishop until the quick-tempered Tugwell had threatened to appeal to the Anglican public in Britain for funds to maintain James Johnson in that position for the Niger Delta Pastorate.[10] Arrangements to put him in the position had been completed before he was informed of it.

He allowed three weeks to elapse before answering the offer. To our surprise, perhaps, he accepted the position he had more than twice rejected. Although in accepting the post of "Half Bishop" he made it plain that for him it was no more than an expediency the act was rather unJohnsonlike. In the past he would not have considered the expedient, even as a starting point for the road towards the ideal; he had insisted on being full Bishop or remain a mere curate. He had refused to compromise. But as will be shown presently, James Johnson had by 1900 begun to mellow in his human relations, in his attitude to African traditional religion and customs and institutions against which he was wont to pronounce on the basis of dogmas before really investigating what they were; he had begun to accept human beings as they were, rather than as they ought to be. Consequently his response to Tugwell's offer was positive, just as his response to Hill's six years before had been blatantly negative.

But it would be misunderstanding James Johnson to think that in accepting the offer he was being inconsistent or that he was abandoning his nationalist objective. For he accepted the post of a second-rank Bishop, not as an end in itself, but as the practical and perhaps the only means available for the achievement of his ultimate goal—the creation of an independent African Diocese in the Niger Delta, the nucleus of his ethereal African Church. He believed that as Assistant African Bishop and with liberty to raise sums for an endowment he would be in a position to infect the Niger Delta Christians and all Africans in West Africa with his nationalist idealism; that he would be able to apply for funds on the platform of Negro nationalism, and that after realising sufficient funds, establish his independent Church. Furthermore he stated clearly his terms—Bishop Tugwell, the C.M.S. and Lambeth Palace must be willing parties to this proposal in a contractual sense.[11] All his terms were duly accepted and the big sum of £10,000 for an Endowment was prescribed. On 18 February 1900 he was consecrated the "Half Bishop" of the Niger Delta, the sermon preached by a man of his own choosing, the Reverend J. B. Whiting. Simultaneously he announced his "Niger Bishopric Fund", the Archbishop ordering that the offertory at the consecration should be contributed to the Fund.

It should be stressed that the Bishopric scheme was not originated by James Johnson. The idea, as pointed out in an earlier chapter, should be credited to Bishop Ingham, who saw in such a scheme the only successful means of stultifying James Johnson's inspired African nationalism in the Yoruba Church in 1887. Ironically the idea was picked up by James Johnson in 1899 for the achievement of the purpose which Bishop Ingham had sought in the eighties to defeat with his scheme. In a sense, then, James Johnson's burgled Bishop Ingham's idea of 1887.

With his consecration James Johnson received the highest tributes of his life. The Africans, who perceived the nationalistic aspect of his Niger Bishopric's scheme, regarded him as a hero rather than as a traitor. The first contributors to the scheme were the Sawyerr brothers of Sierra Leone who jointly contributed £100 and the arch-Johnsonian, R. B. Blaize of Lagos, who contributed £100. Unlike the coldness and apathy with which the consecration of the "traitors" of 1894—Isaac Oluwole and Charles Phillips—was met, that of James Johnson aroused a great deal of interest and support.

Honour upon honour was heaped upon him by Europeans and Africans. The university of Durham conferred on him the degree of Doctor of Divinity. One Canon Tristian and the Dignitaries of the University presented him with a suit of Episcopal Robes "as a mark of their kind interest in me and warm sympathy with my work".[12] The Church Missionary Society made him a Vice President of the Society and the Negro Race was thought to have been honoured when the C.M.S. asked James Johnson to preach the Annual Sermon at St. Brides on 30 April 1900, thus being the first non-European ever to have the privilege. A few weeks later he was received by Queen Victoria. James Johnson's consecration, it is said, came to be perceived by Negroes as "a gradual and larger fulfilment of the prophecy that 'Ethiopia shall soon stretch out her hands unto God' upon which they have long been accustomed, amidst distracting and depressing thought over the terrible misfortunes and disasters that have befallen and oppressed their race, to centre their interests and hopes. . . ."[13] The entire Negro World paid him glowing tributes, through representatives of Ethiopia, Liberia, the West Indies and Negro America. In a long address, beautifully phrased and nicely mounted, the following words occurred: "We are confident, my Lord, that your speeches as a Legislator, your sermons as a missionary, and your position now as a Prelate have tended, and will continue to influence the rising men of our race for good. God grant it. Therefore, we most sincerely congratulate you on your elevation and earnestly hope and pray . . . that excellent accounts of your work of lifting Africa's sons to a higher intellectual and industrial level may be heard of, so to encourage others to follow your footsteps. . . ."[14]

"Half Bishop" James Johnson returned to West Africa as a hero. Never was his prestige and popularity to rise again to the level it did in 1900 and 1901. In Sierra Leone, where he disembarked in September, he was accorded a spontaneous and rapturous welcome. He was received with an hysterical demonstration of joy at the Wilberforce Memorial Hall, under the chairmanship of Sir

Samuel Lewis, the first African in British West Africa to be knighted and an old student of the "Half Bishop" at the Grammar School. An address of eulogies was presented to him. During his stay, which lasted for nearly two months, he preached twice in each of the five principal churches (Anglican) in Freetown. He dined with Governor Cardew, was entertained by the Consul of Liberia and visited Benguema, his village of birth. On 26 September a deputation of the Ijesha Descendants Association, headed by Dr. William Renner, J.P. and Acting Colonial Surgeon, presented him with an address, soliciting his patronage and lauding him for "the deep interest you take in whatever concerns the welfare of your race in general, and your loyal and devoted attachment to the people of your tribe in particular".[15] He was given happy memories of his earlier days in Sierra Leone by a number of women whose morals he had guided over thirty-years before at Pademba. He was gratified by the physical and constitutional changes that had occurred in the Colony, particularly the Municipal Council "dominated by Africans", the "excellent" stone and wooden storey buildings "on all sides" and the railways and telegraphs which he hoped would "contribute much towards a wider diffusion of the Gospel over West Africa".[16] The students of the Grammar School considered his elevation to the position of Assistant Bishop an honour, in the sense that he was the first product of the institution to achieve such a position. On 5 December 1902 his photograph was unveiled with a speech by Sir Samuel Lewis in which James Johnson was described as "a man of firmness and purpose, courage and inflexible will, a kindly disposition and a strong lover of his country and race".[17]

In Lagos there was an even greater and wilder demonstration of joy which culminated in another secession from his Breadfruit Church in sympathy with him. Before his arrival there in November his popularity had brought embarrassment and disgrace to Oluwole. For, James Johnson's consecration for the Niger Delta notwithstanding, the Church Missionary Society believed that James Johnson should not be lost entirely to the Lagos Church. Therefore the suggestion was made to the executive of the Lagos Church, the Church Committee, that he should continue to be Pastor of Breadfruit Church, while at the same time performing his episcopal duties in the Niger Delta. This suggestion was gall and wormwood to Oluwole, the Acting Chairman of the Church Committee. He had hitherto regarded James Johnson's consecration as a godsend that would remove from Lagos the one man whose influence had neutralised his ecclesiastical status. Therefore he rejected the C.M.S. suggestion.

By rejecting this proposal Oluwole stirred up the hornet's nest. He awakened the bitter memories of 1894 against himself. The laity of all the Anglican Churches made it plain that they wanted James Johnson to stay on in Lagos. It seemed to the laity that Oluwole wanted to betray the Negro Race again, that he was back at his tricks again, stabbing the Negro Race in the back by opposing the physical presence of the man they regarded as its perfect representative. The untrue rumour that James Johnson's luggage, which had preceded him to Lagos, was being removed out of the Breadfruit Parsonage earned Oluwole the humiliation of Lagos women marching on him; his attempt to conduct a service at Breadfruit Church earned him the disgrace of the congregation dispersing on him. Even his life was threatened.[18] On James Johnson's arrival he was welcomed by the Christians, the Muslims and the 'pagans'. For months his popularity continued to be a problem for the Anglican authorities who perceived that only his physical removal from the island could bring about a calm atmosphere. To this effect he was instructed by Bishop Herbert Tugwell to depart for his "Diocese" in April 1901.

James Johnson was to be "Half Bishop" of the Niger Delta for the remaining seventeen years of his life. For the second time in his career he had a large area within which to apply his talents. But the Niger Delta was quite different both in geography and ethnography from the Yorubaland he had superintended from 1877 to 1880. Mangrove-ridden and inhabited by relatively small tribes, by 1900 European activity in trade, administration and the dissemination of the Gospel message was still tied to the coastal fringes. This littoral had been the exclusive monopoly of the Church Missionary Society, except the Old Calabar area under the United Presbyterian Church of Scotland, until the last two decades of the nineteenth century when the Qua Ibo Mission appeared in the Qua Ibo River area and the Primitive Methodist Mission in the Ibibio area.

Hardly had he arrived in the Niger Delta than James Johnson embarked on the primary object of his life—that of the spread of the Gospel. Expansion was his watchword. His consecration coincided with the period of military expeditions which forced recalcitrant Edo and Ibo peoples to open their countries to British rulers and traders. Christian missions lost no time in following the Flag. It was the area over which the Edo held sway in the heyday of their imperial power that first attracted his attention. The desire to Christianise the Edo, he declared, had consumed him since his boyhood when his father related to him the cruelties and sufferings he had experienced as a slave in Benin City, the capital of the Edo-speaking peoples.[19] Before his consecration he viewed with dismay the attempts which the Catholic priests of the Society of African Missions seemed to be making to enter the area.

It was in July 1901 that he set out for Benin City. This was four years after the British had brought fire and sword upon the capital. James Johnson did not have the honour of introducing Christianity into the city, having been anticipated by educated Africans and *Saro*, members of the clerical staff of the British administration and independent traders. Consequently there were already pockets of immigrant Christians in Sapele, the chief town of the Urhobo and Warri, the chief settlement of the Itsekiri. But although he was not the torch-bearer of Christianity to the Edo, the Itsekiri and the Urhobo, the credit of initiating and organising churches among these three ethnic groups belonged entirely to James Johnson. For since 1894, when the Itsekiri and Urhobo began to be conquered by the British, and since the Benin Expedition of 1897, Christian missions, including the Church Missionary Society and the Society of African Missions, turned a deaf ear to the repeated appeal of the British administration that they should establish themselves among these peoples. For the C.M.S. Yorubaland and Northern Nigeria were far more attractive than the Edo-speaking areas, whilst the Society of African Missions had practically exhausted their resources in the Ibo area of the Asaba hinterland.

It was to these neglected groups that James Johnson turned his attention, thus becoming the first missionary, European or African, to visit them. After prior consultation with Chief Dogho,[20] the man who had succeeded Nana as paramount chief of the Itsekiri, James Johnson landed in Warri in July 1901 and on 28 July held the first organised service there, with the large number of 230 people attending. He was able to organise a Church here, which henceforth used the Native Council Hall until a proper church building was erected a few years later. In Sapele he was able to organise converts on a similar footing. By 1904 there were some 300 Enquirers there and on 11 June 1905 he dedicated the church that had just been erected. These two stations of Warri and Sapele were to flourish so well that by the time of his death in 1917 each had fifteen congregations affiliated to it. James Johnson succeeded in getting an Itsekiri, Omotshola, to supervise all these churches in Warri and Sapele districts, the agent having been educated at the Hope Waddell Institute, Old Calabar.

James Johnson arrived in Benin City on 13 July 1901. He remained there long enough to collect information on the events leading to the Benin Expedition. He was appalled at the bestialities of Overami, "his very cruel and abominable holocaust, his extravagant waste of human life upon his god—to propitiate that divinity so that he might gain a victory over the British arms".[21] He was particularly stunned by the sacrificing of one Julius Thompson, an educated Edo from Lagos, who was alleged to have

warned Overami that if he was sacrificed the British would capture
and destroy Benin. James Johnson organised the Yoruba and *Saro*
Christians into a congregation which met at the Government School
building until 1904, when a church had been put up and dedicated.
But it was not until 1906 that he was able to put an agent there.
He was the Reverend H. Atundaolu, who had been a Wesleyan
minister for fourteen years. It is remarkable that among the Edo
who became full members of the Church in Benin and who were
baptised by James Johnson were a wife of the ex-king Overami,
her daughter and two grandchildren. James Johnson visited the ex-
king's mother, the Queen Mother, at Ihelu, where she was pro-
pitiating *Orishabunwa* for a return of her son.[22]

Beyond Benin, on the north-west and north-east lie respectively
branches of Yoruba and Edo-speaking peoples. It was the interesting way in which Christianity was introduced into these areas that
persuaded James Johnson to expand his interest in those directions.
He did not have to introduce Christianity into these places. This
had been done by ex-slaves of a different kind from among the
liberated Africans and the *Saros*. They had been captured during
the prolonged civil war in Yorubaland and sold to centres of
missionary activity, where they were converted. After the termination of the Kiriji War they decided to return to their respective
homes to introduce the light they had seen in captivity. In Owo there
was Joseph Doherty who was sold as far away as Lagos. He
gathered a congregation of people like himself in Owo, using the
compound of the Shashere, one of the leading chiefs in the town.
At Iyayun in the Iddo Ani district there was Isaac Tenabe, who
had been sold to Oyo. At Ora, the chief settlement of the Ivbiosakon, an Edo-speaking people, the torchbearer of Christianity
was Elegbeleye, a native of the place who had been sold to Ilesha.
Here he was converted and he acquired the ability to read in the
native tongue.[23]

It was these little-educated ex-slaves who had prepared the way
for James Johnson, when he began to supervise all the areas from
1901 onwards. In Owo there were eventually three stations with a
little more than 100 converts by 1914, when the Church Missionary
Society took over the district from James Johnson, together with
the Iddo Ani area. But up till his death he retained the supervision
of Ora which became the most successful station in the western
part of the Niger Delta. By 1906 Ora had 98 out of 119 full communicants in the territory and 360 out of a total of 988 Enquirers.
Next to Ora was Sapele with eight full communicants and 387
Enquirers. In 1907 there were in the Ora District nine places of
worship and four evangelists, all natives of Ora.

Apart from the area west of the Delta which James Johnson

added to the geography of the Niger Delta Pastorate, he lost no time in pushing the missionary frontier into Iboland. Until the series of military expeditions which began with the Aro Expedition the Ibo had successfully warded off the intruders. On the Niger, penetration into Iboland by Bishop Crowther never went beyond two miles; on the Cross River, the United Presbyterian Mission of Old Calabar never dared to make a westward thrust into Iboland. The main reason for Ibo exclusiveness was fear of the loss of their land and sovereignty. Commercially, of course, they did not want to lose their middleman's position. As late as 1900 Europeans who had ventured as far as Bende were driven away by the dreaded Aros. This news would not deter James Johnson. It was in the interest of his 'diocese' to extend the missionary frontier to Iboland to save the Niger Delta Pastorate from a rapid decline. For more than half of the Delta population were Ibo slaves who at the humanisation of slavery by the British administration might be tempted to return to their "original home". And, as the vast majority of Christians were of the slave class the Pastorate could be reduced to a condition of statistical decline.

The possibility of such an event occurred very early to James Johnson. "It would be our wisdom to anticipate this and seek to acquire a foothold in that interior now," he wrote, "and strengthen ourselves in a district whose importance would eclipse that of the coast."[24] In November 1901 he set out for Arochukwu, the seat of the much-dreaded Long Juju, terror of whom pervaded all Iboland in the pre-colonial period. But he could only reach Akwete, an important oil market at the periphery of Iboland. For the Aro and their military arm, the Abams, attacked Ubago, only fifteen miles away, on 20 November. No less than 800 women and girls were massacred and James Johnson had to join Bonny Christians in the offering of protection to some of the Ubago refugees. Indeed an officer of the British administration advised him to go no farther as the Aro Expedition would soon be launched.[25] It was during this attempted visit to the heart of Iboland that he was shocked by the barbarism of the Ibo in their area of the Delta region. As he claimed, he counted in the houses of "principal inhabitants . . . human skulls heaped together on scaffolds or strung together on a framework of wood and placed in some conspicuous place in the house or premises with the object of their declaring or proclaiming the importance of the householder".[26]

In February 1903, after fire and sword had descended on the Aro, James Johnson renewed the attempt to establish a mission station in Arochukwu. In a tour that lasted two months he was able to see the effects of British rule on the Ibo. The days of oppression by court clerks and "Warrant chiefs" had begun. For people took to their heels, fleeing into the bush, at the sight of him and his party, in the belief that they were representatives of the white man who had begun to exploit and oppress them. In village after village elderly men waited upon James Johnson "with their complaints . . . in reference to the blackmailing from which they and their people had suffered . . . that death from the bullets of British soldiers would be preferable to the very miserable life they had been living since the conquest and of the occupacion of the country by the British military force and the introduction of British rule".[27] In Bende James Johnson succeeded in getting such "miscreants" of the Abam District dealt with by the British Commissioner.

From the missionary viewpoint he was not as successful in Iboland as he had been in the western area. There were no immigrant Christian communities; there were no ex-slave evangelist pioneers. Although the United Presbyterian Mission had had an eye on Bende and Arochukwu James Johnson was the first to preach in many villages and certainly the first to preach in Aba and to distribute copies of the *Ibo Primer* in the interior. In Aba, Bende and Arochukwu he spoke before chiefs and people, who importuned him for teachers, denouncing cannibalism. At Arochukwu he visited the Long Juju and his description of the grove and of the settlement of Arochukwu itself still perhaps remains the best account.[28]

The missionary tours of James Johnson had greater value than the statistical results. They gave him the opportunity to inform himself about the culture and institutions of the Edo and the Ibo, peoples essentially different from those he had known before. The language of the Itsekiri interested him immediately because it possesses morphological similarities with the Yoruba language, a phenomenon that made him express the view reiterated in subsequent years, that both the Yoruba and Itsekiri possessed at some point a common past. The Edo language he did not understand immediately but he regretted that Edo works of art had been destroyed during the Benin Expedition and appreciated the historiographical value of such materials.[29] It was the habits and the customs and the ethnic characteristics of the Yoruba of Owo and Iddo Ani districts, of the Ivsabiokon of Ora and the Ibo of Bende and Arochukwu areas that attracted his attention most. In this respect his recordings must be a mine of information for sociologists and social anthropologists. In the Ibo country he observed the value of ornaments—anklerings, cosmetics, hairstyles, tattoos— among the women, and the indolence of the Ibo and the hard use he made of the woman. But what struck his attention most was the martial spirit of the Ibo which, he said, had been reinforced by "tribal or township jealousies". He admired the resistance they had

S

put forth against the British: "They pass for skilful stockaders and as adepts in the art of riddling a path with sharp pointed spikes against an enemy's approach."[30] In the Owo District he was appalled at the custom of child marriage. He records that girls who refused their husbands were punished by having their ears lopped off or by being drowned. From his records also emerge the facts, later attested by social anthropologists, that twin-infanticide prevailed in the Ekiti country and that among the Ivsabiokon twin albinos and deformed children were usually killed; that among the latter boys and girls of the age of five or six were married.

The missionary programme which James Johnson set for himself was greater than could have been sustained even by the larger, wealthy and organised Christian missions. But the Niger Delta Pastorate was not a missionary society. Indeed James Johnson's inheritance of 1900, the Niger Delta Pastorate, was a problem in very many ways. Although in the period 1864 to 1897 the most liberal Christians and the most zealous evangelists in Nigeria belonged to the Delta, the institution had by 1900 fallen on evil days, hardly able to sustain itself and much less able to sustain others. Consequently the stations he had opened up west of the Delta—Sapele, Warri, Benin City and Sabongida Ora—were not really part of the Niger Delta Pastorate; they were the personal property of Holy Johnson. Not a penny of the Pastorate was ever spent on these stations which James Johnson grouped together as the Benin Mission, nor were the churches ever institutionally or constitutionally a part of the Pastorate.

The Benin Mission was sustained by self-help on the part of the stations, but mainly by gifts and donations from friends and admirers in Britain. In this respect the chief helper was one Miss E. H. Beckwith, "who has been an invalid confined to her house many years now, but whose facile pen and very eloquent pleading from her sick-room have always brought me much valued contribution to my Diocesan Fund for mission extension".[31] Then there was an Irish lady, Miss Susan Atkins, who from 1900 to 1910, when she died, gave him £36 every year. Other "European friends" gave less frequently and the voluntary donations of African admirers all along the coast were erratic. It was from these sources that he employed agents like Omotshola at Sapele, the Reverend C. F. Cole at Warri, H. Atundaolu at Benin City and the agents in Ora.

Nor did the Pastorate have the means to evangelise the Ibo country. All that the Delta Christians were able to do was to organise themselves into bands of volunteers, which worked in Bende and Arochukwu for six-month periods. With quarrelsome people, unattractive geographically and comprised almost entirely of slaves, the Niger Delta Pastorate was impoverished. The institution became poor because the Delta people were victims of historical developments over which they had no control. The frontier of opportunity moved into the interior, killing the middleman's system upon which the Delta peoples had depended for more than four centuries. The days of affluence were over. Profits were extremely marginal. The converts were very generous, giving from 5 per cent to 10 per cent of their earnings and profits. Income rose from £1,012 2s. 4d. in 1902 to £1,604 18s. 10½d. in 1907. But expenditure rose in proportion, leaving hardly up to £100 balance in the Church's treasury in any one year. The effects of the grinding poverty that began to stare the Church in the face were visible in several ways. Salaries of the staff were inadequate and irregularly paid. Moreover it would have been cheaper to run the institution with local people, but for the first ten years all effort by James Johnson to recruit Ijaws failed. The educated Ijaw preferred a career outside the Church which possessed prospects of advancement and higher salaries than could be afforded by the Church. For, as they were relatively poorly educated when compared with the *Saro*, the chances of the local people holding more than subordinate posts were very slim indeed. Consequently the age-long tradition of recruiting agents from Sierra Leone continued, with telling effect on the finances of the institution.

The financial difficulties of the institution may be judged from the fact that throughout his directorship of the Niger Delta Pastorate Holy Johnson had no official quarters. The Church Missionary Society voted a sum of £500, which was expected to be supplemented by the Delta Christians, for a residence for their "Half Bishop". Benin and Old Calabar were mentioned as possible places for his abode. But not only was the Pastorate unable to find funds to supplement the C.M.S. grant, but it was so penurious that it could not bear £20 per annum towards the cost of the Bishop's rent. Consequently James Johnson became an itinerant Bishop renting a house in Lagos, where he resided for three months in the year, moving from one station to another in his 'diocese' for the rest of the year. Needless to say it gave him much personal inconvenience until towards the end of his life he was able to have a personal house, with more than one storey, situated near the old secretariat in Lagos.[32] By 1904 the Pastorate was faced with "outstanding debts to be paid and buildings to be repaired".[33] In 1905 the financial power of the Pastorate was further reduced by the sudden decision of the chiefs to withdraw the aid which they had hitherto given to the Pastorate. Although they never embraced Christianity, which they regarded as a religion fit only for slaves, they had since 1900 made an annual grant of £40. James Johnson's persuasion with them was of no avail. They withdrew the grant "on the plea of a low condition of trade and diminished income to their state coffer especially as they were still practically masters and owners of almost all the members of the Church and the earnings of these persons and others like them are taxed by them".[34]

The unsatisfactory financial situation engaged the attention of Holy Johnson and leaders of the Pastorate from time to time, particularly at the annual conferences. It was debated whether Pastors and the Parochial Committee should be invested with the powers of the chiefs and heads of Houses, in order to enforce the payment of the House Tax on members. Holy Johnson was faced with a problem not dissimilar to the one he had faced in Yorubaland, particularly in Abeokuta, regarding the class fees which he believed should be exacted by force by the Pastors. The way and manner he handled the matter in the Niger Delta indicated clearly that he had mellowed, that after all he could appreciate the peculiar situation of the slave-ridden Niger Delta Pastorate and accept the attainable in place of the ideal. The question was, as usual with him, thrown open. As he recorded: "Some advocated strong discipline by the exclusion of persistent and wilful defaulters from the roll of registered members and the privileges of full communion with the Church; and others a silent passing of their names when the list of members is read out at the weekly Bible class meetings till their obligations are discharged. But the recommendation that was adopted was that whilst it was not doubted that defaulting members of a Society forfeited their claim to continued membership connection by their failure to discharge their obligations to it and whilst Parochial Committees should persist in making their demand upon defaulting members of the Church for a full and regular discharge of their stated pecuniary obligations to it, earnest prayers should be continually offered on their behalf to God who alone can and will make them willing in the day of his power, and impress them with a strong and active sense of their obligations to Christ."[35]

The final judgment, with which James Johnson concurred, was an immense contrast to the opinion he had held in Abeokuta from 1877 to 1880. James Johnson had ceased to be the autocrat who would wish to compel people to behave in a particular way. There was no question of outlawing defaulters, just as there was no question of removing liquor dealers from the roll of communicants. In the Niger Delta he was dealing with a different kind of Christian community, in a different set of circumstances and in a different age. In Sierra Leone the Victorian type of rigidity in moral and religious matters was all right; in Abeokuta, where he was dealing mainly with offspring of liberated Africans like himself, he was in the midst of a free and sophisticated people. But in the Delta he was dealing with the poorest and lowest class over whom he could not impose his own will. Not that his attitude was less fixed; his ideal for a genuine Christian life was pursuing legitimate trade and donating liberally for Churchwork. But in practice he was learning to be pragmatic and to realise that religion was essentially a matter of personal conviction.

James Johnson's "diocese", then, was impoverished. It had no endowments, no wealthy converts. It was thrown upon its own resources, supporting its own ministry, evangelising the 'pagans', training its agents and doing its own translational work. It is against this background of poverty that the achievements and progress of the Niger Delta Pastorate during the seventeen-year directorship of Holy Johnson should be assessed. His first task and success was the integration of the Brass churches into the Pastorate. Although the Brass had sympathised with the rebellion that James Johnson had led in 1891, they did not join the independent Niger Delta Pastorate because European missionaries had promised them that if they stayed on under the C.M.S. the Society would help them to regain the markets which the Royal Niger Company had taken from them. The refusal of the Society to fulfil what the Brass regarded as a pledge had led to the Akassa Raid of 1895 and the desertion of Christianity for the traditional religion. Only a few people remained in the Church. James Johnson found the soil "very hard".[36] Those who had defaulted refused to come back to the Church. Nevertheless he was able to persuade the few remaining Christians to merge with the Pastorate and become self-supporting.

Perhaps James Johnson's greatest success was in the welding of the various churches into a unit. Separated by creeks and lagoons the key churches at Bonny, Brass, Okrika, Opobo, Bakana, and New Calabar had a tendency to be self-governing. The inter-state warfare over markets and the struggle for supremacy in the Niger Delta which had characterised the area in the nineteenth century had left behind a legacy of bitterness. Opobo in particular resented the fact that Bonny, from which it was torn away in 1870, was the headquarters of the Pastorate, whilst the other churches wanted to be free of Bonny control. The surprising thing was not that a monolithic unity was not achieved but that any degree of co-operation by all the churches was made possible at all. Although several of the pastorates were very reluctant to transfer money raised by them to the central Fund at Bonny the bodies that were instituted for central control of all the pastorates survived the strains and stresses of intra-tribal bitterness.

The Executive was the Church Council on which the pastorates were represented and which met twice a year. It was this body that paid salaries and decided the location of agents. But there were annual conferences as well for the clergy and the laity, fixed for February and rotating from centre to centre. To James Johnson's dismay these conferences were usually poorly attended. He had expected that they would serve the purpose of promoting "that feeling of oneness and common interest and that wholesome rivalry which it is desirable for all the several pastorates to entertain and exercise towards each other, the existence and development of which difference of nationality, language, custom and past tribal feuds and warfares are calculated to prevent".[37]

But besides the legacy of intra-tribal warfare of the nineteenth century there were other fissiparous forces that began to militate against the solidarity of the institution. There was, for instance, intra-House feud within each city-state and reflected in the division within the Church. In practically all the churches—Bonny, Opobo and Bakana for example—the solidarity of each church was threatened by this kind of feud. In 1906 the two factions of a House led by communicant members resorted to open fighting in the streets. In Bakana all efforts were of no avail by James Johnson and others to settle the fratricidal conflict between Marion Braid, the paramount chief and the leader of one party and Lulu Will Braid, his nephew and next in rank and leader of the other party, which dated back to the nineties. It was not until 1913, after the disputants had dragged themselves to court and been fined from time to time, that they resolved their conflict and resorted to the Church to "thank Him for the restoration of peace and harmony among them".[38]

He had to deal with another fissiparous factor—that of the struggle for power and control between the laity and the clergy. Since practically all the ordained agents were from Sierra Leone it had an ethnic overtone, assuming the complexion of a conflict between the *Saro* foreigners and the native Ijaws. It was in the premier church, St. Stephen's Cathedral, that this conflict was most acute. Here the Reverend James Boyle, whose connection with the Niger Mission went back to the sixties, was involved in a conflict with non-communicants, who were nevertheless the most influential members of the Church. The latter accused him of monopolising all power, through his lackeys in the Parochial Committee. These embittered powerful members elected their own nominees and refused to attend services or pay dues unless their will prevailed.[39]

Besides these fissiparous factors James Johnson had to contend with other problems as well. The herd-instinct that governs the Ibo people was a matter of anxiety for him at the meetings of the Executive. Individually the Ibo members would not talk at meetings, but later at subsequent meetings they would as a body "resurrect" old matters. "The position", commented the "Half Bishop", "calls always for the exercise of much patience."[40] Then there was the moral degeneracy which accompanied the material decline. For in order to promote their trade interests the Christian converts descended to the moral level of their customers in the interior markets by taking women customers as concubines; they also became polygamists. Nor could they dispense with the trade in liquor. With regard to financial matters James Johnson saw the futility of attempting to compel the converts to observe the injunctions of the Christian faith in sexual matters or his own on the liquor traffic. He could not excommunicate dealers in liquor as he had done in Sierra Leone; nor could he be severe with those guilty of moral lapses. Exhortation took the place of execration; persuasion that of ex-communication. There was no question of winnowing the wheat from the chaff. It should be stressed that James Johnson had no choice to accepting the situation as he found it. The converts he had to deal with now were different from the earlier generation. The latter had been liberated to a very great extent by Christian missionaries and they had taken Christianity literally, to the point that they would never trade on Sundays or even sell palm wine.[41] But the new generation, though still the lowest in society, were born into a good measure of liberty. Naturally their sense of gratitude to the new faith was much less strong than that of their fathers.

It might have been expected that the constitutional arrangement concluded with the Pastorate institution and the placing over it of an Assistant Bishop whose salary was paid by the institution, would persuade the Church Missionary Society to grant some financial aid. But this did not happen. There were two reasons for this. First of all the Society did not forget, or forgive, the rebellion of 1891-92, a matter painful to Herbert Tugwell.[42] Secondly, the institution never abandoned the idea of a full African episcopate, under the inspiration of James Johnson. In other words, as far as Salisbury Square was concerned, the Niger Delta Pastorate was not only conceived out of rebellion but it continued to be an unrepentant and incorrigible rebel. Even when the institution was striving to acquire a theological college all that the Church Missionary Society gave was £5, whilst the Society for the Propagation of Christian Knowledge gave £100.[43] It was not before 1911 that the Bishop Crowther Memorial Institute was founded, largely from local subscriptions and from non-C.M.S. sources in Britain. It is significant that the plan for the Institute was drawn *gratis* by Herbert Macaulay.

It was in the field of education that James Johnson achieved a measure of success. Education had always been a matter of paramount interest to him. Although the Delta peoples were among the early patrons of Western education, the education of women was still frowned upon at the time of James Johnson's appointment. The attitude of the Delta peoples in this regard is worth appreciating. It was purely utilitarian; boys would be an asset as accountants but not girls. By 1906 a quarter of the 764 pupils in the various schools were girls. On 11 July 1904 was founded the first post-primary school for girls in the Niger Delta, the Female High School of Bonny, due to the gifts of English friends and local subscriptions. The headmistress was one E. M. George from Sierra Leone.

There was also a post-primary school for boys, at Abonema. There were only six primary schools, two of which—those in Bonny and Opobo—were being assisted by Government. Not only did James Johnson carry out an annual inspection of all the schools in the Niger Delta Pastorate areas but he laboured to impress on the chiefs and peoples of the area the educational value of the vernacular against which there was prejudice everywhere in contemporary Nigeria. On one occasion he had to address the Delta chiefs thus:

> If I give you a good lock you want a key to open it; if I give you the wrong key, you are not able to open it, and if you use force you will spoil the lock. Children's minds are like locks made to be opened and God gives you the key which is the language of the country; if you refuse to use it, or try other keys or force, you will either never open their minds or spoil them altogether. The English language is the key to open the minds of English children, not German or French and so the Brass language is the key for Brass children. Use then the language of your country to teach your children, and then through their language they will learn to understand English. If the children understand what they learn, they will take a pleasure in it, the work will be easier for the schoolmaster, easier for the children.[44]

In order to press home his point further he interested himself in all the languages of the peoples of the Niger Delta among whom he was working. Until his consecration not much translation work was done in Ijaw but in 1901 he appointed two Translation and Revision Committees—one at Tuwon under the direction of Henry Proctor and the other at Nembe under the direction of J. Wilson. These European missionaries were to have the help of David Ockiya, an Ijaw, and P. J. Williams, a *Saro*. So much was he concerned with vernacular literature that he studied Itsekiri, Urhobo, Ora and Benin and went as far as producing Primers for beginners in all these languages, apart from making translations of portions of the Bible and the Book of Common Prayer.[45] In none of these languages, it should be stressed, was James Johnson proficient; none of his translations exceeded an amateur standard. But the point to note is that he was a pioneer of the literature of these peoples and it was through him that hundreds of people who became Christians first learned their alphabet in their own language.

In spite of his efforts Christianity never achieved popularity in the parts of Southern Nigeria that constituted James Johnson's 'diocese'. All along he attempted to find out the reasons for the non-acceptance of the new religion on a massive scale comparable to the situations in Yorubaland and in Iboland. Apart from the fact that the lethal coastal areas were largely ignored by the Christian missions there were reasons peculiar to the areas under his supervision. According to his experience there were three factors working against his activity in the Edo country. Firstly the British administrators in the Benin area were uniquely secular-minded. Although they did not oppose missionary activity as such they did not encourage it either. Unlike in other parts of Nigeria, where missionaries and administrators were giving the impression that they were birds of the same feather, the administrative officers persuaded Edo chiefs that missionaries were not only a separate class of people, but also a group not indispensable or all that desirable. Thus, to James Johnson's surprise, when he applied for land the Edo chiefs, on the instruction of an administrative officer, urged that land be leased rather than given on freehold terms.[46] This was certainly contrary to the tradition and practice all over West Africa, according to which land was given to Christian missions freehold for an indefinite period of time, as long as it was being used for the purpose for which it had been given. Then there was the misbehaviour of another administrative officer who seized the bell of the overzealous Christians in Benin in order to make a noise with it and persuaded the chiefs to impose a fine on the African minister of the church.

It was natural, therefore, that the chiefs believed that a favourable disposition towards the new religion was not a *sine qua non* for securing the good countenance of the British administration. Moreover the latter established schools which were completely secular. In James Johnson's judgment the absence of religious instruction, that is Christianity, from their curriculum was a disservice to the Edo. The latter, he said, would become atheists and a people without any ability to practise moral principles. The products of these schools, he observed, had by 1904 begun to manifest indifference to Christianity. Then there was the obstacle posed by polygamy. A number of chiefs who in the earlier years began to attend services withdrew in 1905, "alleging as a reason that they could not appreciate a Religion which would require them to relinquish polygamy, dismiss severally all but one of their wives, break up their families and destroy their households in order to become professors of it and Members of its Church".[47]

In the Owo District, which James Johnson described as a hard soil, there was no mass movement because, as a part of Western civilization, Christianity was corrupting morals and upsetting society. The first effect of the white man's presence was the terrific blow administered to the prestige of the Olowo of Owo, who was compelled to dismiss a large number of his slaves and wives. But it was the disturbing effect of Christianity on the home that was distasteful to the people. For several girls, who had been married off by their parents, began to claim the liberty to choose men of their own liking in the name of the Christian religion. Then came a decline in morals. As recorded by Holy Johnson, "All speak everywhere of these days as degenerate days. It is painful to think that a growing corruption and loss of innocence and virtue are a price the interior countries are in many instances called upon to pay for an enforced freer contact and commerce with the coast especially."[48]

Among the Ivsabiokon, where Christianity succeeded most in the western part of his 'diocese', the main obstacle was provided by the chiefs and traditionalists. For by 1905 Christianity had become a disturbing element. Christians began to claim new loyalties and began to renounce traditional ones, particularly those relating to traditional religion. For they began to refuse to participate in the traditional religion; to repair roads leading to groves; to offer animals killed during hunting expeditions for sacrifices or for distribution among the elders as prescribed by traditional religion.[49] In the judgment of the traditional guardians of law and order the votaries of the new religion were turning the world upside down, behaving in a manner that might provoke the gods to bring calamity to the community. Several laws were promulgated against the new religion. Church bells were seized, Christians were compelled to work on roads on Sundays and Church attendance was prohibited. However, far more than in any other part of his 'diocese', Christianity was able to command the respect of the Ora people. For on 10 June 1907 James Johnson was able to summon chiefs, Christians and 'pagans', to the Church at Eme. He succeeded in lecturing them on the barbarity of their ways and the importance of their observing laws and sanitation, including the disposal of refuse and the non-pollution of the springs from which they took their drinking water. He also spoke to them on what was to be a big problem in the future—the loss of interest in agriculture and the movement to other parts of Southern Nigeria for employment.[50]

In the Niger Delta the Church stagnated. By 1906 it had become clear to James Johnson that there was no need for new churches. The chief factor militating against Christianity was sociological. The chiefs had absorbed the idea that Christianity was only fit for their subordinates, people of slave origins who from the beginning had been the main supporters of the religion. Moreover the chiefs could not reconcile themselves to the idea of monogamy. It should be stressed that although many of them passed through mission schools in their boyhood they believed that traditional religion offered them all they required. It was their ambition, noted James Johnson, to be "exalted to the position and dignity of deified ones and honoured with worship".[51] This ambition could be realised only with respect to the traditional religion. Moreover, at a time when it was becoming difficult to amass wealth, through the loss of their middleman's position, the need for them to pay attention to their trade was more imperative than ever. Lastly, many of the chiefs were turned away from Christianity by their "frequent intercourse with ungodly Europeans".[52] It was not until after 1910 that the attitude of the chiefs to Christianity began to change. By 1913 a few chiefs in Okrika had embraced the religion and something like a mass movement to Christianity actually began there.

Throughout James Johnson's 'diocese' the vast majority of the people continued to adhere to traditional religion. In this connection the Edo were perhaps the most unrepentant 'pagans'. Groves and altars were to be found everywhere. According to James Johnson's observation their "heathenism" was "much higher than that of the Yoruba". Although they worshipped several divinities "there is always an altar devoted to Jehovah. The sacrifices offered at this altar are to be perfectly white, the worshippers also are to dress in white."[53] But throughout the 'diocese' certain customs began to give way. In New Calabar printed cloths, which used to be regarded as sacred to Kalabari divinities, could be sold. Mudhouses, hitherto forbidden to human beings by *juju*, began to displace wooden houses. In Okrika the high dowry, which used to be an obstacle to young men who wished to marry, was abolished.

Even if he died without achieving the Christianisation of the majority of the population of his diocese he could claim that he was more than a "Half Bishop". Although in theory he was no more than a mere lieutenant of the Diocesan of Western Equatorial Africa, Herbert Tugwell, yet in practice he often behaved as if he were really independent. In many ways he did not behave as a subordinate in the way Oluwole and Phillips did. In a sense he was more fortunate than these two because his territory was farther away from Lagos and constituted a unit in a way that the areas under Phillips and Oluwole did not. For the residence of Tugwell in Lagos made it easy for the Diocesan to overshadow Oluwole. In fact so patently ridiculous was the latter's position between 1901 and 1904 that it was being seriously proposed that the churches in Ijebuland or Egbaland be put under his control. Unfortunately, however, the missionaries in the latter refused flatly to have an African ecclesiastical master,[54] whilst in the former, until his consecration, James Johnson's control and authority remained unquestioned. Charles Phillips was more independent in the remoter eastern half of Yorubaland, but only in the sense that he conducted an annual visitation and exercised some control over the agents. But his control over the latter was not complete; many of them appealed against his authority to the European-controlled Executive Council.[55] In fact Charles Phillips himself had to report to this body in Lagos, which exercised control and supervision over the administrative affairs of this area.

In contrast was James Johnson. He was a law to himself; he reported to no executive in Nigeria and the reports of the territory which he sent to the Church Missionary Society were his decision. Nor did he do this every year. He was in absolute control of his agents in administrative matters and in ecclesiastical affairs as well, except on the very rare occasions when Bishop Tugwell visited the Niger Delta. James Johnson indicated his independence of attitude in several ways, in a manner tantalising to several European missionaries. Firstly, like a full independent Bishop he began to summon annual conferences at which all the agents and lay representatives were gathered. At every one of these conferences he delivered what amounted to the Bishop's Address, in which he dinned into the ears of his lieutenants his observations on world events, European misbehaviour in Africa, the intransigence and apathy of chiefs towards Christianity, apart from the factors retarding the evolution and progress of genuine Christianity in the Niger Delta Pastorate areas. It should be remarked that of all the Assistant Bishops of Western Equatorial Africa he was the only one who had the daring to set up an organisation of this kind and who never bothered to attend the conferences of the entire Diocese summoned annually by the Diocesan.

Even when in 1906 the Synod, which was expected to give a form of unity to the Anglican community in Nigeria, was founded, James Johnson was the odd man out. He refused to attend any of its meetings until 1909. The point to emphasise is that in spite of his never failing loyalty to the Anglican Communion the ideal of an independent African Church and the independent African Bishop never quite eluded him completely. By his action after his consecration he showed that he interpreted the arrangement of 1899-1900 in his own way. When he began to appear at a few meetings of the Synod his was a dominant, if not a jarring voice. The Synod became for him nothing more than a theatre for the delivery of lectures and the exposition of his views on the necessity of African Bishoprics and the role that independent African Bishops should play.[56]

Although Holy Johnson never deliberately refused to be submissive to the Diocesan there can be no doubt that had his ecclesiastical overlord been any other than Tugwell conflict between them would have been difficult to avoid. But on the contrary the relations between Johnson and Tugwell were very cordial and they communicated frequently. Tugwell understood James Johnson very well and deliberately allowed him liberties that neither Oluwole nor Phillips would have dared to claim. As the Diocesan often asserted, the Niger Delta was a special preserve of James Johnson and it was specifically for that 'diocese' that he had been consecrated. Always at the back of Tugwell's mind was the fact that James Johnson was an excellent man, under whom he had been willing to serve after Crowther's death. It is clear that Tugwell perceived that it was only by allowing him a good deal of freedom that the nationalism this African agitator was advocating in the Church could be contained.

NOTES

1. See Minutes on C.O. 267/369, James Johnson to Sir H. Holland, 26/7/1887; C.O. 147/62, James Johnson to E. Stanhope, 4/1/1887; C.O. 147/147, James Johnson to J. Chamberlain, 27/12/1899.
2. *Jubilee Volume of the Sierra Leone Native Church*, London, 1917 (his Jubilee sermon February 1913), p. 201.
3. *Sierra Leone Weekly News*, 18/11/1914.
4. C.M.S. G3/A3/06, Edward Cantuar to Delta Pastorate Church, 12/10/1893.
5. C.M.S. G3/A3/07, H. Tugwell to C. F. H. Battersby, 12/5/1898.
6. *Ibid.*, Petition by Chief S. Epelle and others to H. Tugwell, 25/4/1898.
7. C.M.S. G3/A3/09, H. Tugwell to F. Baylis, 19/1/1899.
8. *Lagos Weekly Record*, 8 and 15 April 1899.
9. *Sierra Leone Weekly News*, 3/6/1899: text of speech by James Johnson at Exeter Hall, 12/4/1899.
10. C.M.S. G3/A2/09, H. Tugwell to F. Baylis, 22/5/1899.
11. C.M.S. G3/A3/08, James Johnson to H. Tugwell, 5/10/1899.
12. C.M.S. G/AC 4/30, James Johnson to S. W. Fox, 2/3/1900.
13. C.M.S. G3/A2/011, James Johnson to F. Baylis, February 1902.
14. Reported in *The Rock*, London, 20/7/1900.
15. *Sierra Leone Weekly News*, 24/11/1900.
16. C.M.S. G3/A1/02, James Johnson to F. Baylis, 6/3/1900.
17. *Sierra Leone Weekly News*, 7/12/1902.
18. C.M.S. G3/A2/010, I. Oluwole to F. Baylis, 19/9/1900.
19. James Johnson, *A Brief Outline et seq.*, p. 24.
20. C.M.S. G3/A3/09, James Johnson to F. Baylis, February 1902.
21. *Ibid.*
22. C.M.S. G3/A3/011, "Bishop Johnson's Missionary Report, 1907".
23. C.M.S. G3/A3/09, "A Report of a Missionary Journey within and beyond the Southern Nigeria British Protectorate from November 1903 to July 1904" by James Johnson.

24. *Ibid.*, "Report of a Missionary Journey into Interior Iboland Southern Nigeria from February 24-April 8 1903" by James Johnson.
25. *Ibid.*
26. *Ibid.*
27. *Ibid.*
28. *Ibid.*
29. C.M.S. G3/A3/011, "Bishop Johnson's Missionary Report, 1907".
30. C.M.S. G3/A3/09, "Report of a Missionary Journey into Interior Iboland Southern Nigeria from February 24-April 1903" by James Johnson.
31. *Sierra Leone Weekly News*, 16/1/1915.
32. 5 Campos Street. Still a modern-looking house; see photographs.
33. C.M.S. G3/A3/09, James Johnson to H. Tugwell, 23/1/1904.
34. C.M.S. G3/A3/010, Presidential Address to Delta Conference, 20/2/1905.
35. *Ibid.*, "Bishop Johnson's Journal Report, December 1904-July 1905".
36. C.M.S. G3/A3/09, James Johnson to F. Baylis, February 1902.
37. C.M.S. G3/A3/011, "Report of the Niger Delta Pastorate Church and Mission Work 1906" by James Johnson.
38. *Western Equatorial African Diocesan Magazine*, October 1913, pp. 173-176.
39. C.M.S. G3/A3/010, "Bishop Johnson's Journal Report December 1904-July 1905".
40. *Ibid.*
41. For an account of the first generation of slave Christians in the Delta see E. A. Ayandele, *op. cit.*, Chapter 3.
42. C.M.S. G3/A3/011, H. Tugwell to F. Baylis, 22/2/1906.
43. *Ibid.*, D. C. Crowther to F. Baylis, 10/8/1910.
44. Quoted in *Nigerian Pioneer*, 20/7/1917.
45. *Ibid.*
46. C.M.S. G3/A3/09, James Johnson to H. Tugwell, 15/4/1902.
47. C.M.S. G3/A3/010, James Johnson to F. Baylis, 21/7/1905.
48. C.M.S. G3/A3/09, "A report of a Missionary Journey within and beyond the Southern Nigeria British Protectorate from November 1903 to July 1904" by James Johnson.
49. C.M.S. G3/A3/010, "Bishop Johnson's Journal Report December 1904-July 1905".
50. C.M.S. G3/A3/011, "Bishop Johnson's Missionary Report, 1907".
51. *Ibid.*, "Report on the Niger Delta Pastorate Church and Mission work, 1906".
52. *Ibid.*
53. *Jubilee Volume of the Sierra Leone Native Church*, London, 1917, pp. 86-87.
54. J. B. Webster, *op. cit.*, p. 70.
55. See for example in G3/A3/010 the papers on the dispute between Bishop Charles Phillips and Moses Lijadu over policies referred to the Executive Committee in which judgment was given against Bishop Phillips.
56. Ibadan University Library, *Report of the Proceedings of the First Session of the Second Synod of the Diocese of Western Equatorial Africa*, pp. 70-75.

CHAPTER ELEVEN

APOSTLE OF AFRICAN PERSONALITY

> God does not intend to have the races confounded, but that the Negro or African should be raised upon his own idiosyncracies.
>
> James Johnson to Pope Hennessy 24/12/1872

As may have been gathered from the accounts given so far of his nationalist exertions in Church and State James Johnson's behaviour was often the outcome of a process of thinking. There was never any question of his being rash, of his taking a step he was likely to regret or a stand he would be at a loss to defend or explain in rational terms. For he had a tremendous capacity for thinking, a thinking derived partly from his literary education, partly from his unique conversion, partly from his experiences in and observations of Sierra Leone, Lagos, Yoruba and Niger Delta societies and partly from his contact with different classes of Europeans. From the earliest times his thinking developed into ideas, the latter in turn crystallising into principles. It was when he applied these principles to issues, as he invariably did, that he possessed opinions and arrived at judgments that were on several occasions at variance with those of less reflecting, less principled, less dogmatic African colleagues. Hence his loneliness on the independence issue in the Church in Sierra Leone in 1873-1874 and in the State in Lagos in 1889.

But not all his ideas were provocative or controversial or within the realm of action. One of the ideas he conceived very early in his career in Sierra Leone, and which he expostulated throughout his life, remains alive with us to this day. It is the concept of African Personality.

As an ideology that has been investigated in respect of one or two contemporaries of James Johnson and a few present-day African leaders in thought and statesmanship, it is essential to indicate the ideas of African Personality expressed by the latter in order to put the uniqueness of his conception in its appropriate place. Since it came into currency at the beginning of this century the term "African Personality" has never quite meant the same thing as it did to the African patriots with whom it has been associated. For Dr. Mojola Agbebi, about whom Edward Blyden first used the term in 1903, African Personality had a predominantly cultural connotation. African customs and institutions not offensive to humanity, Agbebi stressed for the greater part of his life, should be adopted rather than abandoned as the majority of educated elite in West Africa in the Victorian era tended to do.[1] For Edward Blyden, African Personality meant that Africans must preserve the purity of the Negro Race and the characteristics with which the race was endowed. There should be no intermingling of the races: "Any African who does not contend for the purity of his race is not worthy of a place in the ranks of humanity."[2] For Kwame Nkrumah, a former President of Ghana, African Personality is largely a political philosophy, the implementation of which would exorcise from Africa all forms of imperialism and neo-colonialism. In practical terms, says Nkrumah, its implementation would see the emergence of one Government for Africa as the only institution that would enable Africa to neutralise the subtle attempts of the former colonial powers to maintain an economic stranglehold on the continent.[3] For many African *literati* today, including Leopold Sedar Senghor, African Personality has mainly a psychological and emotional connotation, clearly discernible in their abstract philosophy, songs and poetry.

Common to all the exponents of African Personality is the fact that in their articulation was something of a paradox. Products of the formalised education systems of their colonial mentors they became, inevitably, victims of Western norms, social habitudes, mores and religion. In spite of efforts by many of them to emancipate themselves from the cultural enslavement in which, as they discovered in later years, their education had placed them, their mental orientation remained a puzzle: a curious amalgam of the European and the African. The result, naturally, was their ambivalent attitude to African culture. Invariably they renounced or rejected some traditional customs and institutions, whilst sometimes with an astonishing gusto they appropriated or adopted others. Their media and methods of articulation were all foreign; their language either English or French—as the case might be—even when venerating African culture; their weapons the newspaper, political organisation and the Christian religion.

These African intellectuals were, then, betwixt and between. In some respects they looked towards Europe for their values, inspiration and hopes; in other respects they turned their eyes towards uncontaminated Africa. They envied Europe its literacy, its science, and its technology and wished for their continent an economic development that would raise the material standard of Africans to a level not inferior to that of contemporary European society. But at the same time they were anxious to see preserved all they deemed worthwhile in African culture, which they regretted seeing so battered and badgered by a penetrating European civilisation. In this latter desire they were in search of an identity that would remove from them the stigma that they were not pure Africans but Europeanised or Americanised or hybridized Africans. However their wish was one thing, reality another. It was largely in theory that they wished away the European culture and mode of thinking in which they had been brought up; it was impossible for them completely to identify themselves with uncontaminated Africans. In this sense their claim of personifying Africa is not true. Willy-nilly they found themselves in a dilemma that defied solution.

No apostle of African Personality has had to face this dilemma as much as James Johnson. As hinted in an earlier chapter[4] no one was at such pains as he to paint a romantic account of the virtues and excellence of uncontaminated Africans in the most unrestrained language. But equally no one was at such pains as he to advocate adoption of the means that would bring about a transformation of uncontaminated Africa—by his puritanical outlook, his literal acceptance and his platonic conception of Christianity. For to deprive Africans of their religion was to completely undermine the morality of society and de-Africanise them in the social, cultural and metaphysical aspects of indigenous religion. As he admitted in the later years of his life the religion of the Yoruba achieved moral and social results that must bewilder the moral educationists of today.[5] Indeed, as he also admitted, Christianity had patently failed to produce in its votaries in West Africa a similar level of morality and cohesion, to the extent that he was becoming anxious that Christianity might suffer another effacement in Africa. And yet the source of his credo of African Personality ceased to be Africa with its religion but Christianity with the Bible, together with Christian theology and Christian ethics. As he said, what he wanted in Africa was "to see Christianity and pure Scriptural morality deep-rooted in the African soil".[6] For him Christianity was the only prophylactic for "the woes of a land made wretched by foreign greed of gain".[7]

James Johnson's unyielding commitment to Christianity and its values leavened his conception of African Personality to such an extent that even when he seemed to be on common ground with his contemporaries—Edward Blyden and Mojola Agbebi—his language and emphasis, his passion and opinionatedness, his extremism—gave his ideas an acerbity and a rigidity distinctly his own. No other African intellectual and patriot has been so cribbed, cabined and confined as James Johnson was within the iron walls of Christianity. The result was that he suffered from a myopia that sometimes made nonsense of his apostleship of the African Personality doctrine. Take for instance his conception of the African, the genuine Christian. In this regard he looked upon the *Saro* and the Negroes in the New World—that is the very categories of the Negro Race farthest from traditional religion and the most Europeanised and Americanised—as better representatives of African Personality than the religious traditionalists or Muslims, no matter what features of African-ness were possessed by the latter. Blyden and Agbebi, who were much less inhibited by Christianity, saw the *Saro* and American Negroes in quite a different light—as peoples who had lost the identity of Africans and who must be persuaded to shed the European or American culture into which they had been foisted and return to African culture and mental orientation.

Holy Johnson never alluded to, or perceived, the fact that to a very great extent the *Saro* and Afro-Americans had been de-Africanised, that in several ways they were more European and more American than African. Although he was an exponent of repatriation of Negroes back to the African continent he never expected them to identify themselves with what existed in Africa; rather, he declared, they were to become models for Africans. It was more the racial discrimination they were suffering in the United States that annoyed him, rather than a desire to see the Negroes fall back on African culture or persuade them to demand a separate existence in the country of their exile. Only once did he declare that he would like to see Negroes return to Africa because in the New World "they cannot under any possible circumstances, exist as a distinct nation".[8]

In another way James Johnson's rigid commitment to Christianity made him turn his back against Africa—in the cultural sense. Hence his unreflecting, nihilist and wholesale condemnation of a number of customs and institutions towards which, for instance, the much-less inhibited Blyden and Agbebi were more accommodating. A good example is his attitude to polygamy, an institution which was not a moral issue in African traditional society. Without investigating the true position of this institution Holy Johnson declared a relentless warfare against it. Polygamy, he said, made the African a debased being, less than human. It was "immoral", a negation of Divine Law which all peoples on the terrestrial globe should obey. In James Johnson's opinion, only victims of sensual gratification, voluptuaries, would uphold such an institution. "If polygamy is immoral in Europe," he wrote in 1894, "it is immoral in Asia and Africa also." So much did he loathe this institution that, again without any research, he pronounced that it was an obstacle to population growth and a sap of man's mental vigour; it was the cause of slavery, inter-tribal wars and jihads.[9]

James Johnson's distorted views of polygamy became a disservice to African members of the Anglican Church in 1886. At a conference in Wakefield, England, his views served as a useful weapon for Anglican orthodoxy against the more informed opinion and judgment of Dr. E. M. Bickersteth, Bishop of Exeter, who spoke in favour of admitting polygamous converts to full Church membership. James Johnson's opposing views, erroneously held out as authentically African, were theological rather than African. When in subsequent years he relaxed his attitude to polygamy he did so not because he was in the least prepared to understand it and appreciate its virtues, as Blyden and leaders of the African Church movement in Nigeria did, but because he feared that if Christian missions did not relax their policy Islam would continue to out-rival Christianity. As late as 1908 he repeated his theology of marriage in the following language: In his innocence, he declared, Man was ordained to be monogamous: "The aim of Christianity is I take it, to re-establish everywhere on the earth the original form, Monogamy, and at the same time correct the awful licentiousness which disgraces many a European city where Monogamy is professedly the only form of marriage permitted to its inhabitants."[10]

Nevertheless, his obsessive attachment to Christianity notwithstanding, James Johnson was an early exponent of the philosophy of African Personality in his own particular fashion and in an impressive manner. First, far more than any of his contemporaries, he expressed the view and conviction that Africans were not only a distinct race but that they were in no way biologically inferior to, or different from, other races. In 1900 he said: "I hold it strongly that the black man is the equal of the white, given similar advantages, and his powers of mind will develop equally with those of the white man."[11] The backwardness in which the African found himself, he loved to stress, was an accident of history and the handiwork of geographical environment.

This belief, it should be remarked, was not original. Europeans like Henry Venn, Thomas Clegg and Heinrich Barth, the famous German explorer, had said so earlier and independently, to refute the pernicious doctrine of the racist writers and explorers of the middle years of the nineteenth century. But in West Africa it was James Johnson who reiterated this view intermittently and emphatically from the early days in Sierra Leone until the time of his death. Never did he lose an opportunity to impress this idea on to his fellow Africans. It became his habit to hold before European disparagers samples of Africans who had mastered the white man's skill to the credit of the Negro Race. Thus at the commemoration service of Dr. T. N. King, the first Nigerian medical doctor, he stressed that the deceased, who had Europeans among his clients, "did prove that all things equal, Africans can hold their own with Europeans".[12] It was in the same way that in 1903 he held up Sir Samuel Lewis, who was patronised by Europeans and who enjoyed an undisputed reputation as a legal luminary in British West Africa.

The talent displayed by some prominent educated elite in West Africa reinforced his conviction that the African was capable of standing shoulder to shoulder with the white man. It gave him the opportunity to remind his fellow Africans and to enlighten jaundiced Europeans, for whom the doctrine of biological inferiority of the Negro Race had become a dogma. For him it was shown beyond doubt that the Negro Race was the equal of the White Race. As he lambasted the negrophobists with a list of accomplished West Africans:

They spoke as if Crowther, the first Negro Bishop of the Niger Territory, had not publicly and fully demonstrated in his long life and by his zealous and devoted apostolic labours the capacity of the Negro to embrace and practise Christianity and teach it to his countrymen, or as if Quaker, the first native principal of the Church Missionary Society's Grammar School in Sierra Leone, had not by popular consent and public acknowledgement led it to a higher success than it had before attained after his appointment to and assumption of the post which had for many years before been filled by Europeans; or as if Babington Macaulay and Captain James Davies had not unitedly and with the countenance, sympathy and co-operation of the Church Missionary Society called a grammar school into existence in Lagos, or as if Davies and Horton, the first up to this day since 1858 the only duly qualified negro medical men to serve as Military Doctors in the British Army where they respectively attained to the rank of Principal Medical Officers, had not proved through nearly 25 years of active service, and in the case of one of them through his valuable literary productions on tropical diseases among other subjects also, that the negro can be both a good soldier and a worthy disciple of Aesculapius; or as if the Negro Republic of Liberia had not in Crummel and Blyden and in its poet Hilary Teague been proclaiming in able lectures and inspiring patriotic songs the aspirations for their beloved Africa.[13]

The point to emphasise is that in an age when several educated Africans, who had been dazzled by the technological marvels and the material display of the white man, were diffident about the capacity of their race to stand side by side with the other races of mankind, James Johnson did not only emphasise his conviction in the biological equality of his race with other races, but was also optimistic and in hopes about the future of the Negro Race.

Rather than being diffident James Johnson was extremely proud about many of the endowments of traditionally uncontaminated Africa. In this respect, far more than any of his contemporaries, he was concerned about the physiognomy of the African, which he wanted preserved intact. In primeval Africa, contended Holy Johnson, the uncontaminated African was endowed with manliness, a willingness and joy to endure hardship, "habit of thrift and that self-control and self denial and that physical strength",[14] which enabled him to be self-reliant and self-governing; he paid taxes with joy; he lived long; the urge, power and force of association with others to co-operate communally was very strong in him; he was very religious; he had the moral fibre to resist evil and the standard of his sexual morality was incredibly high.

It was these virtues which, under the instinct of self-preservation, James Johnson wished to see preserved. It did not occur to him that the form of life which inculcated these virtues could only be preserved intact in the traditional environment in which Africans had lived, had moved and had had their being. He did not perceive that once the traditional environment was changed, as he expected it to be changed by Christianity, the virtues must automatically change their shape, if they did not wholly disappear. Here, again, James Johnson was on the horns of a dilemma, posing a riddle he could not solve. In his emphasis on primeval Africa and the virtues he believed it fostered James Johnson gave the impression that all the contact he wished with the European world was that which would give Africans mental cultivation, literacy and technological skill. Christianity, which he expected would sanctify and sublimate these virtues, he did not regard as part of European civilisation. Holy Johnson did not ask himself the necessary questions. How could Africa's contact with Europeans be regulated in the manner he wanted? Could the flood of European civilisation be dammed and only the part he wanted made to flow into Africa?

Rather than recognise the impracticability and absurdity of his ideas James Johnson minced no words in denouncing the deleterious effects of the unregulated contact of the European world with Africa. In many ways, he declared, the white man's presence was eroding the virtues of the uncontaminated African. First, there was the trans-Atlantic slave trade which for centuries had demoralised the African in the coastal area. The result, he said, was a loss of will and power by the African to resist that which he knew was bad and against his intrinsic interest.[15] Second, coming with the European to Africa was his liquor. By the nineteenth century, he opined, the white man's liquor had not only damaged the African's health along the coast but had deadened his reasoning and undermined his being to such an extent that he, the African, could not appreciate the merits of the Christian faith or give up the evil.

Ridiculous as it might seem to us James Johnson believed that he had found in the educated African elite of his time, in the European enclaves of West Africa, the best illustration of the deleterious effects of European contact with the continent. The characteristics of these elite, he observed, were a glaring contrast to the virtues of the uncontaminated Africans. The Europeanised Africans lacked the virtues of self-reliance, self-dignity and the bliss of independence. To this end they would not pay tax; they would not like to become independent at any price; they became shamelessly dependent on the white man's government to do everything for them. Moreover they went on dying at an early age, in their forties, because of the Europeanised atmosphere that had been established in their settlements, an atmosphere that made them sedentary and which determined their attitude of contempt for work, such as farming, that required physical energies. It was in order to arrest the physical decay of such people that James Johnson advocated physical exercise in schools.[16]

The harm of European contact to Africans, James Johnson said, was not confined to destruction of the virtues of primeval Africa. It affected their reproductive capacity as well. For, according to the demographic data which he claimed were based on official sources, the population of Lagos and Sierra Leone Colony refused to grow by natural process, but only by the constant replenishment from the peoples of the interior.[17] Moreover in these enclaves the Europeanised elite lacked a sense of corporate existence and feeling; they were individualistic, hardly in a position to combine successfully to carry out universally-acknowledged worthy projects, such as the Wilberforce Hall in Freetown and the Glover Memorial Hall in Lagos. As he lamented publicly in Lagos on 22 September 1885: "Our life in British settlements on the coast has not been a national one, we are not a nation, but a collection of individuals of different tribes, though of the same race under a foreign government with divergent feelings and aspirations, and whom it has been found difficult to fuse into one and make one great nation of."[18]

In other ways, observed James Johnson, the hybridised Africans were inferior to their uncontaminated countrymen. They were anything but religious; Christianity among them was more professed than practised. In sexual matters their morality was the opposite of the one that obtained in traditional society. It was nothing to wonder at, he said, that the educated elite were in mental slavery, learning European and British History, but unable to appreciate and study African History and its heroes, whose lives had "contributed much to the well-being of their countries".[19]

James Johnson's doctrine of African Personality was unique at that time, in that no contemporary made the physiognomy of the African an important factor, or romanticised primeval Africa and Africans in the way which he did. It was logical that in connection with the moral and physiognomical decay of the African he dedicated himself to the anti-liquor cause. He threw himself into the anti-liquor movement with a zest bewildering to most of his contemporaries. It was he who started and led the anti-liquor organisation in Nigeria until the last years of the nineteenth century, when Bishop Tugwell assumed its leadership.

In Holy Johnson's judgment the liquor traffic in West Africa was essentially not a commercial enterprise; its inspiration and purpose were racial. Through it the white man hoped to wipe Africans off the face of the earth as he had liquidated the North American Indians and the Black Australian Fellows.[20] Evidence for this view—for him a conviction—was the fact that the gin being bartered in West Africa in the nineteenth century was a specially vile concoction which neither the manufacturers nor the European sojourners in West Africa would taste. In the light of this fact, said Holy Johnson, it behoved Africans to see the Gin invasion—as he liked to refer to the traffic—as the action of demons which would "work for Africa a far greater and more serious evil than the trans-Atlantic slave trade with all its hellish horrors".[21]

It is essential to stress that James Johnson's anti-liquor crusade was not solely or primarily due to the neutralising effect of this traffic on missionary activity. His zeal derived as well from his love for Africa and the doctrine of African Personality in the physiognomical sense. Thus whilst practically all Protestant missions who joined the agitation against the traffic were satisfied with restrictions, James Johnson would have nothing less than complete abolition; whilst the missions confined their opinion to headquarters, or dealt directly with the governments in Britain, James Johnson took it as a matter of public interest, and organised opinion at all levels—the Legislative Council, the Lagos and British press, mass meetings in Nigeria, the British House of Commons, the Colonial Office and the European monarchies.[22] In the belief that the liquor traffic was a Sword of Damocles hanging over Africa he spared no publicity medium, whether letters or journals, whether representations or resolutions, whether memoranda or addresses, in denouncing the traffic as the greatest enemy of the Negro Race.

In Sierra Leone, in Lagos, in the Niger Delta, in Britain and at Church Conferences he described the gin invasion in overstatements characteristic of the humanitarian zealots of the Victorian era. The havoc to Africans, he stressed, time and again, was unimaginable. It brought sterility to women; it fomented and intensified warfare among the West African peoples; it was an important cause of depopulation. As he was quoted in a publication of the Aborigines Protection Society in 1895: "It is the vilest manufacture under the sun, so bad that the lowest European trader on the coast would never drink it himself. It is so bad that in West Africa native painters have used it instead of turpentine. One kind they call 'death'. . . . It has a most injurious effect on the people. It weakens the body, it debases the mind, it demoralises the intellect, and it feeds the war element in the country."[23]

No matter where he was he strove very hard to persuade Africans to perceive that it was in their essential interest to refrain from the vile traffic. In Sierra Leone, it will be recalled, he dismissed from membership any communicant who traded in liquor. In Lagos he called for the entire abolition of the traffic, "this death ministering traffic".[24] In Otta, Ibadan and Abeokuta he was depressed by the increase in the consumption of liquor. "The trade is rapidly on the increase," he lamented, "Merchants and traders say nothing sells so well. Consumption is very large; women too share in it and children are indoctrinated. It is the chief entertainment to visitors [in] the hottest day."[25] He wanted the trade boycotted entirely, seeing this as the only way to render ineffective the alleged conspiracy of the white man to blot Africans "out of existence". Those who would not yield to his pleas for abstinence from, and non-participation in, liquor traffic were, for him, the greatest enemies of the African continent and of the preservation of its people's physique and moral stature. In 1887, having attempted to arouse the conscience of Europe through its rulers, James Johnson appealed to unheeding and indifferent educated Africans in West Africa:

Let us protest with all the might we can employ against this deadly traffic by Europe with West Africa, by ceasing ourselves to have any connexion with it in our business, so that we may not ourselves help others for the sake of gain to ruin our own country and people and race. Let the guilt of ruining Africa for gain be that of strangers and foreigners only, if they will persist in the unchristian and dishonourable course. Let us try to diffuse information among our people in the colonies and in the independent native states as to the danger from this traffic to them, their race and their country.[26]

So much did James Johnson regard the liquor traffic as a disaster to African Personality that he would rather have Africa isolated than the benefit of a European presence at the expense of the moral well-being of Africans. As he said as early as 1878: "I rejoice at the liberal and gigantic measures Europe is adopting for the opening up of Africa; but if this is to afford greater opportunities and facilities for swamping it with the intoxicating drinks of foreign countries, it had better always remain a *terra incognita*. I am no believer in the creed that we must accept civilization with all its enervating and soul and body destroying evils together."[27]

James Johnson was alone in his perception and conviction that in the physiognomical and moral senses, African Personality was at stake in the liquor trade. Although Blyden and Mojola Agbebi recognised in the traffic a moral danger to African peoples neither of them viewed it with the kind of obsession and horror in which Holy Johnson held the gin invasion. In the prominence and priority which he gave to the liquor question James Johnson's exposition of the doctrine of African Personality was unique. To the opinion usually expressed by European traders and administrators who had a stake in the liquor traffic, namely that liquor was nothing new in Africa and that imported liquor was of a higher quality than African-made spirits, James Johnson had a firm retort and denial. African beer, he opined, had no deleterious effects on Africans, was never intoxicating no matter the quantity taken and was no disturbance to sobriety in traditional society.[28]

But it was not liquor alone that James Johnson dreaded as a sledge-hammer to the physique and virtues of the uncontaminated African. He considered that the white man and his civilisation undermined African Personality. At a time when extremist anglicised Africans were contending that not only must Africans be ashamed of their past and culture but that they must be ashamed of their colour as well, and were encouraging Africans to disown their colour by widespread inter-marriage with the white in a progressive manner, James Johnson, like Edward Blyden, denounced miscegenation of the white and black. As he said it was not only "unnatural" but "undesirable" as well. "There is nothing to be said in its favour", he declared to a group of British journalists in 1900, "and it would be a great source of weakness to the national life of West Africa if ever it came to fashion."[29]

For in the cultural sense, as may be recalled from his correspondence with Pope Hennessy, James Johnson did not believe in the oneness of the human race. He perceived the fact that history and geography had introduced differences between peoples all over the terrestrial globe; he desired that these differences be not only recognised but also respected. Geography and history, he noted, had been responsible for the evolution of different cultures and civiliza-tions. In the light of this fact he believed that civilization could not be absolute but relative. He did not belong to the group of the educated elite of his day who believed with their colonial mentors that one civilization was superior to another. No mores, or laws or civilization of one people, he said, should be conceived as being of universal benefit and application. What was meat for one people might be poison for another. As he lectured a group of European "civilizers" in an interview in 1900: "It has been forgotten that European ideas, tastes, languages and social habits, like those of other nations, have been more or less determined by geographical positions and climatic peculiarities, that what is esteemed by one country polite may be justly esteemed by another rude and barbarous."[30]

To us today this view is accepted as a self-evident fact. But for the age in which he said it, that is before social anthropology became a serious academic discipline, it was out of tune with conventional opinion. Rudyard Kipling's refrain, that Africa was the white man's burden, had a cultural connotation. Even where administrators—the so-called Indirect Rulers—perceived the value and legitimacy of African culture and the advisability of administering African peoples in the light of their culture they never esteemed African culture as being as high as European civilization. The latter was invariably described as "higher", the former as "primitive".[31]

It was his belief in the excellence of African culture and racial idiosyncracies that made him advocate Indirect Rule. As he declared to a British audience at the beginning of this century: "You English think that your form of civilization is the only one, but you are quite mistaken. We find your clothing quite unsuitable; your own social amenities are good for you, and we respect them but why should we abandon our own? Take for instance your English dances. Our own people think yours uncomely, and prefer their own."[32]

James Johnson was emotionally drawn towards African culture in the way Europeans were drawn towards theirs. Just as the latter were disposed to extol their civilization James Johnson was very proud about several African customs. Indeed he believed that some of these customs were superior to the European customs which the majority of the African educated elite only too eagerly and un-critically patronised wholesale. Speaking mainly of his experience with the Yoruba he admired the orderliness that prevailed in the pre-Scramble era, in spite of the absence of a standing army or police; the absence of theft; the prevalence of chastity, absence of adultery and illegitimate children; respect for elders by the young and a constitution that was not only democratic in form but in its operation—"a popular assembly of the people, declaring their own mind upon any important subject that may be before the Government".[33]

In defence of and respect for African culture, for which Edward Blyden is better known, James Johnson was asking that Africans should know themselves as a people, a race, distinct from other peoples and endowed with attributes unique to themselves. Rightly perceived, contended James Johnson, these attributes were magnificent and should inspire in Africans pride of race. Nothing seemed to him more irrational and unpatriotic than the behaviour of Europeanised Africans who began to thirst after and glory in European culture, in the belief that they, Africans, were nondescript people, without a worthy past and a culture to be proud of.

It is perhaps difficult for us to imagine the degree and extent of the cultural thraldom into which the majority of the African educated elite in British West Africa placed themselves before the First World War. The adoption of European ideas, thoughts and habits of life was regarded and pursued by them not only as an ideal of culture for Africans, but as the means and indispensable requisite by which they would obtain spiritual generation and salvation. As a Lagos newspaper cogently summarised the position in 1897: "One of the most difficult and most pernicious impressions for the so-called civilized African to overcome is that he is not a European."[34]

The contempt for the African past and culture by this class of educated elite, declared James Johnson, was based on a lack of understanding and was the crudest of nonsense. To renounce their culture would be denying to Africa an identity, a separateness, self-dignity and independence. If they took the trouble to examine their past and understand their customs and institutions they would discover that they had racial characteristics and endowments in which they should take pride; their contempt for traditional African culture was due to a state of mental slavery. In the borrowed cultural atmosphere of the Europeans in which they were thinking and revelling they were misfits and out of their element. They could never be, nor was it in their interest to seek to be, Europeans. After all Europeans would not accept them as equals, no matter how much they Europeanised themselves.[35]

So much did Holy Johnson value and venerate what he regarded as the virtues of the culture of uncontaminated Africa that the European presence in Africa was for him at best a necessary evil. He saw in the European no model in moral and cultural matters. Only in the realms of literacy, technology and science were European contact and tutorship desirable and indispensable. It was his hope that once Africans had mastered these skills the white man would withdraw from the continent.[36] It should not be thought that, in expressing the view that the ideal situation that would conduce to the best interest of Africans was one in which Africa should be for Africans, he was consciously preaching a war of race hate. As a Christian he wanted not racial war but harmony. His language, which European missionaries in particular often misconstrued as anti-European, was no more than a plea to the Europeans that as long as their presence was still required in Africa the two races should have mutual respect for each other. This, he said time and again, should be on the basis of racial equality, rather than on the governor-governed basis of the colonial era.

There is no greater testimony of James Johnson's aversion to, and disapproval of, the moral and cultural aspects of the white man's presence in Africa than his relentless criticism of the denationalising effects of European civilization on Africans. As he said, not only did the European presence denationalise Africans, it also decivilized them[37] It is natural that in this respect the bulk of his denunciation should deal with the western forms of education and Christianity as exemplified by the Christian missions.

Right from the seventies, it will be recalled, James Johnson had announced that the best type of education for Africans was one that incorporated their deep religious instincts and transferred these to Christianity. In 1870 he had declared to the British administration in Sierra Leone that any attempt to secularise education—by making grants to schools for secular subjects alone—would be decidedly against the interest of Africans. In his judgment, "education not based upon religion, the religion of the Bible, will be found productive of a race of infidels, atheists, freethinkers, and mere moralists, . . . the greatest evil that can befall a country is to have her education secularised".[38] For the rest of his life in Nigeria he was unhappy about the progressive secularisation of education by the Ordinances. In his characteristically suspicious manner he believed that the secularising policy of the British administration was a deliberate and calculated conspiracy to deprive the African of the moral fibre he derived from religion.

As it appeared to him, the British began to put this conspiracy into effect when the Colonial administration in Nigeria began to found Government schools without any provision for religion. The consequences of this step for Africans, he said, would be calamitous. For divorced from the pre-colonial obligations, laws and sanctions, and exposed to the terrific onslaught of Westernism, the African, he believed, required the prophylactic of religion to enable them to adjust themselves to the new environment being introduced by the European presence and Government, an environment which meant for the African greater material prosperity, new sets of values, obligations and responsibility. As he declared:

> This mode of Education (secular), however it may commend itself to some people in Europe, is entirely unAfrican, and foreign to the traditions of a people with whom Religion is everything, and whose teaching and training of their children are completely interlined with it; and it cannot commend itself to thoughtful Negroes who are anxious to see preserved inviolate the religious instincts of the people, as they know this purely secular Education cannot fail to produce those hybrids of humanity, Atheists, Infidels, and Indifferents which Africa has not yet given birth to.[39]

The two points to note here are James Johnson's perception of African Personality in the African's religious instincts and his desire to see these instincts preserved in the literary education of modern Africa. How he expected these instincts to be divorced inviolate from the traditional religion and how Africans could transfer and integrate these instincts in the Christian faith is a different matter. No analyst of pre-Scramble African society can fail to appreciate the validity of James Johnson's concern about the loss to the African of the ethics and code of behaviour associated with religion, which the colonial educationists tended to ignore. The religious instinct of the African was certainly one of the props of morality, cohesion and orderliness which Africans were doomed to lose at the establishment of European colonial rule. As several colonial administrators perceived and admitted, new ethical laws and regulations were certainly required as a cement to save the social fabric from tottering to ruin. It was the point emphasised by Lugard, really the first British administrator to give education a serious consideration.[40]

Apart from denouncing the British administration in West Africa for robbing African Personality of its religious element through its secularising educational policy James Johnson accused those among the European sojourners, guilty of moral misbehaviour and godlessness, of being a bad example to imitative Africans. In sermon after sermon he regretted that Europe went on sending to the continent a large number of such characters "who have not lived moral lives and are likely to introduce new vices amongst the people and corrupt and degrade them".[41]

The content of literary education, largely in the hands of Christian missions, became a special target for Holy Johnson. Naturally in the pre-Scramble and colonial periods the colonial and missionary mentors adopted curricula and textbooks designed for European societies. The result was the emergence along the west coast of

Africa of hybridised Africans who lost the best of two societies. All their gain from the western ideas, norms, social habitudes, mores and religion into which they had been foisted was the shadow of European civilization; they were rejected and ridiculed by European denigrators as a class of people who would never in substance become Europeans. But at the same time, as "detribalised" Africans they had lost the substance of the culture of the uncontaminated African society which, as outlined earlier in this chapter, commanded the admiration of James Johnson.

As early as 1873 James Johnson had defined in clear terms the type of education he wished to see in Africa. "On the subject of Education," he wrote in a newspaper, "we cannot afford to be indifferent. It has been frequently remarked by those whose opinions we respect, that Africans under foreign culture are generally inferior to their brethren who have not been brought under it. That which we want is an education that will leave undisturbed our race peculiarities. We do not wish to lose them because we have learnt the natural and other sciences in foreign lands, or been taught them by foreign people. The injuring or destroying of such peculiarities is among the greatest calamities that can befall a nation."[42]

For the rest of his life James Johnson missed no opportunity to suggest to the British authorities in West Africa and in Britain how best to achieve an education system that would preserve "undisturbed our race peculiarities". First, he declared, the language of teaching must be the vernacular. Although this was a demand in accord with missionary interest James Johnson advocated vernacular education not just because it was in this way that the Scriptures could become intelligible to adult converts being taught how to read and school children, but because he regarded language as a cardinal part of African Personality. In this respect James Johnson was again unique among the apostles of this philosophy in his generation. Neither Agbebi nor Blyden made the vernacular a doctrinal issue. Nor was this emphasis on vernacular education a popular idea in his age. It was an age when neither the children nor their parents wanted to learn in the vernacular at any level in the school. In Yorubaland and the Niger Delta James Johnson had to contend in vain with a very serious prejudice against the vernacular. However it should be noted that he was not opposed to the English language as a medium of teaching, but he believed that it was a sound principle to impart instruction to children only in their language. It was in this way alone, he said, that they could acquire true knowledge, that is instruction with understanding. To teach children in English or any language but their own from the alphabet, as was the practice of the age, was to make them robots.

It was his faith in the vernacular as the best instrument for

imparting instruction to children that lay behind his effort to persuade a deaf Colonial Office in 1887, 1899 and 1909 to perceive
the imperativeness of the adoption of curricula and textbooks, at
certain levels to be written in the vernacular, that would be based
on African culture, African experience and African environment.[43]
A start, he said, should be made with textbooks in History,
Geography, Botany and Zoology. In the same vein he contended
that the theology being taught African ministers must not be
entirely Christian, that African theology was worth examining and
its textbooks written in the vernacular. In this respect he went
beyond words; he made a theological study of Yoruba religion.
Published in 1899 as *Yoruba Heathenism* it was intended as a
textbook for African agents and Christian converts. Not only was
it well received by his contemporaries, it has been respected by a
leading scholar of African theology.[44] By 1901 he was convinced,
after some study of Yoruba, Edo and Ibo societies, that the Christian doctrines of Atonement, the mediation of Christ and the
Incarnation "are to be found embedded in their [African] religious
system".[45]

James Johnson's pleas on behalf of vernacular and Africa-
orientated curricula and textbooks rested on the principle that in
Africa literary education should form part of African Personality.
In the physiognomical sense he was concerned about the dangers
of Africans going abroad for training. Therefore he sought to
persuade British authorities to establish in West Africa institutions
at which a variety of disciplines, including brickmaking, gardening,
printing and practical engineering, would be taught. In these
institutions, where "respect for the race" would be the watchword,
the students would be saturated with, and hardened in, the virtues
of primeval Africa. After their studies it would be safe to send
them abroad for further training, if necessary, relieved of anxieties
that the ravages of the "trying climate" of Europe and the corrupting morals of European society would affect their physique and
character.[46]

There is no doubt that in his advocacy of an educational system
assimilated to African Personality in its content and perspective
James Johnson was several generations ahead of his time. It was
a unique doctrine of African Personality shared only to a certain
extent by Edward Blyden.

James Johnson was never silent about the European brand of
Christianity being spread in Africa and which he regarded as
another great danger to African Personality. Christianity *per se*, he
was convinced, was a culturally neutral ideology which was capable
of growing in different cultures and environments without losing
its sublimity or compromising its tenets. As he declared at the Pan-

Anglican Congress of 1908: "Christianity is intended to be the religion not of one particular race of people only, but of the whole world. But in different countries it will wear different types, if it is to become indigenous to every soil. It should have in Europe a European type, in Asia an Asiatic type and in Africa an African type—different types of one and the same religion with different formulae of Faith and different ceremonies of worship; for not otherwise can Christianity wear anywhere a national character, not otherwise can its attitude be what it should towards national customs which have much in them to help to promote indigenousness to it."[47]

In other words what Africa wanted was the unadulterated Christianity, the Christianity of the Bible, which would acclimatise itself in the peculiar environment of the continent and produce a form that would bear the unmistakable imprint of African Personality. He did not mean that there should be a fusion of Christianity and African culture. He made it plain that there were specific customs and institutions with which Christianity could not compromise. These were twin infanticide, cannibalism, ordeal for witchcraft and "cruel punishment of offenders".[48] Indeed James Johnson's iconoclastic tendencies were never effaced. For he looked forward to the day when even some customs that were not anti-scriptural would disappear on the grounds that, as he said, they were unprogressive by world standards. Among these were home sepulchres, tattooing of the body, and the wearing of facial marks, family and tribal.[49]

The point to note is that Holy Johnson's view of the racial and cultural neutralism of Christianity was unorthodox for the age in which he lived. Even today it is a doctrine not wholly acceptable in many a European and American mission headquarters.[50] The belief that still persists in Africa today, that Christianity is the religion of the white man, has been inherited from the first generation of Christian converts in the nineteenth century, to whom the European missionaries and their African auxiliaries gave the impression that European culture and Christianity were synonymous. Up to the end of the nineteenth century the tendency among Christian missionaries was to condemn all African customs and institutions as "pagan". It was a nihilist view based upon deliberate ignorance. Take for instance the custom of paying dowries. The dowry—a sum within the reach of every male in the pre-colonial era—was a symbol of union between two extended families. In this sense it was an event intended to remind the couple that, as representatives of respective extended families, they should behave themselves and seek to achieve a successful union. Labelled by the missionaries as "bride price" this social event was given a commercial and racialist interpretation. In their belief the dowry became the price at which the husband purchased his wife.[51] The custom was then condemned as wicked and a demonstration of an incapacity to love for love's sake by the African. Or consider the passion of the African for mirth, joyousness and gregariousness, particularly during marriage ceremonies, wakes and obsequies. Rather than seeing these as racial characteristics missionaries described them as heathenish, under the false and perverted Victorian conception of a Christian being a meditative, meek, gentle and quiet man. James Johnson had to rebuke the Europeanising missionaries of his time. "It has been said," he wrote, "that Africans will lose their nationality—not their language but their national customs—and after that they will become Christians. But is this right or necessary? Cannot God the Holy Ghost operate through the preaching of the Gospel for the Christianizing of the nations of Africa without their being denationalised?"[52]

In the circumstances the belief that gained currency was that conversion to Christianity obliged Africans to adopt European habits and customs. The customs being abandoned or dropped by Africans, which received the attention of James Johnson, included names, clothing, burial, marriage and polygamy. Christian acolytes began to thirst after western ideas, thoughts and tastes. As in the matter of the vernacular James Johnson had to meet with opposition from Christian acolytes, who were incapable of recognising the distinction between the Christianity of the Bible and the adulterated European Christianity.

The custom that made him a *persona non grata* with many families in Yorubaland and a focus of controversy was the one appertaining to names. In the belief that European and Jewish names were superior to native names parents insisted that at baptism ceremonies their children must never bear African names. Even adult candidates for baptism earnestly asked for an exchange of their African names for foreign ones. Characteristically, under the notion that African names were associated with idols, missionaries encouraged converts to adopt European or Hebrew names. In no other part of Africa was this craze for foreign names as prominent as in British West Africa, reaching proportions that confounded the C.M.S. authorities in the eighties of the nineteenth century.

It was in this atmosphere that James Johnson began to fight against "such a practice [which] has been a step in the denationalising of the African".[53] For, on investigation he discovered that African names were meaningful, indicating the circumstances of the birth of a child or of its family: these circumstances a child was expected to be acquainted with and remember always as he grew up. As a name distinguished one person from another, so it

U

often distinguished one family or one ethnic group from another. The use of surnames, as among Europeans, was unknown. Given usually at a family conclave the name of the African was pregnant in meaning both for the family and the child. To Holy Johnson's dismay, it was such names that were being thrown away thoughtlessly by converts to the Christian faith, even when these names had no association with the gods at all. These converts alleged that only by bearing foreign names would they be identified as Christians outside West Africa.

For James Johnson names became an African Personality issue: the casting off of African names by these converts was an act of disrespect to the race, a demolition of a part of the African heritage. It was for this reason that he did all in his power to put an end to the adoption of alien names. In Lagos he incurred a great deal of hostility because he refused to baptise any child to whom the parents were not prepared to give African names.[54] He had a similar experience in Abeokuta. To contemporary European observers James Johnson's refusal to baptise people with alien names was a further evidence of his hatred for the white man, his "anti-English monomania".[55]

To his surprise foreign names did not lose their romance with the first generation of converts in the hinterland of Southern Nigeria either. He had to repeat in the Owo District, which it will be remembered came under his supervision after his consecration, what he had done in Lagos and Abeokuta—reject alien names at baptism services. As he declared indignantly about the craze for alien names "for which there is absolutely no necessity whatsoever":

> Christianity is a Religion intended for and is suitable for every Race and Tribe of people on the face of the Globe. Acceptance of it was never intended by its Founder to denationalise any people and it is indeed its glory that every race of people may profess and practise it and imprint upon it its own native characteristics, giving it a peculiar type among themselves without its losing anything of its virtue. And why should not there be an African Christianity as there has been a European and an Asiatic Christianity?[56]

Another habit of the Europeanised Africans and converts of his day deplored by James Johnson was their avidity for European clothes. In the hot climate of West Africa sense and convenience demanded that its people should clothe themselves sparingly and loosely; decency and taste demanded that various patterns and forms should be devised for various occasions. The style of dress and the materials used were intended for the tropics. But as

Christianity spread European forms of dress and materials suitable for the colder climate of Europe were introduced. Again, unreflectingly, the converts identified European forms of dress with Christianity. The majority of educated Africans adopted this alien form of dress, in their eyes a symbol of respect, its personal discomfort notwithstanding. James Johnson regretted the craze of the times in a public lecture in 1909: "There is too much made by young men and young women of European form of dress, or senselessly high stiff collars, corsets and hats and boots and silk and other attractive dresses, suitable or unsuitable to us in this our hot African climate."[57] In Sierra Leone where the first effort in British West Africa was made to renounce European dress in favour of the traditional one James Johnson addressed the Dress Reform Society in 1887, praising them for exhibiting a spirit of independence.[58] In 1908 he declared at the Pan-Anglican Conference the ridiculous idea that, "The adoption and constant use of this form of dress [European] are just regarded as one of the principal contributors" to the physical degeneracy which "has set in upon the African communities on the coast especially, and is shortening their lives and threatening them with extinction".[59]

The question of African marriage began to receive James Johnson's attention only from the last decade of the nineteenth century. He saw nothing wrong with African notions of marriage and the ceremonies connected with it. African ideas about the institution, he said, were admirable. Marriage was looked upon as a lifelong affair; there was no illegitimacy, no marriage by cousins; divorce was rare and concubinage outlawed. As in other matters the missionaries substituted the marriage customs and ideas of their countries, which they described as Christian, "although Christ our Lord, the Founder of Christianity, has prescribed no marriage custom or ceremony for his followers".[60]

In some ways the marriage prescriptions by the Church contravened African laws. For instance the vow which the converts married in the Church were made to take, endowing his wife with his worldly goods, was an affront on the law of inheritance in Africa where life was communistic and not individualistic. For the African law of inheritance prescribed that the property of the deceased should be inherited by the most senior member of his extended family, in trust for the children and the family as a whole. The law of inheritance sanctioned by oath in the Church, declared James Johnson, was British custom and unbiblical. What the Church should do was to adapt its marriage laws and vow to African customs. As he told the Pan-Anglican Congress: "Would it not have been better if the Missionary, to increase the effectiveness of his work and avoid leaving any room for any denationalising process, but contented himself with the native form of marriage for his converts, only helping them to remove from it whatever is calculated to bear hard upon the poorer ones in the matter of expenses?"[61]

Even with respect to polygamy James Johnson was disposed to be more tolerant in his attitude towards the end of his life. Although, as mentioned earlier, his theology never changed, yet he perceived that the situation in Africa deserved a special treatment and the sympathy of the Christian world. For the first time in his life he was prepared to abandon dogma in favour of reality. African polygamy, he became convinced after investigation, could be explained in rational terms. It symbolised prestige; it created large families; it ensured marriage for all women in a society in which women outnumbered men; it had become "a national custom"; it guaranteed "special protection" for women; "polygamy is the rule, and monogamy the exception". James Johnson regretted that he had been so passionately against polygamy in the past and pronounced the view that for a long time to come polygamy would remain part and parcel of African culture.[62] It therefore behoved the Church, he said, to come to terms with this institution, the dogma notwithstanding, and to revise the decision that had been made in 1888. He pleaded that polygamist converts should be admitted into full Church membership.

James Johnson perceived that European Christianity was not alone in the denationalising of the African. The Colonial Administration also tended to erode African Personality, in the sense that the large number of Europeans who went to the interior introduced vice and loose living, thereby rooting out the high sexual morality that had existed before. In Yorubaland, for instance, sexual immorality, he said, was introduced by the "Yoruba Battalion", the soldiers introduced by the British administration. It was made up of men determined to "injure the morals of the country" in which there had been long in existence "a code of morals which cannot fail to command respect from those who know it, and which with the strong public opinion which prevails among the people protects the chastity of the woman, ensures respect for marriage, and sets its face strongly against illegitimacy".[63] In the same manner he denounced the damaging effect of railways, telegraphs and roads upon traditional morality.

So much was James Johnson disenchanted with and suspicious of European civilisation that he ascribed to it effects that have not been proved by researches. European clothing, he believed throughout his life, was responsible for the high rate of infantile mortality and the relative shortness of the span of life of the educated elite in West Africa; European liquor, he remained unyieldingly convinced all his life, increased militarism in West Africa and caused sterility among the women. However he was prejudiced in favour of African brands of beer drinks tapped from palm trees, banana and corn which, he declared, "are absolutely non-intoxicant and wholesome".[64] When the bicycle was introduced into Lagos his reaction was one of horror, believing that Africans who began to patronise this means of transport might be inviting early demise.[65]

Much as James Johnson denounced the effects of European civilisation on Africans he remained in several respects more of a theorist than a practising apostle of African Personality. For instance he never changed his European name in spite of jibes by several Europeans that he should demonstrate his identity as an African by doing so.[66] Nor did he ever wear African clothing. Rather he wore European clothing and the heavy English vestments unsuitable for the tropics. He did not perceive the fallacy of his views on European clothing by the fact that he lived long to be an octogenarian in spite of his European clothing.

But in other respects he was more than a theorist. It was his joy and pride to have his salary paid from the sweat of African labour rather than from C.M.S. funds. When in 1887 he was prostrated by illness in a London hospital he would not have the C.M.S. or any English friend pay his bill.[67] He never took alcohol. Never did he genuflex to any man on account of the "accident of colour". Humble but confident, he never felt himself inferior to a white man in spiritual fervour, in moral probity and in mental capacity. In the international congresses which he attended he participated in a manner that impressed representatives of other races. In every respect James Johnson saw himself as a representative of the Negro Race. At the Pan-Anglican Congresses, in the Keswick conventions, at Exeter Hall meetings, he succeeded in leaving a permanent impression on the European audiences as an African possessing virtues and merits which sceptics were wont to deny were beyond the reach of a Negro. Whilst he was in England in 1887 he and the educated African elite felt that the Negro Race was honoured when James Johnson received "special invitations"[68] from the British Government to the Jubilee Thanksgiving Service of Queen Victoria in Westminster Abbey on 21 June and to Her Majesty's Garden Party at Buckingham Palace on 29 June.

Nothing displeased him more than the failure of Africans to measure up to the standards of other peoples, particularly of the Europeans, in moral, material and artistic matters. Thus he wished Africans to be better Christians than Europeans in order to demonstrate that Africans were not incapable of understanding and practising a religion which it had become the habit of the denigrators of the Negro Race to allege was too demanding for the African. Thus he wished that Africans should not be mere producers for the European manufacturers but inventors and manufacturers sending finished products to the European market. Thus he was annoyed that in the Indian and Colonial Exhibition of 1887 the "native African made cloths exhibited . . . were of the poorest and most meagre description", manufactured by the Europeanised and contaminated people along the West African coast, rather than those from the uncontaminated peoples in the interior, whose products, he believed, would have compared well with those of other parts of the British Empire. As he lamented on the occasion: "I know of no intelligent Native African who saw the Exhibition who did not feel ashamed of and was not humiliated by it."[69]

James Johnson was also a fervent advocate of the international pan-African movement. According to Duse Mohammed, the Egyptian pan-Africanist whose career saw him in Britain, the United States and Nigeria, founder and editor of *The African Times and Orient Review*, James Johnson participated actively in all such organisations during his visits to England in the first decade of this century.[70] James Johnson did not only participate actively in the first Pan-African Conference which took place in London in July 1900 but he was already judged and respected by representatives of the Negro Race from other parts of Africa and the New World as an inspirer of pan-Africanism. Indeed he was honoured with an address.[71] In this respect he was the first person in British West Africa and the first product of the African environment to receive such an honour on the international plane.

NOTES

1. E. A. Ayandele, *op. cit.*, pp. 254-256.
2. Ruth Holden, *op. cit.*, E. W. Blyden to J. H. Wilson, 1/6/1900.
3. Kwame Nkrumah, *Africa Must Unite*, London, 1960, pp. 216-222.
4. See chapter three.
5. James Johnson, *Yoruba Heathenism*, London and Exeter, 1899, p. 51.
6. C.M.S. CA2/056, James Johnson, Annual Report, 1878.
7. *African Times*, 1/10/1887.
8. C.M.S. CA1/0123, James Johnson to M. Taylor and others, 19/4/1873.
9. *Lagos Weekly Record*, 17/3/1894.
10. James Johnson, "The Relation of Mission work to Native Customs". Paper read at Pan-Anglican Conference, 1908, London (S.D. Group 6), C.M.S. Library.
11. *Lagos Weekly Record*, 4/8/1900.
12. *The Eagle*, 12 and 26 September 1885.

13. James Johnson, *Address delivered at Wesley Church, Olowog-bowo, Lagos at the Memorial Service . . . in honour of the Late Hon. Sir Samuel Lewis*, Exeter and London, 1903, p. 6.
14. C.M.S. G3/A1/02, James Johnson to F. Baylis, 28/11/1900.
15. C.O. 520/89, James Johnson to Colonel J. E. B. Seely, 14/1/1909.
16. C.M.S. G3/A1/02, James Johnson to F. Baylis, 6/3/1900.
17. C.O. 147/62, James Johnson to E. Stanhope, 4/1/1887; 267/369, James Johnson to C.O., 26/7/1887.
18. *The Eagle*, 12 and 26 September 1885.
19. *Ibid.*
20. *African Times*, 1/10/1887.
21. C.O. 147/62, James Johnson to H. Holland, 18/3/1887.
22. *African Times*, 1/10/1887.
23. A.P.S., *Poison of Africa*, Papers No. 1, p. 3.
24. C.M.S. G3/A2/04, James Johnson, Memorandum to C.M.S., January 1887.
25. C.M.S. CA2/056, James Johnson, Annual Report, 1878.
26. *African Times*, 1/10/1887.
27. C.M.S. CA2/056, James Johnson, Annual Report, 1878.
28. C.O. 520/89, James Johnson to Colonel J. E. B. Seely, 14/1/1909.
29. *Sierra Leone Weekly News*, 28/7/1900 (reproduces interview).
30. *The Negro*, 1/1/1873.
31. See in particular C. L. Temple, *Native Races and Their Rulers*, Cape Town, 1918; reprinted Frank Cass, 1968, with a new introduction by Mervyn Hiskett.
32. *Sierra Leone Weekly News*, 28/7/1900 (reproduces interview).
33. *Ibid.*
34. *Lagos Weekly Record*, 5/6/1897.
35. *Ibid.*, 27 October and 3 November 1917, quotes speech by him in Lagos, 19 June 1909.
36. *The Negro*, 1/1/1873.
37. *Ibid.*; C.O. 147/147, James Johnson to J. Chamberlain, 27/6/1899.
38. C.O. 267/317, "The Fifty-fifth Annual Report of the Sierra Leone Auxiliary Bible Society, Bible Society, 1871" by James Johnson.
39. C.M.S. G3/A3/09, "A Report of Missionary Journey within and beyond the Southern Nigeria British Protectorate from November 1903 to July 1904" by James Johnson.
40. M. Perham, *Lugard: The Years of Authority*, London, 1960, pp. 489-511.
41. *Niger and Yoruba Notes*, July 1900, p. 15.
42. *West African Reporter*, 17/4/1873.
43. C.O. 520/89, James Johnson to Colonel J. E. B. Seely, 14/1/1909.
44. E. B. Idowu, *Olodumare God in Yoruba Belief*, Longmans, 1962, pp. 32 and 147.
45. *Sierra Leone Weekly News*, 28/7/1900.
46. *The Methodist Herald*, 26/5/1886.
47. James Johnson, *The Relations of Missions et seq.*
48. *Ibid.*
49. *Ibid.*
50. E. B. Idowu, *Towards an Indigenous Church*, O.U.P., 1965.
51. C.M.S. G3/A2/09, "The Sanctity of Marriage and Influence of Home Life" by Thomas Harding.

52. James Johnson, *The Relations of Mission et seq.* cited.
53. C.M.S. G3/A3/010, "Bishop Johnson's Journal Reports, December 1904-July 1905".
54. J. O. Lucas, *op. cit.*, p. 26.
55. C.M.S. G3/A2/02, A. Mann to R. Lang, 28/9/1883.
56. C.M.S. G3/A2/010, "Bishop Johnson's Journal Report, December 1904-July 1905".
57. Quoted in *Lagos Weekly Record*, 27 October and 3 November 1917.
58. *Sierra Leone Weekly News*, 17/12/1887.
59. James Johnson, *The Relations of Mission et seq.*
60. *Ibid.*
61. *Ibid.*
62. *Ibid.*
63. C.O. 147/147, James Johnson to J. Chamberlain, 27/6/1899.
64. C.O. 520/89, James Johnson to Colonel J. E. B. Seely, 14/1/1909.
65. Quoted in *Lagos Weekly Record*, 27 October and 3 November, 1917.
66. *Sierra Leone Weekly News*, 17/12/1887.
67. C.M.S. G3/A1/L10, R. Lang to Bishop Ingham, 9/2/1887.
68. *African Times*, 1/8/1887.
69. C.O. 267/369, James Johnson to H. Holland, 26/7/1887.
70. *The African Times and Orient Review*, Vol. 5, No. 1, 1917.
71. Published in *The Rock*, London, 20/7/1900.

CHAPTER TWELVE

VISIONARY

The West Africa Native Bishoprics Fund affords a great and exceptional opportunity for a practical exercise of that intelligent interest in and desire for the elevation of the Negro Race and for an independent and self-governing native Church life which have grown in many among the people generally in order to secure to the race as such a position of no mean value in the Christian Church.

James Johnson to F. Baylis, 3/10/1900

IN the last seventeen years of his life, when he was achieving so much as "Half Bishop" of the Niger Delta Pastorate and President of the Lagos Auxiliary of the Aborigines Protection Society[1] James Johnson was expending much energy and all his resourcefulness in the pursuit of a shadow—an independent African episcopate for all West Africa. For when he was being consecrated on 18 February 1900 he was in very high spirits; his joyful mood emanated from the conviction that the golden fleece—complete independence from European religious imperialism—was not only within reach but also within sight. As he believed, there already existed a firm arrangement, a contract, solemnly entered into by the C.M.S., Lambeth Palace and himself, that as soon as he could obtain the sum of £10,000 the Niger Delta would be constituted into an independent African Bishopric. In his judgment the existence of such an ecclesiastical institution was the noblest, the most sublime and the grandest achievement for Africa. For, as he believed, it would prove to be the harbinger of political freedom and the key to the realisation of all the aspirations of the Negro Race.

Among the leading educated elite in British West Africa only James Johnson continued to be hypnotised by an illusion of this kind in 1900. In a sense it may seem strange that he learned nothing and forgot nothing. Apart from the realities of the Scramble era around him that had begun to make nonsense of his vision and hopes, he never learnt the palpable lessons of the experiences he had undergone continually for a quarter of a century. Rather he continued to be a Don Quixote charging at the mills. That this was so can be explained. Firstly, Holy Johnson was not the man to accept defeat. As illustrated by his acceptance of the position of "Half Bishop", the means and the approach might be changed but never was the sight of the end lost. It requires an indomitable will in an individual to go on contending with irresistibly overwhelming forces over which he could never have control. And indomitable will and resilience James Johnson had in plenty. Secondly, James Johnson was never aware of the limitations of the individual in society. As a solitary individual gifted with spiritual impulses and moral outlook that placed him on Olympian heights, head and shoulders above the rest of society, it ought to have occurred to him that he was alone, that he could not compel society to bow to his will, his ideas, his thinking; that such moral laws and Christian principles which were all-important to him and which he wished to see become the dynamics of West African society were impersonal and imperceptible forces that could be recognised or accepted by a few men only. Hence the sort of Christian society he wished to see in West Africa has never existed in human annals. In societies where Christianity had flourished for centuries there had never been a time when the sublime verities and lofty demands of the Christian faith had succeeded in conquering human nature to the extent of turning all men into saintly and holy figures like himself.

In his ideas, and his emphasis on what he thought ought to be rather than what really was, Holy Johnson was the Plato of West Africa. His philosopher-king, the sinless man with a soul in eternal communion with God, never emerged. Everywhere he was surrounded by peoples, "sinners, lost souls, needing salvation . . . naturally estranged from God, utterly barren of holiness and demanding nothing short of divine power to convert them into gardens which will be a delight to the Lord".[2] Throughout his life he was aware of the big gulf separating him and his ideas from the rest of society. Consequently he occupied a position similar to that of the prophets of old, condemning the moral lapses of his age, emphasising the sinfulness of man and the necessity for him to return to the true worship of Jehovah. The contrast between his idea of what ought to be and what really was in West Africa is contained in practically all the sermons and addresses he delivered. The following, part of the annual sermon he gave to the Lagos Church Missions in 1888, is quite representative:

We are converts from heathenism, or the children of those who are so. We do not fail to show marks of the complete hold Satan had had over us, and of the severity of the bondage in which we had served. Old habits have not all forsaken us altogether. Superstitious fear and dread, worldly ambition, the worship of mammon, selfishness, an unforgiving temper, a revengeful disposition, feverish anxiety as to what we shall eat and what we shall drink, malice, a desire to get on at the expense of others, resort to heathen oracles in times of perplexity, fear of man, of greater readiness to trust in man than in God, lying, quarrelsomeness, want of brotherly love, patience and forbearance, a too great love of pleasure and excessive frivolity too often mar the beauty of our Christian profession. We do not much resemble the Master and too often fail to show that Christianity and its Great Teacher are higher than Mohammedanism and Mohammed, and than heathenism and its babalawos.[3]

In a sense Holy Johnson had been a visionary since his spiritual experience in Kent. That there was a gap between him and Sierra Leone society has been examined. In several ways there continued to be a gap between him and the society around him in the Nigeria of the last quarter of the nineteenth century. In Lagos, where he mourned the low level of morality and the mere churchianity of the Christian community, contemporary observers shared his apprehension about the standard of life of the Christians. Very few people took Christianity as a way of life in the literal and serious manner of Holy Johnson. As a European observed of the Church in Lagos on 2 April 1889: "It would be better to have the Church almost empty, than filled as it is: you see it crowded on communion Sunday in a wonderful way, but two-thirds of the communicants leave the communion table laughing at the whole thing, to cheat and lie like the rest on Monday".[4] Then, whether in Lagos, or in the interior of Yorubaland, or in the Niger Delta, missionary appeal awakened a response only among the lowest strata of society. In Lagos the *Saro* and liberated Africans from Cuba and Brazil and their offspring constituted almost entirely the whole Christian community; in Yorubaland only the *Saro* and slaves paid attention to the spiritual aspect of missionary enterprise, whilst in the Niger Delta the Church consisted entirely of slaves. In all these areas there was nothing dignifying through being a Christian in the pre-colonial era. Chiefs and freemen continued to adhere to their indigenous religion which they regarded as best for themselves and their society; they resented the religious interference of missionaries.

But in 1900, over the Niger Bishopric question, James Johnson did not believe that he was dreaming, or that he was being a visionary. It is abundantly clear from the records that neither the C.M.S. nor Lambeth Palace nor Bishop Tugwell was as honest with him as he was with them, that they more or less decoyed him into accepting the position of "Half Bishop" without ever entertaining the thought that the conditions he laid down, and to which they agreed, would ever be fulfilled. For James Johnson made it plain that he would not accept the position unless he was allowed to launch a Fund, a sustentation fund, which would make it possible for him to have the Niger Delta converted to an independent African diocese, and that Bishop Tugwell, the Church Missionary Society and Lambeth Palace must give their consent to this proposal.[5] These terms were accepted by all the parties and the substantial sum of £10,000 was mentioned.

In order to assure James Johnson further of its goodwill the Committee of the Society held a meeting with him shortly before his consecration and dangled before him high hopes and glittering prospects that awaited not only the Niger Delta but the whole of West Africa. As recorded by him, with no denial by the Society: "The arrangement, practically, makes the subordinate Episcopal position to which I have been after previous refusals of it about six years ago invited and to which I expect to be consecrated on the 18th inst. D.V. a temporary one. Whilst the opinion and purpose expressed contemplate the unifying of all the different sections of the West African Church, and making of them one strong Church with a metropolitan at its head, giving it the position of a Province, conferring on it synodical powers and creating separate Dioceses independently presided over by Native African Bishops."[6]

The bright prospect of an independent Diocese in the Niger Delta, and the fact that the Church Missionary Society was thinking of signing a Self Denying Ordinance, handing over all dioceses in West Africa to Africans, with the area constituting a Province under an African Archbishop—a dream that even up to now has not become a reality in post-independence Africa—made James Johnson so elated that he thanked the Society profusely for its magnanimity. By this "arrangement", said Johnson, the Churches in Africa would begin to unite. His reaction to the "arrangement" is best put in his words: "If you will kindly allow a little personal reference here, I would say that my own measure of satisfaction is that of a man who had long toiled over a hard task, a task that seemed to grow harder with the times, amidst great difficulties and discouragements and much disappointment and weariness—but who at last is privileged to see a very appreciable measure of success to his undertaking and a clear prospect of a larger and complete success."[7]

In the light of the steps taken by the C.M.S. after the death of Bishop Crowther; in the light of the fact that a European successor had been appointed in 1896 after Bishop Ingham's retirement; and in the light of the fact that European missionaries all over West Africa began to increase in number and to seize control of Mission Churches, it would have been nothing short of a miracle if the Church Missionary Society had decided so summarily and so suddenly to liquidate itself in any part of Africa. It should be stressed that by 1901 leaders of European thought in West Africa had begun to regret that Africans had ever been raised to the status of Assistant Bishop. The situation in Yorubaland, it must be conceded, was very rare. In no other part of Anglican West Africa was an African raised to this level. Crowther had become a Bishop largely because of Henry Venn's determination and pressure; Oluwole and Phillips had become Assistant Bishops because of the agitation fomented and led by James Johnson after Crowther's demise; that James Johnson became "Half Bishop", as shown already, was the sole initiative of Bishop Tugwell. One of the European missionaries, who expressed the popular view of the Scramble era, declared: "There is no doubt to my mind that what is essential, and will be essential for many years to come in this mission is European supervision of carefully trained native agents. I do not believe that the time has yet come for the consecration of native Bishops. Though I trust we may be made to feel that we have made a mistake in going as far as we have done in this respect. But as for an *Independent* native Bishop:—they are very very far from being able to guide and direct themselves leave alone others."[8]

The significant point is that neither the C.M.S. nor Lambeth Palace challenged the contractual interpretation given by James Johnson to the "arrangement" concluded before his consecration. When he recapitulated the substance of the "arrangement" the Society did not deny its authenticity, although it is clear that the Society would not implement it. As Eugene Stock, the Society's man through whom most correspondence for over thirty years had passed, declared: "I think I may say we have never before seen so much light upon West African prospects: and how is that? Simply through the idea of federating the dioceses and thus unifying *the white and black bishops and clergy into the Synod for all West Africa.* And whence came that idea? From the discussions in the Native Church Sub-Committee: or rather from the thoughts that got *expressed* in those discussions. If only we hold fast to that *principle of union*, pace bear G.T.S. we shall get similar enlightenment presumably in India."[9]

As for Lambeth Palace, since 1893 there had been glaring inconsistency in its attitude to the Delta Pastorate and to the question of an independent African Bishop. The Archbishop shifted ground as one condition after the other was being fulfilled. In 1893, following the gloomy forecast of the Hill Report, Lambeth Palace had declared in categorical language that once the Delta Church was in a position to pay the salary of a Bishop an African would be consecrated as an independent African Bishop.[10] A year later, behind the scenes and unknown to James Johnson and Africans, Lambeth Palace had begun to change its mind. For the financial statement of the institution put before the Archbishop had satisfied the condition of 1893. This earlier condition was now discountenanced and fresh ones added. These were, that Bishop Tugwell would have to report well about the institution, that the Church Missionary Society would have to recognise the Pastorate and that the institution must accept the C.M.S. "as having the property in trust for the Native Church".[11]

Unaware of the climate of opinion and thinking well of the C.M.S. and of Lambeth Palace, James Johnson began to emphasise the nationalist significance of his scheme. Every event from his consecration to his departure from England in August 1900 pointed to the fact that the parties to the contract were faithfully fulfilling the terms. On the day of his consecration the offertory, £10 2s. 4d., made at this service was directed by the Archbishop to be the nucleus of the fund for the independent diocese of the Niger Delta. As if it was intended to speed up the ecclesiastical freedom of West Africa the Society unilaterally changed the original name to West Africa Native Bishoprics Fund,[12] which, as interpreted by James Johnson, was a logical step that would eventuate in the creation of a West African Province. It did not occur to him that the change of title had very serious implications. For one implication of the new title was that the scheme could be said to be "West African" and no longer a "Niger Delta" one. The argument which the Church Missionary Society began to employ subsequently was that the realisation of £10,000 did not guarantee the creation of a particular diocese, but that such a sum must be contributed for each of the dioceses into which West Africa should be divided before James Johnson's wish could be realised. Unaware of the implication of the change in the scheme's title James Johnson believed that not only had he won ecclesiastical independence for himself but also for all prospective dioceses in West Africa; that once his diocese was created in the Niger Delta any other diocese that could boast of £10,000 would become automatically an "independent African diocese". Indeed some of his admirers in England began to contribute to the Fund and a Committee was set up to obtain gifts from Christians in West Africa,

Europe and America. Among the collectors of subscriptions in England were Fowell Buxton, a member of the famous philanthropist's family and the Reverend James B. Whiting, the Afrophile member of the Parent Committee with whom James Johnson corresponded for over thirty years and whom he had asked to preach the sermon on the occasion of his consecration.[13]

It was in the belief—which ultimately became an illusion—that he had won independence for all West Africa that James Johnson slipped into an ecstatic mood and made his triumphal ride back to West Africa after his consecration. For him his Ethiopian dream was on the threshold of achievement. He announced that his new project was neither an ecclesiastical nor an Anglican affair, "but one connected with African Christianity generally and as a national and racial one", to which 'pagans', Muslims and all Christians should subscribe. He declared characteristically that "the credit of the Negro Race" depended on the success of the scheme.[14] The nationalist aspect of the scheme was clearly grasped by the educated Africans. Hardly had it been announced than prominent Africans began to contribute to the Fund. The first contributors were the Sawyerr brothers of Sierra Leone who jointly contributed £100, and R. B. Blaize who contributed the same amount. In Sierra Leone where he arrived on 11 August 1900, the West African Native Bishopric Fund was launched formally with a fan-fare eighteen days later under the chairmanship of the Mayor, Sir Samuel Lewis, with the press supporting the scheme.[15] The Governor, Sir Frederick Cardew, contributed £5, but he was the only European who supported the scheme financially. Before Johnson left Sierra Leone on 24 November over £2,020 was either collected or promised, one S. B. Thomas, an old colleague of his in the Grammar School, donating £500. As James Johnson described Sierra Leone's reaction to the Fund: "Throughout the whole of the Religious history of the Colony which covers nearly a century, it is not known that there had been any movement which had been received and supported with the readiness, heartiness, willingness, unanimity, liberality, and enthusiasm which have been accorded to the West African Native Bishoprics Fund by the general Native Christian community."[16]

In Lagos James Johnson was not in a position to launch the Fund. Months before his arrival there he had become the centre of a movement which was to culminate in the biggest secession from the Anglican community in Lagos. Various forces combined to make the creation of an independent African Church by a respectable person like him imperative. He had become a symbol of the restless and inquisitive spirit among the educated Africans in Church and State. In the State the educated Africans seem gratified with the constitutional progress that was being achieved. For in 1899 a

Moloney-like administrator from New Guinea, Sir William Mac-gregor, began his rule in Lagos by increasing the number of edu-cated Africans on the Legislative Council from two to three in 1900 and to four in the following year, when he nominated respectively Dr. Obadiah Johnson and Sapara Williams, the latter being the best-known lawyer of his day. By 1901 the nominated unofficial members of the Council equalled in number the official members. Although power still lay in the hands of the European majority the constitutional position was an advancement on that of the days of Moloney and Carter. Then Macgregor, fulfilling a demand of the Lagos Press, which had been made to unresponsive governors since 1896, for the necessity to rule Nigeria "indirectly", appointed Henry Carr as Assistant Colonial Secretary for Native Affairs, "for purely native affairs".[17] This liberal policy was followed up in 1901 by the launching of the *African Institute* with Sir William Mac-gregor as President, Henry Carr as a Vice President and the Reverend J. H. Samuel, later Adegboyega Edun, as the Secretary. The *Institute* provided a forum for the educated Africans to under-stand government policy and for the British administration to understand African feelings and needs. The educated Africans consequently began to believe that these developments indicated that the British form of parliamentary government was being visibly established in Nigeria.

In the Church, where the European yoke could be cast away with impunity, discontent increased with the toppling of Africans from leadership. As examined already James Johnson himself was the centre, and inspirer of this discontent. Oluwole grew more and more unpopular with clergy and laity. Up to 1900 James John-son had survived the secessions that had occurred in his church largely through his inspiration. Unlike the amalgamation of Churches he had sought to effect in 1891, the U.N.A. was rather unpopular. It carried no prestige and by making polygamy an open question the African Church sought to "debase" Christianity, in the judgment of the majority of educated Africans. Indeed both in the Legislative Council and in the press James Johnson attacked this organisation as being unchristian because of its toleration of polygamy.[18] When, four years later, another group left his Church to form the Church of God, on the grounds that denomin-ationalism was unscriptural, they received less publicity and less support than the U.N.A. For they too decided to accept poly-gamists into full membership.

But the situation in 1900 was quite different. If he was to pre-serve his prestige among his admirers he must cease to be a theorist and be a man of action. He was expected to found his much-discussed undenominational African Church in 1901. The

theme of his West Africa Native Bishoprics Fund scheme was basically similar to the one which he had hitherto led his admirers to believe was his main objective. Hardly had he arrived in Lagos than
he reported to the Christian community the circumstances of his
acceptance of the position of "Half Bishop" and the purpose of
the West Africa Native Bishoprics Fund "which seeks to promote the formation of several separate independent Dioceses presided over by African Bishops as had been the case before the
unification of the separate African Church into one great West
African Church".[19] Moreover the atmosphere was ripe and con-
genial; the revolt that occurred in Breadfruit against the authorities
of the Anglican Church and in which other churches and denominations shared actively, was in sympathy with him. For in spite of
his being an autocrat in theological and moral matters his rule was
accepted throughout his tenure as Pastor. As had happened with
James Johnson in all the churches over which he had been pastor,
the parishioners of Breadfruit did not want him to abandon them
even for the higher office of Assistant Bishop.

In the normal course of things James Johnson's consecration
would not have provoked the crisis that arose in Lagos in 1900
and which continued for the greater part of 1901. He would norm-
ally have moved his seat to Bonny, or some other place in the
Niger Delta, to direct the affairs of the Niger Delta Pastorate for
which he had been specifically consecrated. But for a number of
reasons the Breadfruit parishioners and leaders of Anglican laity,
who had their own ideas of James Johnson, used the occasion
provided by the Church Missionary Society to bring about the
crisis. For the latter advised the executive of the Lagos Church,
the Church Committee, to retain the services of James Johnson
in Breadfruit as minister-in-charge whilst paying episcopal visits
to his 'diocese'. This bona fide suggestion looks very absurd on
the surface: James Johnson would be behaving like an absentee
landlord, in a manner similar to that for which Bishop Crowther
had been criticised. The Niger Delta Pastorate could hardly have
been well administered from a distance of several hundreds of
miles. But the C.M.S. were motivated by the desire to preserve
James Johnson's spiritual inspiration and influence in Lagos. As
the Society put it, "we think that all things considered it would
be a pity for the present to take him away from Lagos".[20]

This suggestion had been made in April 1900, that is several
months before James Johnson was expected back in Lagos. The
suggestion could hardly have been entertained by the Church
Committee of which Herbert Tugwell, the Diocesan, was Chairman and Isaac Oluwole was Vice-Chairman. At the time the former was away on a missionary foray into Northern Nigeria,

leaving Oluwole in a position to influence the decision. If anything Oluwole welcomed the consecration of James Johnson with
delight. After all since 1893 the latter had completely overshadowed him in spite of his superior ecclesiastical status. That
Oluwole was overshadowed by Holy Johnson is clear from surviving records of the Lagos Church Missions, in which no compli-
ment of any kind whatsoever was paid to the former, in contrast
to the profusion of compliments enjoyed by the latter. As long as
James Johnson was in Yorubaland Oluwole's authority and influence could not be effective.

Perhaps Oluwole could have acted with impunity against the
suggestion of the C.M.S. had the matter been really confidential.
But leakage of the suggestion by the Society came through James
Johnson's friend, the Reverend J. B. Whiting. By private corres-
pondence with J. A. Payne, the most consistently ardent disciple
of Holy Johnson, the Lagos Christians became acquainted with
what had happened.[21] The result was an unparalleled commotion in
Lagos in favour of the C.M.S. decision and in support of James
Johnson. A long memorial, signed by 227 representatives of the
Anglican community, including the late Alake of Abeokuta, Sir
Ladapo Ademola, was sent to Bishop Tugwell, who had just come
back from Hausaland. The appeal was that the decision of the
Church Committee should be set aside. The fact that no apparent
residence had been arranged for James Johnson increased sym-
pathy for him.

By the time Bishop Tugwell returned to Lagos Oluwole had
become an eyesore, considered as a traitor. He had suffered one
humiliation after another. It was alleged that he was anti-Johnson.
The Church Committee, it was held, had lied to the C.M.S. that
the parishioners of Breadfruit would not have James Johnson.
The rumour that gained ground was that so much was James
Johnson hated that the Church Committee had decided that all
pulpits in Lagos had been closed against him; that he would not
even be allowed to land in Lagos but would be rushed on to the
Niger Delta.[22] As Oluwole put it, "many boisterous meetings"[23]
were held, his life was threatened and even women rushed at him
when they heard the rumour that some luggage for James Johnson had arrived but was not allowed to be kept in Breadfruit
Parsonage.

The decision of the Church Committee, though proper in principle, was hasty in detail and execution. Its hastiness provided
ample ammunition for the explosion that finally occurred. The
decision to regard his pastoral care of the church as having terminated at the end of March 1900, that is just a month after his
consecration, was ill-advised. Many members of Breadfruit began

to wonder whether the Church Committee ever wanted their Pastor to bid them good-bye "in the usual and proper form".[24] Had the Church Committee been patient and waited until James Johnson had arrived many people might not have read anti-Johnson meaning into its decision. There was also the human factor. With no proper arrangement made yet for his residence, a point well grasped by the Church Missionary Society, the parishioners of Breadfruit could hardly have accepted tamely what they regarded as a shabby treatment of their much-beloved Pastor.

Whilst James Johnson was being ecstatically welcomed in Sierra Leone all effort by the laity and the Church Committee to resolve the crisis failed woefully. The six representatives of Breadfruit Church, viz. D. A. J. Oguntolu, J. B. Dawodu, J. K. Coker, Ben Roberts, J. A. Adebiyi and S. A. Jibowu, who had meetings with the Church Committee, were applying skilfully the principles of democracy that had been fostered in them by James Johnson through the system of classes and Leaders' Conferences. Their sympathy was unconquerably for their Pastor. To the principle that in the Anglican canon a Bishop could not be a Pastor these representatives flung in the face of the Committee the principle of "no taxation without representation".[25] Never before had the authorities of the Lagos Church dealt with so argumentative and so truculent a laity; never before had the Church Committee had to endure the sting applied to them by this band of Johnsonians from Breadfruit. Take for example the following statement by Dawodu:

> As the whole Lagos Pastorate churches do not approve of the Local Committee's Resolution, should the Committee persist and refuse to reconsider the matter? The representatives in Parliament are responsible to their constituents and are therefore to seek their interest as much as lies in that power. Why should the opinion of twelve outweigh that of thousands of people to whom they are responsible? The point is that if the Lagos Church Committee cannot grant this petition, what must the Lagos Church do! Must they go and please themselves?[26]

Or take the remarks of Oguntolu, who pleaded that the resolution of the Church Missionary Society should be implemented in full. They show what James Johnson meant to his parishioners and the nadir to which Oluwole's influence had fallen. Not only did he hear himself labelled as Aachan who would bring calamity upon the Lagos Church but he had the bitter experience of listening to this lecture, in Yoruba: "It is not impossible for men to err. When a man sees his fault and makes amends, he receiveth blessing of God; but whoever wilfully shuts his eyes and refuses to make amends suffers. Had Bishop Johnson been absent for three years without being made a Bishop it is obvious that his post will still be open to him on his return. Bishop Johnson will not accept anything that will not work well. This Committee is responsible to the Church and to God, but we want you kindly to let the Bishop return to the pastoral charge of Breadfruit."[27]

The failure of the Church Committee to resolve the crisis—Oluwole having told the irate parishioners to please themselves—left the direction of affairs to one man, Bishop Herbert Tugwell. He was singularly unfit to settle a dispute of this kind; as a Diocesan he was occupying an office inherently authoritarian in the Anglican hierarchy. But there was also venom in his tongue. His immediate reaction was that he must maintain the authority of the Church Committee at all costs and uphold Oluwole against the pro-Johnson forces. The European missionaries saw the crisis as one of a struggle for supremacy between Oluwole and James Johnson.[28] Having consulted with the Governor, Sir William Macgregor, Bishop Tugwell cast his lot with Oluwole, the "hearty appreciation" of whom was expressed by the Governor.[29] For the European missionaries James Johnson was "a lawless Bishop".[30] As should be expected their choice was Oluwole. It should be remarked that European opinion on Oluwole was not based on evidence that he showed any ability or competence in the performance of his duties. Eight years after his consecration Bishop Tugwell had to express disappointment that "he [Oluwole] has not got the grip of the work I hoped he would have got ere this: he does not originate new work and develop fresh plans".[31]

Herbert Tugwell lacked the tact and patience necessary to consider in a sober manner the delicate matter put before him. From the beginning to the end he bungled it and added fuel to the fire. The documents show clearly that he did not grasp the situation fully before acting. He succeeded in further alienating the irate parishioners by giving the issue a racial dimension. His tongue was anything but soothing. On one occasion he declared the pro-Johnson supporters as "rebels" from the pulpit—"these filthy dreamers defile the flesh, despise dominions and speak evil of dignities. These are murmurers, complainers; walking after their own lusts; and their mouth speaketh great swelling words, having men's prose in admiration because of advantages."[32]

The Johnsonians replied in kind, heaping insults upon him. On the basis of Hebrew 3 : 17, "obey them that have the rule over you", Tugwell gave Oluwole and the Church Committee a blank cheque. The Johnsonians knew their Bible well, retorting that in his stand in the matter Tugwell had acted against the injunctions in I Peter 5: 2-3 and Ephesians 6: 4 "And ye fathers provoke not your children to wrath."[33]

Throughout the crisis, which lasted to October 1901 when the majority of Breadfruit parishioners broke away in sympathy with James Johnson, the European missionaries were convinced that all the trouble had been caused by this African agitator, that not only did he foment it but that he was responsible for the momentum it had for over one year and the success which it achieved. Bishop Tugwell's conviction in this regard was based upon four points. Firstly, that although James Johnson resigned his appointment of Breadfruit yet he remained in the Parsonage for several months afterwards, in spite of the Bishop's order that he should vacate it. Secondly, that James Johnson had the power to restrain his supporters but he did not do so. Thirdly, that his supporters confessed to Bishop Tugwell that they did not hate the Reverend Nathaniel Johnson, the person chosen by the Church Committee to succeed him, but that all the row was "about Bishop James Johnson. They do not want him to be driven away."[34] Fourthly, that James Johnson's farewell address positively incited the opposition, was "practically a declaration of war against constituted Authority". As Tugwell told James Johnson: "You practically cast your shield over the disaffected whom you represented as the oppressed. You have condemned those in authority: you have upheld those in Rebellion."[35]

That James Johnson was the central figure of the "Rebellion" is beyond dispute. But it is extremely doubtful whether he was the sole cause of the storm. He was no more than a symbol, through his exposition of the ideology of an independent African Church and as an opponent of injustice of any kind from any quarter. The evidence shows clearly that James Johnson was not at any stage disloyal to the Church Missionary Society. He continued to stay on in Breadfruit Parsonage in obedience to the instruction given by the Society.[36] Moreover he did everything he could to restrain his supporters before and after his return to Lagos. For instance he asked his parishioners to apologise for the insult of walking out on Oluwole. Also on more than one occasion he told them to obey Bishop Tugwell.[37]

The point to recognise is that the cause for which the Lagos Anglican community stood was greater than an individual. There was the confidence and conviction of the laity that they should be in charge of affairs, that the ministers of religion were no more than their servants. Then there was the genuine conviction of a number of people that a truly African Church should be founded, that the authoritarianism being displayed by Tugwell with impunity would not have been possible under an African Bishop.

In a sense James Johnson had strands of all these factors in him and in the doctrine he had been preaching for more than a genera-tion. But in the actual events of 1900 to 1901 all that could be said against him is that he was absolutely neutral. Certainly he was popular with the leaders of the agitation in his favour, but he refused to curb them or prevent them from behaving as they liked. But the fact that he did not join hands with the authorities of the Church made Tugwell and others misconstrue his neutral position as collusion. To be sure James Johnson sympathised with many of the demands of the agitators and he had his grievances against the Lagos Church Committee for the hasty and peremptory man-ner in which he had been treated. But there is no evidence that he incited his supporters against authority. Sympathy for him remained long after he had left for the Niger and the final break-ing away occurred months after he had left Lagos. Bishop Tug-well summarised the position of James Johnson in the crisis in October 1901 very well when he declared to the Executive Com-mittee of the Yoruba Mission: "There is an impression abroad that James Johnson is being unfairly dealt with reference to this question. Complaints are made to me (i) that he is being ejected from Lagos (ii) that no provision has been made for his House Accommodation. How far Bp. Johnson is responsible for the existence of this impression in men's minds I am not prepared to say, but I am aware that he feels he has grounds for com-plaint."[38]

The death of his wife on 19 May 1901, at the height of the crisis, sharpened the personal element in the whole drama. For his sup-porters the unpleasant affair and the ill-treatment meted out to the Johnsons, who had been forced to vacate Breadfruit Parson-age before he went off to the Niger Delta in the previous month, contributed to her death, said to have been brought about by "an unexpected apoplectic attack which brought on her immediately a paralysis of the whole of her right side and deprived her at once of her consciousness and the power of speech".[39] The condolence shown on the sad occasion was universal, touching and profound. Almost every flag in the town was at half-mast. Preparations for the burial had been completed before James Johnson could re-turn from the Niger Delta. In fact she would have been buried before he could come were it not that his admirers chartered a special branch steamer to fetch him from the ship off the bar. Her funeral procession was said to be quite a mile long and it included all classes of the community, Christians, Muslims and 'pagans'. Indeed death was busy in his wife's family in that year. Earlier Dr. Leigh Sodipe, a brother of his wife, had died. A few months after his wife's death her mother followed her two children to the grave, "she being crushed out of this life by the very severe and offensive weight of her grief and sorrow".[40]

In October 1901 two-thirds of Breadfruit parishioners broke away from the Anglican community in Lagos in sympathy with James Johnson and founded the independent Bethel African Church. To the consternation of his admirers, who believed he was with them in their anti-Oluwole and anti-Tugwell feelings, rather than head the new Church which represented the ideas he had hitherto expressed in strong terms, he listened to Tugwell's bitter indictment of him, packed his bags and went off to the Niger Delta.

The papers of one of the leaders in the Breadfruit Church crisis, J. Kehinde Coker, illuminate the position he occupied in the hearts of the founders of the Bethel African Church. His career and "saintliness" in Sierra Leone, in Lagos, and in Abeokuta they stressed, had been a veritable inspiration to them in the last quarter of the nineteenth century. Many of them had been under his teaching in Abeokuta and in Breadfruit Church for well-nigh a generation. They had all along sympathised with him as the European missionaries unfolded their hostility towards him. By 1899 the personal attachment they had for James Johnson was very strong indeed and they expected and believed sincerely that in 1900 and 1901 Holy Johnson would give them leadership. Indeed many of them had expected him to declare independence from the Church Missionary Society in the last days of his superintendence in the interior of Yorubaland. As J. K. Coker lamented, Holy Johnson "failed to lead his people";[41] "he was the teacher of the African Church". James Johnson was "the teacher appointed by God to teach the establishment of the Independent African Church".[42]

But not only did James Johnson fail to "lead his people" in 1900 and 1901 but he became a great opponent of the African Church movement. It is significant that he coined the term of ridicule, "Bo da o wa"[43] (If you are rejected by other Churches come to us) for the U.N.A. which, it will be remembered, came into existence in 1891 as a result of his failure to institute an undenominational African Church in that year. Indeed he missed no opportunity to attack this organisation in the Legislative Council and in the press. Nor did he spare the Bethelites either. Almost every year he attacked them in his annual presidential address to the Niger Delta Conference, and he also used the press to oppose their attempt to intrude into his Benin Mission territories. Holy Johnson went out of his way to try several times to persuade the leaders of the Bethel African Church to return to the Anglican fold. Quite rightly the Bethelites persuaded him to perceive that he, James Johnson, had been responsible for their movement. As J. K. Coker declared:

> I brought his life to mind. In 1872 how he pleaded to obtain the Native Pastorate in Sierra Leone and later likewise in Lagos. To Abeokuta—as Superintendent of whole Yoruba Mission with the distinct understanding that he might eventually become the Bishop of Abeokuta in a purely native state and how he was persecuted without a cause and among other things for the training of the Abeokuta Church into independence which plans he inaugurated for the training of myself and others for 23 years. I told him that God appointed him to teach the African Church and not to lead it, therefore he should not on account of the love we have for him push us out of the path [on] which God has placed us.[44]

It was the bitter truth that James Johnson could not deny. Since then he never asked the Bethelites to return to the Anglican fold.

Nevertheless the leaders of the African Church never broke from James Johnson as a person. He too responded in a very impressive way. For the former Holy Johnson remained "a father", the "spiritual father", "the good man". Largely through the influence of J. K. Coker, James Johnson had acquired by 1907 a large area of land, fifty-four acres, at Ifako on which cocoa, rubber and kolanut were cultivated. His overseer on this farm was J. K. Coker and James Johnson never worked on it personally. James Johnson saw the plantation as a practical demonstration of his idea of education of the Hand, but he also looked upon it as a resort on which he intended to erect a house to which he could retreat for rest away from the humdrum of Lagos life.[45]

The events of 1900 to 1901 in Lagos have been examined in detail in order to reveal the grand opportunity available to James Johnson for a partial implementation of his Ethiopian programme. He was in these two years, so to speak, the idol of Lagos. Never was his prestige so high; never were events and time so ripe and so excellent for the achievement of part of the dream he had been having for a generation and yet never had a man so disappointed his admirers by failing to take the opportunities they put at his disposal in 1901. His actions were illogical and he paid the price with his prestige. Once more James Johnson betrayed his unbreakable attachment to the Church Missionary Society. For him the Anglican Church was the only legitimate nucleus of his visionary continental African Church. He would therefore not lead an African Church that was not a projection of the Anglican Church and the child of the Church Missionary Society.

Perhaps at sixty-four James Johnson had reached an age when

a radical rethinking was impossible and sentimental attachment to a body he had been associated with for so long a period of time blurred his objectivity. There was also the fact that the fanfare with which he had been received in England in 1899 and 1900, an experience that eluded even Bishop Crowther, had made a deep impression on him. He certainly would not have liked to leave a Society that counted among its supporters pro-Africans like the Reverend James Whiting, Dr. R. N. Cust, who resigned from the C.M.S. Executive over the shabby treatment of Bishop Crowther and the appointment of a European successor to him, and F. Buxton, a descendant of the famous philanthropist. Indeed after 1899 European missionaries observed that James Johnson was friendlier towards them than hitherto.[46] With him the days of bitter anti-European invectives were surely over.

For years after the events of 1900 to 1901 James Johnson regretted that the Bethelites broke away from the Anglican communion, on the grounds that their action was accentuating sectarianism. In his judgment they were trying to work for another death of the African Church, similar to that experienced by the early Church in North Africa. As he declared: "We should not lose sight of the fact that endless sectarian divisions among professors, the mutual active antipathies, and the spiritual and moral weakness they had given birth to were among the causes that had prepared the way for the downfall of the North and North East African Christianity of history and contributed to make it incapable of resisting the aggressive invasion of Mohammedanism which eventually destroyed the greatest portion of it. Can we in view of this serious historic catastrophe, the spiritual and moral weakness which the long-standing divisions among us have contributed with other circumstances to produce . . . be indifferent to so serious a split as that which has occurred within our own Communion in Lagos?"[47]

By not leading the Bethelites James Johnson lost the opportunity of taking the tide at the flood, thereby abandoning certainty for uncertainty. For the founders of the Bethel African Church were realists who were aware that African leadership and independence in religious matters could not be obtained within Christian missions in Colonial Nigeria. The only step open, it was clear to them, was to break away and to pursue the ideas and ideals which James Johnson had been advocating for a generation. Indeed they were fully aware that it was only a Church founded in this way, without the co-operation, goodwill and assistance of the white man, that could become truly independent and free to hold its future in its own hands and to make Christianity win the affection of Africans in an African environment, harmonising the sublime verities of the Christian faith with compatible African customs and institutions. There was certainly substance in the boast of one of the founders, that "we are now building a church in conjunction with our fellow African brethren (who desire Ethiopia to stretch forth her hand to God) in order to establish a strong native African Church to be supervised solely by Africans".[48]

In contrast to the Bethelites was James Johnson who believed that through the West Africa Native Bishoprics Fund scheme he would achieve the programme he had been advocating for so long. It was, to say the least, an uncertain scheme dependent on the hope that Africans would willingly subscribe the substantial Endowment of £10,000, that both the Church Missionary Society and Lambeth Palace would interpret the "arrangement" concluded before his consecration in a legally contractual sense, that Bishop Tugwell, who had every cause to deplore the role James Johnson had played in the Breadfruit Church crisis, would stand by his pledge. His scheme, too, was also visionary in the sense that it envisaged a self-liquidation of the Church Missionary Society in West Africa and a surrender of his authority and control by the Archbishop of Canterbury.

If anyone ever misplaced confidence in the white man then James Johnson did so with respect to the West Africa Native Bishoprics Fund scheme. Neither Bishop Tugwell nor the Church Missionary Society nor Lambeth Palace intended to grant him the terms of the "arrangement". Rather it was thought by all of them that the terms were unattainable and that in this sense the "arrangement" would prove the death-knell of his nationalism in the Anglican Church. But as subscriptions began to be made in a manner that confounded the parties to the "arrangement", they began to retract, first privately and then publicly. As early as May 1900, that is the month in which James Johnson was being congratulated by members of the Negro Race in London, Bishop Tugwell shuddered at the response that James Johnson's appeal began to evoke in Africans. He therefore wrote that the raising of sufficient funds for a bishopric did not mean that a bishopric would be created and that the Archbishop did not entertain such an idea at all.[49] It was also stated privately by a C.M.S. spokesman that the step being envisaged by James Johnson had never occurred to the Society.[50] And yet as late as 21 January 1902 Bishop Tugwell declared publicly that he had entered into a pledge that on James Johnson's consecration he should raise a Niger Bishopric Endowment Fund for the establishment of an "Independent African Bishopric" in the Niger Delta. As he admitted: "To that great Mission Bishop Johnson stands pledged, and I stand pledged to support him. I ask the prayer of the Conference on his behalf, for health and strength, for grace and courage."[51] And, fearing that the crisis of 1900-1 would be aggravated if James Johnson was allowed to launch his Fund in Lagos, Bishop Tugwell urged him not to do so, saying that he, Tugwell, would raise funds for him in Lagos and Yorubaland and that if James Johnson would not accept this condition their relations would be terminated.

In innocence and completely oblivious of the real mind of the parties to the "arrangement" James Johnson left Lagos for the Niger Delta in April 1901. He lost no time in organising subscriptions for the Fund outside Lagos and Yorubaland. Indeed for the rest of his life the scheme became the most important subject of his conversation, his sermons, his addresses and his interviews with Lambeth Palace and newspapers and of his exhortations to Africans. His missionary tours were designed to educate the chiefs of the Niger Delta, Benin, Sapele, Warri, Sabongida Ora and the Owo district on the virtues of the independence that the scheme would confer on Africans and to persuade them to subscribe generously to it. For James Johnson the scheme cut across religion, denomination, ethnic group and status. He did not reject subscriptions by members of other races as well.

In April 1902 James Johnson went to the Gold Coast on behalf of the scheme. Although the Europeans there were apathetic, the response of Africans, even though the latter were mainly Wesleyans, was astonishing. Cape Coast, he wrote, "has responded very generously and nobly, Wesleyan gentlemen being among the foremost and most liberal supporters".[52] Collections were also organised in Accra and Axim, which he also visited. In December 1903 he went to the Spanish island of Fernando Po. At a public meeting at the church of the Primitive Methodists at Santa Isabel the Fund was launched. So warm was the reception accorded to the scheme that, according to James Johnson, "even Roman Catholic Native Africans, some persons of high position and influence, would not deny themselves self-governed and independent Native Churches presided over by African Bishops though these be of a different communion to their own".[53] He visited the Cameroons, then under German rule, twice—in 1904 and 1905. On 3 January 1905, the Fund was launched at Baseke Anglican Church in Duala. At the meeting were King Monga Bell and King Acqua of Bell and Aqua Towns and other important aborigines were among the glad and willing subscribers to the Fund. He was gratified at the response, "a handsome one", in spite of the poverty of the people.[54]

James Johnson's organisational method for Fund raising was

the setting up of Committees, one for male and another for female where possible, under the leadership of important local people. For instance until his death in 1903 Sir Samuel Lewis was chairman of the Sierra Leone Committee whilst the Secretaryship and Treasureship devolved on the Honourable J. J. Thomas. In Cape Coast the Reverend N. H. Boston was Secretary as well as co-Treasurer with Chief R. A. Harrison. The Accra Committee was under the secretaryship of R. E. Quartey, whilst the Fernando Po Committee was under the guidance of J. Barleycorn, a Bubi who had been trained in Spain. In the Niger Delta the Reverend James Boyle was both Secretary and Treasurer.

The point to emphasise about the West Africa Native Bishoprics Fund scheme is that it assumed an international complexion, a reflection of the cosmopolitanism that characterised the educated elite of the Victorian and Edwardian generations. That the scheme awakened support at all, following the founding of the Bethel African Church, is sufficiently surprising and shows the immense prestige commanded by James Johnson along the West African Coast. That the subscriptions promised or paid up in Sierra Leone and the Gold Coast alone within two years amounted to nearly £7,000 must be regarded as a spectacular achievement and a credit to the ability of James Johnson to arouse African support. His success can be explained by the fact that, left to themselves, the majority of Christians deplored secession as the means to obtain religious freedom. They would prefer a mutual separation, a negotiated independence that would not involve recrimination and racial bitterness. The Henry Venn formula was all that they sought to see implemented, and that in a peaceful manner. For most of his supporters the "arrangement" concluded with their ecclesiastical masters by James Johnson arose out of a genuine conviction regarding both the C.M.S. and Lambeth Palace, that the more than fifty-year presence of European leadership had been long enough and would be terminated. Such a Church would carry prestige. As a Lagos newspaper editorialised: "The reason for this universal enthusiasm [for the Fund] was that the people saw in the movement the realisation of a long-cherished hope, the foundation upon a solid basis of a Church managed and controlled by Natives and free from the leading strings of foreign supervision. This is what the missionaries of the C.M.S. have all along declared to be the end of and aim of their labours in Africa, viz. that their presence among us and their interference in spiritual matters were only for a time and until the Native Church was strong enough to stand alone. . . . Surely if there is ever to be a consummation of what the agents of the C.M.S. always declared to be the object of the Society's labours, and what native Christians everywhere have hoped and prayed for, the time cannot be riper than it is at present."[55]

Perhaps the most significant feature of the West Africa Native Bishoprics Fund scheme is the fact that it provided James Johnson with the opportunity to convince the unlettered, the chiefs and the ordinary folk, of the virtues of independence at a time when the unlettered were unhappy that the white man had come to rob them of their sovereignty.

There is no better illustration of James Johnson's success than the dramatic change of attitude of the Church Missionary Society to the scheme. Probably fearing that not only would the target sum be realised by James Johnson but that it might be oversubscribed, the Society announced in an Editorial of the *Intelligencer* of October 1902 that the funds being collected would not be used for any specific bishopric, but for West African Diocesans "wherever and whenever they may be appointed". Furthermore it ruled out the idea of an independent Bishopric under an African, emphasising that whenever a diocese was created such a diocese must be in communion with the Church of England.

The effects of the C.M.S. view and veto were electric. Hitherto the African subscribers, including a Mr. J. W. Sey in the Gold Coast who donated £500, had supported the scheme on "racial grounds" for one particular scheme—that of the Niger Delta— and it had been thought that once the target amount of money had been realised its creation would be automatic.[56] It had also been believed that the diocese would be truly independent, completely rid of alien control. The reaction in Lagos, Old Calabar, Cape Coast, Accra and Freetown was sharp and emphatic. Many who had made promises declared that they would not fulfil them; others who had offered subscriptions regretted that they had ever done so and several demanded a refunding of their money.[57] It was now that the implication of the unilateral change of the title from "Niger Bishopric Fund" to "West African Native Bishoprics Fund" was perceived. It was not until now, too, that the Bethel Church began to look respectable in the eyes of several admirers of James Johnson. It began to be argued that the Bethelites, after all, were more radical and committed to the achievement of aims grander than those envisaged in Holy Johnson's scheme. No amount of ink or oratory by James Johnson would revive African enthusiasm in the scheme. He betrayed his unbreakable attachment and loyalty to the Church Missionary Society when he openly admitted that the "independent" African Church that would be established in the Niger Delta would be in communion with the Church of England, had been what he had been working for since 1872 and that: "This was exactly the position held

by the ancient Churches in Africa, the Churches of Cyprian,
Augustine, Cyril and Athanasius which when they were self-
governing and independent, and whilst they spoke severally at
what are known in history as the general Councils of the Christian
Church as independent Churches and gave their votes accordingly
were in communion with the older churches of Jerusalem, and
Rome, and Constantinople and also represented on these Councils."[58]

It would have been thought that the sharp reaction of African
supporters to the C.M.S. veto and withdrawal of support for the
scheme should have opened James Johnson's eyes to the realities
of the situation and persuaded him to abandon it, and the dream.
But he remained undaunted and continued to live in hopes until
he breathed his last. Curiously enough he did not detect the lack
of faith so clearly demonstrated by all other parties to the
"arrangement" of 1900. Rather he believed that it was Africans
themselves who were to blame because they would not contribute
the target sum. As late at 1913 he declared in the West African
press that the realisation of African Bishoprics "depends upon
ourselves, our steadfastness, perseverance, persistence, determination, liberality and self-denial",[59] in terms of subscriptions.
Although he did not see the wide credibility gap in the public
statements of both Tugwell and Lambeth Palace there was ample
evidence that ought to have convinced him that he was pursuing
a mirage. For one thing all attempts by him to persuade the C.M.S.
to retract the damaging veto of October 1902 failed. But more
glaring was the fact that Bishop Tugwell never redeemed the
promise he had made, that he would launch the Fund in Yorubaland. Not a penny was ever collected by Tugwell.

The evidence is overwhelming that from the beginning to the
end James Johnson was deceived by Bishop Tugwell and Lambeth Palace. There were many differences between what was discussed in private and what was publicly announced. Throughout Herbert Tugwell was consistent in his private view that the
question of an independent African Bishop should be ruled out.
On 22 September 1908 he had a meeting with a Special Committee of the C.M.S. at which he proposed that Yorubaland, the Gold
Coast, Iboland and Northern Nigeria should be constituted into
separated Dioceses, under European Bishops. When questioned
about African national susceptibilities his reply, as recorded, was
"that the Lambeth Conference made it clear that the day for
Native Bishoprics should wait for the day of Native resources for
their income; and he was of [the] opinion that that day in West
Africa had not yet come. And on other grounds he seemed to be
unable to recommend an independent African Bishopric at pre-

sent".[60] And this was the very man who not long afterwards had a meeting with James Johnson and the Archbishop on the same matter in which the principle of African episcopate was reaffirmed.[61] At this meeting Dr. T. R. Davidson, the Archbishop, expressed surprise that Africans had been so incapable of raising £10,000. Therefore he would be magnanimous by reducing the target sum to £8,000, with the understanding that after a Bishopric should have been created the remaining £2,000 should be raised gradually and added to the Fund.

So eager were Tugwell and the Archbishop, it seemed to James Johnson, in their desire that the scheme should be a success that he was told that once Africans could fulfil their part two Church societies in England had offered to help. In a printed paper dated February 1909 the Committee in charge of collection in England published the text of a letter to one of its members, T. H. Baxter, dated 28 January 1909, in which the principle of an independent African principle was reiterated: "Before independent jurisdiction can be given to our African Bishop for the Delta, some adequate provision should be forthcoming, or in immediate prospect, to secure proper training of clergy and teachers."[62]

As long as James Johnson was alive Bishop Tugwell could not disclose to the West African public the fact that the African agitator was being deceived all along. For by 1909 when James Johnson had begun to express "deep disappointment" at the failure of the Archbishop of Canterbury and the C.M.S. to fulfil their pledge on the Bishopric scheme, his idea had begun to infect the African clergy and laity in a manner disconcerting to Bishop Tugwell. In 1909, the first time when James Johnson attended the Synod since its inauguration, a resolution supporting the scheme was formally adopted[63] and reiterated in subsequent years. Even the eternally submissive Oluwole had begun to indicate resentment at the form that European leadership in the Church had begun to assume. Although in 1908 he declared secretly to Bishop Tugwell that he was not in favour of an African being a full Bishop yet he would not like to have another ecclesiastical master besides Bishop Tugwell.[64] The latter had to be careful what he said in public.

For apart from the Yoruba clergy and laity the Delta Pastorate and Sierra Leonian Christians began to show increasing interest in the scheme. No occasion was ever lost by the Pastorate to draw the Archbishop's attention to the fact that their desire and hope remained fixed on the issue of an African Episcopate. In order to meet the new condition about facilities for the training of clergymen the Bishop Crowther Memorial Theological Training Institute was completed and officially opened in 1912. At the annual conference a vote of confidence and congratulations was passed

in support of James Johnson's exertions for the Fund and a resolution was passed (which was sent to Lambeth Palace) reaffirm-
ing "its desire for the appointment of a Bishop of African descent,
who being in full communion with the Church of England shall
possess full Episcopal powers in the Diocese in which the Niger
Delta is situated, so soon as such a Diocese can be separated from
the present Diocese of Western Equatorial Africa".[65] In Sierra
Leone T. F. Victor Buxton, the C.M.S. representative at the Jubilee celebration of the Church of Sierra Leone had to admit *that
the facts stated by Bishop James Johnson with reference to the
sincerity of the Church Missionary Society for the creation of
Native Independent Bishoprics in West Africa were perfectly correct but that actions were hanging fire because the Funds had not
yet been raised, and that in that respect the matter rested with
Africans*.[66]

To the dismay of Bishop Tugwell African faith in the scheme,
naturally, began to revive. In 1912 Mrs. C. O. Obaso, daughter of
the deceased R. B. Blaize, generously added £200 to her father's
gift of £100.[67] Even an undisclosed Englishman contributed £30.
The Lagos press urged Africans to contribute the remaining £3,000
"in order to see the beginning of the realisation of our highest
Christian aspirations".[68] Tugwell lost no time in persuading the
Archbishop, who even before receiving the resolution of the Conference of the Niger Delta Pastorate had declared that the institution had "a great future and that a Native Pastorate, headed in
due time by a Bishop of African descent, will be able in the Providence of God to do more for the people of that region than can
ever be done by those who are not themselves of African birth or
upbringing".[69] This Pastorate, he declared, did not deserve the
Archbishop's sanguine hope because the ministry was that of alien
Africans and not of the genuine natives. In order that Buxton and
other liberal-minded members of the C.M.S. Committee might stop
thinking that James Johnson's dream would ever be fulfilled, Tugwell wrote:

Possibly the impression may get abroad that if the sum of £8,000
or £10,000 be raised, the appointment of an African Bishop of
the Delta would immediately follow. We have no assurance
from the Archbishop that this would be the case, and speaking
for myself only for the moment I should not be able to recommend to the Archbishop the adoption of such a course. There
are several matters which must be dealt with before such action
can be taken (1) No earnest endeavour has hitherto been made
to instruct the people in the vernacular scriptures in large portions of the Delta, e.g. the Ibo section (2) Native clergy must be

trained (3) The Church must manifest a Missionary spirit (4) The funds of the Church must be in a more satisfactory condition. . . . Nor could I recommend the taking of such a step, even if those conditions were fulfilled until the creation of a Province is a practical question.[70]

The deceit practised on James Johnson by Tugwell and Lambeth Palace was greater than the credibility gap of their public statements. It had been decided as early as 1907 that the Fund would be controlled by the Diocesan for a purpose contrary to that for which it was established. James Johnson was persuaded to accept a Trust Deed made with terms flexible enough to make the Diocesan employ the Fund to pay Bishops in West Africa irrespective of their race. For although term Two declared that the Fund "shall be applied towards the stipend of a Bishop of African descent in communion with the Church of England" term Four specified that the trustees "may at any time, with the approval of the Bishop of the Diocese and of any such committee as aforesaid, transfer the Fund to the Colonial Bishoprics Fund, or when a Synod shall have been formed in and for the Diocese, it shall be lawful for the trustees, with the consent of the Bishop, to transfer to that Body".[71] In 1908 five trustees were appointed by the London Committee, out of whom only one was an African. They were Alfred Fowell Buxton, Rev. H. L. C. De Caudole, Rev. J. B. Whiting, T. H. Baxter and the Hon. Kitoyi Ajasa, a Lagos lawyer and, perhaps, the most pro-C.M.S. and pro-white man of his age. Hardly had James Johnson died than the Fund was transferred to the Colonial Bishoprics Fund from which Assistant Bishops of all races henceforth came to be paid.

In preferring the West Africa Native Bishoprics Fund scheme to founding an independent African Church of his own James Johnson was an incorrigible visionary, a man incapable of distinguishing the possible from the unattainable. Only a man of his type could after 1900 believe that African leadership in an institution like the Church would be encouraged by Christian missions, that the era of Bishop Crowther's African episcopate would not only be revived but exceeded in favour of African patriotism. The scheme showed too that James Johnson was also incredibly naïve. Why did he make Lambeth Palace the prop of his scheme? Why did he believe that Tugwell and Lambeth Palace would or should give him the ecclesiastical independence he wanted? How could a Church that required the authority and blessings of the Anglican Church be truly independent? Never did James Johnson become free from the myopia of Anglicanism.

But it would not be sufficient to dismiss him as a visionary on the West Africa Native Bishoprics Fund scheme. There was also his simplicity, his incapacity to distrust others. This characteristic of his was fully exploited by Tugwell and Lambeth Palace. James Johnson was not a diplomatist; he could not deceive; he could not say one thing and mean another; he could not conspire; he knew no trickery; he was like a child. So much did he trust Tugwell that he went on reporting to him details of his progress in the collection of the Fund, in spite of Tugwell's signal failure to redeem his pledges over the Fund.[72] In their dealings with James Johnson over the Bishoprics scheme there can be no doubt that Tugwell and the Archbishops—E. W. Benson and F. Temple—were anything but straightforward, that they did not put all their cards on the table. Although they admired the sterling qualities of James Johnson, which made him excellent exhibition material to mission-supporters in Britain as a pious and exemplary Christian, an ardent evangelist and an able African leader, yet they found his patriotism irritating, if not offensive. For them, it should be repeated, the Bishopric scheme was the best instrument for the sapping of his patriotism in the Church.

In the way it was conceived by James Johnson, notwithstanding the deception by Herbert Tugwell and the Archbishop of Canterbury, the West Africa Native Bishoprics Fund project had only the remotest chance of succeeding. It rested on an ideology long abandoned in Christendom—that not only Church and State would be administered by the same personnel but the Church would determine the form of the State. In the pre-colonial era the missionary was invariably the most educated, the leader of enlightened opinion and the most important social figure in the interior of West Africa. The Church, too, was the most important institution around which African aspirations crystallised. In one way or another the Church was the main theatre of struggle for supremacy between the African and the white man. Even grievances for transmission to the Colonial Office were often channelled through Church leaders and missionary headquarters. Thus James Johnson not only led agitations on behalf of vernacular education and the sovereignty of Yorubaland against the incursion of Dahomey in 1882 and 1890 respectively but he asked for the endorsement and support of Salisbury Square.[73] In fact, in a way they were never to do in the Colonial era, European missionaries participated actively in agitations, such as those for social improvements in Lagos and against the activities of the Royal Niger Company.[74] When in 1887 the arch-Johnsonian, Otunba Payne, founded the Civil Service Prayer Union, which was perhaps the first union of African civil servants, he saw to it that it was tied to the apron strings of the Church Missionary Society.[75]

But in 1900 things had begun to change. Church and State had begun to drift apart. In 1896 the Bishop of Sierra Leone ceased to be a civil servant and the Colonial Chaplaincy was abolished. Eight years later, to the chagrin of James Johnson, the Colonial Chaplaincy of the Gold Coast was abolished. Certainly James Johnson was aware of the increasing gap separating Church and State. His pleas with the Colonial Office from 1887 to 1899 that Church and State be linked through Chaplaincies were brushed aside. The godlessness of Europeans early in the century received his condemnation from time to time, to the extent that in 1905 he and Oluwole had to lead a delegation to Governor Egerton on the disregard of Sunday by the European inhabitants of Lagos.[76]

It seems an unspoken maxim that he who controls the State also controls the Church. Black secular government and black religious leadership made Crowther's episcopate possible in the realms beyond colonial frontiers. Inside the European frontiers a white bishop ruled. With the overthrow of African government all over West Africa there was no hope of an independent African bishop.

The British establishment—the Colonial Office and Lambeth Palace—knew that an independent African bishop in a colony would set the stage for a real battle between Church and State. Inevitably white bishops in Africa had to sacrifice the interests of the Church in the overall interests of the British empire. Could an African, especially James Johnson, sacrifice the interests of the Church in the overall interest of an alien rule he had never wanted for Africa? Also could the British contemplate a Church which would stimulate and be the guardian of African feelings and patriotism? It certainly could not, and yet James Johnson believed that this was the only way the Christian Church could really sink its roots into West African soil in a vital manner. Everywhere in Europe the Church was the embodiment of the State. Anglicanism reflected the English character, Lutheranism the German. But in West Africa the Church was carefully prevented by the missionaries from securing this dual position. Thus as the partition advanced and white secular control was extended everywhere there could be no hope of James Johnson's scheme being implemented.

It should be noted that at the same time that the British Government in Nigeria was refusing to make Christianity or the Church the basis of the constitution, indigenous religion was being divorced from the political functions it had hitherto performed in traditional government. Traditional religion had virtually ceased to be the *primum mobile* of society in colonial Africa. And this was exactly what James Johnson had always wanted and was what he affected to expect the Bishopric dream to achieve. Religion *per se* was becoming of lesser and lesser importance for administrators and peoples alike. Attitudes were becoming more and more secular.

Economic and political matters in their own right had begun to demand greater attention.

The greater emphasis on secularism was clearly reflected in the emergence of purely secular organisations as vehicles for the articulation of Nigerian nationalism. With his consecration, although he was often in Lagos and he remained the most revered patriot, the Lagos Native Pastorate whose platform used to be an excellent instrument for the propagation of his nationalist ideas, was no longer available to him. For the first decade of the century nationalist articulation was largely confined to the press. And when organisations began to emerge, they had nothing to do with religion and the Church. In 1909 Obasa and Randle, who formed the People's Union, made it plain that it was their objective to look after the welfare of Lagos community as a whole, irrespective of their religious allegiances.[77] That the Church had ceased to be of practical usefulness to the nationalist movement is clear from the fact that in the following year, as will be analysed in the next chapter, James Johnson himself had to accept the presidency of a secular, though philanthropic organisation—the Lagos Auxiliary of the Aborigines Protection Society. In the light of these facts, then, the West African Native Bishoprics Fund scheme, with its hope of an independent African Church that would be followed by other forms of independence for Africa, was but a chimerical dream.

NOTES

1. See next chapter.
2. C.M.S. G3/A2/09, "Lessons to be learnt from other Mission Fields, such as Uganda, Tinevelly and China", paper read at C.M.S. Conference, Ibadan, 1899, by James Johnson.
3. *The Seventh Report of the Lagos Church Missions, for the year 1888*, Exeter, 1889, pp. 12-13.
4. C.M.S., G. W. Brooke's Diary in F4/7.
5. C.M.S. G3/A3/08, James Johnson to H. Tugwell, 5/10/1899.
6. C.M.S. G/Ac4/2, James Johnson to S. W. Fox, 14/2/1900.
7. *Ibid.*
8. C.M.S. G3/A2/010, N. T. Hamlyn to F. Baylis, 22/4/1901.
9. C.M.S. G/Ac4/2, Eugene Stock to S. W. Fox, 16/3/1900.
10. C.M.S. G3/A3/06, Edward Cantuar to Delta Pastorate Church, 12/10/1893.
11. *Ibid.*, "Memorandum of Interview of Group III Committee with Bishop Tugwell, 20/4/1894".
12. *Lagos Weekly Record*, 10/1/1903.
13. C.M.S. G3/A3/011, "West African Native Bishoprics Fund", February 1909.
14. *Ibid.*, James Johnson to F. Baylis, February 1902.
15. *Ibid.*, same to same, 3/11/1900.
16. C.M.S. G3/A2/011, James Johnson to F. Baylis, 3/11/1900.

17. C.O. 143/144, W. Macgregor to J. Chamberlain, 10/9/1899.
18. *Lagos Weekly Record*, 10/3/1894.
19. Quoted in *Lagos Weekly Record*, 1 and 15 December 1917.
20. C.M.S. G3/A2/010, F. Baylis to Nathaniel Johnson, 10/4/1900.
21. *Ibid.*, I. Oluwole to F. Baylis, 19/9/1900.
22. *Ibid.*
23. *Ibid.*, I. Oluwole to F. Baylis, 19/9/1900.
24. *Ibid.*, Petition to Lagos Church Committee by Breadfruit Parish, 21/8/1900.
25. *Ibid.*, Minutes of Meeting, 13/9/1900.
26. *Ibid.*
27. C.M.S. G3/A3/011, Minutes of Meeting with six representatives, 13/9/1900.
28. *Ibid.*, T. Harding to F. Baylis, 27/12/1900.
29. *Ibid.*, H. Tugwell to F. Baylis, 20/3/1901.
30. *Ibid.*, N. T. Hamlyn to F. Baylis, 10/2/1901.
31. *Ibid.*, H. Tugwell to F. Baylis, 8/4/1901.
32. C.M.S. G3/A3/010, quoted in T. R. Phelam to H. Tugwell, 4/10/1901.
33. No. 13 in *Lagos Standard* (Special Issue), 8/11/1901.
34. C.M.S. G3/A2/010, Interview with James Johnson by H. Tugwell, 15/10/1901.
35. *Ibid.*
36. *Ibid.*, H. Tugwell to F. Baylis, 11/11/1901.
37. James Johnson to Breadfruit Church, 17/10/1900, No. 10 in *Lagos Standard* (Special Issue), 8/11/1901.
38. C.M.S. G3/A2/010, Statement by H. Tugwell, dated 14/10/1901.
39. C.M.S. G3/A3/09, James Johnson to F. Baylis, February 1902.
40. *Ibid.*
41. The Coker Papers, (G), J. K. Coker, "to my dear Christian brothers", October 1912.
42. *Ibid.*, (R), *African Hope*, February 1922.
43. *Ibid.*
44. *Ibid.*, March 1922.
45. *Ibid.*, (J), James Johnson and J. K. Coker, 21/8/1914.
46. C.M.S. G3/A3/08, Henry Proctor to F. Baylis, 8/3/1901.
47. C.M.S. G3/A3/09, James Johnson's Presidential Address to the Third Annual Delta Church Conference, 25/1/1904.
48. *Lagos Standard*, 4/12/1901.
49. C.M.S. G3/A9/01, H. Tugwell to F. Baylis, 25/5/1900.
50. *Ibid.*, quotes C. F. H. Battersby.
51. C.M.S. G3/A2/011. See copy of his Address in Lagos, 21 January 1902.
52. C.M.S. G3/A3/09, James Johnson to H. Tugwell, 15/4/1902.
53. *Ibid.*, "A Report of Missionary Journey Within and beyond the Southern Nigeria British Protectorate from November 1903 to July 1900".
54. C.M.S. G3/A3/010, "Bishop Johnson's Journal Report, December 1904-1905".
55. *Lagos Standard*, 17/12/1902.
56. *Ibid.*, 10/12/1902.
57. *The Gold Coast Leader*, 27/12/1902.
58. *Lagos Weekly Record*, 10/1/1903.
59. *Sierra Leone Weekly News*, 8/3/1913.

60. C.M.S. G3/A2/013, Memorandum of Meeting by Special Committee with Bishop Tugwell.
61. C.M.S. G3/A3/011, "Extract from Notes of Honorary Secretary's Interview with the Archbishop of Canterbury", 21/1/1909.
62. *Ibid.*, "West African Native Bishoprics Fund", February 1909.
63. *Ibid.*, "West African Native Bishoprics Fund", February 1909.
64. C.M.S. G3/A2/013, Memorandum of Meeting by Special Committee with Bishop Oluwole.
65. C.M.S. G3/A3/013, for Copy of Resolution.
66. *Sierra Leone Weekly News*, 8/3/1913.
67. *Ibid.*, 8/3/1913.
68. *Lagos Weekly Record*, 22/2/1913.
69. C.M.S. G3/A3/013, Archbishop of Canterbury to H. Tugwell, 11/12/1912.
70. *Ibid.*, H. Tugwell to Victor Buxton, 1913.
71. C.M.S. G3/A3/011 for copy
72. C.M.S. G3/A3/09, James Johnson to H. Tugwell, 23/1/1904.
73. Cf. C.M.S. G3/A2/01 and G3/A2/04.
74. *Lagos Observer*, 26/5/1888.
75. *C.M. Intelligencer*, 1887, p. 511.
76. C.M.S. G3/A2/012, J. Mackay to F. Baylis, 26/9/1905.
77. A.P.S., Dr. J. K. Randle to Rev. J. H. Harris, 21/12/1910.

CHAPTER THIRTEEN

LAST YEARS

Thank God, I have finished my work, my heart is clear.
James Johnson's last words, Bonny 17 May 1917

ALTHOUGH James Johnson in 1910 had exceeded the Biblical life span of seventy years his physical energy and mental vigour seemed those of a youth. He was endowed with a hard body. His health was ever splendid and but for the British winter that sent him to a hospital in early 1887 he was never prostrated by illness. He had his own recipe for sound health and long life; he considered both hygiene and regular physical exercise to be very important. The hardness of life in traditional African society, he said, was responsible for the superior physique and relatively long life enjoyed by Africans who had not come in contact with the comfort and ease of European civilisation.[1] Educated Africans of the second and third generations who were observed to be dying in their forties, he said, owed this to the ease and comfort of the Europeanised enclaves on the Atlantic seaboard. Consequently he was a consistent advocate of physical exercise being introduced into West African schools. He himself led a hard life, abstemious in matters of liquor, women and luxuries. He trekked a lot, along tortuous paths in Yorubaland and travelled extensively in canoes in the pestiferous mosaic of creeks in the Niger Delta. In 1878 he completed a manuscript on physiology. Intended mainly for schools its aims, declared James Johnson, were to persuade Africans to correct "their habitual and general violations of the very elementary laws of health and [prevent] the injury to the country and race thereby".[2]

But notwithstanding the astonishing physical power and alert mind which he continued to exhibit, Holy Johnson could not escape the effects of old age. By 1903, when he was about sixty-eight years, he was feeling the first effects of age. His body ceased to be the precise and perfect machine it had been before.

But old age did not diminish his ardour on behalf of "God and my country". Apart from the mirage of the West Africa Native

Bishoprics Fund and the burden of the administration of his 'diocese' James Johnson packed a great deal into the last decade of his life. They were years full of limited achievements, unfulfilled hopes, disappointments and frustrations. The key events of these years to which attention will be devoted in this chapter are his participation at the Pan-Anglican Conference in London in 1908, his Presidency of the Lagos Auxiliary of the Aborigines Protection Society, his activities in Sierra Leone, where he recovered his health from 1912 to 1915, the messianic movement that rent his 'diocese' in pieces, and the circumstances of his death.

James Johnson paid his last visit to Britain in 1908, in connection with the Pan-Anglican Congress of that year. As on previous occasions he was the showpiece of the Church Missionary Society and the cynosure of Church dignitaries. As a churchman observed: "Amongst the many Bishops of the Anglican communion who have visited England during this year none has aroused more interest than Bishop Johnson. A native of Africa, the son of parents who had experienced the worst horrors of slavery, he took his place at no disadvantage on the score of personality, intellect or spiritual discernment with the best products of English piety and learning."[3] Not only was he invited to speak in different parishes throughout the Congress period but his life was deemed rich and worthy enough to be recorded. He gave an account of his life which he was persuaded to deliver in Mullaglass Parish, Newry, Ireland, and it was suggested that this be published. It appeared as *A Brief Outline of the Story of My Life* and ran into a second edition within months in 1908.

At the Congress Holy Johnson was no mere observer. He contributed to discussions and produced a paper entitled "The Relation of Mission Work to Native Customs" in which he castigated the Westernising attitude and methods of Christian missions in Africa. The very opening paragraph of the paper sums up the substance: "Christianity is intended to be the religion not of one particular race of people only, but of the whole world. But in different countries it will wear different types, if it is to become indigenous to every soil. It should have in Europe a European type; in Asia an Asiatic type; and in Africa an African type;—different types of one and the same religion with different formulae of faith and different ceremonies of worship; for not otherwise can Christianity wear anywhere a national character nor can its attitude be what it should towards national customs which have much in them to help to promote indigenousness to it."[4] The significant thing to note is that by this date James Johnson was much less inhibited by Western ideas on institutions such as slavery and polygamy, which in early years he had denounced in uncompromising terms.

Perhaps the most significant feature of Johnson's paper was that in it he admitted that polygamy in an African society is not a moral question and that Christian missions had been irrational in their attitude towards it. In 1894 he had strongly urged that the Lagos Government should withhold recognition of, and financial assistance to, the United Native African Church on the grounds that it countenanced the institution. This African institution, declared James Johnson, was a negation of "Divine Law", the cause of slavery, inter-tribal wars and jihads and a manifestation of human depravity.[5] But in 1908 James Johnson was prepared to accept that polygamy was not a basic evil, a debasement of human nature. While acknowledging that monogamy was the ideal to which the Church should encourage African converts to aspire, he recognised the moral, economic and social advantages of polygamy in African society, from which was absent the "awful licentiousness which disgraces many a European city where Monogamy is professedly the only form of marriage permitted". Johnson called on the Anglican world to accept polygamist converts into full membership of the Church, an advice still unheeded by Christian missions all over the world.

As was his habit James Johnson used the occasion of his visit to draw the attention of the Colonial Office to what he considered to be the grievances of the Nigerian peoples. In contrast with his petitions in 1874, 1887 and 1899 his petitions of 1908-9 were non-political; they were entirely social. On 16 December 1908 he had a meeting with Colonel Seely, Under Secretary of State for the Colonies. He dwelt at length upon the deleterious effects of the liquor traffic on the Nigerian peoples and demanded, as he had done several times before, that it should be abolished. Then he raised the major topic of education. The British Government, he repeated, had not been doing enough for the Nigerian peoples. First of all the emphasis upon the English language as the medium of teaching was wrong; the vernacular should not only be recognised but given due prominence. Secondly he condemned the textbooks being used in Nigerian schools as unsuitable for the Nigerian environment. Thirdly he deplored the indifference of the British administration in Nigeria to teacher training. Lastly he condemned the secular atmosphere of Government schools.[6]

As before his petitions aroused little sympathy. On the liquor question it was decided to appoint a Commission of Inquiry to study the problem, not because of James Johnson's representations but because the anti-liquor movement and the weight of the Pan-Anglican Congress were irresistible. His presentations on education were dismissed summarily. As an official minuted, the vernacular languages were of little value because there was no literature in them. Therefore English must continue to be the medium of teaching. "The sooner we can make English—even if it must be 'pidgin English'—the common speech of W.A., the better," the official concluded.[7]

The fanfares and meetings with Church and State dignitaries which James Johnson had enjoyed during his last visit were followed by what he described as a shock on his way back to West Africa. He became a victim of "race antipathy" which had become more marked in the relations between educated Africans and Europeans at the beginning of the century. He was the only African passenger of the *Aro*, the Elder Dempster ship that took him to Sierra Leone, and his seat at breakfast was placed at the table of four Europeans, two of whom had lived for several years in America whilst the two others were young Englishmen just going out to West Africa. These white men thought that the arrangement was "an insult to the dignity of Europeans, and especially Englishmen and members of an Imperial Race and a demand was made that such an arrangement should on no account be repeated and that a separate table should be laid out for me".[8] On Sunday when he attempted to hold a service no one was disposed to listen to him. For two weeks he was ostracised and saw himself treated as "an unclean leper".

In Sierra Leone, where he stopped for a brief period, his prestige soared very high. On 8 March he was addressed many times, and he held meetings with the Committees in charge of the West Africa Native Bishoprics Fund scheme. He was also made a Trustee of the Agriculture Institute, covering an area of 1,000 acres, which was founded with the £60,000 left for the training of Africans in scientific farming by S. B. Thomas, his old colleague who had donated £500 to his Bishoprics Fund.[9] In Nigeria his attention was absorbed immediately on arrival by the evidence he had to give before the Mackenzie Commission of Inquiry on liquor. The deliberations of this body were of considerable importance for James Johnson in two ways. Firstly, although the anti-liquor movement in Nigeria had found a new and ardent crusader in Bishop Tugwell, it was James Johnson who had launched the movement in August 1877 and was its undisputed leader until 1898. Moreover, whilst in Britain, the memorandum he had sent to the Colonial Office on the liquor traffic had been deemed important enough for the Commissioners to be given copies for their attention. Secondly the Niger Delta, his diocese, was notorious as the most liquor-ridden area in the world.

He gave evidence before the Commission on 17 May.[10] Of the 171 witnesses James Johnson's evidence was the second longest, next only to that of Bishop Tugwell. His performance before the Commission was not calculated to obtain their sympathy. Long before the Commission set out their duty had been made plain[11]—they were a fact-finding body and every step was taken to choose men who held a favourable opinion of the Administration which depended upon customs duties on liquor for more than fifty per cent of its revenue. The conflict of opinion between him and the Commissioners emerged clearly. First of all his extremist views, by no means based on empirical data, were of little value to the Commisioners who wanted facts and figures. As the Chairman had to remark, James Johnson tended to deliver sermons rather than present concrete facts.[12] Gin, James Johnson declared, had done incalculable harm to the coastal inhabitants of western Africa generally but to the inhabitants of the Niger Delta in particular. It had made the Delta peoples mentally sluggish, and evidence that the liquor traffic caused physical deterioration, he said, was provided by the Ibo. In Sierra Leone they were inferior only to the Yoruba but in the Niger Delta the Ibo were much inferior to the members of their race in Sierra Leone. At Sapele he saw "women and children reeling about just like drunken men in the streets" and in the Government school at Warri 60 out of 75 children of 8-16 years of age admitted that they were already addicted to drink.[13] But in no circumstances was he able to supply precise details.

Moreover the way and manner he spoke was different from that of the other African witnesses. He told A. Cowan and T. Welsh, two of the Commissioners who had an interest in the liquor trade in Nigeria, that their opinions, which contradicted his own in very many particulars, were of little value because they were "strangers", that is non-Africans. Nor could Captain C. H. Elgee, the administrator of Ibadan, have been impressed by the way he was being told that he, Elgee, was not necessarily speaking the truth. Even the Chairman was scandalised by the views Johnson expressed of European traders in Nigeria. Declared James Johnson: "What indication do they give there that they have an interest in the welfare of the country? They would destroy the country and make money out of the people's lives."[14]

The Commissioners, who had to consider the aversion of the people to any direct form of taxation, did not accept James Johnson's view that the traffic should be abolished. James Johnson did not abandon the principle of taxation but he was disposed to be more sympathetic than usual, saying that it should be "very light". But even now, as on previous occasions, educated and unlettered Africans in Nigeria did not want any form of direct taxation. Although there had been considerable mass support for the movement for the abolition of liquor in Southern Nigeria, all support for it ended the moment it became clear that the only alternative to prohibition was direct taxation.[15] In fact no other witness, besides

Tugwell, advocated prohibition at any cost as James Johnson did. But the fact that James Johnson did not carry his propaganda beyond the venue of the Commission's sitting in Lagos resulted in no deterioration in his relations with the people. Indeed Herbert Macaulay and the Lagos leaders of opinion had worked up the mind of the people against the liquor traffic movement and the man with which it was associated outside the Commissioners' venue was Herbert Tugwell.

In the final report, which emphasised the overall sobriety of the Nigerian peoples, James Johnson did not come out very well. It was beyond doubt that he was guilty of over-statements and that his memory had failed him in particulars. For instance he told the Commission that there was no Visitor's Book in the Government School at Warri but not only was this book found but James Johnson's entry in it as well. James Johnson's assertion that the kolanut was no longer being eaten or used for entertainment was contradicted by the expanding cultivation of the kolanut in the Ijebu country and its wider circulation. Also the statistics for Lagos for the years 1906 to 1908 could not sustain the assertion made by James Johnson that in not one year from the sixties had the number of births exceeded that of deaths.[16]

Whilst the Report of the Commission of Inquiry into the liquor problem in Southern Nigeria sealed his hope of a teetotal Nigeria he became useful again in the nationalist movement. Perhaps the most important nationally significant event between 1900 and 1914 was the founding in Lagos in 1910 of the Lagos Auxiliary of the Aborigines Protection Society. It was founded to serve as a watchdog of Nigerian interests in British Nigeria. As its name suggests it was a daughter to the Aborigines Protection Society in Britain. Unlike the People's Union, which had been founded in 1909 on the narrow basis of the interests of Lagos inhabitants, the Lagos Auxiliary had, at heart, the welfare of Nigeria as a whole. It had the uniqueness of being non-religious, non-sectarian, non-sectional, embracing both the high and the low, the rich and the poor, and ultimately acquiring "a singular position and a very great influence in and for the country",[17] even though being under the guidance of the educated Africans. It was a recognition of James Johnson's leadership and achievement in Church and State that at the inaugural meeting Herbert Macaulay (the great grandson of Bishop Crowther), who had become a thorn in the side of the British administration, proposed him with the eulogy: "the foremost patriot in West Africa who has done much for the good of the people."[18] He was unanimously elected as Chairman of this body. In 1915, when another election took place, he was re-elected. Under him were to serve leading educated elite who were to play significant parts in the nationalist movement in Nigeria. Dr. Mojola Agbebi, leader of the Native Baptist Church and an ardent crusader on behalf of African culture, was for some time a Vice President; Herbert Macaulay was the first Secretary, with Adeyemo Alakija (later knighted) being elected to the post in 1915.

Before examining the achievements of this organisation in the nationalist movement it is important to appreciate the strategic position occupied by James Johnson as President of this organisation. He was the central force that welded together the mutually antagonistic nationalist leaders of the decade before the First World War. For instance the older and more peaceful Dr. Oguntola Sapara found it impossible to work with the much younger and more fiery Herbert Macaulay.[19] It is clear that the latter, who had had some personal relationship with James Johnson since the 1890s, would not assume the Secretaryship of the organisation except under James Johnson's presidency. Then there was the bitter antagonism between Dr. Mojola Agbebi and Sapara Williams, the most eminent legal practitioner of his day, who factiously disputed the Vice Presidency with the former. Personal bickerings were so prejudicial to the interests of the organisation that it was on the verge of collapse all the time that James Johnson was away in Sierra Leone from 1913 to 1915. But he was respected by all parties who corresponded with him. Eventually he was able to dispose of the bickering lieutenants when they were found wanting in integrity. For in 1914 Herbert Macaulay was convicted of forgery. Much as James Johnson loved him, declaring that at a future date a petition for pardon might be sent to the British Government, he did not hesitate to dismiss him.[20] Not long afterwards Dr. Agbebi was accused of cheating illiterate members of the organisation in the Itsekiri country. James Johnson lost no time in ordering an inquiry to probe the integrity of all the members under suspicion.[21] During this time Dr. Agbebi was removed. As for Sapara Williams, death removed him. Thus when he returned to Nigeria in 1915 practically all the officers of 1910, except himself, had been removed and new men had been brought in.

His presidency of the Auxiliary fulfilled another function in the history of the nationalist movement in Nigeria. Through the inspiration he infused into people like Herbert Macaulay, Mojola Agbebi, A. Folarin and Adeyemo Alakija, he served as a bridge between the Victorian type of educated Africans in Nigeria and the more fiery, more assertive and more vocal Georgian type of Nigerian elite. The former were predominantly Christian in their outlook, relatively docile, pro-British and profuse in their thanks to the British; the latter, more secular and highly critical of the British administration in Nigeria. Although both Herbert Macaulay and Osho Davies willingly served under James Johnson they had by 1917 given the indication that his Ethiopian brand of nationalism, that in which the religious and nationalistic fused, was becoming a thing of the past.[22] But on the other hand both Agbebi and Johnson remained leaders until they died in 1917.

The achievements of the Lagos Auxiliary of the Aborigines Protection Society were considerable. One of its declared objects was "to educate and organise public opinion in Nigeria upon the principles which govern the activities of the Parent Society". They looked to the latter for support in their conflict with the local administration, "whose purpose at the present day, it would seem, is to treat the coloured man as a creature of no consequence and whose aim it may not be amiss to say, is to enslave in their own country, those whom your Forefathers have set free".[23]

Perhaps the greatest single act in which the interest of all the people of Southern Nigeria was at stake was their exertion over Land Tenure. When the British Government appointed the Belfield Land Commission in 1912 Lord Harcourt, Secretary of State for the Colonies, had announced that the Commission would gather African evidence on the spot. This was unacceptable to the educated Africans who feared that African witnesses in Nigeria might either be frightened from giving evidence, or frightened into speaking in favour of what British officials and merchants wanted—a European concept of land ownership and alienation of Nigerian lands to concessionaires, as had been the case in the Belgian Congo and British East Africa. For in 1909 many British officials and merchants had actually forced many Nigerian witnesses into speaking in favour of the liquor traffic before the Commission mentioned earlier.

The question of land, as has been mentioned in an earlier chapter, received the attention of James Johnson early in the century. Under the direction, and through the Parent Body, Lord Harcourt agreed to receive in London a deputation who, as James Johnson put it, would appear before the Commission "to give evidence on the question" and thereby contribute "towards ensuring to the people the continued independent ownership of their land—a matter on which they have been always most sensitive, and which is of the highest value to them".[24] The extreme importance of the question to the people may be gathered from the fact that, as James Johnson observed, "in spite of the poverty of the country and the cry of hard times to be heard on all sides", the peoples of Southern Nigeria sent a delegation of twenty. The delegation consisted of chiefs or representatives of chiefs, representing the Yoruba, Ijaw and Efik tribes. It was the first occasion when so many tribes stood on a common platform and presented a common front on any matter in the history of Southern Nigeria. The delegates were able to discharge their duties. As the Parent Body reported to James Johnson: "we are happy to inform you that the members of the deputation have made the happiest impression upon all they have met, including the authorities of the Colonial Office, members of Parliament and leaders of public opinion".[25] The fear of the danger to the African ownership of land in West Africa was removed.

The fate of Ovonranwen, the Oba of Benin whom the British had exiled after the expedition of 1897, attracted James Johnson's attention. It will be recalled that he had visited the ex-Oba's mother and that some members of Ovonranwen's family were baptised into the Anglican Church in Benin. From the time he first visited Benin James Johnson had believed that Ovonranwen had not been treated fairly. For according to the investigations he conducted Ovonranwen advised against the decision to massacre Phillips' party in 1897. In any case, contended James Johnson, Ovonranwen had been more than punished when his palace was "wrecked" and he himself was disgraced and humiliated. His removal from the throne, he discovered by investigation in the villages, had never been popular and the Edo desired to have him back rather than continue to be under British rule.[26] It was in 1908, on the occasion of his visit to the Pan-Anglican Conference, that he spoke to G. W. Neville, one of the directors of the Bank of British West Africa and Cathcart Watson, M.P. The latter pleaded in the Commons for Ovonranwen's release. But rather than release the ex-Oba, "stronger chains" were forged anew on him, for detention was added to deportation. No solicitor was allowed to plead his case before the Court. The detention was in fact illegal. It was not until 1911 that Governor Egerton summoned the Legislative Council to pass the necessary Ordinance to legalise both deportation and detention that had taken place for several years, after Ovonranwen's solicitor had attempted to obtain a writ of *Habeas Corpus*. In James Johnson's judgment, the British had not only contravened moral and natural justice, but they had also broken their own law. As he protested: "It seems most strange that the Government should have suffered itself to be guilty of the serious fault of an unlegalised and unlawful detention throughout so long a period . . . manifested no manifestation to temper judgment with mercy if at all there had been justice on its side."[27] In 1913 he brought the matter to the notice of the A.P.S. who in turn got in touch with the Colonial Office. However, before anything could be done the ex-Oba expired in Old Calabar.

The Auxiliary was the main vehicle of nationalist agitation throughout the years of the First World War. It fell on this body to denounce the propaganda of the Empire Resources Development Committee, an organisation which tried to persuade the British Government to allow commercial corporations to develop the resources of British West Africa for the benefit of Britain. The elite were also incensed by the attempt of the British Government to impose export duties on Nigerian commodities. This fiscal measure, the Auxiliary declared, would "hamper the profitable development of the country's resources to their highest possible limit", would "reduce the producers to moral slavery . . . unsettle the country, retard its development, demoralise the aborigines and ultimately affect adversely the Revenue of the West African colonies".[28]

Although it was not in all respects that the Auxiliary achieved its aims (for instance James Johnson could not persuade the Parent Body to appreciate the grievances of the educated elite about Lugard's exclusion of lawyers from the Provincial Courts) yet the organisation achieved much that is still to be recognised. Well could the President, James Johnson, rejoice that the Auxiliary "has been mercifully used by God to perform most valuable services to the country [of Nigeria]".[29]

In the meantime James Johnson was involved in other matters. The Jubilee celebrations of the Native Church of Sierra Leone, that is the Native Pastorate which had had such a modest beginning in 1861, was a big occasion for which long preparations had been made. James Johnson, it will be remembered, had fought energetically in the sixties and seventies for this institution, which he then expected to be the nucleus of an African Church and the precursor of a pan-African State. It was a recognition of his pre-eminence in the West African Anglican Church that not only was he asked to represent the Anglican Community in Nigeria but he received a special invitation from the institution and was given the biggest assignment—the preaching of the Jubilee sermon. By 5 February 1913, when he landed at Freetown in the *Dakar*, he was becoming physically very weak. On medical advice he had been told to abandon the onerous burden of his diocese for a while in order to restore his health.

But he could not heed this medical advice until after the Jubilee celebrations. He threw himself into the celebrations with characteristic bewildering energy. The great part he had played and the high respect in which he was held in the hearts of men were clear from the Jubilee's proceedings. For apart from his pre-eminence in the Church his position as the greatest living patriot in West Africa became undisputed at the death of Edward Blyden on 7 February 1912. Holy Johnson probably had his finest hour on 11 February 1913 when he performed "the greatest event of the celebration" of the Jubilee, the delivery of the Jubilee Sermon. Never in the history of Sierra Leone had St. George's Cathedral, the venue of the event, been "so inconveniently crowded" as on the occasion, when, as the newspaper put it, "for sixty-five minutes [James Johnson] rivetted the attention of the congregation, who hung on his lips. . . . It was an elaborate discourse, exhaustive, most instructive and most inspiring."[30] That only he could do it was the universal verdict. The Nigerian press expressed pride in him, describing him as second to none in the Yoruba saying: "Ko si meji Ajanaku ninu Igbo," that is, "there are no two animals of the elephant's size in the forest".[31]

The speech was the finest of his published sermons and is important and unique in several ways. He did not consider himself as speaking exclusively to West Africans or Africans but to Christendom in general. The greatest threat to the Christian religion, he observed, was the arrogance of several in European society who, he said, were flying in the face of God by denying His existence and Man's need of Him "under the influence of pride and self-conceit over some very important and valuable discoveries which either they themselves or some other members of their race have made of the secrets of nature and their great ability to harness some of her forces to mankind and because of abounding prosperity".[32]

The gap separating James Johnson from contemporary society in West Africa and in other parts of an increasingly secular and materialistic world will be clearly understood from the fact that his theology and views on Christology, the Church and what ought to be the primary concern of men, had not changed an iota since his dramatic conversion in Kent fifty years before.

His sermon contained recurring themes such as the failure of the visible Church, forebodings that the Church in Africa might suffer another effacement, as had happened several times before, the imperative independence by an African Church, the tide of hatred for Negroes by the white race, Christian moral philosophy and lamentation on the loss to Africa of "the simple virtues of truthfulness, honesty, filial piety, respect for age and reverence for authority and chastity".

The Jubilee was an occasion to awaken nostalgia in James Johnson. Not only did he go to the villages of the Colony that he had known so well as a boy and as a Catechist but he received overwhelming publicity, greater than that accorded to Victor Buxton, whom the C.M.S. had sent there as its representative. In all places James Johnson reminisced. In Waterloo representatives of his boyhood Church, St. Matthews, in Benguema, met him and he dwelt upon his early days in life and spoke about his parents. At Regent, where he spoke for one hour, his emphasis was on the needs of the

z

Niger Delta Pastorate with particular emphasis on the phenomenal success of the gospel at Okrika. At Wilberforce he concentrated on the activity and achievements of the West African Methodist Church in the thirties of the nineteenth century, in the hope that his listeners would be inspired and become affected by the desire of the earlier African Church in the Colony for independence and self dignity. In several places James Johnson spoke against the liquor traffic with traditional vehemence and he did not miss the opportunity of reviving interest in the West Africa Native Bishoprics Fund scheme.

For the first time since he had joined the C.M.S. service in 1858 James Johnson took a long rest, which lasted two years. Throughout 1913 and for the most part of 1914 he heeded the medical advice and performed no public functions. But he did not rest completely, as his correspondence with the Lagos Auxiliary of the A.P.S. and the Parent Society in these years shows. Also he spent his time as a peace-maker in homes and families. It is said that in this period he succeeded in re-uniting "several husbands and wives that have long parted asunder".[33] It was also a period when gratitude was evinced by people who believed that he had been the instrument for their Christian life. Some people claimed that James Johnson had planted the seed in their hearts thirty years before when he went to Sierra Leone as a Missioner.[34] But of particular interest was the position he continued to fill in the hearts of the Ijebu Remo, to whom it will be remembered he was a torch-bearer and guide for nearly a quarter of a century. The Church there had developed to the extent that in 1914 it achieved the status of a Provincial District Council. The status, maturity and growth attained were credited to Holy Johnson, as the following excerpt testifies: "Your humble children in Christ now represented by the Remo Provincial District Council on behalf of all the Churches of this Mission in connection with the foundation and promotion of which your dear name shall ever be memorably associated and respected, earnestly desire me hereby heartily to inform the Bishop how far God has helped them. . . . How the Council wished the Bishop were present . . . to see the first bloom of his earnest, self-denying zeal, labour and prayers, so much promising and good harvest."[35]

Towards the end of his stay in Sierra Leone James Johnson was associated with one of the major events in the Colony during the First World War, the activity of the African Movement, a Negro organisation dedicated to self-improvement and in several respects a predecessor of the well-known movement led by Marcus Garvey after the War. Its declared objectives were similar to the ones for which James Johnson had stood all his life, namely patriotism, pro-

motion of self-help by Negroes in industrial and commercial projects, and propagation of the Christian faith.[36] The African Movement was able to own a number of ships and it revived interest in
the settlement of Negroes in Africa. In 1915 about two hundred
Negroes intended for settlement in some part of the Gold Coast
were carried in the *Liberia*, one of the ships of the organisation,
under the leadership of Chief Sam, Judge Sobrel and Professor
Orishatuke Faduma. James Johnson's knowledge of the last, a
Yoruba of Ife origin and a *Saro* who was to transfer himself to the
New World, dated from 1887 when Faduma was a member of the
Dress Reform Society of Sierra Leone.

When the Afro-American delegates anchored off Fourah Bay and
the local Anti-Slavery and Aborigines Protection Society decided to
accord them formal welcome on 23 December 1914 it was James
Johnson who was chosen to be its spokesman.[37] It was an occasion
calling for a revival of the ideas he had held of the Negroes and the
role they should play in Africa. Since 1872 he had followed the
progress of these Africans in exile, as he regarded them, in self-
help and in the cultivation of the virtues of self-denial, self-dignity
and the search for an identity. James Johnson thought that not
only would American Negroes be of immense value in instilling
these virtues in Africans, if they returned to Africa, but he believed also that the regeneration of the African continent was better
left in their hands than in those of Europeans. In other words, in a
sense, James Johnson considered the Negroes of America and the
Saro higher than uncontaminated Africans and the class of Africans
in whose hands the future of Africa should rest. He emphasised the
common grounds of the American Negroes and the *Saro,* how they
were co-exiles, co-victims of European wickedness and greed in the
age of the trans-Atlantic slave trade and how, by being co-beneficiaries of contact and association with the white man, the leadership of Africa would be theirs. As he opined, the Negroes of the
New World "are evidently intended by God, the Father of all, to
be with us fellow missionaries and fellow workers for the upbuild-
ing of our desolated Aboriginal Homeland, the repeopling of it, the
regenerating of West Africa religiously, intellectually, morally,
socially and otherwise".

Never did James Johnson perceive or comment upon the denationalising aspects of the Negroes in the New World. Rather he
perceived and emphasised the skills and knowledge they had
learned in exile and which Africans should seek to acquire. As he
told the representatives of the African Movement:

We have learnt with much pleasure and delight and pardonable
pride of the great progress and advance in several directions

which you and the myriad brethren of our common Negro race
have made in America since Emancipation of your Elementary
Negro schools, your Secondary Schools, your Colleges and Uni-
versities with their Negro Professors your Industrial Institutions,
your self-supporting and self-governing Negro Churches and
Pastorates, with their many Mercantile Establishments, and
several Negro Banks etc., achievements that you have effected in
a country where you had been despised and cruelly oppressed
slaves, and in spite of the prejudice of the white man that has
persistently dogged your steps, and the severe limitations that
attend and seek to depress Negro life in America. We say to
ourselves: "If, in spite of these oppressive drawbacks you have
achieved so much what would you not have done under more
favourable conditions?" (Cheers)

Ever a dreamer, the occasion gave James Johnson the opportunity
to dream. He saw visions of the economic independence of Africa
and the mass emigration of Negroes to Africa, through the agency
of the African Movement. His dream is worth quoting *in extenso*:

With steamships of our own, traversing the ocean to and fro
between West Africa, America and England, in the interest of
commerce, we shall, in respect of carrying power, be in a great
measure commercially independent. With acquired ability for
converting some of the raw materials which we are in the habit
of exporting into foreign markets into properly manufactured
articles and improving upon that rudimentary and fundamental
manufacturing knowledge and skill which many of our aboriginal
peoples already possess and which has long been waiting for
development, and also carrying on trade in them with our own
people in the interior countries and others, and with agriculture
properly learned and diligently and extensively followed (and we
are willing and ready to learn from you who have from your
exile acquired knowledge that we have not) we shall be in a very
important measure industrially independent; whilst the possession
of vessels of our own could connect West Africa with Black
America and greatly facilitate the gradual return of many of our
exiled brethren in America, with all the enlightenment they have
acquired, to the great Fatherland, the ancestral home which they,
we understand, are longing for, and which has on her own part
been very long waiting for them. Thus Rachel would be com-
forted over the very long painful and cruel bereavement which
it has been her lot to endure, and some interpretation would be
afforded her of that mysterious Providence which has made her
life one of so much bitter suffering.

But when, early in 1915, James Johnson left Sierra Leone for Nigeria for the last time he was a disillusioned man. Sierra Leone society was in conflict: brother was against brother, family against family and section against section. The last two years of his life were full of sorrow, disappointment and bitter experience. The failure of the West Africa Native Bishoprics Fund scheme disappointed him profoundly. For at Synods all that was being done was to pass ineffective motions in its favour. When in May 1915 Africans were angered that the Fund was being relegated to the background James Johnson had the mortification of being told that his hope would never be achieved in his lifetime. For Tugwell carried a unanimous vote, that the Fund was only "for the future of the Church", and that it did not deserve priority attention. Although the Diocesan praised James Johnson as the greatest labourer in West Africa "devotedly in the interests of the Church in West Africa", yet there was enough to cause him despair when Tugwell declared:

People sometimes speak in such a way as to convey the impression that the raising of a sum of £8,000 or £10,000 would immediately be followed by the appointment of a Bishop for the Delta of the Niger possessing full Diocesan powers. The Native Bishopric's Fund contemplates the taking of such action, and since it has received the sanction and support of the Archbishop of Canterbury, it is to that extent an assurance that the taking of such a step is seriously contemplated; but the Fund does not carry with it a guarantee that such a step shall be taken at any particular time. Such action rests entirely with the Archbishop of Canterbury, who alone can determine when such action shall be taken.[38]

Two major events absorbed what remained of his life, one in the State and the other in the Church. In 1916, as has been analysed, Ijebu fury was provoked by the utter disregard for immemorial laws and customs governing the appointment and coronation of the Awujale by the British administrator. But hardly had Ademolu been restored to his throne than a paroxysmal eruption occurred in the Niger Delta Pastorate, threatening to undo Johnson's efforts of the past fifteen years. In his long experience, full of troubles, he had never seen one like it. Garrick Sokari Marian Braide, an unlettered canoe-maker and a seer of visions, launched a prophetic movement that reduced James Johnson's Diocese in size and number by more than 50 per cent within three months—November 1915 to February 1916.

While Johnson had been aware of Garrick Braide's unusual powers and piety since 1908 he had not foreseen the eventual schism which occurred. His attitude to the seer at the beginning was positive and constructive. James Johnson believed that the gift to heal without the aid of medical science was possible as a divine gift. As early as 1899 he had declared in *Yoruba Heathenism* that mortals could be gifted with powers to perform miracles and to see visions and he was to believe this for the rest of his life. But at the same time he stressed that such powers were legitimate only insofar as the people so endowed recognised that they owed these powers to God and used them for valid ends.

He believed this to be the case with Garrick Braide, who for seven years was to use his gift to win converts for the Church without taking a penny from the cured. Moreover the Garrick Braide movement was a statistically successful evangelistic organisation. He was able to achieve what the British investment in men and money and James Johnson himself could not achieve. For in order to prove their adherence to Christianity the chiefs brought out their great ancestors' heirlooms, which they valued and regarded as their protectors and to which sacrifices had always been offered. Even the great divinity of the Kalabari branch of the Ijaw, *Awoniekaso* (protector of the country), who was worshipped with sacrifices on behalf of the people every eighth day by a chief priest, was discarded and its images and all its paraphernalia were thrown away. Lastly, both James Johnson and Garrick Braide found a common platform over the liquor question. Never before had a people responded as they did to Garrick's call for an end to liquor taking, in spite of the fact that gin-drinking had long been an endemic habit. People who had been healed stopped drinking and whoever ignored the warning died immediately. Even the chiefs refrained from alcohol, with serious consequences for Europeans and native traders. So serious was this that the British administration faced a deficit of £576,000 in 1916, a loss which was ascribed to the people's abstinence from liquor.

Never in Nigeria had a religious movement as that associated with Garrick Braide occurred. In impact, in manifestation and in form it was similar to that being led from 1910 to 1915 by the ill-educated Grebo preacher, William Waddy Harris.[39] In type it anticipated by a decade the Aladura movement led by Orimalade.[40] Garrick Braide was born of 'pagan' parents and became a native of Bakana. An illiterate to the extent that he could not even speak the pidgin English commonly spoken in that part of the world, he also stammered. Full of zeal, earnestness and energy he was of humble and quiet disposition. A member of St. Andrew's Church he belonged to the District Council and Board and was a licensed lay preacher.

The remarkable thing about Braide was that he *was* a seer and a miracle-maker. As early as 1908 his pastor, the Reverend M. A. Kemmer, recorded that Garrick had predicted calamities that would befall people who did not believe him or who disobeyed his advice and warning; he had caused rain to descend in order to shame *dibias* (Ibo magicians) whom a play-club at Bakana had invited to seal the clouds against rain; he had become skilled in the art of healing the sick by faith and prayer.[41] So popular had be become, by late 1915, as a healer by prayer that the sick from all over the Delta and the interior of the Ibo country flocked to him and procured a cure either through his prayers or through the use of a few words of prayer dictated to them by him, or through a mere touch of his hand upon them. Under the impression that he was under the mantle of the Holy Spirit Garrick Braide claimed that he was the prophet Elijah II spoken of in Malachi IV: 5. He had two lieutenants, Ngiangia, another native of Bakana formerly a Government clerk and subsequently a school-master, and Moses Hart, an agent of the Niger Delta at Bonny. Both of them arrogated to themselves divine virtues, the one calling himself a "son of the prophet" and the other "a servant of the prophet". Belief in their prophetic character and divine mission became so universal that it shook the institution of the Niger Delta Pastorate to its foundations.

Although it seems that Garrick Braide did not originally intend to break away from the Pastorate yet he became the most convenient focus for the crystallisation of a number of forces that had been working against the Niger Delta Pastorate since its birth in 1892. First of all was the unsatisfactory and incomplete rebellion that had been led and inspired by James Johnson. In that rebellion the Ijaw of the Niger Delta had been imbued with the cosmopolitanism that characterised the outlook of the educated elite in the pre-colonial era. They had stood by Bishop Crowther and his agents, all of whom were *Saro*, as fellow Africans under the tyranny of the C.M.S. They, the Ijaw, were not at that time fighting on the platform of Ijaw nationalism. It was natural that once the European yoke was removed the Ijaw should resent the *Saro* yoke in turn, particularly with the increase of the educated elite among the Ijaw and their consciousness of their financial power upon which their alien pastors depended entirely. Once more, then, as had been his experience with the Egba, James Johnson was to become a victim of localised nationalism.

As early as 1905, as can be gathered from the tension that developed between the clergy and the laity in most parts of the Delta, anti-*Saro* feeling had become very strong indeed.[42] It is not easy to ascertain how far blame for the non-Ijawlisation of the Native Pastorate can be ascribed to James Johnson. For not only did he recognise the advisability of encouraging the natives to be trained but he consciously pursued a policy of promoting Ijaw agency. As he emphasised time and again the cheapest and most effective way of administering the Diocese lay in the use of local people.[43] But for several years the gap between the *Saro* and Ijaw agents remained; it was never narrowed. In the absence of a secondary grammar school and a theological seminary until the second decade of this century, the Ijaw agents held subordinate posts. James Johnson did not consider the ethnic nationalism of the Ijaw a primary factor; merit and merit alone carried weight with him. Consequently throughout his directorship of the affairs of the Niger Delta Pastorate the pattern of *Saro* leadership and Ijaw followership remained unaltered. In the name of efficiency the practice of recruiting the *Saro* never ceased and was never relaxed.

But there was another side to the coin. Educated Ijaw who could have competed with the *Saro* would not take up a career in the Church. Eventually even several Ijaw agents found the better prospects in Government and mercantile establishments irresistible. In 1903 alone four of them—Stowe, Jacob Pepple, Alfred Hart and Samuel Allison—resigned posts in the Church for secular appointments.[44] It is important to note that one of them, Alfred Hart, had been sent to Sierra Leone Grammar School by the Pastorate with the prospect of being ordained. By 1907 James Johnson was so concerned for the Ijawlisation of the leadership of the Delta Pastorate that greater importance was placed on the idea of a theological institution. It was this concern that inspired the founding of the Crowther Memorial Institute in 1911. It is essential to note that this was no mean accomplishment. The training institution was the only one in West Africa which was erected, staffed and supported by a Native Church. By 1917 the number of Ijaw agents had increased to more than ten, six of them about to be ordained.

The Delta Christians could not have been expected to rationalise and appreciate the effort being made by the *Saro* leadership to encourage indigenous agency. It seemed to the Ijaw that *Saro* imperialism had replaced that of the Europeans. It was thus a convenient soil on to which fell the seeds of the movement led by Garrick Braide. Garrick Braide became a symbol, a charismatic leader for all Ijaw, Christians and 'pagans' alike. Moreover, after November 1915, the prestige of Garrick Braide came to be higher than that of Holy Johnson in the eyes of the chiefs and people of the Niger Delta because the "prophet" had supernatural powers. His impact upon the Niger Delta was also greater than that of James Johnson. Thousands of 'pagans', including chiefs, surrendered their gods and announced their conversion to Christianity.[45] In other words Garrick Braide achieved in three months what the Church

Missionary Society had not attained in half a century. Idols were dumped in streets and set on fire. Most of the members of the Niger Delta Pastorate deserted their *Saro* leaders and recognised the divine claims of Garrick Braide and his lieutenants. The *Saro* leaders, as can be expected, found the prophet's claims unacceptable on theological grounds. But any Ijaw who did not recognise these claims was labelled as unpatriotic. For them it behoved the Ijaw nation to be thankful for the honour which, it was believed, God had conferred upon them by raising up sacred people like Braide and his assistants. If the denial came from a *Saro* it was regarded as a token of prejudice and jealousy. The spell of Garrick Braide on the Ijaw was incredible. Holy Johnson watched with amazement:

> Garrick's person is considered as so sacred and so filled with power that even the water he bathes in is regarded as charged with healing and other virtues, and is readily drunk or washed with. It is eagerly sought after or scrambled for by chiefs and people, rich and poor, sick and whole alike; and it has even been drunk by Church agents. The vegetable matters with which many, especially women, used often to rub their bodies for adornment are now being commonly dispensed with in favour of the clay which earth makes when mixed with this water, either on account of the healing and other virtues believed to have entered into it, or as a charm to bring good luck or to secure protection against evil. The same can be said of the persons of his assistants.[46]

The cumulative Ijaw national feeling was a strong factor that gave the Garrick Braide movement the force and character it possessed to the discomfiture of James Johnson and the alarm of the British administration. But it was also a severe judgment on the inadequacy and ineffectiveness of the Anglican brand of Christianity for which James Johnson had stood all his life. For the refusal of the chiefs and 'pagans' to embrace Christianity lay mainly in the fact that, as it was presented to them, Christianity had little meaning or relevance to their lives. It was patently impractical. In the experience of the Ijaw abstract prayers to an unseen God yielded no visible results, nor did Christianity allay the universal fear of the unseen malevolent forces and witchcraft; the white man's faith, they experienced, left diseases and afflictions uncured. In contrast to the irrelevance of the white man's religion was the religion proclaimed by Garrick Braide and the prayers he offered. His prayers produced quick and visible result, healing diseases at a rate greater than that of native or European medical science. In the belief that there was a logically necessary connection between sin and suffering Garrick Braide adopted the practice of compelling the sick to make confessions of their sin and to undergo penance.[47] Once the sick did this they were assured of a complete cure within weeks by praying seventeen times daily. Thinking about the movement convinced James Johnson of the necessity for the Christian Church to make the Christian faith meaningful and relevant to its adherents. As he told the Delta Board in February 1916:

> The whole affair is a very sad one, and it indicates an awfully defective knowledge, or an entire ignorance of the very elementary truths of Christianity in very large numbers of people that are called, or call themselves Christians, and an alarming weakness in the Native Church especially in view of the shortness of time barely three months, within which the movement, with all its serious drawbacks, has acquired control and mastery over a very considerable section of it. It calls for deep humiliation before God on the part of us, the clergy; its Teachers, Shepherds and Leaders, and for a thorough overhauling of our work in every one of its departments, and the methods of procedure which we have followed in it, with a view to a considerable amendment.[48]

James Johnson watched his Diocese falling apart, as the Church founded by Garrick Braide in 1916—the Christ Army Church of Native Delta Church—took away two-thirds of the Niger Delta Pastorate adherents. No station was unaffected but those that were worst hit were Bonny, Abonema and Bakana. Even those who remained loyal to the Anglican Church were not prepared to write off the movement as an entire evil and emphasised the following good in it—morning and evening prayers in every town, the ending of drinking and selling of spirits, due observance of Sundays, the giving up of charms and bad medicine, and the restoration of peace and harmony amongst the people by putting an end to litigation.[49]

All was well between James Johnson and Garrick Braide as long as the latter regarded himself as a mortal and no more than an instrument for the fulfilment of divine will. But Johnson was totally unaware of the potential danger and of the way Braide was heading and by January 1916 Garrick Braide and his lieutenants had begun to make claims and behave in a manner that compelled James Johnson to revise his attitude. The seer began to claim that he was a prophet. This claim touched James Johnson at his tenderest spot. For him no man was divine; no man could be divine. Garrick Braide, Ngiangia and Moses Hart became in his view heretics who were committing a sin against the Holy Ghost for which there could be no forgiveness. In James Johnson's judgment, Braide and his lieutenants usurped the position of God by posing as confessors and presenting themselves to the people as divines who could redeem and forgive sins. Thousands of people obtained a cure through them as their redeemer and not "through the atoning death of Christ on the Cross as a sacrifice for the world's sin".[50] Holy Johnson could hardly believe his ears when he was told of the reception accorded to Braide as he moved from place to place. He was venerated and even deified. The following is the account by James Johnson on how Braide was received at Abonema on 6 January 1916:

> Crowds upon crowds came out to greet him and do him homage. Chiefs, masters of the country, several of them of great importance, crawled along the ground to where he sat, and bowing with their heads to the ground did obedience to him, he stretching out his right hand in a stately fashion to raise them up. They vied with each other in entertaining him, each striving to outrival his neighbour in doing honour to one who was almost accounted a guest from heaven. When he went from the house of one chief to that of another, very large numbers of men, women, and children attended him singing his praise. A chief's compound, after the great guest's entrance into it, would be crowded with a seething mass of humanity packed together as herrings in a barrel, many of them occupying a prostrate position for long spells of time. At other times when Garrick is on the march, a herald precedes him, and every one that passes by falls on his knees and remains in the position till he has passed.[51]

James Johnson could hardly have been expected to bear with a situation like this. In February 1916 he summoned Garrick Braide to Bonny to discuss the movement. That his summons was honoured by the "prophet" was a mark of respect for Holy Johnson but there was little ground for agreement between the two. Braide commanded the allegiance of his people, whose chauvinism he had greatly aroused, James Johnson that of the *Saro* "imperialists". Braide was the founder of a heretical movement, James Johnson was the rock of Anglican orthodoxy. It hardly occurred to Holy Johnson that the erstwhile submissive canoe-seller of Bakana, who had been under him for years, could no longer regard James Johnson as a superior. It cannot be surprising, then, that the meeting was a failure before any discussion could take place. Holy Johnson's anger reached fever height when Bonny and Bakana chiefs introduced Garrick to him as a "prophet". James Johnson retorted to the contrary in so strong a manner that Garrick "left me in an abrupt, disrespectful and disgraceful manner".[52]

From now on James Johnson declared total war on the movement which "is filled with corruptions". The movement became theologically unacceptable to him in other ways. Thousands of the prophet's followers, he said, were not true converts. They had not understood the content and implications of the new faith they were professing. They were no more than nominal Christians whose mouth profession was based entirely on the cure they had obtained. Even on the theological basis, Garrick emphasised the danger of liquor to the body rather than to the soul. Offensive to James Johnson's notion of hygiene was the fact that the water in which Garrick had taken his bath people sought because of their belief in its healing virtues. The devil, he said, had entered into Garrick and his lieutenants.[53]

James Johnson cannot escape part of the responsibility for the persecution and oppression meted out to Garrick Braide and his followers by the British administration from February 1916 to early 1917. The administration could not have welcomed a movement preaching against liquor upon which most of the British trade in Southern Nigeria depended, but James Johnson's opposition to Garrick Braide presented the British officials with the moral support which made it impossible for a dissentient voice to be raised in Britain against the ruthless suppression of the movement. The administration was uncomprisingly reactionary. Occurring during a global war and at a time when war was being fought with the Germans in the Cameroons, it was easy for the administrators to see the Garrick Braide movement as a kind "of South African Ethiopianism, or the Chilembwe movement in Nyasaland". The movement, most of the officials believed, was politically and racially motivated and its aim was to expel the white man and his rule from the Niger Delta. In one of his addresses Garrick Braide was alleged to have claimed that he could put a stop to the war and that "power is now passing from the whites to the blacks".[54] No effort was spared to discourage the movement. The churches were burnt down by fanatics of the Niger Delta Pastorate, heavy fines were imposed, and mass arrests and imprisonments made. Garrick Braide was given various six-month prison sentences, which were later halved by the Lieutenant-Governor.[55] In November 1918, however, to the delight of the *Saro*, who claimed that James Johnson had predicted God's wrath for him if he failed to fulfil the divine will, Garrick Braide met his death by a stroke of lightning. Previously, James Johnson's death had been mourned by members of the Christ Army Church and several years after 1917 his memory continued to be cherished by Patriarch J. G. Campbell, the Nigerian nationalist who assumed the directorship of the Church after the death of Garrick Braide.

By January 1916 the Niger Delta Pastorate was only a ghost of its former self. The Garrick Braide movement had developed into a settled Church. Persecution did not affect its growth, popularity and organisation. Its membership was put at the fantastic figure of one million. The Reverend S. A. Coker, a one-time Anglican minister who had joined the African Church organisation and was currently President of the Congregational Union of West Africa, was invited to organise the new Church, the Christ Army Church. The start of a ministry was made with the ordination of Josephus D. Manuel, a native of Abonema, formerly a first-class clerk in the service of the British administration. Also application was made to join the world-wide organisation, the Evangelical Alliance.[56]

James Johnson opposed the new Church until his death. Throughout his last episcopal tour, from February to May 1917, the theme of his discussions was a plea that the Delta people should never have anything to do with the Christ Army Church.

However, these last two years were not entirely taken up by the challenge and frustration of the prophet movement of Garrick Braide. In November of 1916 he was Missioner at Breadfruit Church in Lagos, in connection with the National Mission of Repentance and Hope organised by the Lagos Church. His soul-stirring sermons attracted huge congregations. His last sermon in Lagos was delivered at St. Peter's on 18 February 1917, when his audience was thrilled with the text: "Sin no more lest a worse thing come unto thee."

When he left Lagos on 21 February 1917, after a very successful revival mission to his old Church, James Johnson was aware that his end was not far away. Two days before he had made a Will, to the effect that his volumes of *Encyclopaedia Britannica* should be given to the library of Fourah Bay College, that £350 should be given to each of his two sisters and their children (should they have any), that £300 be given to his niece, but that should the latter die childless then this sum be paid over "to the Authorities of the Church Missionary College Fourah Bay in Sierra Leone aforesaid towards the formation of a Fund to be designated *The Bishop Johnson's Scholarship Fund* the income from which should go towards helping some deserving and needy youth to acquire a university education with a view to entering the ministry of the Anglican Communion".[57] His dedication to the Bishoprics Fund scheme remained strong. For on 20 February he helped in arranging for a meeting which the Lagos Ladies Committee of the Fund was to hold "soon".

This journey back to the Niger Delta was overland, by foot, across the Yoruba country through Oyo and Oshogbo. For the first time he had the opportunity to visit Ilesha and Akure, places of importance for his paternal connections. He performed episcopal duties at Sabongida Ora and Benin City. It was a journey which might well have tried a man only half his age. By the middle of March he was presiding over the annual meeting of the Delta Church Board, (formerly called the Conference) at which he presented a very long presidential address. Almost immediately he began an episcopal tour which took him to practically all the stations. The confirmation services alone which he held in every station were sufficient to sap his energy, and these were apart from exhortations and other ecclesiastical functions. The number of people confirmed in each station were as follows:

Toun	...	...	...	125	Buguma	...	...	62
Queenstown	...	...		25	Abonema	...	...	71
Okrika	...	...		57	Bakana	...	...	12
Opobo	...	...	...	99	Nembe	...	...	76
Egwanga	...	...		35	Ibile	...	...	...	13

As he moved from station to station by canoe, he corresponded with Lagos. On 26 March, from Okrika, he wrote to Tugwell "at considerable length",[58] and as Tugwell claimed: "There was nothing to indicate any loss of vigour or power." On 15 May he arrived back in Bonny. He complained that he had lost his appetite and was feeling some pain in his side. But in spite of his physical ailments he confirmed 89 candidates on 17 May, a herculean task which, the writer was told, has been a lesson to Anglican Bishops ever since that confirmation of too many people at a time could result in a Johnsonian death! Indeed Holy Johnson still hoped that on 18 May he would be fit enough to go to Old Calabar by *S.S. Elmina*.

By 17 May he was painfully aware that his end was drawing near. At the service held on that day in Bonny, he chose as his text Job 19: 25, "I know that my Redeemer liveth". In the course of his sermon he told his congregation that it was his last service and he appealed to both chiefs and people to have nothing to do with the Garrick Braide movement. As he left the service for his room he exclaimed: "Thank God, I have finished my work, my heart is clear." After this he lay down, evidently weak and tired. One Dr. Seiger was summoned to attend to him. He was restless during the night, refusing to take anything except cold water. In the following morning he showed no signs of death but took some milk and soup. At 4 p.m. he began to breathe heavily and twenty-five minutes later his heart failed him completely and he passed away quietly.[59] Thus Holy Johnson died in harness as he would have wished to do.

His death evoked a deep, spontaneous and genuine sympathy in Bonny among Europeans, Africans and chiefs. He was buried in a coffin which a non-native resident had ordered in anticipation of a relative's death. It was a coffin the like of which Bonny had never seen. Though in a remote and isolated place James Johnson's death was no ordinary one and he received all the honours a great man should receive. The Union Jack flew at half mast on Government buildings. On the morning of the funeral a contingent of marines carried the coffin. This was a very high honour. Four Europeans were present at the funeral. They were Captain Purdon, the Director of the Marine Department, who represented the British administration and brought his marines with him in uniform; H. P. Doules, who represented the merchants; Watson, who represented the Cable Company and Hyde, Inspector of Schools, representing the Education Department.[60]

The news of his death circulated along the West African coast within twenty-four hours. Memorial services were held throughout "all the centres in Nigeria which are in telegraphic communication with Lagos".[61] A most impressive service was held in English in St. Paul's Church at which about 3,000 people were present. A second service was held in Yoruba the following Sunday. In Sierra Leone services were held in Freetown, Waterloo and Benguema. The memorial service in the last place, which took place on 27 May, was organised by the Benguema Descendants' Association who had by that date erected the marble statue of Johnson in the east end of St. George Cathedral in Freetown.

Never before had a West African died with such universal sympathy and acclaim. Being the country of his birth, Sierra Leone wished his body to be interred there; as the place where he spent the greatest part of his career Yorubaland, particularly Lagos, wished that he be buried in Lagos. Tributes, which continued on for months, poured into newspapers from Europeans and Africans alike, from Christians of all denominations and Muslims. In the opinion of Herbert Tugwell who knew Holy Johnson well: "His name will long live as that of one of Africa's most devoted sons."[62] The Church Missionary Society summed him up as follows: "The late Bishop was a wholehearted man of God and has left a distinct mark on the Church in West Africa, both by the saintliness of his life and by his rigid adherence to principles of righteousness, combined with a deep sympathy with African thought and African aspirations."[63]

The two most prominent characteristics of his career and life —saintliness and African patriotism—were emphasised by virtually all who knew him intimately. In the view of a former Wesleyan missionary in Nigeria, J. M. Elliot, "No one who knew him intimately, as it was my great privilege to do, could doubt either his goodness as a Christian or his patriotism as an

African."[64] Bishop J. Walmsley, the European Bishop of Sierra Leone, believed that the following words of Robert Browning, the English poet, defined James Johnson's character, particularly his courage:

One who never turned his back but marched breast forward,
Never doubted clouds would break,
Never dreamed, though right were worsted, wrong would triumph,
Held we fall to rise, are baffled to fight better,
Sleep to wake.[65]

The press extolled him to the sky. The *Lagos Standard* declared: "So deep also was his love for his race and so intense his religion that all natives of West Africa from the Gambia, whatever their religious persuasions regarded him as a great, patriotic and Christian African. In Sierra Leone, the Gold Coast and in Nigeria his name was a household word. Crowds flocked to hear him preach. . . . The father of us all, our guide and adviser of our wordly troubles and spiritual difficulties is no more."[66] The *Lagos Weekly Record* paid him an even greater tribute:

He departs from our midst our Grand Old Man in Church and State, a zealous and steady worker in the Master's vineyard who prayed daily to die in harness—in the holy and delightful task of winning souls for Heaven. Truly had a Prince and great man fallen from Israel. . . . In the galaxy of West African heroes or celebrities whose golden deeds shall be written in the sands of Time; whose blessed memories shall be consecrated by tradition and revivified by the laws of association for the express purpose of inspiring the youths of succeeding ages to still greater and nobler achievements when "Ethiopia shall stretch forth her hands unto God", the name of Bishop James Johnson the Grand Old Man in Church and State, the one possible healing and mediating influence within the whirligig of our social existence—the name of Bishop Johnson (we venture to predict) shall live in fame through all ages—*Nomen Episcopi Johnsonis per omnia secula vivet fama*. Peace to his shades.[67]

In Sierra Leone they felt that James Johnson had left behind a gap which would be difficult to fill for a long time to come. In the words of the *Sierra Leone Weekly News*: "In the death of Bishop James Johnson, Negro West Africa has sustained a loss which may not be made good for the next fifty years . . . Bishop Johnson was not an ordinary minister. He was born to an end, sent into the world for a great purpose."[68]

Far away in London the *African Times and Orient Review*, a paper owned and edited by an Egyptian Muslim intellectual, Duse

Mohammed, declared: "Bishop Johnson was ever in the fore-front of West African native spiritual, intellectual, and political advancement; although a Christian Bishop, he possessed the entire confidence of the Muslims of Nigeria. He was not only a native but a welcome figure at the many conferences and congresses in London."[69]

NOTES

1. C.M.S. G3/A1/02, James Johnson to F. Baylis, 28/11/1900.
2. C.M.S. CA2/056, James Johnson to H. Wright, 27/8/1878.
3. Foreword J. Johnson, *A Brief Outline et seq.*
4. Cf. C.M.S. Library S.D., Group 6.
5. *Lagos Weekly Record*, 17/3/1894.
6. C.O. 520/89, James Johnson to Colonel J. E. B. Seely, 14/1/1909; same to same, 20/1/1909.
7. *Ibid.*, Minutes dated 6 February on James Johnson to J. E. B. Seely.
8. C.M.S. CA2/013, James Johnson to F. Baylis, 30/3/1909.
9. *Ibid.*
10. Cd. 4707, *Southern Nigeria Report of the Committee of Inquiry into the Liquor Trade in Southern Nigeria*, Part II, Minutes of Evidence, pp. 244-254.
11. C.O. 520/67, W. E. Egerton to Earl of Crewe, 27/11/1908.
12. Cd. 4707, cited p. 250.
13. *Ibid.*, p. 247.
14. *Ibid.*, p. 250.
15. *Lagos Standard*, 14/10/1908.
16. Cd. 4906, Part I, Report of the Commission.
17. James Johnson to Dr. M. Agbebi, 13/9/1913, reproduced in *Nigerian Chronicle*, 7/11/1913.
18. *Nigerian Chronicle*, 9/9/1910.
19. M.P. F9, O. Sapara to E. Morel, 16/10/1912.
20. James Johnson to Dr. M. Agbebi, 13/9/1913, reproduced in *Nigerian Chronicle*, 7/11/1913.
21. A.P.S., James Johnson to Dr. M. Agbebi, 31/8/1913.
22. A.P.S., A. Folarin to Travers Buxton, 10/7/1916. They formed a political organisation called Nigerian Reform Association.
23. *Ibid.*, J. L. Harrison to Travers Buxton, 29/5/1912.
24. *Ibid.*, James Johnson to T. Buxton, 17/6/1913.
25. *Ibid.*, A.P.S. to James Johnson, 23/6/1913.
26. *Ibid.*, James Johnson to T. Buxton, 17/6/1913.
27. *Ibid.*, James Johnson to T. Buxton, 17/6/1913.
28. *Ibid.*, A. Alakija to T. Buxton, 20/10/1916.
29. James Johnson to Dr. M. Agbebi, 13/7/1913, reproduced in *Nigerian Chronicle*, 7/4/1913.
30. *Jubilee Volume of the Sierra Leone Church*, London, 1917, pp. 59-60.
31. *Lagos Weekly Record*, 3/8/1913.
32. *Jubilee Volume et seq.*, p. 198.
33. *Sierra Leone Weekly News*, 9/6/1917.
34. *Western Equatorial Africa Diocesan Magazine*, September 1917, p. 255.

2A

35. *Sierra Leone Weekly News*, 16/1/1915.
36. *Ibid.*, 26/12/1914.
37. *Ibid.*, 23/1/1915 (contains entire speech).
38. *Report of the Proceedings of the First Session of the Fourth Synod*, Lagos, May 1915, p. 74.
39. G. M. Haliburton, *The Prophet Harris and His Work in Ivory Coast and Western Ghana*, Ph.D. London, 1966.
40. H. W. Turner, *History of an African Independent Church*, 2 Volumes, Oxford, 1967.
41. Letter to James Johnson, 1908. Reproduced in *Lagos Weekly Record*, 24/2/1917.
42. C.M.S. G3/A3/010, Bishop Johnson's Journal Report, December 1904-July 1905.
43. See Reports 1903-1907. See in particular C.M.S. G3/A3/011 for 1906.
44. C.M.S. G3/A3/09, James Johnson to H. Tugwell, 4/2/1904.
45. *Lagos Weekly Record*, 10/2/1917.
46. James Johnson, "Elijah II", *Church Missionary Review*, 1916, pp. 455-462.
47. *Ibid.*
48. *Western Equatorial African Diocesan Magazine*, August 1917, p. 212.
49. *Minutes of the Proceeding of the Second Session of the Fourth Synod*, 1916, p. 62.
50. James Johnson, "Elijah II", *op. cit.*
51. *Ibid.*
52. *Minutes of the Proceeding of the Second Session of the Fourth Synod*, 1916, p. 84.
53. James Johnson, "Elijah II", *op. cit.*
54. *The Times*, 22/6/1916.
55. H. W. Turner, "Prophets and politics: A Nigerian Test Case", *The Bulletin of the Society for African Church History*, Vol. II, No. 1, December 1965, pp. 112-117.
56. C.M.S. G3/A3/0, Joseph Manuel to the General Secretary Evangelical Alliance, 6/1/1917.
57. T. J. Thompson, *The Jubilee and Centenary Volume of Fourah Bay College*, Freetown, 1930, Copy of Will, pp. 154-155. One beneficiary of his Scholarship Fund was to be Archdeacon R. A. Ashley-Dejo.
58. C.M.S. G3/A2/017, H. Tugwell to G. T. Manley, 18/5/1917.
59. *West Equatorial African Diocesan Magazine*, August 1917, p. 217.
60. C.M.S. G3/A2/017, H. S. Macaulay to H. Tugwell (undated).
61. *Ibid.*, H. Tugwell to G. T. Manley, 30/5/1917.
62. *Ibid.*, same to same, 18/5/1917.
63. Quoted in *Nigerian Pioneer*, 20/7/1917.
64. *Lagos Standard*, 23/5/1917.
65. Robert Browning, *Asolando*, Epilogue; quoted in *Nigerian Pioneer*, 20/7/1917.
66. 23/5/1917.
67. 26/5/1917.
68. 26/5/1917.
69. *African Times and Orient Review* (Special Anniversary Number), Vol. 5, No. 1, Mid July 1917.

CHAPTER FOURTEEN

SOUL MARCHES ON

Armed as if with power from on high, his admonitions and exhortations seemed to breathe words of living fire; for his predictions more or less came to pass, thus vividly reminding one of the *Thus saith the Lord* of the ancient testament, since that which he cursed seemed to be cursed; and that which he blessed seemed to be blessed.

The Lagos Weekly Record 26/5/1917
Obituary of James Johnson

ALTHOUGH James Johnson died on 18 May 1917, his soul was never to rest in the grave. Fifty years after Holy Johnson's death African nationalists were to struggle in the direction of the goals he had upheld—Pan-Africanism, political and religious independence, mental emancipation, and cultural renaissance.

But ironically, by the time he died, James Johnson was in some ways more ahead of his age than in the 1870s. Within British West Africa the Colonial powers were firmly in the saddle at the time of his death. In Sierra Leone the writ of the British Government began to run throughout the hinterland after the suppression of the Hut Tax rebellion in 1898; in the Gold Coast the Union Jack had begun to wave over the heads of the Akan Ashanti, whose last resistance in 1900 had been smashed in an exemplary manner; in Nigeria fire and sword had assimilated into the British Empire an hinterland of nearly a thousand miles. Effective administration and effective exploitation of the economic resources of these territories were being carried out under the unchallengeable control of the white man. Assertiveness by the educated elite in Church and State was being discouraged; the orthodox doctrine that gained currency in government, in commercial houses and in the Church, was that the educated elite must be content with subordinate positions only. As an embittered, independent and accomplished Johnsonian put it: "We know what is proposed in certain high quarters with reference to our future education; it is that we must be educated otherwise we will prove dangerous . . . and a supply of lower grade clerks for Government and merchants as well as unskilled workmen will always be required: but that the education must be of a strictly limited kind and by no means technical, lest we compete with the British workmen. . . . It fully explains why Civil Engineers if Natives of West Africa cannot find posts in Government Service. Why fully qualified Medical men are held to be unfit for the service while their foreign compeers, with even inferior diplomas and less acquainted with the diseases of the country are eligible and also why all are classified as 'aliens' or 'Native foreigners' in their fatherland, and bear the disabilities of the nomenclature."[1]

The heterodoxy, if not heresy, of the biological equality of the African with the European and of the moral necessity of the Europeans to observe the principle of Africa for the Africans, which James Johnson emphasised all his life, can be appreciated in the light of the prevailing circumstances indicated above. Although the West African press became unsparingly virulent against the consolidation of the imperial grasp on the territory, there was not wanting a number among the educated elite who accepted the doctrine of African subordination in the colonial establishment as right and just. In this class of educated elite was a grandson of a Lagos chief, Kitoyi Ajasa, whose newspaper disseminated the bitterest post-mortem criticisms and reflections on Holy Johnson.

A lawyer of mediocre ability and a strong Anglican Churchman, Kitoyi Ajasa saw the *Pax Britannica* in Nigeria as a providentially-ordained event and the British administration as an establishment for which the educated elite should be eternally grateful. After all, in his view, the educated elite were the creation of Afro-European contact. Therefore the virulence against the presence and authority of the white man in Church and State, which reached a crescendo in the Lagos press during the opening decade of this century, was to him a manifestation of the base ingratitude by the educated elite.[2] He accepted the credo that in the colonial situation Africans were not yet fit to rule themselves. So much disturbed was he by the anti-white poise of the newspapers that he decided to found a newspaper of his own which would be the arch-defender of the British administration and the Christian missions.

It was in these circumstances that he founded the *Nigerian Pioneer* at the outbreak of the First World War. In the early years it was printed at the C.M.S. Press in Lagos and European missionaries rejoiced that they at last controlled a newspaper.[3] Hardly had the tributes and obituaries about Holy Johnson been completed than a scathing review of his career was made. One theme ran through the series of seven editorial articles—his African nationalism made him the rock on which the monolithic unity of the Anglican Church in West Africa foundered. Holy Johnson, it was stressed several times, was the father if not the architect of the secessions that paralysed the Lagos Church up to the time of his death; he was the relentless and zealous advocate of premature independence for Africans; by introducing the principle of nationality into the Church he incited the laity against "constituted authority". Why should this principle have been evoked at all? Why should the authority of the white man be rejected because it was "foreign"? What evidence was there that they —the African Church leaders led by Holy Johnson—were ready for freedom? It behoved them to realise that "unless they were ready for freedom independence was not a blessing but a curse". In the concluding remarks of the *Nigerian Pioneer*: "It must be admitted that this desire for an independence which only leads to anarchy and which is supposed to have its sanction in the spirit of nationality is largely the result of a low level of general intelligence and a lack of sufficient instruction in the principles of Christianity."[4]

The orthodox doctrine enunciated in the *Nigerian Pioneer* had been heeded *in toto* by the African clergymen in the Church Missionary Society in Nigeria two decades before James Johnson's death. He had in these years been the odd man out. Never was there to emerge another such thorn in the side of Anglican authorities in West Africa. After his death the white man's rule was accepted as a matter of course. Not that Africans were not given higher education. In fact there began a programme of training in Fourah Bay College for a large number of Nigerians but in spite of the fact that the Anglican Church boasted of a large number of graduates never had there been such a silence about the white man's activity in Church and State. They showed no interest in public and political affairs. As an irate African Church leader recorded "None of my countrymen has ever written a pamphlet or a book or even subscribed an article in the press whose educative value is worth a place in one's library" since the death of James Johnson, in whom "we have lost a saint and a patriot; he loved God and loved his people also".[5]

It may be remarked that the absence of a successor to James Johnson in the propagation of his ideas was not peculiar to the Anglican Communion. It was also characteristic of the other

Churches under the control of the white man. In the Southern American Baptist Mission, which had merged with the Native Baptist Church of Dr. Mojola Agbebi in the Yoruba Association, conceding the leadership of the latter to the African, the death of Agbebi in the same year as James Johnson removed from the organisation the only man who had inspired the ideals of self-government. Among the Wesleyans the only man who could have continued to challenge the white man's leadership, the Reverend W. Euba, the only graduate of the organisation until after the First World War, had in 1912 resigned in bitterness against the authoritarianism of Oliver Griffin, the European Chairman.[6]

Nevertheless the spirit of James Johnson did not stay in the grave: it continued to haunt African men and women who had found in his holiness and patriotism a veritable inspiration. Ironically those who picked up the challenge posed by his death were the leaders of the break-away African Churches he had fathered. By the end of 1917 not only had the call been made that a biography of "the acknowledged greatest West African Divine of his time" should be written but a pamphlet entitled *Elegy on the Late Right Reverend Bishop James Johnson M.A., D.D., Native of West Africa*, by S. T. Jones, a retired Chief Clerk of the Secretariat Southern Nigeria, was already in circulation. A twenty-five verse composition, it was dedicated "to the rising Generation of Africans in British West Africa".[7]

At a meeting of the Women's Branch of the Committee of the West African Bishopric's Fund, which James Johnson had inaugurated early in 1917, it was decided, immediately after his death, that a portrait should be painted, every woman in Lagos contributing no more than a shilling. It was agreed that the portrait "should be placed in a public building in Lagos, as a memorial in honour of him". In due course the sum of £48 was raised. The portrait was painted by the first western-trained artist, Chief Aina Onabolu, at a cost of about £24 and a further sum of £8 was spent to obtain twenty-four smaller copies which could be purchased by the friends and admirers of Holy Johnson. The portrait, which still hangs over the main entrance to the rebuilt Glover Memorial Hall, is 45 inches high and 32 inches wide. In sepia wash and water-colour, it was laid on canvas and framed in oak with a gold inset. It represents Holy Johnson in his closing years—standing upright, a tall gaunt figure in episcopal robes, ascetic in appearance, with the light of battle in his eyes and his aged face worn deep with the lines of thought, struggle and sorrow. At the ceremony in which it was placed in a cynosural position at the entrance of the old Glover Memorial Hall, and which took place on 26 November 1918, the speaker was no less a person than Henry Carr, the finest intellect of his day who had been sent by his parents to Fourah Bay College in 1879 at James Johnson's persuasion. The occasion was witnessed by the Governor General, Sir Frederick Lugard.[8]

In Bonny, the Ijaw nationalism unleashed by the Garrick Braide movement notwithstanding, James Johnson's memory continued to be cherished. On 23 October 1922 a monument was erected over his grave. For the minister who had to perform the ceremony, the Right Reverend A. W. Howells, who had two years before been raised to the status of Assistant Bishop, the life of James Johnson was full of inspiration but his demands for independence and the manner he had antagonised the Europeans continued to be offensive. His address on the occasion, at which some Europeans were present, was an unblushing re-echo of the orthodox doctrine as defined by the *Nigerian Pioneer*. Immediate independence, declared A. W. Howells, was not desirable; European presence was still required, cherished and indispensable.

Europeans were assured that "our endeavour towards self-realisation and self-determination" would not be undertaken "in the spirit of a Marcus Garvey, a Ghandi or a De Valera".[9] In a cryptic criticism of the man whose memory was being honoured he went on "To you, my fellow countrymen, whether you hail from Sierra Leone, the Gold Coast or Nigeria, I would add one word of caution. Let us make haste slowly and do nothing that could alienate and estrange the good will and sympathy of those whose help we still need for years to come in our aspirations and laudable aims in all that makes for the uplift and progress of the race".[10]

However, adverse observations on James Johnson receded between the wars among the African clergymen of the Anglican communion, as will be seen presently. By 1930 it had become the habit of clergymen sent to Fourah Bay from Nigeria to make a pilgrimage to Benguema, the birthplace of James Johnson.[11] As late as 8 January 1940, in spite of the attention claimed by the Second World War, the Ijebu remembered and honoured James Johnson by unveiling a very beautiful painting of this ecclesiastical nationalist who had done so much for the Ijebu people.[12] In the tributes made to him on the occasion he was described as the most illustrious son Ijebuland had produced to that date.

By the thirties the soul of James Johnson had begun to march on in three important directions. Firstly the scales had begun to drop from the eyes of his African critics within the Church and they came to regard him as a farsighted advocate of African interest; he had become the main fountain of their inspiration and desire to escape from the ecclesiastical imperialism of the Church Missionary Society and Lambeth Palace. Secondly the Pan-African movement became a progressively virile force after his death. Thirdly education and its importance for the evolution of the African continent came to be more and more widely understood in the sense and along the lines he had attempted to indicate in his life-time.

By the thirties African clergymen in the Anglican Communion in West Africa had begun to perceive and regret that the white man's yoke in the Church seemed to assume an appearance of permanence. From 1894, the date of the rebellion led by James Johnson, to 1937 there were never more than two African Assistant Bishops, and these were always chosen from amongst the Yoruba. By the same date there were nine European Bishops and Assistant Bishops. In 1937 Sierra Leone had its first African Assistant Bishop, who was T. S. Johnson, a nephew of Holy Johnson. In 1944 there were eight European Bishops and Assistant Bishops, as opposed to four African Assistant Bishops.

In the circumstances in which they found themselves the African clergymen began to invoke the spirit of James Johnson by giving the West African Native Bishoprics Fund scheme the emphasis, meaning and importance that James Johnson had accorded it. The agreement of 1899 which James Johnson had made with Bishop Tugwell, Lambeth Palace and the Church Missionary Society, they began to contend, had been entered into on behalf of Africans as a whole. On 16 June 1932 the entire African clergy of Sierra Leone forwarded a strongly worded memorandum to the Church Missionary Society, expressing a yearning of Africans for ecclesiastical independence and emphasising the ephemerality of a Church not controlled by the indigenous people.[13]

As they declared, it was in order to prevent a Congo-type effacement of Christianity that "the Parent Committee of the C.M.S. thirty-two years ago did enter into the following solemn and sacred agreement with us through our ever-to-be-lamented brother, the late Bishop James Johnson, that if we, on our part, could undertake to raise a certain required and agreed amount of money to create the said Endowment Fund, they [i.e. the C.M.S. authorities in London] would undertake on their own part, to grant in the said full and independent West African Native Bishop". The power to be held by the African Bishop, they emphasised, was precisely defined in the agreement with James Johnson—"full, complete and unrestricted ecclesiastical powers and jurisdiction, spiritual, temporal, or otherwise over the Protestant Church either throughout or in prescribed portions of West Africa".[14]

The Church Missionary Society authorities were accused of departing from the original agreement in the sense that when the target sum of £10,000 was reached they began to use it for "an ASSISTANT NATIVE BISHOP", "a complete misuse or misapplication of the said Trust money, absolutely contrary and diametrically opposed to the intention of the sponsors, organisers, promoters of the same Trust Fund and the purpose for which the same has been raised, created and constituted".[15]

These views, so strongly expressed, were reinforced in a letter by the African clergymen in Nigeria.[16] It is significant that the C.M.S. authorities did not refute the charges levelled at them. All appeals were ignored. No African was consecrated Bishop until the fifties, when self-government was beginning to be granted to Africans in the State of British West Africa. And when in 1951 West Africa was constituted into a Province, a demand Holy Johnson had made as early as 1900, there was no question of an African being chosen for the position of Archbishop. Since then, in spite of the achievement of full independence by all the countries of West Africa, no African has up to this date been considered fit for the appointment to the highest post in the Anglican Province of West Africa.[17] It is significant to note that the desire for the complete Africanisation of all positions in all the Churches in West Africa remains very strong indeed. In this sense Holy Johnson's soul marches on.

In the same manner the Pan-Africanist ideology which James Johnson had expressed from his early days in Sierra Leone persists, though not in the sense and form in which he perceived it. The Christian Church, upon which James Johnson believed a continental African state would be built, was dropped from the Pan-Africanist programme in the first half of the twentieth century. The idea of one religion becoming the *primus mobile* of human life in a state, how much less in a continent, has long been out of fashion, even in the Christian world before his death. But even in this respect, religion, albeit Islam, is the basis upon which the "Black Nationalist" movement in the United States in recent years hopes to achieve emancipation—cultural, racial and political —from the white man.[18]

Nevertheless the idea of one State for the entire continent, which seemed quixotic in the pre-Scramble era, has been revived in our day by pan-Africanist zealots like Kwame Nkrumah and has begun to find an institutional expression of some kind in the Organisation of African Unity. From James Johnson to Kwame Nkrumah, then, it might be said, the ideological wheel has turned full circle. The latter's idea of a monolithic State and unity for Africa is essentially a revivification of James Johnson's dream. The difference between the two dreamers lies only in the means that would be employed to bring about this goal. James Johnson expected Christianity to achieve his vision, Nkrumah the secular agency. Though still an ethereal dream the fact that more and more post-independence African statesmen pay lip service to this idea and seek to put it into effect through regional groupings, emphasising more those things that unite, rather than those that divide, is a clear manifestation that Holy Johnson's soul is, with respect to the Pan-African movement, still marching on.

And yet in another sense the idealism for which James Johnson stood—in the realm of education—is a major pre-occupation of post-independence Africa. Education, he emphasised throughout his life, was the task of the secular administration. To this end, he contended, private agencies like Christian missions should not be regarded as being in charge. Education, too, should train the Head, the Heart and the Hand; Africa should produce her own technocrats and agriculture should be thoroughly mechanised. With respect to education some part of his dream is being achieved. Poor but clever children are now being awarded scholarships by the state up to university level; teacher training, which he had regarded as vitally important since 1870, was taken seriously after the First World War in all British West Africa; the education of women had to wait until after the Second World War. However vernacular education and the amalgamation of indigenous and foreign cultures in a satisfactory manner are still to be fully achieved.

No less important than the challenge of his career to present-day African society is the challenge of his moral probity, integrity, sympathy towards the poor and underprivileged, his honesty and firmness of purpose, all of which should influence and be adopted by African statesmen in Independent Africa. James Johnson knew no fear, expressing his opinions and the truth as he perceived it with equal vigour, whether they were popular or not. He was never daunted nor disheartened by opposition or by misrepresentation, whether by Europeans who found his tongue too venomous or by Africans who were envious of, and overpowered by, his virtues. His was a proud tenacity of purpose, an unyielding will and an undefeated perseverance.

Yet masterful and firm though his temper was, he possessed a gentleness and unmistakable courtesy, a pathos and transparent sphinx-like honesty and saintliness which never failed to inspire awe and affection for him among his opponents at critical moments as in Abeokuta in 1879, in Lagos in 1900 and 1901, and in the Niger Delta Garrick Braide crisis, 1915-1917.

Infinitely sympathetic, he knew no social distinctions in his courtesy. He was accessible to all who cared to approach him and was uniformly affable to all—rich and poor, high and low, educated and unlettered, Christian and non-Christian. He made himself the tribune of the people, sometimes at the expense of his personal interest. On no occasion did he ever turn away anybody seeking his help. As a man, not given to exaggeration, who knew him very well, Henry Carr, observed: "He was admitted into every home as a familiar friend. He was the consoler of many sad hearts, the inspirer of not a few broken lives. In all the vicissitudes of human affairs he remained the unfailing friend of the unfriended man and of the fallen woman. There was no man of his time who was the depository of so many confidences from all sorts and conditions of men and women; there was no man of his time who had his advice so frequently asked on questions of the greatest difficulty and delicacy. Only a man whose presence infuses trust and reverence, only a man who is possessed of singular abilities, could have wielded his influence or established the empire he acquired over so many hearts."[19]

Holy Johnson was self-effacing, never boastful and extremely humble. He considered service to humanity in whatever community he found himself in a very broad sense. There could be no question of his deploying his resourcefulness and talents in the religious sphere alone. Rather throughout his life he was a man of affairs. He took great interest and an active part in all political social and philanthropic movements. To his thinking no man was a good Christian if he were not a good citizen and a fervent patriot. With all the energy of his body and soul he sought to make the Christian life a reality in all the departments of the life of his country. Christianity to him was profitable unto all things, having the promise not only of life which is to come, but of the life that now is.

All this is not to say that Holy Johnson was not without his weak points. One of his greatest faults was that his religious prejudices caused him to be a poor judge of others. In the manner characteristic of humanitarian zealots the slimmest evidence was sufficient for him as the basis for opinions and judgments that could hardly be sustained by careful investigation, as is seen in his beliefs about the havoc of the liquor traffic. His judgment was not necessarily based on a careful sifting of empirical data—take for instance the danger he was prepared to ascribe to the bicycle and the brevity of life he ascribed to European civilisation. Also he was often sandwiched within the inevitable conflict between morality and the principle of nationality. For instance morality demanded that his loyalty to the Church Missionary Society, which meant all the world to him in a sense, should never be illtreated, and yet the principle of African nationality demanded the emergence of an African non-sectarian Church for the sake of Christianity and the welfare of Christians. Or consider the conflict he could not resolve with respect to the Ijebu Expedition. His attachment to Christianity demanded that he should rejoice at an event that was bound to hasten the Christianisation of this people, but at the same time his patriotism demanded that the intrusion of the British into Ijebu society should never be allowed.

Nevertheless, his weakness notwithstanding, it is clear from this work that there is substance in the judgment of Henry Carr that Africa should be grateful for "the priceless gift of such a notable man [James Johnson] to our race—a man with so great a part in West Africa and whose name is so memorable in the annals of his country".[20] To ardent African Christians who find the ecclesiastical imperialism of alien Christian missions the obstacle to the evolution of indigenous African Church in Africa Holy Johnson remains an inspirer. To the dreamers of a united Africa Holy Johnson's literal belief in the prophecy of Ethiopia stretching forth her hands to God is a message of hope. To frustrated members of the Negro Race there is solace in James Johnson's conviction that "the latter days of the Negro Race shall exceed the former". To the tribal jingoists in Africa who are not only undermining the unity of Africa, but of individual States in the continent, James Johnson conveys a message. To historians James Johnson's papers are a mine of information on many aspects of West Africa. And yet although he was a keen student of history it is an irony that history is just doing him a tardy justice.

NOTES

1. Herbert Macaulay Papers, MSS, Dr. O. Johnson to E. Morel, 18/12/1912.
2. M.P. F9, Kitoyi Ajasa to E. D. Morel, 16/10/1912.
3. C.M.S. G3/A2/015, M. Jones to G. T. Manley, 27/1/1914.
4. *Nigerian Pioneer*, 21/9/1917.
5. J. G. Campbell, *Lagos Awake on the Election Question*, p. 124.
6. E. A. Ayandele, *op. cit.*, p. 272.
7. Printed by Bosere Press, Lagos, December 1917. See Appendix B.
8. *Nigerian Pioneer*, 10/1/1919.
9. Hist. S. Dept. Ibadan University, Fombo collections, Appendix U, p. 272.
10. *Ibid.*
11. For instance Bishops S. O. Odutola and I. G. S. Jadesinmi.
12. It now hangs at the Reading Room, Ijebu-Ode.
13. T. S. Johnson, *The Story of a Mission*, London, 1953, pp. 120-123.
14. *Ibid.*, pp. 122-123.
15. *Ibid.*
16. *Ibid.*, p. 123.
17. In August 1969, after this book went to press, Bishop N. C. O. Scott of Sierra Leone, became the first African Archbishop of West Africa.
18. E. U. Essien Udom, *Black Nationalism* (The Rise of the Black Muslims in the U.S.A.), Pelican, 1966.
19. *Nigerian Pioneer*, 10/1/1919.
20. *Ibid.*

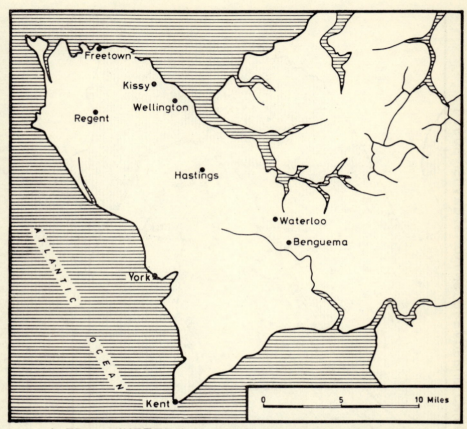

A FEW NINETEENTH CENTURY SETTLEMENTS IN
SIERRA LEONE COLONY

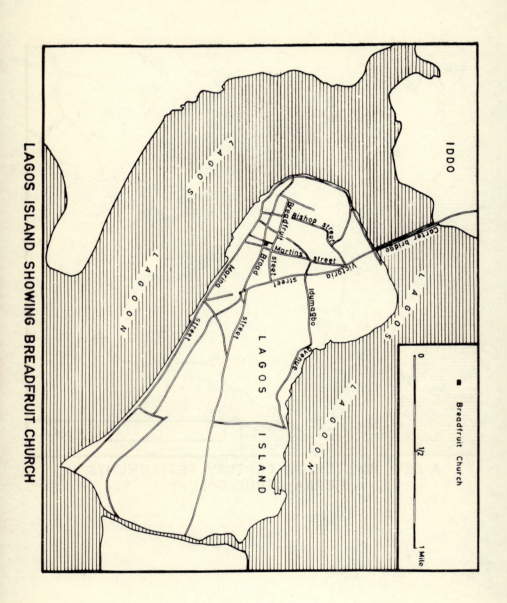

LAGOS ISLAND SHOWING BREADFRUIT CHURCH

IDDO

Carter bridge

Bishop street

Breadfruit street

Martins street

Victoria

Broad street

Idumagbo avenue

Marina street

Bamgbose street

LAGOS LAGOON

LAGOON

LAGOS LAGOON

LAGOON

LAGOS ISLAND

■ Breadfruit Church

0   1/2   1 Mile

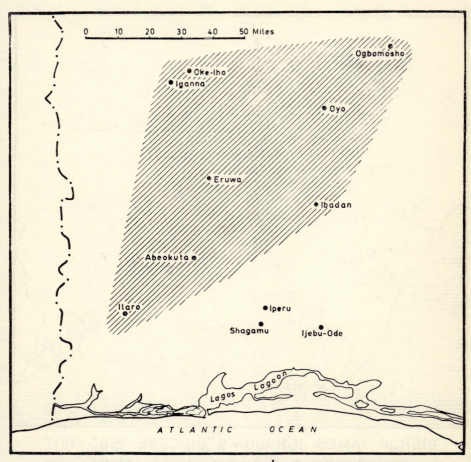

AREA UNDER JAMES JOHNSON'S SUPERINTENDENCE
1877 – 1880

BISHOP JAMES JOHNSON'S 'DIOCESE' 1900-1917

APPENDICES

APPENDIX A

RESOLUTIONS PROPOSED AND ADOPTED IN RE. C.M.S. NIGER DELTA
CHURCHES AT A MEETING OF A FEW NATIVE CHRISTIAN GENTLEMEN
AT THE BREADFRUIT PARSONAGE ON 17 APRIL 1891

1. Resolved that having learnt of the position of the Niger Delta
Churches and Church buildings under the auspices of the Church
Missionary Society, and having in view of the late Niger Mission
difficulties in connection with the Society's decision upon them,
and its new arrangement for the future conduct of the Mission
which are a practical announcement against the efficiency of the
Episcopal Supervision of our much revered friend, Bishop Crowther, the founder of that Mission under it, and of the subordinate
leadership of the Native Ministry and of other Native Agency
which he had worked from the beginning, and also having in view
the fact that these arrangements by which the whole Mission in
spite of Bishop Crowther's presence in it, and of official connection
with it as Bishop, is placed under the direct supervision of the
Society's European Secretaries have reduced Bishop Crowther's
Episcopal authority to a mere shadow, and held up the whole of
Native Ministry, rank and file before the world as incapable of
living and working by itself without the active presence, direction and control of a European in spite of long years of teaching, an opinion the meeting does not share in, and having also in
view of the fact that these arrangements would place the Native
Churches and the Native Ministry under Eurpoean tutelage for an
indefinite period which experience has shown from the way it has
been hitherto employed, is calculated to prevent the healthy
growth of self-reliance and manly independence, this meeting is
of opinion that it should be respectfully suggested to Bishop
Crowther that it is desirable for him both in the interest of his
office—the general Native Ministry and the Native Churches to
take steps to effect an arrangement at once with the C.M.S. to
relieve it of any further pecuniary responsibility in connection with

the Niger Delta Churches to assume to themselves the work of self-support and the responsibilities and privileges connected with it.

2. Resolved:—That having heard from reliable sources that £700 in round number would be required annually from outside to supplement the efforts of the Niger Delta Churches to support their own Church work, and thankfully acknowledging God's blessings upon the Lagos Church generally, and the Christian obligation of giving help to those who are in need, this meeting undertakes to raise annually £350 by private subscriptions for five years towards the amount in the hope that by the end of the time D.V. the native Christians in the Niger Delta may be able to raise themselves the whole amount needed for the sustentation of their work. The above contribution from Lagos will be subject to a gradual reduction as the contributions from the Niger Delta Churches grow.

James Johnson (Chairman)

APPENDIX B

ELEGY ON THE LATE RIGHT REV. BISHOP JAMES JOHNSON, M.A., D.D., NATIVE OF WEST AFRICA

by Mr. S. T. Jones Lagos 1917

(a retired Chief Clerk of the Secretariat, Southern Nigeria) Dedicated to the rising Generation of Africans in British West Africa.

1

The pealing bells announced the mournful news
Of the good Bishop having passed from sight;
The howling winds did waft and not refuse
The plaintive note to spread with all their might

2

The rolling waters heaving high their surf,
Did calm become in their recesses deep;
They listened how the measured toll died off—
Throughout the day the bells did ringing keep

3

Love, honour, and respect his memory dear,
From hearts of young and old so well deserves;
Thus, with each fellow-worker we must share
His sorrows and his joys through which he serves

4

Iconoclastic in his pagan home—
His moral strength here had its first great test;
That overpow'ring force which did become
The mighty impulse that throbbed high his breast.

5

So early in his life did he give proof
Of will determined and his mission true,
When he from idol worship stood aloof:
His heart was gravely touched, so he withdrew.

6

The Niger Delta countries felt the stroke
Of his victorious sword—the word of God,
Gradually their rude idols all he broke:
The people worship now Creator, Lord.

7

His tribes ancestral did slay all twin-breed,
And twin-born he, that was his cruel doom:
But when the blood of Christ did intercede,
His tender life was spared for future bloom

8

Like perfumed flowers shedding fragrance sweet
So strewed he seeds of kindness everywhere;
Though now his form revered we ne'er shall greet
His lasting influence fills our atmosphere.

9

His thoughts were great, and broadcast he diffused
His love profound, exhaustless, deep, and clear.
Sublime ideals his great life infused,
And him inflamed to lead his country higher.

10

Great always was the throng that pressed to hear,
His weighty Sermon, Speech, or grandiose discourse
The truth to utter was his prime desire,
And *that* he dauntless did whate'er the cause

11

Sincere and grave in language word of tropes,
His God-sent message fervently he spoke
His hand was pure, his heart was full of hopes
To free his land from Satan's cursed yoke.

12

He captured hearts of all that heard him speak,
Made them to sob and smile, just as he pleased:
His modest bounty nursed the poor and weak,
And those that raved with anger he appeased.

13

And those on whom Dame Fortune gladly smiled,
As well as those on whom she sadly frowned,
His seasoned counsels, homely, hopeful, mild,
Refreshed and cheered with life more to abound.

14

Himself and all he did the hall-mark bore,
Of sweet simplicity and grace divine;
The garb of self-repression which he wore,
His flowing vestments brightly did outshine

15

His words and works rhymed with angelic grace,
Scarce dots of human frailty could be seen;
He stands a *beacon* to our struggling Race,
To pour bright flashlights on its paths unseen.

16

Such men as he are heroes for all time;
They gently lead and guide their nation's growth,
The gladsome winds their names and deeds shall chime,
True Patriots they; self-seeking do they *loathe*?

17

Quite conscious of his end he breathed his last,
'Thank God, I've done my work, my heart is clear'
These were his dying words, let's hold them fast—
Our watchword let this be *My heart is clear*

18

Perhaps in yonder Hall of this famed land,
His image dignified will ne'er be seen,
Down to posterity his name to hand,
Yet shall the Negro's history bear the sheen.

19

Thus, not a few of Afric's worthy sons,
Their names to skilled Fine Arts have left unknown;
It was their lot to tread this world of thorns,
Their deeds to inscribe on deathless hearts alone

20

These are as well the jewels of our sky,
And suns no less that gladden it with light;
They are rich fountains, gushing truth that lie
In layers hidden deep from common sight.

21

From the dear spot where his rare bones are laid,
Continually shall rise quintessence pure;
Whilst ever-greens, and not fair wreaths that fade,
That Spot shall mark and not at all obscure.

22

Shall rise, I say, quintessence ever pure.
To inspire and nerve all Negroes far and nigh
To worthier deeds than done in days of yore.
To dare to do as he, or dare to die.

23

The task is done: How nobly hast thou trod
This toilsome earth with joy and sorrow blent:
Son of the soil, or purest Negro blood,
How great thy sacrifice of life well-spent:

24

O mighty dead: Let now thy mantle fall
On us who sojourn still this wilderness;
Let Afric's sons and daughters, one and all
Feel its descent, then homes and lives to bless.

25

Praise to the God of Heav'n who gave him *ours*,
And all like him, so noble, true and bold;
Come day, come quickly, when in plenteous showers
Our land shall teem with Negroes of such mould.

S. T. Jones

APPENDIX C

Church House,
Freetown, Sierra Leone,
16 June 1932

The Secretary,
Church Missionary Society (African Section),
4 Salisbury Square, London, E.C.4.

Sir,

We the undersigned, members of Sierra Leone Anglican Clergy,
on behalf of ourselves and of all the West African Natives Concerned, respectfully beg to bring through you to the careful notice,
consideration, and action of the Parent Committee of the Church
Missionary Society in London, the following matter which we,
being deeply mindful of the work, and thoroughly obsessed with
a grateful appreciation of the past labours of our white Missionaries in West Africa, honestly believe and are fully convinced
is of so vital importance that unless it is urgently taken up,
seriously considered, and promptly settled, we fear may eventually
lead to a situation which may gravely endanger the future stability
and other interests of the C.M.S. work in West Africa.
2. That the said matter is concerned with the founding and
establishing of a West Africa Native Independent Bishopric Endowment Fund, for the express purpose of establishing, founding, retaining, creating, and maintaining in West Africa an independent Native Bishopric with full, complete and unrestricted
ecclesiastical powers and jurisdiction, spiritual, temporal, or otherwise over the Protestant Churches of England either throughout or
in prescribed portions of West Africa.
3. That in order to carry into effect the aim and object in paragraph 2 above, the Parent Committee of the C.M.S. thirty-two

years ago did enter into the following solemn and sacred engagement with us through our ever-to-be-lamented brother, the late Bishop James Johnson, that if we, on our part, could undertake to raise a certain required and agreed amount of money to create the said endowment Fund, they (i.e. the C.M.S. in London) would undertake on their own part, to grant in the said full and independent West African Native Bishop.

4. That the said Endowment Fund, having been first of all duly sanctioned by the C.M.S. in London to be raised, was started, sponsored, launched out, organised, promoted, and developed to a point by our said brother, the late Bishop James Johnson, and continued to be developed after the latter's death.

5. That the said Endowment Fund has now been raised to the required, full and agreed amount, which has since been duly and properly constituted a Trust Fund for the said express purpose of keeping, maintaining, and paying A FULL AND INDEPENDENT WEST AFRICAN NATIVE BISHOP and not for keeping, maintaining, or paying AN ASSISTANT West African Native Bishop or otherwise.

6. That the present use to which the said Trust Fund is devoted, as we understand it, namely, for paying and maintaining an ASSISTANT NATIVE BISHOP in West Africa, is, in our opinion, impression, and conviction, a complete misuse or misapplication of the said Trust money, absolutely contrary and diametrically opposed to the intention of the sponsors, organisers, promoters, and creators of the said Trust Fund, and to the purpose for which the same has been raised, created and constituted.

7. That we, having already fulfilled and completed our own part of this solemn and sacred engagement by having raised the necessary fund, therefore most respectfully, earnestly, and solemnly pray, petition, and implore our beloved, most respected, and august Parent in the Lord, the C.M.S. in London, to the end that the said West Africa Native Independent Bishopric be granted us in the Delta Pastorate, Nigeria; lest, if otherwise, it be considered a breach on their part of their solemn engagement with us and a failure to fulfil their sacred obligations to us.

8. A copy of this letter has been handed to our Bishop here (the Rt. Rev. Bishop G. W. Wright), who having been first of all consulted in the matter advised that the Parent Committee in London be written to.

Other copies have been sent to His Grace the Archbishop of Canterbury, His Grace the Archbishop of York, the Rt. Rev. Bishop Melville Jones of Lagos, the respective C.M.S. Secretaries in Nigeria, Sierra Leone, and other authorities concerned in the matter.

9. Praying that our heavenly Father may send His Holy Spirit from above to direct you and the authorities concerned as well as ourselves in this all-important matter, and earnestly awaiting your kind reply.

> Believe us to be
>   Sir,
> Your humble and faithful fellow
> servants in the Lord
> (Sgd) E. T. Cole, Archdeacon of Sierra Leone
> and others.

BIBLIOGRAPHY

I PRIMARY SOURCES

The field work undertaken in Sierra Leone in parts of July and August 1967 was quite fruitful. Many of the settlements outside Freetown, founded by the Liberated Africans in the first half of the nineteenth century, were visited to an advantage. The emotional value of visits to Hastings, Waterloo, Kent, Benguema and Brookfields—all scenes of childhood experiences or earliest activities of James Johnson—and of the meeting held with the Reverend James Ingham Johnson of Liverpool Street, Benguema, a retired Methodist Minister, was great. The latter was a Lokoh adopted by J. B. Johnson, a cousin of James Johnson, he grew up in the home of the Johnsons. He showed me the spot where the house of the Johnsons was located; it has returned to bush. His reminiscences on the Johnson family were stimulating and refreshing.

In Freetown it was a great pleasure meeting the Reverend Eva Johnson, a son of late Bishop T. S. Johnson, the first 'half bishop' of Sierra Leone and a nephew to James Johnson. One other name is worthy of mention. Canon M. D. Showers of 38 Campbell Street, Freetown, was the only surviving *Saro* recruited into the Niger Delta Pastorate by James Johnson. He went to James Johnson's 'diocese' in 1909 and stayed on there till 1947, returning to Sierra Leone in the latter year. He featured prominently in the Garrick Braide movement and in spite of his old age—over 80 years—and feeble memory the charismatic figure of the Ijaw nationalist and prophet remained prominent in his memory.

A. MISSION SOURCES

i. *Church Missionary Society Archives*
   (a) This is by far the richest source. James Johnson has two files for the period before 1880. These are CA1/0123 (Sierra Leone) and CA2/056 (Yoruba Mission). From 1880 onwards James Johnson's letters and journals are to be found in G3/A2/0 and G3/A3/0 series. Practically every material in these series up to 1917 were consulted. On his Sierra Leone days the following files are, in addition, relevant:

CA1/02	CA1/09(a)
CA1/03	CA1/023
CA1/07	CA1/024
CA1/08	CA1/025(e)

CA1/064	CA1/0169
CA1/088	CA1/0178
CA1/094	CA1/0178(a)
CA1/0129	CA1/0228
CA1/0144	

Also

CA1/I
G3/A1/L10
G3/A1/L11
G/AC 4/2
G/AC 4/3
G/AC 4/26
G/C 4/30

(b) *The Brooke Papers.*
(c) *Committee Minutes Book, Vol.* 40.
(d) *Magazine and Journals.*
    Church Missionary Record, 1863-1875
    Church Missionary Intelligencer, 1849-1906
    Church Missionary Review, 1907-1917
    Western Equatorial Africa Diocesan Magazine, 1893-1917
    Yoruba and Niger Notes, 1893-1900
    The Sudan Leaflet
    The Delta Pastorate Chronicle, 1897-1906

ii *The Methodist Missionary Society.*
    Sierra Leone Boxes 1812-1834 and 1868-1873.
iii *Society of African Mission Archives*, Rome.
    A few files on Yorubaland.
iv *Lambeth Palace.*
    The Tait Papers.

B. SIERRA LEONE ARCHIVES

Liberated African Department Letter Book 22 August 1837 to December 1842, Volume 7.
Record of Manager for the 2nd Eastern District 1842-1854.
Local Letters to Governor 1869, Box No. 7.
Local Letters to Governor 1870, Box No. 8.
Confidential Enclosures to Governors' Despatches (Box 1868–1885).
Report of the Commissioners of Inquiry into the State of the Colony of Sierra Leone 1827.

C. FOURAH BAY COLLEGE LIBRARY

James Pope Hennessy, *Papers dealing with John Pope-Hennessy's administration of the West African Settlements.*

D. NATIONAL ARCHIVES, IBADAN

C.M.S. (Y) 2/5.
The Coker Papers.

E. IBADAN UNIVERSITY LIBRARY

The Henry Carr Papers.
The Macaulay Papers.
Reports of Synods (1906-1917).
The Fombo Collections.
The Annual Reports of the Lagos Church Missions 1879-1917.

F. PUBLIC RECORD OFFICE, LONDON

C.O. 147—Lagos Despatches.
C.O. 149—Legislative Council Minutes (Lagos).
C.O. 520—Southern Nigeria Despatches.
C.O. 267—Sierra Leone Despatches (1831-1843; 1868-1874; 1887).
C.O. 270—Legislative Council Minutes (Sierra Leone).
C.O. 272.
C.O. 806/357.
C.O. 879/8.

G. PARLIAMENTARY PAPERS

Cd. 4477 Further Correspondence Respecting the Affairs of the Gold Coast 1885.
LXI Correspondence Respecting the war between Native Tribes in the interior and the negotiations for peace conducted by the Government of Lagos, 1887.
Cd. 4906 Report of the Committee of Inquiry into the Liquor Trade in Southern Nigeria Part I.
Cd. 4907 Part II Minutes of Evidence.

H. RHODES HOUSE, OXFORD

The Lugard Papers.
The Aborigines Protection Society Papers.

I. NEWSPAPERS

(a) *Published in Sierra Leone.*
The Warder, 1868.
The Day Spring and Sierra Leone Reporter, 1869.
The Negro, 1873.
The West African Reporter, 1873.
The Methodist Herald, 1886-1887.
Sierra Leone Weekly News, 1887-1917.

(b) *Published in Lagos.*
Lagos Times, 1880-1883.
Lagos Observer, 1882-1888.
The Eagle and Lagos Critic, 1883-1887.
Lagos Weekly Record, 1891-1917.
Lagos Standard, 1895-1917.
Nigerian Chronicle, 1908-1914.

Nigerian Pioneer, 1914-1920.
African Hope, 1922.

(c) Published in the Gold Coast.
   The Gold Coast Leader, 1903.

(d) Published in London.
   African Times, 1863-1898.
   African Times and Orient Review, 1912-1917.

J.   BOOKS

E. W. Blyden, *The prospects of the African*, London, 1874.
—— *Africa's Service to the World*, London, 1880(7).
—— *The Return of the Exiles and the West African Church*, London, 1892.
—— *A Chapter in the History of Liberia*, Freetown, 1892.
—— *The Lagos Training College and Industrial Institute*, Lagos, 1896.
—— *Africa and the Africans*, London, 1903.
——*The Significance of Liberia*, Liverpool, 1907.
——*Christianity, Islam and the Negro Race*, London, 1887; new edition, Edinburgh, 1967.
J. G. Campbell, *Lagos Awake on the Election Questions*, Lagos.
   Church Missionary Society, *The Church in the Yoruba Country its Needs and its Difficulties*, London, 1887.
R. Clarke, *A Description of the Manners and Customs of the Liberated Africans*, London, 1846.
Adeoye Deniga, *African Leaders Past and Present*, Lagos, 1915. Vol. I.
J. B. Horton, *West African Communities and Peoples*, London, 1868.
—— *Letters on the Political Conditions of the Gold Coast*, London, 1870; reprinted with a new introduction by E. A. Ayandele, Frank Cass, 1970.
James Johnson, *Yoruba Heathenism*, Exeter, 1899.
—— *Address Delivered at Wesley Church, Olowogbowo, Lagos by the Rt. Rev. James Johnson at the Memorial service held on Sunday the 19th July, 1903 in Honour of Late Hon. Sir Samuel Lewis*, Lagos, 1903.
—— *A Brief Outline of the Story of My Life*, London, 1908.
—— *Ora Primer*, Exeter, n.d.
—— "Elijah II", *Church Missionary Review*, 1916, pp. 455-462.
T. S. Johnson, *The Story of a Mission*, London, 1953.
S. T. Jones, *Elegy on the Late Right Rev. Bishop James Johnson, M.A., D.D., Native of West Africa*, Lagos, 1917.
W. K. Knight, *Memoir of Henry Venn*, London, 1882.
J. O. Lucas, *Lecture on the History of St. Paul's Church, Breadfruit, Lagos*, 1946.
Kehinde Okoro (ed.), *Views of some Native Christians of West Africa on the subject of polygamy*, Lagos, 1887.
R. B. Seeley (ed.), *A Memoir of the Rev. W. A. B. Johnson*, London, 1852.
A. B. C. Sibthorpe, *The History of Sierra Leone,* Third Edition, London, 1906; Fourth Edition, Frank Cass, 1970.

(Sierra Leone Government) *Eminent Sierra Leonians*, Freetown, 1961.
(Sierra Leone) *Industrial Exhibition at Sierra Leone*, London, 1866.
(Sierra Leone) *Memorial of the Celebration of Her Majesty's Reign and of the Centenary of Sierra Leone*, London, 1887.
L. J. Thompson, *The Jubilee and Centenary Volume of Fourah Bay College*, Freetown, 1930.
A. E. Toboku-Metzger, *Historical Sketch of the Sierra Leone Grammar School 1845-1935*, Freetown (n.d.).

II SECONDARY SOURCES

BOOKS

E. A. Ayandele, *The Missionary Impact on Modern Nigeria 1842-1914: A Political and Social Analysis*, Longmans, 1966.
J. S. Coleman, *Nigeria: Background to Nationalism*, Berkeley and Los Angeles, 1958.
D. C. Crowther, *The Establishment of the Niger Delta Pastorate Church*, Liverpool, 1907.
Phillip Curtin, *The Image of Africa*, London, 1965.
E. M. T. Epelle, *Bishops in the Niger Delta*, Aba, 1964.
Esere, *As Seen Through African Eyes*, 1916.
E. U. Essien-Udom, *Black Nationalism*.
K. Ezera, *Constitutional Development of Nigeria*, O.U.P., 1960.
Christopher Fyfe, *A History of Sierra Leone*, O.U.P., 1962.
J. D. Hargreaves, *A Life of Sir Samuel Lewis*, O.U.P., 1958.
Ruth Holden, *Blyden of Liberia*, New York, 1966.
E. Hutchinson, *The Lost Continent: Its Rediscovery and Recovery*, London, 1879.
E. B. Idowu, *Olodumare God in Yoruba Belief*, 1962.
B. Idowu, *Towards an Indigenous Church*, O.U.P., 1965.
Robert W. July, *The Origins of Modern African Thought*, London, 1968.
J. H. Kopytoff, *A Preface to Modern Nigeria*, Wisconsin, 1965.
Hollis R. Lynch, *Edward Wilmot Blyden* (Pan Negro Patriot 1832-1912), London, 1967.
Kwame Nkrumah, *Africa must Unite*, London, 1963.
M. Perham, *Lugard: The Years of Authority*, London, 1960.
L. S. Senghor, *Liberté, Négritude et Humanisme*, Paris, 1964.
G. Shepperson and E. Price, *Independent African*, Edinburgh, 1955.
E. Stock, *The History of the Church Missionary Society*, London, 1899. Vol. III.
B. G. M. Sundkler, *Bantu Prophets in South Africa*.
P. A. Talbot, *The Peoples of Southern Nigeria*, O.U.P., 1926. Vol. I, reprinted Frank Cass, 1969.
C. L. Temple, *Native Races and Their Rulers*, Cape Town, 1918; reprinted, with a new introduction by M. Hiskett, Frank Cass.
H. W. Turner, *History of an African Independent Church*, 2 Volumes, O.U.P., 1967.

J. B. Webster, *The African Churches Among the Yoruba 1888-1922*, O.U.P., 1964.

J. Wheare, *The Nigerian Legislative Council*, London, 1949

—— *Anglo-African Who's Who*, London, 1910.

—— *Report of Proceedings at a Banquet to Sir Guilbert Carter*, Liverpool, 1893.

—— *Conference of West African Missionaries*, Gabon, 1876.

ARTICLES

J. F. Ajayi, "Nineteenth Century Origins of Nigerian Nationalism", *Journal of the Historical Society of Nigeria*, Vol. 2, No. 2, 1961.

E. A. Ayandele, "An Assessment of the place of James Johnson in Nigerian History 1874-1917", Part I 1874-1890, *Journal of the Historical Society of Nigeria*, Vol. 2, No. 4, December 1963.

—— Part II 1890-1917, Vol. 3, No. 1, December 1964, pp. 73-101.

—— "James Johnson: Pioneer Educationist in West Africa", Part I, *West African Journal of Education*, Vol. XII, No. 2, June 1968, pp. 92-98.

—— Part II, Vol. XII, No. 3, October 1968, pp. 174-180.

C. Fyfe, "The West African Methodists in the Nineteenth Century", *The Sierra Leone Bulletin of Religion*, Vol. 3, No. 1, 1961, pp. 22-28.

Robert W. July, "Nineteenth Century Negritude, Edward Blyden", *Journal of African History*, Vol. 5, No. 1, 1964, pp. 73-86.

Hollis R. Lynch, "The Native Pastorate Controversy and Cultural Ethnocentrism in Sierra Leone, 1871-74", *Journal of African History*, Vol. 5, No. 3, 1964, pp. 395-413.

G. Shepperson, "Notes on Negro American Influences on the Emergence of African Nationalism", *Journal of African History*, Vol. I, No. 2, 1960, pp. 299-312.

H. W. Turner, "Prophets and Politics: A Nigerian Test Case", *The Bulletin of the Society of African Church History*, Vol. 2, No. 1, December 1965, pp. 97-117.

III UNPUBLISHED THESES

A. B. Aderibigbe, *The Expansion of the Lagos Protectorate 1861–1900*, Ph.D. (London), 1959.

E. W. Blyden, III, *Sierra Leone: The Pattern of Constitutional Change* (1924-1951), Ph.D. (Harvard), 1959.

S. H. Brown, *A History of the People of Lagos 1852-1886*, Ph.D. (Evaston, Illinois), 1964.

G. M. Haliburton, *The Prophet Harris and His Work in Ivory Coast and Western Ghana*, Ph.D. (London), 1966.

J. E. Peterson, *Freetown: A study of the Dynamics of Liberated African Society*, Ph.D. (Northwestern), 1963.

INDEX

2a*